THE KEYS TO DOWNING STREET

by

Tom Fisher

The Conrad Press

The Keys to Downing Street
Published by The Conrad Press in the United Kingdom 2024
Tel: +44(0)1227 472 874
www.theconradpress.com
info@theconradpress.com
ISBN 978-1-916966-51-2
Copyright ©Tom Fisher 2024
All rights reserved.
Typesetting and Cover Design by: Levellers
The Conrad Press logo was designed by Maria Priestley.
Printed and bound in Great Britain by Clays Ltd, Elcograf S.p.A.

I would like to thank Professor Allan Lichtman for granting me his kind permission to adapt his 'keys' forecasting method to the British political system. I would also like to thank my friend Christian Scott for kindly lending me some books on recent British political history, which have proved most useful. I dedicate this book to the triumph of substance and competence over hype and spin in our political life.

Contents

Introduction 5

Chapter 1 The Keys 10

Chapter 2 1945-51 54

Chapter 3: 1951-64: 84

Chapter 4 1964-1979: 127

Chapter 5: 1979-1997: 194

Chapter 6:1997-2010 269

Chapter 7:2010-2024: 331

Chapter 8: questions and criticisms 432

Chapter 9: Counterfactuals 440

Chapter 10: The lessons of the Keys 501

Introduction

<u>The keys to Downing Street</u>

Are the Tories finished? Is Keir Starmer destined to become Britain's next Prime Minister? Is Rishi Sunak a dead man walking? Is it all pre-determined or is it still up for grabs? These are the questions we hear every day in the media and online, but is there any way of knowing in advance? Most pundits simply follow the polls. Others follow the betting markets, which themselves at least partly follow the polling.

Well, in the three hundred odd pages that follow, I will be setting out a system that can predict the political fortunes of our main parties from the perspective of the governing party in power. It is a system that I have directly adapted from Professor Allan J Lichtman, the American historian who has been accurately predicting every US presidential election since 1984. Professor Lichtman has kindly authorised me to write this book, and it has been a great pleasure to do so.

The system has yet to be tested in a UK election ahead of time, and I am fully aware that I may end up with egg on my face at any time over the next year or so! Having said that, I see no reason why the British electorate should be any more or any less rational than their American counterparts, and I believe it is more than just hubris on my part, that gives me confidence in accurately predicting the next general election this side of the pond.

Although I can boast no prior publications of historical papers, my interest in politics goes back over thirty years. My parents were always interested in it, and The Guardian, BBC news and Radio 4 formed the familiar background of my formative years. My first memories of political events were of the miners' strike of 1984-85. Battles between police and flying pickets dominated the TV news for exactly a year. I also clearly recall the Brighton bombing that nearly killed Mrs Thatcher during that same period.

A measure of both my early naivete and the apparent impregnability of Thatcher's dominance was my astonishment at about the age of twelve, upon learning from my mother that Labour could actually form the government if they won an election. 'Do you mean to say that Neil Kinnock would be Prime Minister and Thatcher would have to sit on the opposition benches?'- I said, or words to that effect.

A year or so later, around the time of the Poll tax riots in March 1990, my awareness grew to a more mature perspective, and I had a pretty shrewd idea of what was going on during the Tory leadership contest towards the end of that year.

My first attempt to intuitively predict an election result was precociously brilliant. In the run-up to the 1992 election, as a fourteen-year-old schoolboy, I guessed that the Tories would win with a majority of twenty. On the fateful April evening itself I recall my father saying, 'leave the country!' when the exit poll was announced. I also recall him shouting at the television the next day, when John Major spoke of his party's achievements in government. My dad shouted, 'you've achieved nothing!' and 'bilge!'

In the ensuing years I attained a degree in English, a PGCE in Post-Compulsory Education and finally a degree-diploma in acting. I worked for three years in the MOD civil service and then moved to teaching English as a Foreign language and later acting. All the while my interest in politics continued, and around the time of the Brexit referendum I began following a diverse range of online personalities, broadening my political perspective. I also studied philosophy in my spare time and dramatically deepened by understanding and perspective.

One of the personalities I discovered online was Allan Lichtman, whom I stumbled across in September 2016, when I was following all manner of political threads on YouTube. That year was an American election like no other. All the commentators were saying that Trump had no chance, that he was a buffoon, a joke candidate, or at best, merely a protest candidate with no hope of winning. But then I saw how Lichtman was predicting a Trump win, and more than that, was explaining exactly why it would happen. I had never come across such a forecasting system, and was instantly hooked. I viewed all the YouTube videos I could find on Lichtman's forecasting system, and then I bought his book, *The Keys to the Whitehouse*, and studied it minutely.

When election-day came and went, I was not all that surprised at the result; which like Brexit five months earlier, convulsed the liberal media on both sides of the Atlantic and beyond. 'How could this happen!' went the cry of outraged progressives the world over; but as the keys answered - actually very easily. Elections are not really about a beauty contest between two candidates or parties, they are simply referenda on the government in power. The old adage that 'Oppositions don't win elections, governments lose them' was true after all. Yet could this system translate to other countries?

The following June I made £45 betting on a hung parliament in that strange British general election, though as yet, using intuition alone.

Then in September 2020, whilst on a very long walk in the Isle of Wight (from Carisbrooke to the Needles) I began to apply the Lichtman system to the British political scene in my head. Suddenly it all seemed to slot into place, more or less. I adapted it, by substituting a few keys for ones more suitable to the UK, and by adding in several special keys.

I continued this for the next eighteen months, adapting the results to every UK election since World War Two. I had twenty to work with, and gradually I fine-tuned the system.

Of course, the biggest difference between the British and American systems was that the UK's is not a presidential one, but a parliamentary one. Therefore, my system had to predict seat numbers in the House of Commons. There were significant other differences which I will go into later in this book, but overall, the retroactive results were impressive.

Polling has not had a good past decade on either side of the Atlantic. In Britain. The pollsters were way off the mark in 2015 when they seemed to predict a hung parliament with both parties roughly level. In fact, the Conservatives won a majority of ten. The pollsters also played down the imminent demise of the Liberal Democrats. In fact, they went from fifty-eight seats to only ten. That year they over sampled younger people and ended up with too many young people who were interested in politics. In 2017 they over-corrected and downplayed the youth vote. That year, many pundits were predicting a comfortable majority for Theresa

May's Tories. In the actual result, they failed to win even a bare majority.

They fared no better with predicting the Brexit referendum, with most polls predicting Remain at least a few points ahead. In fact, they were four points behind.

In the US, pollsters got egg on their collective faces five months later, when they issued probabilities of more than ninety percent for a Clinton win. They fared a bit better four years later in 2020, but still over-estimated Joe Biden's margin of victory.

Failure of pollsters is of course nothing new or surprising. In Britain they famously slipped up in the elections of 1970 and 1992, when they predicted Labour victories in vain. In 1974, a year of two elections, they first predicted a Tory win, only for Mr Heath to lose power, and then in October, predicted a Labour landslide, only to see Harold Wilson squeak back in with only a paltry majority of three!

American pollsters fared no better, famously predicting the electoral demise of Harry Truman in 1948, and failing to See Reagan's landslide in 1980. Perhaps we should have turned to Nostradamus...

Allan Lichtman's brilliant system was devised back in 1981 and has proved correct ever since. And now, after having obtained the kind authorisation of its famous author, I have adapted it to the United Kingdom.

Chapter 1 The Keys

THE MAIN PRINCIPLE OF THE SYSTEM

The main principle behind my adapted system is essentially the same as in Professor Lichtman's model; i.e. that elections are not contests between competing parties or candidates, but are referenda on the party in power. The opposition is very largely irrelevant, and that they can do very little to help themselves win power. Perhaps because the UK is a parliamentary rather than a presidential system, the quality of an opposition party does seem to have rather more impact on elections in the UK than in the States. It seems that oppositions can only influence the election result in two ways: either by selecting a charismatic leader, which is the same as in the American model, or by becoming unelectable. If the opposition party is somewhere in between these extremes, then nothing they say or do in the campaign will make any real difference.

There certainly seem to be more ways in which an opposition can 'Shoot themselves in the foot,' then they can seriously improve their chances. As my later chapter on counterfactuals will try and show, had certain oppositions been more effective, then certain electoral outcomes would have been quite different.

I will go into greater depth towards the end of the book on the lessons of the keys. In my system, as in its original American system, the keys consist of true or false statements to be answered from the perspective of the government in power at the time of the election. Each key carries equal weight. If one key is more important than the others, then it will trigger other keys indirectly. For example, following British victory in the 1982 Falkland's war, the only key to turn directly was Foreign Policy/Military Success Key nine. However, this military success also hugely boosted Margaret Thatcher's stature, securing her the Incumbent Leadership Key three. It also united the then quite fractious Conservative party, saving Party Unity Key two. However, there may be an exception to this rule which we will come to in a moment.

In Professor Lichtman's system there are thirteen keys. In mine there are thirteen principal keys and three special keys. We have six political keys, two economic keys, two foreign policy keys, one policy change key and two problem keys.

The keys also fall into two broad categories; the causative keys and the indicative keys. The causative keys are those that refer to areas of government policy and performance that have a direct bearing on whether people will vote for or against the governing party. For example, the Short-Term Economy key measures the perceived state of the economy at the time of the election. If this is poor, then it will have an impact on government support.

The indicative keys are those that act as a barometer of popular discontent with the government and do not influence the result in themselves. There is only one purely indicative key and that is the By-elections key; since people do not decide to vote for or against the governing party on the basis of how many by-elections they have won. However, if the government has lost more than a third of the by-elections it has contested during the term, then that is a barometer indicator of government unpopularity. The Third Party Key and the Civil Unrest Key are partly causative, partly indicative.

This is because civil unrest and surging third parties are both barometer indicators of public discontent, but will also directly influence the election result in themselves.

The only key from the American model without a British counterpart is the Incumbency key. This is because the leader of the governing party in the UK is now automatically the sitting prime minister.

I said earlier that there may be an exception to the rule that all keys are weighted equally. This would be the Third Party Key five. If a government is besieged by two separate third parties, both coming from different sides of the political spectrum, and both voicing different sets of concerns, and appealing to different sections of a party's coalition, then a double Third Party Key could in theory be called.

This would certainly be the case if both third parties were clearly and significantly eating into the government's support; and therefore, would be causative keys and not purely indicative ones. If for example the Conservative government of Rishi Sunak (or whoever is leading it into the next election) is faced with a revitalised Liberal Democrat party attacking from the left, and an insurgent Reform party attacking from the populist, identitarian right; then a double key could be called against the government. [1]

For that to happen, the Liberals would have to appear ahead of their 2019 performance by five points in the national polls, or on course to gain fifteen seats at the constituency level; and Reform UK would need to be surpassing their parent Brexit party's 2019 vote by the same amount. At the time of writing (November 2023) Reform are exceeding eight percent across most polls and are in double figures in some. It has also been found that around two thirds of Reform supporters are ex-

Conservatives, so they are having a differential impact against the Conservatives.

The Keys are:

1) By-Elections Key:

The incumbent party has won at least two thirds of the seats it was defending at by-elections since the last election.

This key works on the assumption that a government's balance sheet of by-election wins and losses is a fairly reliable barometer of its popularity. The equivalent in the original Lichtman model is the Mandate key. That key is concerned with governing party gains and losses in the House of Representatives.

The UK does not have an equivalent mid-term vote, so by-elections are the nearest indicator in Britain. One possible advantage the by-elections have over the Congressional elections in their predictive capacity, is that by-elections are ongoing, so reflect government fortunes over the whole duration of the term; whereas the bi-annual Congressional votes are more of a snapshot, leaving out changes in presidential popularity during the second half of the term.

The UK by-elections key is however a bit more complicated to operate than its American counterpart. The rule is that the governing party has to win at least two thirds of the seats that it is defending in by-elections over the course of the term.

There is a caveat though. If the government can actually take a seat from an opposition party, then that cancels out one of the losses it has suffered during the term. For example, if the government is contending nine seats in by-elections during a given term, then it must normally win six of them in order to keep the key. If however they only manage to win five, but also score a direct win from the opposition, then the government win wipes out one of the losses, leaving the government with a win rate of six out of nine, thus securing the key.

2) Unity Key:

the incumbent party is not seriously divided at the time of the election campaign

This key measures whether the governing party is broadly unified or is suffering serious internal division. It is the counterpart to the American Nomination Key. In the Lichtman model, that key turns against the incumbent if there was a significant contest for the nomination of the presidential candidate. There is no equivalent situation in the UK system, so I have replaced it with the Unity key, which essentially measures the same thing; namely division within the governing party. It is admittedly more subjective than its American counterpart, yet as Professor Lichtman acknowledges, a certain level of subjectivity is unavoidable when making forecasts of this kind.[2] It is really about making an informed judgement on the political situation.

When the governing party is seriously divided, then the party's fortunes are always damaged as a result. Divisions can be ideological, such as the bitter left-right division in the Labour party at the time of the 1950 and 1951 general elections, and the bitter schism in the Conservative party over Europe during the 1997 election. Division can also be centred around personality and power struggles at the very top of the party, such as the rivalry and suspicion between Tony Blair and Gordon Brown at the time of the 2005 election. It can also be between the grassroots and the leadership of the party.

It does generally tend to be ideological in nature, even when it is focussed on a specific policy, such as British involvement in the Iraq war for example. It still reflects a clash of underlying values; in that particular case, issues of pacifism, international law, and anti-Americanism versus pro - Americanism and interventionism.

3) Incumbent Leadership Key

The Prime Minister is charismatic, a national hero, or a strong and commanding Prime Minister

This is the equivalent to the charisma key in the Lichtman model, though its interpretation is a little more difficult than in the US. Firstly, Britain is not a presidential system, with the Prime Minister leading the government under the principle of collective cabinet responsibility and so must command the confidence of the cabinet and Hose of Commons in order to continue to govern.

It is much easier to drive a Prime Minister from power than it is with an American President. Only one President has ever resigned, and none have been removed from office by the impeachment process. Since 1945, seven British Prime Ministers have been forced out of power by their own party for political reasons during their term of office. Two more have retired for personal or health reasons.

Therefore, the British premier is expected to be a national leader in a different way to the occupant of the White House. Not so much an elected monarch, but a manager of a team. The media focus is also not on the individual leader in quite the same way. However, British politics has become more presidential since 1945, with the Thatcher, Blair and Johnson governments in particular, steering the political culture in that direction.

In modern Britain the candidates for next Prime Minister at an election are always the leaders of the two main parties and so there is rarely any surprise in the election year as to who the leaders will be. As the leaders are already running either a cabinet or shadow cabinet, the general impression is of a more bureaucratic, managerial political figure, than the somewhat more regal grandeur of a presidential candidate.

Through being more involved in the day to day running of the government, Prime Ministers tend to lose charisma more quickly than the relatively detached US Presidents. Familiarity breeds contempt. When he first took office, Boris Johnson was advised by Cabinet Secretary Mark Sedwill that a Reaganesque, presidential, hands-off style would work well for him. Johnson apparently stared blankly and ignored what was excellent advice. [3]

Additionally, whilst an American president is through being both head of state and head of government, the embodiment of the nation, a British prime minister is only head of government, and therefore is not viewed in quite the same patriotic light.

It is also true that the British do not really tend to produce charismatic figures like John F Kennedy and Barack Obama. It could well be that a small country tends to skew towards more reserved personas. In *The Abolition of Britain*, Peter Hitchens writes that, 'High-octane American ways of behaving and speaking are simply too powerful for this much smaller and narrower country.'[4] Also, that 'Britain's smallness and its settled class system have compelled us to be polite, restrained, or face chaos.'[5]

In an American presidential contest, the media focus is very keen, the campaign fund enormous and the rhetorical heat therefore more intense. It takes an exceptional level of personal charisma to make a difference. In the UK, the political temperature is a little cooler and so the leaders need reach a lower threshold. Margaret Thatcher for instance was recognised in her time and now as a major political figure and formidable personality; yet she was never charismatic in the way that JFK or Obama were charismatic. However, she still wins the key for reasons we shall soon come to.

What exactly is charisma? Most dictionary definitions are along the lines of a kind of personal magnetism, a compelling charm that enables one to attract, impress, inspire and influence others. It is a quality of natural leadership, though it can be to some extent developed. It is associated with great personal confidence, and of having something to sell, whether it be political or religious ideas or a performance artist selling their craft, such as singing or acting. This is not the same thing as charm, or of just being popular.

Charm is a quality of projected agreeableness and likeability, which makes a person able to put others at their ease and feel good about themselves. It is a form of social finesse and can be false or manipulative. Charismatic personalities though are magnetic. Such people tend to combine strong powers of oratory, persuasion, vision and authority; as well as something to sell apart from their own personalities. [6]

Examples of charismatic leaders from modern British history would include: Gladstone, Disraeli, Lloyd-George, Churchill, Blair and (for a time) Johnson. Although Clement Attlee effected great change, he was too mild-mannered a man to make this particular category. As someone unkindly commented, 'He was a modest man, with a lot to be modest about!'

Anthony Eden certainly had charm. He was a good speaker, telegenic and imposing. He could boast high approval ratings, even during the disastrous Suez episode. [7] However, he did not really inspire people or mesmerically attract people to hear him speak, and did not really have a clear message to sell.

The second category is that of the national hero. This, as Professor Lichtman has defined, is someone recognised for playing a crucial role in a critical national endeavour. Leading the nation in war is the most obvious example of this. In Britain, Churchill would be the last party leader to meet this category.

The third category is the Strong and dominant Prime minister. Prime Ministers can win the Incumbent Leadership without being truly charismatic or a national hero; though they must have a limited quality of the two. My definition of the strong and dominant Prime Minister is that they must have the following qualities.

1) the leader is seen to be competent and in command of events

This is most important. No leader who is blown about by events like a leaf in the wind can hope to win this key. Examples of success include Churchill's wartime performance, Margaret Thatcher's handling of the Falklands war and Macmillan's skilful rebuilding of Britain's reputation and Anglo-American relations post-Suez. Leaders can also achieve this during the good times. Wilson achieved this during his first short term of office, until the July 1966 economic crisis. Blair had a longer period of such dominance, which was only really ended by the war in Iraq.

Clement Attlee, though a remarkable leader in many ways, was still seen as struggling against the difficult economic fallout from World War Two. He therefore does not win the key. Needless to say, that hapless and unlucky Prime Ministers, such as Wilson, (Post-devaluation) Heath, Callaghan, Major, Brown and May, do not win the key. Liz Truss is perhaps the ultimate in failure, losing heavily in every category outlined here.

> *2) the leader must have the confidence and unity of the cabinet, parliamentary party, party membership and likely supporters in the country*

They must in other words command the support of their side of the political spectrum. Obviously, a divisive leader such as Thatcher or Johnson cannot expect to get approval ratings of sixty or seventy percent, but they do not need them in order to win big. In Britain it is perfectly possible to win a majority with under forty percent of the vote and to win a landslide with under forty-five. Any leader with a party that is badly divided at any level cannot expect to win this key.

> *3)the leader must extend the appeal of their party beyond narrow sectarian lines - at least to some extent*

This mirrors Allan Lichtman's condition for awarding the Charisma key in his system. For example, Trump did not win the key, as his support-base was too narrow, and he was detested by large swathes of the American electorate. Examples of this being achieved in British politics include the more aspirational sections of the working class who switched from Labour to support Margaret Thatcher in the 1980s. Tony Blair drew many moderate Conservatives into his New Labour fold a decade or so later. Macmillan also broadened the Conservatives appeal during the late fifties, boasting that the class war had now become obsolete. Boris Johnson briefly (it seems) won the Labour 'red wall' in the election of 2019.

4) The leader has strong communication skills

This too is vital. The leader does not have to be truly charismatic, but a strong capacity for connecting with the British public, or at least with their half of the political spectrum is vital. Thatcher could certainly do it, and excelled as a kind of missionary for her free market doctrine. Heath, Major, Brown, May, Truss and Sunak could not. Blair was an excellent political actor in all situations. Macmillan too was highly effective and conveyed a strong but affable patrician image. Boris Johnson could also connect with his Brexiteer half of the electorate until he was discredited by scandal. This ability must manifest in speeches at the party conference, speeches on the campaign stump, televised speeches to the country as a whole, TV interviews and of course, performance in the chamber of the House of Commons.

5) the leader must wrong-foot and out-smart the opposition

The successful Prime Minister must look like the only game in town. For example, Thatcher and Blair made their opposition leaders look irrelevant and reactionary, eccentric and archaic.

(Although Messrs Foot, Hague and IDS did a lot of the work themselves.) Any Prime Minister will struggle to win the key if there is a popular viable opposition leader snapping at their heels. Home in 1963-64 and Major in 1994-97 are obvious examples.

Of course, just because someone is strong at one point in time, does not guarantee they will always be so. For example, Tony Blair was no longer strong and dominant after the unpopular invasion of Iraq in 2003. In Margaret Thatcher's case the situation was reversed; she was very unpopular until victory in the South Atlantic transformed her standing.

Although Macmillan was very popular in the 1959 election campaign, by the time of his resignation in 1963, he was beginning to look like a dinosaur; an elderly Edwardian in the swinging sixties.

Fortunes change and people are perceived differently over time. For example, although since 1945 he has been remembered as a charismatic leader, Churchill was not seen in this light prior to becoming wartime Prime Minister in 1940. In the thirties he was seen as a rather old-fashioned figure whose time had passed.

Additionally, it must be said that a leader's popularity inevitably reflects public satisfaction with the current state of the country. They would hardly be super-popular if they led detested and failing governments.

Thus, key three is also a general barometer indicator of the current state of the nation, and efficacy of its government.

One situation that does not win the key is when personal popularity is largely a reflection of novelty in the post. Examples include Anthony Eden who called an election just sixteen days after becoming premier, Gordon Brown in 2007 and Theresa May in 2016-17. Such popularity tends not to last very long, since there was never any solid basis for it in the first place. In all the aforementioned cases, people projected what they wanted to see.

In Eden's case, he was personally popular because of his charm, dapper appearance and debonair image. Yet he had not had time to establish himself as an effective Prime Minister, so the public support, reflected in high poll ratings was superficial, and thus did not win the Tories key three. Within two years he was out of office and a discredited figure. In Brown's case, Labour supporters were hoping that he would offer them real socialism combined with integrity and competence, instead of Blairite triangulation and spin. In May's case, Brexiteers projected their desire for whatever kind of Brexit they wanted, and Remainers projected theirs for a watered-down Brexit in name only. In all cases, such hopes were painfully disabused.

Polling is of very limited benefit in calling this perhaps most subjective of keys. A consistent rating of above sixty percent would indicate popularity though not necessarily charisma or a commanding political figure. A truly abysmal rating of under thirty percent would seem to rule charisma or competence out.

However, a number of formidable and successful Prime Ministers have had only mediocre ratings. Margaret Thatcher for instance, only occasionally got more and only slightly more than fifty percent approval in the polls. [8] It is the same in the States. Ronald Reagan is widely regarded as a charismatic president; yet his mean approval ratings when in office were not particularly impressive. [9]

There is another reason why British premiers do not need to meet the high level of charisma that Allan Lichtman calls for in the American mode. It is due to the much higher strength of third parties in the UK. This means that main parties can win a majority with fewer votes than in the states. In all elections between 1974 and 2015, there had been a third party getting more than ten percent of the vote, and on four occasions more than twenty percent. Therefore, it is possible for a party to win a workable majority with fewer votes than in the USA.

Both of Thatcher's landslides in the eighties were achieved with under forty-five percent of the vote, as were Blair's 1997 and 2001 triumphs. In the States, unless there is a strong third party candidate such as Ross Perot in 1992, the winning candidate normally has to reach close to fifty percent. Major landslides such as Reagan's 1984 blow-out, require closer to sixty percent.

The upshot of this is that it is easier for divisive leaders to win power in the UK.

4) *Opposition Charisma Key*

the opposition leader is not charismatic or a national hero

If the leader of the opposition is charismatic, highly-effective or a national hero this key turns false for the government. It is harder for a UK opposition leader to be highly credible than it is for the serving Prime Minister, as a Prime Minister can draw upon their competence in running a government, whereas most opposition leaders are untried and untested.

The exceptions are former Prime Ministers running for election. Churchill in 1950 and 1951 would qualify here, as a recently minted national hero.

Harold Wilson was a highly compelling leader in 1964, combining a thrusting dynamism, with a modern, man-of-the-people image and highly effective use of both TV and rallies. Tony Blair, a third of a century later was another charismatic leader of the opposition in 1997. He was the first British prime minister of the JFK mould; youngish, exciting, and with a full head of hair. David Cameron attempted to repeat the trick for the 2010 general election, but unfortunately for him, fell a little short of turning the key.

5 *Third Party Key*

there has been a significant increase in third party support, which is not the result of any split in the opposition

This key is activated if there is a sustained increase in the support of a third party by five percent or more, or indications that such a party is likely to take fifteen or more parliamentary seats off the government. The exception is when the third party surge is clearly resulting from a split within the opposition party. (See key 5A) In general, a sharp rise in third party support is a barometer indicator of general popular discontent, and this is almost always bad news for the party in power. Sudden rises in third party support have usually come from the Liberal party. This happened in the elections of

1964, February 1974 and in 1979. In 2015 the third party in question was UKIP. At the time of writing (November 2023) it seems that Reform will be turning a second Third Party key against the Conservatives.

Another way in which the key can turn, is in the case of tactical voting. In the 1997 election the Liberal Democrats more than doubled their seats total, whilst suffering a slight decline in the popular vote. This was due to anti-Conservative tactical voting, wherein Labour supporters voted for the Liberal Democrats in seats that Labour could not win, and vice versa.[10]

I have decided not to add a tactical voting key to our armoury of political forecasting tools. This is because any significant increase in tactical voting inevitably involves some increase in third party support, as it is brought about by vote switching between supporters of the main opposition party and third parties. Any large-scale trend towards tactical voting would show up in advance of the general election in the form of by-election and local election results. Additionally, it is already covered by the balance of negative keys reflecting increasing government unpopularity.

My system awards progressively larger swings against the incumbent party for each additional negative key that turns against them after the fifth key. This anticipates tactical voting, as the more accident prone and unpopular an administration becomes, the more desperate people are to get rid of them - by any means necessary.

It is not always easy to predict a rise in third party support. Polling is an obvious metric, but it is not enough, especially if the third party increase is due to tactical voting or localised swings, and therefore may not necessarily be reflected in national polls. There are polls of marginal constituencies as well, but several other metrics.

If a third party has been performing well in by-elections and local elections, then this can often be a guide. Performance here does not only mean winning seats; a dramatic rise in vote share at by-elections is also significant. Additionally, the number of candidates being fielded by the party is also a relevant indicator. An increased number of candidates obviously suggests an increased potential vote share. It also is reflective of increased third party confidence as well as the confidence of party donors.

Other indicators to look out for are the popularity and visibility of the third party leader. For example, the Liberal leader Jo Grimmond was able to connect with voters in the run up to the 1964 election; thus, combined with other factors, turned the key against the Tory government.

Another factor is whether or not there is an ideological convergence between the third party and main opposition party. For example, in 1997 there was a clear ideological convergence between Tony Blair's New Labour party and the Liberal Democrats. Specifically, New Labour's interest in constitutional reform was clearly appealing to many Lib Dem voters.

These indications must of course be weighed against the strengths of the main parties, especially the party in power. Such signs are obviously more potent for third party success if the governing party is weak in the polls and has many keys against it. For instance, the Liberal Democrats enjoyed significant by-election wins during the 1987-1992 parliament yet reaped disappointing results in the 1992 election. Over the course of the following parliament, they also fared well in by-elections, but enjoyed an outstanding result in May 1997.

The main difference of course was that the Conservative government had twice the number of negative keys against it in 1997 than it did five years earlier, even before we added the Third Party key. It was also around ten points lower in the polls, suffered very poor performance ratings, as well as being pilloried in the media.

The question of how to call this key when a third party has been doing better than historically normal over a long period of time is a hard one. The best way to call it is to look at whether the third party is having a disproportionate effect on one of the two main parties. This is also not obvious. Polling can be a guide. For example, in the 1992 general election, polling suggested that Liberal Democrat supporters were roughly equally suspicious of the two main parties, and not obviously more closely aligned to one than another.[11] Therefore, in such a situation it is best not to turn the third party key.

In the case of the election of October 1974, the Liberals were still very strong seven months after the previous election at the end of February. Should the key be automatically turned against the minority Labour government of Harold Wilson? I decided not to. Owing to the extreme shortness of the third Wilson ministry, the high Liberal polling was essentially a hang-over from the troubles of the Heath government; oil crisis, recession and three-day week.

Occasionally the key can be turned in the event of a dramatic decline in a third party that will disproportionately benefit the principal opposition party. This eventuality occurred in the election of October 1951 when the Liberals found themselves unable to field more than a quarter of the candidates that they had at the previous election due to financial problems. This could have been predicted to benefit the Tories, since Liberal voters leaned slightly to the right at that time, and the Labour government already had five keys turned against it. In this election it was enough only to effect a half-turn of Key five, since the Liberal support was dropping from a low base.

6: *Cyclical Incumbency Key*

The incumbent party has already been continuously in power for longer than three full terms (fifteen years)

This key reflects the feeling that a party has been in power for too long and it is now time for a change. In the UK, this occurs once the party in power has occupied Downing Street for more than fifteen years by the time of the general election. This key has only turned once since 1945, during the election of 1997, when the Conservatives had been in power for eighteen years.

There does not seem to be a significantly strong 'time for a change' movement to warrant turning the key after twelve or thirteen years. The system accurately predicts the outcomes of the 1964, 1992 and 2010 general elections without recourse to this key, when the incumbent party sought a fourth term.

The difficulty in turning the key comes when a party's tenure has been made up of irregular-length terms, such as in the post 2015 era. However, the current government cannot go beyond January 2025, so falling just short of fifteen years in power.

7: *Short Term Economy Key*

the economy is not perceived to be in recession during the election campaign

This key is the first to be exactly the same as in the American model. In fact, from now on, all the keys are identical to those of their American counterparts. If the UK economy is perceived as being in recession during the election campaign, then the key turns false. As in the States, it is not always an easy question as to whether to turn the key are not. Accurate GDP data may lag behind a fast-changing economic situation, such as the banking meltdown of autumn 2008. The best way of reading the key is whether there is a public perception of an economy mired in recession. Polling is vital here. The key is determined by the last decisive change in the public perception of the economy.

After any recession this key will be false, until there is a clear recognition that the economy is moving again. For example, in May 2010 the economy was no longer technically contracting, but the public mood was clearly one of living through very hard economic times, and so the key remained false for Gordon Brown and his administration.

8: *Long term Economy Key*

Mean GDP over the term is equal to or greater than the mean GDP over the previous two terms, or if not, has been growing consistently throughout the term without a major financial crisis, or serious public concern about the economy.

This key at first glance appears the most objective of them all, but is in fact one of the most complex to turn. This key is true if mean GDP growth over the course of the term is equal to or greater than that of the preceding two terms. Equal in this case would mean within one tenth, (0.1) of one percent. This is because growth accumulates over the course of time, giving a slight additional boost to the growth of two terms compared with one. For example, in a four-year term in which annual year-on-year growth were exactly three percent, the average growth per annum over the whole four-year term would actually be 3.34% However, if this year-on year growth of three percent were maintained over two four-year terms, then the average growth per annum over the whole eight- year period would be 3.45%.

If the key is true, then it is a good indicator of governmental electoral success. However, things are more complicated if it is prima facie false.

If GDP growth over the term is less than its two predecessors, the key does not automatically turn false. It will turn false however if the slower growth is reflective of any of the following:

A) Any kind of recognised recession.

B) Any other serious economic crisis, (e.g. currency devaluation.)

C) Any widespread, sustained and serious public anxiety about the economy. (E.g. over Brexit)

Examples of elections when the key was called false would include: 1950, following post-war contraction, rationing and devaluation, 1970 following devaluation, 1979 following recession, industrial unrest and a bail-out by the IMF, in 1983 following deep recession and mass unemployment, in 2010, following the banking crisis and recession.

If none of the above criteria have been the case, growth has been consistent, and the lost key is only technical and relative, (i.e. a strong term following two even stronger ones.) then the key will remain true. For instance, at the time of the 2005 election, GDP growth was significantly below that of the previous two terms. However, there had been no tangible economic crisis during the term. Growth had been very consistent, unemployment, interest rates and inflation had remained low. There was never a widespread belief that the economy was in serious trouble. For that election, I consider the key as still being true.

If we were to apply the original American model to the UK, then we would have the bizarre situation of calling the key true in 1992, despite a major recession, high unemployment and a house-price crash; but false in 2005 despite no recession, low unemployment, a booming housing market and a mood of complacency towards the economy.

In the 2019 election the key turned false again. Although there had been no recession, the economy had experienced slow growth, with major anxieties over the impact of Brexit, as well as uncertainty as to what kind of Brexit we would have, and indeed if it would happen at all. This confirmed the key's falsity.

In other years the picture is more mixed. For example, in the elections of 1959 and 1966, there had been some quarters of contraction, against a background of concern the over the balance of payments and possible devaluation. However, there had been no actual recession or major crisis. In these situations, we have to call a Half-turn; as I shall explain later.

9: *Foreign Policy/Military Success Key*

The administration has achieved major success in foreign policy and/or military affairs.

This key is true if the government of the day have achieved a major foreign policy or military success that furthers the interests or image of Britain. Examples since the war include Mrs Thatcher's stunning victory in the Falkland's War, Edward Heath's success in bringing Britain into the EEC and Tony Blair's achievement of securing peace in Northern Ireland following the Good Friday Agreement. Such a success has to achieve public recognition, not merely recognition from experts in the field or media pundits.

A highly divisive policy venture such as Brexit, with roughly equal numbers of supporters and opponents will not turn the key. Neither will a venture that generates a slew of positive headlines, and then is soon forgotten.

10: *Foreign Policy/Military failure*

The administration has suffered no major failure in foreign policy or military affairs

This key turns false if the government suffers major failure in military or foreign affairs. Examples include the Suez debacle of 1956 that ended Anthony Eden's premiership, the rapidly deteriorating situation in Northern Ireland during the early 1970s, Britain's humiliating defenestration from the European Exchange Rate Mechanism (ERM) on Black Wednesday in 1992 and her participation in the Iraq War from 2003. Failed initiatives do not necessarily meet the threshold. For example, the failed bids to join the Common Market in the 1960s do not turn the key against the MacMillan or Wilson governments. It has to be something that significantly damages the interests or prestige of the nation.

11: *Policy Change Key*

the administration has effected major change in policy

This key is one of the hardest to turn, since any government must effect at least a small degree of policy change, unless it falls within weeks taking office. In order to win the key, the changes have to be significant, either involving a change in the direction of previous policy or achieving major innovation.

This has nothing to do with whether the changes are popular or even successful. There has to be a major change from the policies of the previous term. Examples include the major nationalisations and decolonisation policy of the Attlee government, Margaret Thatcher's anti-union and privatisation agenda of the 1980s, and Tony Blair's constitutional reform, social liberalism and pro-Europeanism of his first term.

It can be quite hard to determine if a change is big enough to qualify, so the bar is set quite high. What is important is the changes must be recognised as significant at the time, and by the general public. It is not enough for reforms to only be recognised by experts or media pundits - or indeed by historians fifty years later!

One question that comes up with the change key is does the passing of legislation turn the key in itself, or does the policy have to be implemented in practice? The answer is that legislative reforms are enough to turn the key when passed through both houses of parliament and gaining the Royal ascent; provided that they are understood and there is reasonable public confidence that they will be enacted.

Reforms of a more concrete nature, like increased government spending and the building of infrastructure, will turn the key only when they materialise in the real world. Thus, Tony Blair's Constitutional Reform Act of 2005 contributes to the partial turning of the key at the 2005 election, whereas his promises to fund and reform the public services sounded too much like hot air at the 2001 election; they had to be enacted in practice to turn the key on their own.

Brexit was in a bit of a special category regarding this key. Although Article fifty had been invoked by the 2017 election, the government still needed to secure a deal with the EU, and have that deal ratified by both houses of parliament. Therefore, the Change key did not turn at the 2017 or 2019 general elections. Additionally, there was so much deep scepticism and cynicism as to whether the Remainer forces in parliament and the legal system would obstruct Brexit, or water it down to what Nigel Farage called 'Brexit in name only,' that the policy had to be enacted in both name and practice for the change key to be turned. Therefore, not till after December 31st 2020.

12: *Civil Unrest Key*

there has been no widespread civil unrest

This key turns false if there is widespread, sustained and major protest against the government. This includes mass demonstrations, riots, strikes or even terrorism and civil war. The unrest either has to be ongoing at the time of the election campaign, or still uppermost in the public mind, and with the issues behind it unresolved. This key has only turned fully twice since the war. This was in the election of Febraury1974 and again five years later in 1979. On both occasions it was due to strikes.

Unrest that occurs earlier in the term and peters out will not turn the key. For example, there was major rioting in both 1981 and 2011; yet by the time of the subsequent elections the streets were peaceful again. Had Thatcher been forced to call an election in the autumn of 1981, then the key would probably have turned against her ministry, but by June 1983 the tensions had faded into the background.

The unrest has to be obviously manifested in the form of public disorder for the key to be turned. There was widespread bitterness and resentment over the Brexit impasse, but it did not manifest in the form of frequent massive protests or riots. Thus, the key did not turn in 2017 or 2019.

13: *Scandal Key*

the administration has not been tainted by major scandal

This key turns false if the administration is tainted by major scandal. Such scandals normally either involve the office of the Prime Minister, or appear to be pervasive throughout the parliamentary party. Isolated incidents involving one MP or minister will not turn the key. For example, the unfortunate incident involving Welsh Secretary Ron Davies on Clapham Common in 1998 did not turn the key against the Blair administration.

This key has turned false four times since 1945: firstly, during the election of 1964 when the Tory government was tainted by the Profumo affair, secondly in 1997 when the Conservative administration of John Major was engulfed in multiple allegations of 'sleaze,' thirdly in 2005, when a clear majority of the British public believed that Tony Blair's government had lied over the existence of weapons of mass destruction in Iraq, and fourthly in 2010 when Gordon Brown's Labour Government was tarnished by the expenses and 'Cash for Coronets' scandals. It looks almost certain to turn again at the next election, following Boris Johnson's misconduct during 'Partygate' and the Owen Patterson affair.

It can be hard to judge if a scandal will succeed in toppling the key. As a general rule, if the government seems clearly damaged by allegations, then the key turns. Conversely if nobody seems to care, then the key stays true. A partial example of the latter was in the election of 2001, when a number of scandals failed to completely permeate the Teflon coating of Tony Blair's first administration.

A good measure for assessing whether the severity of a scandal is sufficient to topple the key, is whether its recognition as a scandal crosses partisan lines. If only the opposition parties and the more partisan commentators in the media are talking about it, then it is probably not sufficient to topple the key. If the government is clearly losing supporters and facing criticism from its own side and from normally favourable commentators, then the key looks set to turn.

Additionally, scandals that prove here today and gone tomorrow are most unlikely to turn the key.

SPECIAL KEYS

The following keys are special keys which come into play occasionally. They all act as bonus keys that effectively reduce the balance of negative keys turned against the government.

4A) *Opposition Implausibility Bonus Key*

the opposition is widely seen as unelectable

If the principal opposition is widely perceived to be unelectable then the government of the day is awarded a special bonus key. This has the effect of cancelling out one of the negative keys against them, thus reducing their balance of negative keys by one. An opposition can render themselves implausible through the adoption of extreme or unpopular positions, for being badly divided on grounds of either ideology or personality, through manifest incompetency, or through a deeply unpopular, or implausible leader, or via a combination of these factors.

Moreover, because there are far greater parliamentary swings in the UK than occur in the States, it is not uncommon for losing parties to become so depleted and devastated in elections that they are simply not taken seriously for a long time afterwards. For example, in the 1997 election, the Conservatives lost half their seats. Labour had also been reduced to half their Blair-era peak by cumulative losses between 2005 and 2019.

Therefore, in eras when the opposition is very weak, such was the case for Labour in the 1980s and the Tories in the 2000s, the main opposition party is often rather ignored by the media and it can be a struggle for people to imagine an opposition leader as Prime Minister, standing in front of the door to number 10 Downing Street.

The key is activated when the principal opposition party is bankrupt of political capital. The opposition implausibility key has been activated four times since the Second World War. It has happened twice with the Labour opposition, firstly in 1983 under Michael Foot, and again in 2019 under Jeremy Corbyn. The Conservative party was also a useless opposition in 2001 under William Hague and again in 2005 under Michael Howard.

The criteria for calling this key is whether media and public opinion in general, do not regard the opposition party as credible, and cannot envisage them winning and forming a government. If the party is seen as a joke, most people find it very hard to visualise their leader standing outside number 10 Downing Street. Therefore, although Ed Miliband was widely pilloried during the 2015 election campaign and the months leading up to it, there was widespread media speculation that Labour could win, or at least come first in a hung parliament. It was this feeling that prevented the key from turning in the government's favour that year.

4B) *Opposition Complicity Bonus Key*

The opposition are complicit in enabling and/or defending a highly unpopular government policy.

This key is activated if the principal opposition party is complicit in supporting or defending an unpopular government policy, therefore throwing away the opportunity of gaining votes resulting from that policy's unpopularity and/or failure. This key has only turned once; in the general election of 2005. In that election cycle the Conservative opposition voted with the government to authorise British participation in the American-lead invasion of Iraq in 2003. It was only due to the support of the Conservatives under Ian Duncan Smith that Tony Blair avoided a crushing defeat at the hands of his own back bench rebels.

Duncan Smith's successor Michael Howard continued to defend the controversial decision to go to war for the rest of the term, including during the election campaign itself. This prevented the Tories from gaining the anti-war protest votes that could have come their way had they opposed the invasion.

5A: *Third Party Bonus Key*

There has been a significant change in third party support or behaviour that is clearly detrimental to the main opposition party and/or directly beneficial to the governing party.

This key is turned for the government if the performance of a third party actively benefits the party in power. This happened in 1983 and 1987 due to the Alliance between the new Social Democratic Party (SDP) and the existing Liberal Party. The Alliance took crucial votes away from Labour, but owing to the First-Past-The-Post system, yielded only a disappointing return for the Alliance. Ergo, the Conservatives of Margaret Thatcher were the clear beneficiaries.

It can also be the case that a sudden collapse of third party support can benefit the government. In 2015, the widely predicted implosion of the Liberal Democrats due to their support of unpopular coalition policies such as rising tuition fees, gifted David Cameron around twenty-five seats. This was ample to both give him the key and secure a majority.

Another situation that can turn this key is an alliance between a third party and the governing party. This happened during the early post-war years, when the National Liberals merged with the Conservatives at the constituency level in 1947. This meant that the Tories were boosted by additional National Liberal MPs at the elections of 1950, '51, '55 and '59. After this, the National Liberals went into decline and their effect was insufficient to turn the key in 1964 or '66. Thereafter they merged completely with the Conservative Party.

OTHER DIFFERENCES FROM THE LICHTMAN MODEL

The main difference between my UK model and the original American model devised by Allan Lichtman, is that his system is based on predicting the popular vote, whereas my method directly predicts the strength of the governing party in the House of Commons. This roughly corresponds with the popular vote, but it is nowhere near an absolute. For example, in the 1951 general election, the Labour party won a plurality of the popular vote, but the Tories won a small majority in the House of Commons. A system that predicted the popular vote would therefore not have been able to forecast the Conservative victory. My system predicted that Labour would lose their majority, with five-and-a-half false keys stacked against them. Given the extreme weakness of the Liberal party and the alliance between the National

Liberals and the Conservatives, I could also have predicted the Conservatives being the largest party, with a probability of them achieving a majority.

In 1974 a similar thing occurred. The Conservatives won marginally more votes than Labour, yet Labour won slightly more seats, and was able to form a minority government. My system predicted the Tories would be well short of a majority with six false keys, and therefore the result would be a Labour government of some sort.

In 1992, the Conservative majority was cut despite the party receiving almost exactly the same share of the vote as in the previous three elections. My system predicted a much-reduced Conservative majority with four negative keys. Therefore, the British electorate seem to be able to directly translate government performance into seats, irrespective of the popular vote.

Another difference between the British and American models is the existence of Special keys. These special keys are effectively 'bonus' keys and it is even possible for a government to have a positive net balance of keys. This was the case for the election of 2001. In 1983 the balance was zero. Since the UK is a parliamentary democracy, each turn of the keys represents a loss of a certain number of seats. A balance of four or fewer false keys indicates that the government will retain a majority in the House of Commons. A balance of five or more false keys indicates that they will lose their majority.

In calculating the number of seats, I have decided that each turn of the keys costs the governing party fifteen seats. However, when six keys are turned that loss increases to twenty. This is because of the piling-on effect of more and more people wanting to give an unpopular government a good drubbing at the polls. This is also manifests in anti-government tactical voting which is also accounted for by this key. Each misfortune has a compounded effect in terms of lost seats. At seven negative keys the number of seats lost rises to twenty-five, and at eight keys it is thirty, and at nine it will be thirty-five and so on.

HALF-TURNED KEYS

An additional difference between my system and Professor Lichtman's is that I have an allowance for situations in which the keys are hard to call. I have 'Half turned keys', when a key seems indeterminate. I only use this when I genuinely find it difficult to call it. For example, in the election of 1970, the Policy Change Key was not obvious. The Wilson administration had effected considerable liberalising social change; for example, the decriminalisation of male homosexuality and abortion, the Equal Pay Act, no-fault divorce and the abolition of many grammar schools. The reforms were clearly more than those of many other governments, but at the same time, less than the changes effected by the Atlee or Thatcher governments. The key seemed partially true. Therefore, the government lost half of the value of the key. As this election was a five key election with one other half-turned key, that meant they would fall significantly behind Edward Heath's Conservatives in the parliamentary arithmetic.

The government's other 'half-turned key' happened to be the Civil Unrest key. There had been mounting wild cat strike action throughout the Wilson term, and also significant student demonstrations against British support for the American war in Vietnam. There had also been right wing agitation following Enoch Powell's 'Rivers of blood' speech in 1968. All of this resulted in levels of social unrest greater than was normally the case in the UK, but falling short of the level necessary to topple the key. The strikes were nowhere near as disrupting as those during the Three-Day Week in 1973-74 or 'Winter of Discontent' in 1978-79. The 'Civil Unrest' key seems to be a particularly sensitive barometer of popular discontent.

This half-turned Key results in a loss of half that key's value. In 1970, there were five lost keys. So had the civil unrest been worse, the complete loss of that key would have cost the Wilson administration twenty seats. Therefore, the halving of that key cost them half of that - ten seats. Other examples of half-turned keys are to be found in the elections of 1959 and 1964. Here, the long-tern GDP was less than that of the two preceding terms. However, there had been no recognised recession or major economic crisis. There was also no mood fear or despondency concerning the economic situation. On the other hand however, there were moderate concerns about the balance of payment, and some quarters of contraction. Ergo, the key turned halfway each time, costing Macmillan and Wilson, seven seats respectively.

Other examples of half-turned keys include the Policy Change Key in 2005 and 2010. Blair's creation of the Supreme Court, increased public spending and public sector reforms fell just short of turning the key fully – but were still significant. The same situation resulted from the Bank Rescue Package at the 2010 election.

There is a greater necessity for having weakened and compensated keys when forecasting British, rather than American elections. This is because it is a parliamentary system based on complex arithmetic. There is a possibility for hung parliaments and this grey area means that extra precision is required. The American presidential system is of course a binary one, so less fine-tuning is needed.

Finally, it is worth noting that if there are two half-turned keys in an election, then their combined effect is the same as one wholly false key. This happened in the 1970 election, in which there were five false keys and two half-keys; thus, a final balance of six false keys.

keys and majorities under the current House of Commons

650 seats. 326 required for majority

Keys:	*strength of governing party*
one positive key	majority of 165
zero balance of keys	majority of 135
one negative key	majority of 105
two negative keys	majority of 75
three negative keys	majority of 45
four negative keys	majority of 15
five negative keys	318 seats 8 short of a majority

six negative keys   298 seats 28 short of a majority

seven negative keys   273 seats 53 short of a majority

eight negative keys 243 seats 83 short of a majority

nine negative keys 208 seats 118 short of a majority

ten negative keys   168 seats 158 short of as majority

This precise calculation of seat numbers is of course modified by any
half-turned keys. It is also modified slightly by the campaign.

GUAGING STRENGTH OF THIRD PARTIES

Due to the nature of this predictive method, the exact strength of the losing parties cannot be quite so accurately predicted as can that of the victor; but can still be closely estimated, based upon the projected strength of the winning party. Polling, together with local and by-election performance remains the best guides for the estimation of third parties.

Professor Lichtman's rule for predicting the strength of third parties is to find their best weekly polling average and then halve it. This does not work well in the UK, probably because third parties are stronger and more numerous here, and so voting for one of them seems less of a futile gesture than in the US. Generally, they do under-perform compared to the polling, but only by a little and even then, not always.

CAMPAIGN

Generally speaking, election campaigns in Britain make very little difference to the result. Unless one party clearly campaigned more effectively than its rival, then the campaign shall be deemed as making no measurable difference whatsoever to the result. If however, one side is clearly performing better than the rival party, then it makes a small difference. If the difference is significant but not dramatic, then the projected government majority is either raised or lowered by five seats. For example, if the government is doing better in the campaign, then their projected seat tally will rise by two or three, and hence their majority will rise by five seats and if badly, then vice versa.

If however one party is campaigning brilliantly and the other disastrously, then the more successful party will gain five seats as a result, changing the projected government majority (if one is forecast) by ten. For example, in the election of 1983, the Conservatives were fighting a very slick campaign under the campaign wizardry of Sachi & Sachi. Labour under the hapless Michael Foot, were fighting a badly organised and old-fashioned campaign, led by a man who did not own a television set. This increased Mrs Thatcher's forecast majority from 135 to 145. (Actually, they got 144.)

The only time when a campaign has made a really significant difference was in the strange election of 2017. In this surprise snap election, Theresa May entered the campaign with some exceptionally good approval ratings after having just triggered article fifty to leave the EU.

However, her campaign was so inept and clueless, and her performance so stiff and uncomfortable that the Incumbent Leadership key was turned false during the course of the campaign itself; thereby providing the fifth false key that erased her majority.

However, all the campaign really did was to expose May's serious lack of communication skills, that had already been present, but so far invisible to the public and media. The lesson from that debacle is that any very recently elected leader, who goes into an election still basking in their political honeymoon, should tread very carefully indeed!

CALCULATION FOR DIFFERING TERM-LENGTHS

In US presidential politics the term is a fixed one of four years, with the exact date of the election known long in advance. This is not, and has never been the case in Britain. Until 1911, terms could be up to seven years long. Since then, the maximum length has been five years, though four is still considered a full term. However, terms can be very short indeed. In 1974, the third Harold Wilson administration lasted for just seven months before facing a fresh election. Therefore, how do we apply the keys for elections of differing length?

For the purposes of calculating long term economy, any term of at least twelve months will count as a term. If one of the last two terms is under a year, then the last three shall be used to work out the Long-Term Economy key referral period. Any incoming government that has been forced to call a general election before its first year is up will be judged only on the basis of short-term economy and not long-term economy. For example, the administration of Harold Wilson in 1974 had to go to the country after only seven months in office. Therefore, the Long-Term Economy Key would be considered void in that election.

If a pre-existing government is forced to call an election less than twelve months into its second or subsequent term, then the Long-Term Economy Key would include the whole period of the previous term, plus the months since the last election. For Example, if the government of John Major had lost a no-confidence vote following Black Wednesday and been forced to hold an election in November 1992, then the Long- Term Economy Key would have applied to the whole period of the previous term up till the election; therefore, from June 1987 to November 1992.

In the case of a new government forced to go to the polls in under two years, then failure to achieve major policy change or major foreign policy success will not count against it. If it does achieve either or both of these, then they shall count as a bonus key, erasing other negative keys, and perhaps even pushing the balance of keys into positive territory. For example, the first Wilson government of 1964-66 called an early election in March 1966, following only seventeen months in office. In that case, the failure of the government to achieve major policy change, or a major breakthrough in foreign policy did not turn any keys against it, as it would have done for a government in office for longer than two years.

In the case of a pre-existing administration forced to call an election after less than two years of a new term, then failure to achieve foreign policy success or policy change will count against them. This is because policies put into place during the previous term, could reasonably have borne fruit in the current term. For example, the second Attlee administration of 1950-51 failed to match the spectacular policy changes of the first Atlee government. This turned the Policy Change Key against it.

In the case of calculating the Long-Term economy key, the two previous terms are counted for the calculation of average GDP. All terms of at least one year will count as full terms. If however, one of the previous two terms has been under one year in length, then the previous three terms will be included. For example, when calculating the Long-Term Economy key for the 1979 general election, the reference period would include the very short term in 1974, the Heath term of 1970-74 and the second Wilson term of 1966-70.

THE WIN RATE OF THE INDIVIDUAL KEYS

How often the incumbent party wins a majority with the individual keys being true or loses when it is false. Half-turned keys are counted 'true' for Civil Unrest, Long-Term Economy, but 'false' for Policy Change.

By-Election Key 1:

Win Rate if True: 70%
Loss rate if False: 56%

Unity Key 2:

Win Rate if True: 64%
Loss rate if False: 44%

Incumbent Leadership Key 3:

Win Rate if True: 100%

Win rate if False: 57%

Opposition Leadership Key 4:

Win Rate if True: 69%
Loss rate if False: 75%

Third Party Key 5:

Win Rate if True: 67%
Loss rate if False: 80%

Cyclical Incumbency Key 6:

only false once

Short Term Economy Key 7:

win rate if true: 63%
loss rate if false: 50 %

Long Term Economy Key 8:

win rate if true: 62%
loss rate if false: 50%

Foreign/Military Success Key 9:

win rate if true: 70%
loss rate if false: 44%

Foreign/Military Failure Key 10:

win rate if true: 75%

loss rate if false: 50%

Policy Change Key 11:

win rate if true: 86%
loss rate if false: 50%

Civil Unrest Key 12:

win rate if true: 67%
loss rate if false: 100%

Scandal Key 13:

win rate if true: 69%
loss rate if false: 75%

Opposition Implausibility Special Key 4A:

win rate if true: 100%

Opposition Complicity Special Key 4B:

only true once.

Third Party Bonus Special Key 5A:

win rate if true: 100%

In these statistics, 'winning' is defined as being re-elected with an official majority. It has to be borne in mind that of the twenty elections being considered in this book, twelve saw the re-election of the incumbent administration with a Commons majority. Therefore, the overall win rate is sixty percent. In order to find the most effective individual keys, we should therefore look for win rates well above sixty percent and loss rates well below forty percent.

I have excluded the cyclical incumbency key six and the Opposition Complicity Key 4B, as they have each only come into play once since 1945. The Civil Unrest key twelve has only turned false twice since World War Two, but each time the government was ejected from office, giving it a loss rate of a hundred percent. However, if half-turns of the key are counted, the win rates drops to just sixty percent, suggesting the half-turned key is valuable only in providing the bigger picture and not in isolation.

The Incumbent Leadership Key three, and the Opposition Implausibility Key 4A and Third Party Bonus Key 5A, also have a 100% rate of predicting the outcome – in this case, government re-election. Obviously, if a government is heading towards the electoral rocks, then it is highly unlikely that the Prime Minister would still be perceived as charismatic or strong. Still, there were many people predicting the defeat of the Conservatives under the popular Harold Macmillan in 1959, and indeed the formidable Margaret Thatcher in 1987.

The predictive rates for the two Foreign Policy keys are perhaps surprisingly good considering Britain was no longer a first rank world power in this period. Also note the very high win rate for the Policy Change Key. Short Term Economy Key seven is perhaps less effective a prognosticator than we might have imagined at only fifty percent. Here though, one of the two incumbent victors in tough economic times was the government of Harold Wilson that had only been elected seven months previously. Voters probably still blamed the recession on the recently ejected Heath government.

What is even less effective in isolation is the Long-Term Economy Key 8, with a loss rate of only fifty percent. However, if we simply defined 'false' as meaning technically false, with the years 1959, '66 and '05 counted false, the win rate would drop to just thirty-three percent, suggesting that my more nuanced interpretation works better – in the UK at least. However, were the key to be removed, the system would work much less well as a whole, confirming that the bunch of keys is greater than the sum of its parts!

Chapter 2 1945-51

THE ATLEE YEARS: SOCIALISM, DE-COLONISATION, AND COLD WAR

'We live in a state of society where the vast majority live stunted lives – we endeavour to give them a freer life.' Clement Attlee, to his brother Tom in 1918. [12]

For Six years Britain was subjected to a bold new socialist experiment that had permanent effects on the way the country would be governed, and on the relationship between the British people and their government. In these short years, Britain gained a National Health Service and a welfare state, and began to lose an empire. After the terrible sacrifices of fighting the Second World War, the British people were determined to have a peace worth fighting for. Now, the privations and inequalities of yesterday were no longer tolerable. Britain needed to become a land of opportunity for all.

Although the British public were grateful for the wartime leadership of Winston Churchill, they were inspired by a Labour leader who had a real vision for the country's future, which the Conservatives lacked. After the bullish, charismatic Churchill, who embodied a nation's defiance in the face of such a grave threat, Britain's new leader was a laconic, mild-mannered man with a plan for tomorrow. Proving that style and charisma are not everything, Clement Atlee transformed Britain to a degree rivalled by very few leaders.

Labour also proved far-sighted and wise in their acceptance of Indian independence and recognition of the danger posed by Stalin's encroaching Soviet Empire.

The wisdom of expanding the welfare state has been a bone of bitter contention down the years, as has the struggle within the Labour movement between its right and left wings. Neither have been resolved.

Although much of the nationalisation programme of this government would be undone by Thatcher forty years later, the creation of the National Health Service is still with us, and is generally regarded as Labour's finest single achievement.

1945-50

'The British have the distinction above all other nations of being able to put new wine into old bottles without bursting them.' Clement Attlee [13]

In July 1945, Labour won a majority for the first time in Britain. They won a sensational landslide majority of 146 seats. Churchill had been reluctant to go to the country before victory was assured over both Germany and Japan. However, Home Secretary Herbert Morrison and the rest of the Labour party opposed this, and an election was called after the German surrender on VE day, but several weeks before the Japanese surrendered on VJ day.

The election of July 1945 could not have been forecast using the keys system, as it was a case of the different parties in a coalition government deciding to go their separate ways. No one party could therefore take all the credit, or all the blame for what had happened over the previous five years. Both main parties were heavily involved in the wartime coalition, but both campaigned for different programmes after its dissolution was announced.

Labour essentially campaigned on implementing the Beveridge Report of 1942. This widely read and highly popular report, proposed the creation of a welfare state, nationalisation of healthcare, national insurance and the expansion of state education. According to polling, forty-one percent of respondents thought that housing was the single most important issue facing the country, followed by fifteen percent who believed it was employment. [14]

The Conservative campaign complacently relied on Churchill's personal popularity to win them votes, and failed to articulate a clear plan for the peacetime era.

Labour meanwhile cleverly drew the distinction between Churchill and the party he led, and their respective records in office.

Labour attacked the Conservative failings of the pre-war era; notably the high unemployment during the Depression, and the appeasement of Hitler at Munich and failure to re-arm against him.

Winston Churchill made a serious blunder when he accused Attlee of authoritarianism during the campaign. He claimed that Attlee 'would have to fall back on some form of a Gestapo,'[15] in order to implement his socialist programme.

The scale of Labour's victory was not widely anticipated. Opinion polling did indicate a big Labour win, but it was still in its infancy and not yet taken seriously. Even the left-wing Manchester Guardian expressed the opinion that 'the chances of Labour sweeping the country and obtaining a clear majority... are pretty remote.' [16] Yet this Labour did, achieving an overall majority of 146 - the first in Labour's history. The

Conservatives faced their worst result since 1906 and the Liberals were pushed towards the edge of extinction.

On receiving news of the result on July 26th - three weeks after the actual election, Winston Churchill drove to the King and resigned. He was at least magnanimous in defeat, declaring: 'The decision has been recorded. I have therefore laid down the charge which was placed upon me in darker times. It only remains for me to express my profound gratitude for the unflinching support they have given their servant through these perilous years.'[17] His successor, Clement Attlee was characteristically laconic with, 'We are facing a new era. Labour can deliver the goods.'[18]

Several of the most senior figures in the Labour team had all been key players in the wartime government. Clement Attlee had been the Deputy Prime Minister, in fact the first official holder of that office, and had held the fort when Churchill had been overseas. Ernest Bevin had been the Minister for Labour, Stafford Cripps had been leader of the House of Commons, in order to take the workload off Churchill, since previously Prime Ministers had held both posts simultaneously. Herbert Morrison, the former leader of London Council (and grandfather of future 1st Secretary of State Peter Mandelson) had been Home Secretary.[19]

The biggest problem facing the Attlee administration was the economic cost of the war. This had exhausted about a quarter of Britain's national wealth. This was clearly unsustainable, especially when combined with the need to counter the growing Soviet threat, and fund the enormous re-building programme at home - half a million homes had been destroyed by the bombing. Things were so bad that economist John Maynard Keynes described the situation as a 'Financial Dunkirk'[20].

During the war, the USA had supplied Britain with food, oil and other materials as part of the Land-Lease Programme. This had provided roughly two thirds of the funds necessary to support the war effort. This however, unfortunately came to an abrupt end when the war finished. In the words of Alan Bullock, Bevin's Biographer, the news 'fell on Whitehall like a V2 - without warning.' [21]

For three months after the Japanese surrender, Keynes led a frantic British delegation to negotiate an alternative form of American financial assistance. This finally bore fruit in the form of the Anglo-American Loan. This provided $3.75 billion dollars, plus a $650 million-dollar final settlement. This was to come with an interest rate of two percent that would be charged for five years; the same point that the first repayments would have to be made. The British government would have fifty years to repay the total amount. In fact, the last repayment was not made until 2006.

The Anglo-American-loan would come with one unfortunate condition though; the pound would have to become fully convertible to US dollars. This led to a sterling crisis in 1947, with convertibility having to be suspended after only five weeks. Fortunately, the United Kingdom was also able to benefit from the Marshall Plan, so the country narrowly avoided economic collapse - which would have been the result of the failure to secure the American loan.

The net result of these problems was the continuation of wartime rationing into the mid-1950s, with severe shortages during the first four years of the Labour government. The wartime rationing actually got worse, not better in the immediate aftermath of the Second World War. Bread rationing was introduced for the first time in 1946, in order to avoid famine in British-occupied Germany. This was after the petrol ration had been brought back and rations for meat, oil and soap had all been cut at the end of the war, a year earlier.

The country was also very low in coal reserves, with less than seven million tons of coal in reserve at any one time, as against an annual, national consumption of two hundred million tons. This was a particularly serious problem, since nearly everything was coal-powered at that time.

In the winter of 1946-47 fate dealt the Attlee government a devastating blow, with the coldest, snowiest winter in most people's memory. From the end of January till mid-March, much of the country was blanketed in deep snow and frozen in a permafrost. The effect was disastrous. Due to transport disruption and power-shortages, unemployment increased from 400,000 to 1.75 million. The Thames froze over, as did the North Sea, trapping much-needed coal-boats. The coal mines themselves froze up and the railway networks were paralysed. The RAF had to distribute food parcels to cut-off rural communities and even Big Ben froze up and stopped chiming.

With the power shortages came the return of wartime blackouts; cooking on electric stoves was banned between nine am and noon, and between two and four pm. Offices were reduced to working by candlelight and even traffic lights were switched off.

Even the end of the big freeze was not without new chaos: the sudden thaw led to major flooding, and the resultant contamination of water supplies left a million Londoners without drinking water.

Post-war Britain certainly still felt in the grip of crisis. The cold winter crisis was exacerbated by a hauliers' strike, which resulted in the army being called in to deliver food supplies to the capital.

The major economic problems facing Britain in the aftermath of the world war, caused the economy to contract badly from 1944-47. Although growth returned at a reasonable rate of three percent from 1948 onwards, this was nowhere near enough to save Labour the loss of the Long-Term Economy Key.

In September 1949 the country suffered another devaluation of the pound, to the tune of thirty percent against the dollar. Devaluations are normally very bad for incumbent parties and presage a loss of support. Here was no exception. However, the dire predictions made about inflation did not come to pass, and the recovery continued through 1950 and beyond. The improvement was sufficient to save the Short-Term Economy Key.

Rationing continued throughout the remainder of the term, with only bread and clothes rationing being brought to an end. The latter was abandoned only because black marketeers had made rationing impossible to enforce.

The main thrust of the Attlee government's agenda was the nationalisation of the British economy, the expansion of the welfare state, and the creation of the National Health service.

The Beveridge report of 1942 had stated that the aim of the post war government should be the maintenance of full employment, which would itself provide the revenue for a welfare state. It contained a Dickensian warning against the 'Five Giants': want, ignorance, squalor, disease and idleness. The report proved very popular and influential, and all parties committed to it in principle. However, Labour were seen as the party best placed to put the recommendations into practice.

Labour embarked on a major programme of nationalisation, bringing the Bank of England, coal, electricity, haulage and the railways into public ownership in 1946-47, the hospitals in 1948, and then gas in 1949.

Additionally, they introduced major improvements to workers' rights, regulating hours, pay and conditions. Coal mining in particular enjoyed major benefits following the creation of the National Coal Board. Children were banned from being sent down the mines, and miners enjoyed compulsory training, sick pay and even baths installed at pitheads.

The Fire Services Act and the Electrical Act provided better conditions for firemen and electricians, whilst the Shops Act provided breaks for all shop workers. The Merchant Shipping Act, The National Dock Labour Board and the Agricultural Wages Board offered increased pay for workers in their respective industries as well. The Dock Labour Scheme of 1947 also guaranteed work for dockers, as well as improving working conditions.

The government also repealed The Trades Disputes and Trades Unions Acts of 1927, thus allowing secondary strikes.

The National Health Service was established by former Welsh miner, Nye Bevan in 1948, in the teeth of fierce opposition from the medical establishment. This free at the point of use service is still in existence and is widely regarded as Labour's greatest ever achievement.

The idea of a nationalised health service had first been mooted by Beatrice Web in 1909, and was advocated again by the minority government of Ramsay Macdonald twenty years later, before being proposed a third time in the Beveridge Report of 1942.

The healthcare situation before the Attlee government had been one of a patchwork of charitable and local authority municipal hospitals that lacked a central directing hand. The National Health Service Act of 1946 authorised the nationalisation of hospitals in Britain, the setting-up of regional boards and the re-allocation of doctors to under-provided areas. It also led to the establishment of local health centres to house group practises, as well as the provision of state care for sick, aged and disabled people in their own homes.

The act was opposed vociferously by the British Medical Association, (BMA) despite Nye Bevan's considerable charm and skills of persuasion. In 1946, the BMA voted against accepting the bill by fifty-four percent. Dr Alfred Cox, a former secretary of the BMA even compared the NHS to Nazi health policy, calling Bevan a 'Health Fuhrer.'[22]

However, early in 1947 the presidents of the three royal colleges signalled compromise. Bevan then moved to secure the support of consultants by allowing them to maintain pay beds in NHS hospitals for their own private practice, whilst giving them NHS salaries. Bevan quipped that he had 'stuffed their mouths with gold.' [23]

The BMA finally capitulated in April 1948 after Bevan agreed to a ban on salaried service and also promised extra pay for maternity work. The National Health Service was formally set-up on the 5th July 1948, and ninety-seven percent of the British public signed up for it, as did ninety percent of doctors. In the words of historian Peter Hennessy, 'The NHS was and remains one of the finest institutions ever built by anybody, anywhere.' [24]

With the creation of the National Insurance Act 1946, funding was levied from all workers to provide for sickness benefit, pensions and unemployment benefit. Like the NHS it is still very much with us today.

Additionally, the government improved the rights of women by removing unfair legal obstacles to them obtaining inheritance, and by removing the marriage bar in the civil service which prevented married women from working in that institution.

The Labour policy on housing was ambitious, with election-time pledges to build 3-4 million new houses. In reality, one million new homes were built during the term. Although this fell short of the wild promises, it was still a considerable achievement.

Labour also made major educational reforms, implementing the recommendations of the 1944 Education Act. Secondary education was now a right, with fees eliminated for state grammar school pupils and the school leaving age raised to fifteen in 1947. There was also a major programme of school building, as well as upgrading and repair of existing schools; many of them damaged in the blitz.

In addition to this, the government assisted thousands of ex-servicemen to go to college, and provided scholarships for poorer people to get to university. Government generosity also extended to the provision of free school meals and milk.

All of this was achieved under the creation of a Ministry of Education, replacing the somewhat more limited Board of Education. On the cultural front, the Attlee government set up the Arts Council to promote the arts in Britain.

Constitutional reform was comparatively limited, but one thing the Labour party did achieve was the elimination of Plural Voting, wherein graduates were allowed to vote twice; once in their home town, and once in the university town where they graduated. The Parliament Act of 1949 reduced the amount of time the House of Lords could delay bills, from two years to one.

All this tremendous amount of reform clearly won Labour the Policy Change Key for the 1950 general election.

Regarding foreign policy, Labour had to deal with three major issues; the reconstruction of Europe following the ravages of World War Two, the new Cold War with Stalin's USSR and the disintegration of the British Empire.

On face value, the British Empire stood at its peak in 1945, occupying and controlling an unprecedented amount of the globe.

This included having partial control of occupied Germany and Italy, as well as much of North Africa, the Mediterranean, Greece and southern Iran. All this was of course in addition to the pre-existing Empire.

Indeed, Britain had just achieved a mighty victory against the imperialist ambitions of Germany and Japan. As the horrors of the Final Solution and Japanese POW camps became exposed to the world, Britain seemed to be on the side of right and progress; the demise of her empire was then, by no means an inevitable or even desirable conclusion.

However, her territorial over-reach was simply not economically sustainable, especially when the cost of Labour's nationalisation programme was taken into consideration. In the words of Peter Hennessy, Britain was 'Morally magnificent, but economically bankrupt.'[25]

It was also the case that occupation by the Japanese, increased nationalist sentiment throughout those affected colonies, and a desire to be rid of all foreign interference. Yet, the complete liquidation of the empire was not Labour policy, nor was it widely foreseen at the time. In 1943, future Prime Minister Harold Macmillan was observing a victory parade of British troops in Tunis.

It struck him that the 'jolly, honest, sunburnt, smiling English, Scottish or Irish faces seemed on that day masters of the world and heirs to the future.' [26]It was not to be. Within two decades, very little indeed would be left of the British Empire.

Attlee, Bevin and many others continued to see the Empire as a force for good in the world, and in fact many of the African colonies were now ruled more directly from London than before. It was however on a different continent that the winds of change first began to blow.

One of the most momentous developments of this period is the independence of India and Pakistan in 1947. Clement Attlee had earlier been Labour's expert on India, after sitting on the Simon Commission in the late 1920s, which had been set up to examine the feasibility of Indian independence. He had subsequently been in charge of India during the war. Although far more sympathetic to the independence movement than Churchill and the Conservatives, the Labour manifesto only called for 'the advancement of India towards responsible self-government.' This fell a little short of advocacy for full independence.

However, because Britain was so financially weakened after World War Two, and also required many troops to counter the growing Soviet threat in Eastern Europe, it simply did not have the resources necessary to pacify further Indian revolt. Viceroy Wavell said he would require seven army divisions to contain violence if independence negotiations failed. The surrender of the 'Jewel in the Crown' was probably as much due to expediency as it was to ideological change.

It must also be said that as Britain had just fought the world war on the platform of freedom and respect for national sovereignty - the latter being codified in the UN charter; it seemed hypocritical to continue to deny the sovereignty to the peoples of the Indian subcontinent. Additionally, there was also pressure for Britain to decolonise from the United States, in order to open up new markets to American trade.

At the end of the war in 1945, Viceroy Wavell released future Prime Minister Nehru and the other senior congress party leaders from jail. (They had been locked up due to their opposition to the war.) With the change of government in the UK, India was now set on the path to some kind of self-government. However, talks on establishing such a government soon foundered on the Muslim insistence on creating a state of their own. (This of course became realised in the form of Pakistan.) Clement Attlee's response was decisive. In his own words; 'I decided there was only one thing to do – give them a deadline and tell them, "On that date we go out, so you'd better get together right away." [27]

In February 1947, Lord Mountbatten was appointed the final Viceroy of India, to maintain order during the transition to independence. He was given special 'plenipotentiary Powers.' With Mountbatten's appointment came a shortening of the transition period: Independence Day was brought forward from Summer 1948 to August 1947.

The Indian Independence Act was passed by the British Parliament on August 15th 1947, splitting the 'Jewel in the crown' into a Hindu-dominated India and a Moslem-dominated Pakistan. The latter being the first country to be named after an acronym: P-Punjab, A-Afghanistan, K-Kashmir, S-Sindh and Stan from Baluchistan. This involved dividing Bengal and Punjab between the two. It also involved splitting the Indian army, just when it would be most needed.

The 565 Princely States were nearly all persuaded to be subsumed into either India or Pakistan. Although in the case of Kashmir, the dispute led to war between India and Pakistan, and the region is still disputed and unstable to this day.

The speed of this decision was sometimes derided as a 'scuttle', and there was some Conservative opposition to its desirability in the UK. Churchill was so disgusted with the whole process that he avoided coming into the House of Commons while it was being debated.

The immediate consequence of independence was the bloody Indian Civil war between Hindus, Moslems and Sikhs which cost between half a million and a million lives, and ended with the assassination of Gandhi himself in 1948. Independence was also granted to Burma (now Myanmar) and British Ceylon (now Sri Lanka) in 1948.

Despite some critics on the right, Indian independence was generally very popular in the UK, with the former Conservative Secretary of State for India, Leo Amery calling it a 'personal triumph' for Attlee. [28] The Manchester Guardian hailed it as the product of Attlee's 'creative zeal.' [29] Therefore, the policy clearly wins the Foreign Policy/Military Success Key nine. In addition, it also contributed to the winning of the Policy Change Key eleven.

Britain had to deal with trouble elsewhere in the decaying empire. Violence erupted in Malaya in 1948 with the killing of three European plantation managers. A state of emergency was declared and the conflict escalated. The communist Malayan National Liberation Army led by Chin Peng began a long guerrilla campaign to drive the British out of Malaya and to establish a socialist government.

The rebels were based in the jungles, and carried out attacks against plantations, military and police bases, mines and the railway network to cripple the colonial economy and force the British out. The British sent troops to counter the threat, and UK force levels reached 35,000 at their peak. Counter-insurgency methods included scorched-earth policies, and mass internment of up to a million civilians in concentration camps, euphemistically labelled 'New Villages,' to isolate the population from the rebels. Agent Orange was also used to burn down foliage in a foreshadowing of Vietnam. In another incident often compared with that later conflict, the Scots Guards shot dead twenty-three unarmed men in what is known as the Batang Kali massacre – sometimes dubbed 'Britain's Mai Lai,'

The conflict was called the 'Malayan emergency' so as insurance companies would compensate plantation holders and other settlers for losses; which they would not do in a recognised civil war. This conflict would drag on for many years, but at the time of the 1950 election was neither an obvious military failure or success.

An even more pressing international problem was Palestine. The British Mandate in Palestine had existed since 1922. The fall of the Ottoman Empire, following defeat in World War One, led to the territory coming under British control. Palestine was then a primarily Arab-populated area with a small but growing Jewish minority. However, in 1917 the British government had in the Balfour declaration, promised the establishment of a Jewish homeland in Palestine.

Partly as a result of Zionist expectation, Jewish immigration to Palestine increased steadily during the inter-war years, accelerated in the 1930s by Nazi persecution in Germany. Conflict between Arabs and Jews became a persistent problem during this period. This era also saw the creation of the Jewish paramilitary groups Haganah and Irgun and the Arab Revolt of 1936-39.

In the wake of the Holocaust there was natural sympathy for the Jewish people and increased support for the idea of a Jewish homeland – especially from the United States. A rising stream of Jewish immigration was accompanied by a Zionist insurgency after the Second World War, leading to the British abandonment of Palestine in 1948. Terrorist attacks included the bombing of the British Palestinian Headquarters at the King David Hotel, and the killing of two British Sergeants who had been taken hostage by Irgun.

Although the United Nations had proposed partitioning Palestine between the Arabs and the Jews, the former group refused to accept the idea, plunging Palestine into an Arab-Israeli civil war in 1947-48, which made the territory ungovernable. The Labour government decided to relinquish control in September 1947 and handed Palestine over to the United Nations.

When the British Mandate finally expired in May 1948, the leader of the Jewish Agency David Ben-Gurion declared the existence of a Jewish state. The result was the immediate attack by multiple Arab countries, in what is known as the Israeli War of Independence. This process led to the expulsion/exodus of 700,000 Arabs from the state and Israeli victory. The conflict still burns on to this day – essentially unresolved despite the best efforts of multiple world leaders and conferences.

Clement Atlee struck up a productive working relationship with new US president Harry Truman and he could justly claim some credit for the implementation of the Marshall Plan, which helped rebuild the war-torn European continent.

In the developing Cold War with the USSR, Attlee initially wanted to give Stalin the benefit of the doubt, believing that if we treated the Soviet Union as an enemy, then it would become one. In a later-criticised good-will gesture, the British government sold the Soviets twenty-five Rolls Royce Nene Jet Engines in 1947-48. Although there was an agreement for the Soviets not to use them for military purposes, they managed to reverse-engineer them to create their very own MiG-15 Interceptors. These were deployed effectively against western forces during the Korean War.

Following Stalin's expansion through Eastern Europe, Attlee realised the wisdom of Ernest Bevin, who had been a staunch anti-communist following his experience of dealing with communists in the unions - and so his government embraced the Truman Doctrine of resisting communist expansion.

The Labour government co-operated keenly with President Truman in defeating the Soviet Union's attempt to starve West Berlin into surrender during the Berlin Blockade of 1948-49. For almost a year, Joseph Stalin cut off road, rail and canal links to the land-locked West Berlin, refusing to open the borders unless the allies withdrew the recently introduced Deutsche Mark from the territory.

The RAF and US Air Force delivered round-the-clock supplies to the city, thus defeating the Soviet siege and avoiding the outbreak of World War Three.

Labour, and in particular Foreign Secretary Ernest Bevin also played an important role in the foundation of NATO - the alliance of western powers established in 1949 to defend Western Europe against the growing Soviet threat. The origins of the treaty lay in the Treaty of Dunkirk, a mutual assistance pact signed by Britain and France in March 1947. This led to the Treaty of Brussels the following year, which included Belgium, The Netherlands and Luxemburg. Talks broadened to include the USA, and the formation of NATO was further facilitated by the Berlin-Airlift and the re-election of President Truman in 1948.

These achievements combined with Indian independence and Britain's involvement in the establishment of the Marshall Plan, easily secured for the Attlee government the Foreign Policy/Military Success Key.

One important area of foreign policy that Attlee acted decisively on was the development of nuclear weapons. At the time of the dropping of the first A-bombs on Hiroshima and Nagasaki in August 1945, there appeared to be a kind of loose gentleman's agreement between Churchill and Roosevelt about the sharing of American nuclear know-how.

However, although the Combined Policy Committee formed in 1945 had urged full cooperation between the two countries, the Secretary of State James Byrnes decided that the matter best be decided by Congress. In 1946, Congress responded by passing the Atomic Energy Act which forbade the sharing of nuclear secrets with all other countries. This led Attlee to take the decision that Britain was going to develop her own nuclear deterrent.

The Labour cabinet was split on the policy with Dalton and Cripps objecting to the huge cost. However, the Prime Minister found support from Bevin, who exclaimed that, 'We've got to have this thing over here whatever it costs... we've got to have the bloody Union Jack on top of it.'[30]

Clement Attlee however, decided to circumvent the full cabinet and form a secret committee codenamed GEN 163 – which met for the first and only time on 8th January 1947, with Attlee, Bevin, and the Defence Secretary A.V. Alexander, the only people in attendance. This finally bore radioactive fruit with the testing of the first British A-bomb under Churchill's watch in 1952.

The country suffered from industrial strife during this term, with lorry drivers striking in 1947 and a dockers' strike in 1949 having to be ended by troops. Violent clashes between Communists and far right Mosleyites also led to a three-month ban on political marches in the capital. The level of unrest fell somewhat short of that needed to topple the Civil Unrest Key. However, it was still significant, enough to lead to a Civil Unrest Half-turned key, costing the Labour party eight seats in the election.

The Labour government also avoided any really damaging scandals, but there were a few. In 1947 the chancellor Hugh Dalton had to resign after divulging the contents of his budget to a journalist before it was publicly announced. Another one involved John Belcher, the Parliamentary Secretary for the Board of Trade. He was found guilty of taking bribes in return for withdrawing the prosecution against a corrupt football promoter. However, these isolated incidents were clearly insufficient to taint the government as a whole, and so the Scandal Key also was saved.

However, the government was hit by tragedy as well. In January 1947, the Education Secretary Ellen Wilkinson caught pneumonia whilst opening a new school in the freezing cold and died. This was days after securing cabinet agreement to the raising of the school leaving age.

Let's take a look at the first six keys, the political keys. Regarding by-elections, the Labour party did not lose a single one, thus keeping the first key. The second key, that of party unity fared less well, since one problem that did blight the party was internal division.

In the 1947 crisis, Attlee's leadership came under attack from Cripps and Dalton, who plotted to replace him with Ernest Bevin. Bevin however refused to move against his leader, reportedly saying, 'I'm sticking with little Clem.' [31]. Clement Attlee defused the plot with a deft reshuffle, which promoted Cripps to the newly created post of Minister for Economic Affairs – taking considerable responsibilities away from Morrison. (Lord President) Thus buying off one rival and clipping the wings of another. He also promoted right-winger Hugh Gaitskell to Fuel & Power, and the thirty-one -year-old future Prime Minister Harold Wilson to the Board of Trade.

Attlee additionally came under attack from backbench rebel Ian Mikardo, who had a little list of complaints; accusing his leader of lacking 'leadership, fire and passion.' and that his cabinet of being, 'ill-coordinated.'[32] Nye Bevan also caused trouble for his party with his unguarded comments about the Conservative party; calling them, 'lower than vermin,' [33] in 1948. This earned him a rebuke from the Prime Minister.

During the term, a left-right split was emerging between the Bevanites represented by the Weekly Tribune, the majority of the cabinet and TUC leadership; versus moderates such as Clement Attlee, Ernest Bevin and Hugh Gaitskell. In 1947 a pamphlet entitled *Keep Left* was published by left wingers, Michael Foot, Ian Mikardo and Richard Crossman, calling for more overtly socialist policies and in particular, distancing from the United States in matters of foreign policy. The Keep Left group which named itself after the pamphlet would represent the left of the party during the next decade.

Tensions came to the forefront of political life after the watering down of Labour's programme for the forthcoming election. These tensions would grow much worse in the short second term of the Attlee government.

However, this ideological battle and leadership rumblings would be enough to topple the Party Unity Key for the 1950 election.

The next key is Incumbent Leadership, and although Clement Attlee had achieved great things during his four-and-half year term, being a charismatic figure was not one of them. He was so monosyllabic that his Economic assistant Douglas Jay remarked that, 'He would never use one syllable where none would do.' [34] As Trevor Burridge said, 'If he (Attlee) had got up in the commons and announced the revolution...it would have sounded like a change in a regional railway timetable.' [35] Therefore, key number three was also lost.

The next key to consider is the opposition charisma key, and here again is bad news for Labour. Although the Tory leader Winston Churchill was ageing rapidly and past his wartime best, he was undoubtedly a national hero in the eyes of the British public. Therefore, key number four was also turned against the administration.

Lastly, the Third Party Key was more conducive to Labour success. The Liberals were reduced to a pitiful twelve seats in 1945 and showed no sign of recovery in 1950. Thus, the Third Party Key remained firmly fixed in the government's favour.

One factor that helped the Conservatives but did not directly affect Labour is the alliance between the National Liberals and the Conservatives. This boosted the Conservative seat total by sixteen at the 1950 election.

The election campaign itself was highly polemical, with the Conservatives attacking the Labour government as 'a bureaucracy brooding over a dispirited, broken people.'[36] However, the Conservatives ceded some ideological ground to Labour by promising to make the maintenance of full employment a top priority. In the end, neither side achieved an obvious advantage, and it likely made no significant difference to the result.

Let's take a look at the balance of keys for the February 1950 election.

February 1950 UK general election

1) *By-election key*	true
2) *Unity Key*	false
3) *Incumbent Leadership Key*	false
4) *Opposition Charisma Key*	false
5) *Third Party Key*	true
6) *Cyclical Incumbency Key*	true
7) *Short-Term Economy Key*	True
8) *Long-Term Economy Key*	false
9) *Foreign Policy/Military Success Key*	true
10) *Foreign Policy/Military Failure Key*	true
11) *Policy Change Key*	true
12) *Civil Unrest Key*	half-turned
13) *Scandal Key*	true

balance of negative keys: 4 ½

forecast: knife-edge Labour majority of zero seats

campaign differential: nil

tally: 312 Labour seats C. 300 Conservative seats.

actual result: Labour majority of five seats

315 Labour seats 298 Conservative Seats

1950-1951:
'Democracy means government by discussion, but it is only effective if you can stop people talking.'
Clement Attlee. [37]

Labour were returned to power in February 1950, but with a much reduced majority, and the Tories were already saying 'One more heave and socialism is dead.'[38] Attlee found the results very disappointing, but his administration soldiered on, continuing to make some reforms; for example the nationalisation of iron and steel in 1951. However, the government was becoming exhausted and no radically new policies were implemented; thus, costing the party in power the Policy Change key.

On the international front, the period was dominated by the Korean War. In June 1950, communist North Korea invaded the pro-Western South. The USA, Britain and France rallied together to create a taskforce to repel the invasion. This found United Nations authorisation; though this is less impressive when one realises that communist China was not yet admitted to the UN, and that the USSR boycotted the UN in protest of China's exclusion; thus, depriving itself of a vote and allowing the western countries to prevail.

Initially, the western allies pushed the communist forces back, and then expanded the war aims to include regime change in the North. This unfortunately brought China into the conflict and the allies were driven out of North Korea and had to re-group and counter-attack; with the result that by July 1951, both sides were roughly back to the 1950 border and had fought themselves to a standstill.

Two years of stop-start ceasefires punctuated by new offensives failed to change the dynamic of the war, which was finally ended by an armistice in June 1953. Britain's role was significant, contributing 14,000 troops at any one time and suffering over a thousand fatalities.

The most memorable episode for the British was the heroic stand of the Gloucestershire regiment on hill 235 above Imjin. Their capture by the overwhelming Chinese forces was a tragically ironic consequence of British-English versus American-English misunderstanding. Their commanding officer used British understatement to describe their position as 'a bit sticky.'[39] Their American commanders thought he was describing minor difficulties, and so failed to send the back-up that was needed to salvage the situation

At the time of the October 1951 general election, the war in Korea was in a kind of stalemate, so did not amount to either a foreign policy success or failure. The conflict in Malya had escalated significantly, with the British High Commissioner for Malaya, Sir Henry Gurney being assassinated by rebels during the British election campaign. However, the rebels were still a very long way from any kind of conclusive victory, so the keys were split, with the Foreign Policy Success key false and Foreign Policy Failure key true.

European integration was also becoming a significant issue at this time. Its prime motivation was to avoid another devastating war in the continent. The move to creating a federation of Western European countries had begun almost as soon as the Second World War finished. In 1946 Winston Churchill publicly called for the creation of 'a United States of Europe' at the University of Zurich. At around the same time, a number of organisations appeared that began calling for

European integration such as the Union of European Federalists.

The Hague Congress in 1948 led to the European Movement International. From this came the Council of Europe, founded in May 1949, and led the following year to the European Convention on Human Rights.

The Schuman Declaration of 1950, called for the establishment of a supranational community in Europe. Named after the French Foreign Minister Robert Schuman, its first stage was to involve the merging of coal and steel resources in order to improve efficiency. This would lead eventually to 'ever close union' of the European countries. In 1951 France, Italy, Belgium, the Netherlands, Luxemburg and West Germany signing the Treaty of Paris. From here came the European coal and Steel Community, which attempted to avert a future war by merging control of these war-supporting industries between several countries. This paved the way for the High Authority, which was the forerunner of the European Commission, and the Common Assembly, which developed into the European Parliament.

The Attlee government could not agree to join in the proposals, as they were in conflict with its conception of a planned economy. However, the danger remained of Britain becoming sidelined and left out of a growing European market. This issue has still yet to be satisfactorily resolved.

The economy was continuing to grow at a respectable rate with both unemployment and inflation at low levels. In contrast to the very high unemployment experienced in the aftermath of the First World War, the aftermath of the second, saw consistently very low levels of joblessness. Chancellor Hugh Dalton saw this as his greatest achievement. Overall, GDP was considerably better than the average of the war years and the first Labour term, so both economic keys were true.

Industrial unrest also declined somewhat during this more settled period and so the Civil Unrest Key was firmly held by the government.

Although the political world was rocked by the defection of spies Guy Burgess and Donald Maclean to the Soviet Union in 1951, no direct culpability was traced to the cabinet itself.

Another episode that did the Attlee government no credit was the 'Groundnuts scandal,' in which the Ministry of Food undertook the responsibility of setting up vast peanut plantations in East Africa, which would have been used to produce cooking oils etc. The plan, originally devised by the United African Co, was ill-thought out in the extreme: soil conditions and rainfall were not taken into proper consideration, as was the supply of resources such as tractors. The scheme was finally abandoned in 1951 with £37 million of taxpayers' money wasted. These embarrassments remained far short of the threshold needed to topple the Scandal key, and so key thirteen remained in the government's favour.

The Labour government also avoided any by-election losses, thus preserving key one. However, the divisions in the Labour party grew yet worse during the second term. In April 1951 matters came to a head when Nye Bevan, the Minister of Labour, resigned along with the President of the Board of Trade and future Prime Minister Harold Wilson, over the recent budget of Chancellor Hugh Gaitskell. The main issue was the increase in defence spending and imposition of charges for spectacles and false teeth. This clearly kept the Party Unity Key false for the upcoming general election.

The administration also suffered from ageing and illness. Stafford Cripps resigned as Chancellor due to cancer in October 1950 and would die in 1952. Ernest Bevin died in April 1951, soon after stepping down as Foreign Secretary. Bevin's contribution to the creation of NATO was very significant and during the war, his role as Minister of Labour, made him second in importance only to Churchill. The latter contributed a humorous though rather unkind epithet to the puritan, vegetarian, teetotal Cripps: 'There but for the grace of God, goes God.' [40]

Cripps's successor was future party leader Hugh Gaitskell; a right-winger, later dubbed a 'desiccated calculating machine,' [41] by Nye Bevan. This only further fuelled the right-left civil war within the party.

Austerity remained the order of the day, although petrol and soap rationing had ended. The economy was growing and stable, and Labour tried to project a more positive national mood with *The Festival of Britain*, in the summer of 1951. This exhibition/fair, using twenty-six acres of bombed-out land on London's South Bank, was the creation of Foreign Secretary Herbert Morrison, who wanted to showcase Britain's achievements, in an event marking the 100th anniversary of the Victorian Great Exhibition. Although the economy was recovering in the wake of the second major currency devaluation in 1949, most of the country still felt impoverished.

With Attlee and Churchill still holding their respective posts, both the charisma keys remained negative for the Labour government. Attlee's commitment to the job remained strong, but his speeches continued to be on the dry side. Isaiah Berlin unkindly noted that, 'he touches nothing that he cannot dehydrate.'[42]

This election provides an interesting example of Third Party key five being turned against the government as the result of a sharp decline in the level of a third party's support, which had an inordinate benefit for the principal opposition party. The Liberal party suffered a sharp loss of votes, mostly due to it being unable to get insurance against losses, and therefore being unable to field many candidates. The party fielded only 109 seats in 1951, compared with 478 in 1950. This drastic reduction in candidates would inevitably lead to a drastic reduction in the Liberal vote.

At the time, and in fact until the 1980s, it was generally believed that Liberal voters were more likely to prefer a Conservative government to a Labour one. With five keys already being turned against Labour, a strong swing of ex-Liberal voters to the Tories would be predictable in advance.

With the number of Liberal candidates being reduced by more than three-quarters, a loss of six or seven percentage points of support could be forecast. Bearing in mind that a shift of five points is required to turn Third Party key five, and that not all former Liberal supporters would break for the Tories, it would seem reasonable that Key five would experience a half-turn against the Labour government.[43]

The election campaign, like its immediate predecessor was not particularly dramatic and made no significant difference to the result.

<u>*October 1951 UK general election:*</u>

1) *By-election key*	true
2) *Unity Key*	false
3) *Incumbent Leadership Key*	false

4) *Opposition Charisma Key* false
5) *Third Party Key* half-turn
6) *Cyclical Incumbency Key* true
7) *Short-Term Economy Key* true
8) *Long-Term Economy Key* true
9) *Foreign Policy/Military Success Key* false
10) *Foreign Policy/Military Failure Key* true
11) *Policy Change Key* false
12) *Civil Unrest Key* true
13) *Scandal Key* true

balance of negative keys: 5½

campaign differential: nil

forecast: Conservative majority of 14 seats

tally: 305 Labour seats Conservatives c. 320 seats

actual result: Conservative majority of 17 seats

295 Labour seats 321 Conservative seats

The efficacy of the keys in predicting this result is especially striking, as Labour actually out-polled the conservatives in this election. Labour in fact won the highest share of the popular vote in its history, securing more votes even than in 1945. (48.8%)

It also secured support from the highest share of the total electorate in British political history. (Although it has since been surpassed in absolute numbers.)

The continuing alliance between the Conservatives and Liberal Nationals increased the Tory total by nineteen seats in the 1951 election and gave them their majority.

This shows that elections are won and lost on the basis of government performance in office, even if that leads to statistically peculiar results.

It also shows that the British electorate are very good at making the first-past-the post system work, and reflect their true wishes.

Over six years, the Labour government of Clement Attlee made huge and lasting changes to the country that can justifiably be described as the foundations of modern Britain. No Conservative government until Thatcher had seriously challenged the nationalisation legacy, and none till this day have reversed the National Health Service, welfare state or National insurance policies. (Though some have reformed them.) This achievement is all the more remarkable given the extraordinary pressures and adversities that the government had to face. Clement Attlee's economic adviser Douglas Jay, perhaps described his boss's predicament the most accurately:

The picture drawn, or imagined, is of a great man sitting down in his office, pulling great levers, issuing edicts, and shaping events. Nothing could be further from the truth in the real life of number 10 as I knew it. So far from pulling great levers, the PM at this time found himself hemmed in by relentless economic or physical forces, and faced with problems which had to be solved, but which could not be solved.[44]

Chapter 3: 1951-64:
THE LONG FIFTIES: CONSERVATIVE CONSOLIDATION, COLONIAL CRISES AND CONSUMERISM

The thirteen years from 1951 to 1964 saw a long period of Conservative rule, and is often remembered as a period of stability. This is only partly correct. Although the social turmoil of the sixties was yet to come, this era witnessed the disintegration of the British Empire and with it the realisation that Britain was no longer a superpower. This lesson was dramatically underscored by the disastrous Suez adventure in 1956. It also saw the chilling rise of the new nuclear threat, some of the first major waves of non-white immigration to Britain, the first youth culture phenomena with Rock'n'roll and the rapid rise of television.

Economically it was a period of relative stability, with the early years of the period witnessing the end of the wartime rationing and the beginning of an unprecedented consumer boom. There were no great economic crises during this period to rival the Great Depression, the post-war contraction or the 1973 oil shock.

This period of British government saw relatively few major innovations or dramatic changes in ideology. Generally speaking, the Labour party's right gained the upper hand and the Tories remained a one-nation party, largely accepting the changes of the Attlee Government such as the welfare state, National Heath Service and nationalisation of parts of the economy. This became known as 'the Post War consensus' which was to remain very largely intact until 1979.

1951-55

'Around us we see the streets so full of traffic and shops so splendidly presented, and the people, cheerful, well-dressed, content with their system of government, proud as they have their right to be, of their race and their name. One wonders if they realise the treacherous trap-door on which they stand.' Churchill. [45]

In October 1951 the Tories rode back to power. This was partly thanks to the alliance with the National Liberals, whose sixteen seats secured a Tory majority of seventeen.

At seventy-six, Churchill was past his best and had already suffered several minor strokes, but still commanded enormous respect from the British public and the world. Initially, Churchill was inwardly daunted by the enormous scale of the economic challenge he faced. He privately described the economic situation as 'almost irretrievable: the country has lost its way. In the worst of the war, I could always see how to do it. Today's problems are elusive and intangible.'[46]

His government did not try and reverse the momentous changes wrought by Labour, but merely was content to provide a period of stability as Britain recovered from the after-effects of war. Although the Conservatives privatised the steel and haulage industries in 1953 and oversaw the end of rationing a year later, Churchill's Post-war term was not one of dramatic policy change, with the government accepting the NHS, welfare state and the bulk of the nationalisations; therefore, forfeiting Policy Change Key eleven.

Having said that, there was a scaling back in the level of public spending seen under Labour. NHS funding dropped from 3.74% of GDP in 1949-50 to 3.24% of GDP in 1953-54. [47]The new Chancellor Rab Butler also announced a moratorium on school building, provoking accusations from his Labour predecessor George Tomlinson of 'the murder of his own child.' [48] A reference to Butler's alleged betrayal of the 1944 Education Act bearing his own name.

Butler himself proposed something far more radical, the policy known as Operation ROBOT. The policy name was an amalgam of the first two letters of the names of the three civil servants who had been in favour of the idea. The idea of ROBOT was to allow the pound to float freely on the currency exchange, in order to find its own natural level and be convertible. This was to counter issues surrounding the depletion of Britain's gold reserves and balance of payments.

However, it was feared that if implemented it would mark a sharp departure from the Keynesian policies of the past decade and lead to more expensive imports, leading to inflation and rising unemployment. The idea was abandoned by the cabinet in February 1952 as being potentially too dangerous.

One change to the system of government was the introduction of overlords. These were a layer of co-ordinating ministers, between the Prime Minister and the other cabinet ministers. They oversaw several different departments, in the face of civil service opposition. After two years the idea was abandoned in the autumn of 1953.

There were other changes that deserve a mention. In 1954, the Television Act paved the way for the emergence of ITV, three years later. Contrary to popular belief, the surge in the popularity of Television was in fact first triggered by the TV coverage of the funeral of George VI in February 1952, sixteen months before the coronation.

Then, many more, approximately half a million sets were bought in anticipation of Queen Elizabeth's coronation; an event that was watched by an estimated 20 million people from only 2½ million TV sets. Overall though, Churchill's peacetime government fell far short of achieving the kind of change needed to secure key eleven.

One policy change that had begun with the Attlee government but was accelerated to completion under the Tories, was the abolition of rationing. Churchill had no idea of the scale of privation the British people were suffering from. This was illustrated nicely when the Minister for Food, Gwillym Lloyd George, presented the premier with a mock-up of the current weekly rations. Churchill looked at it and said, 'Not a bad meal.' When he was told that this was not the rations for a single meal, nor a single day, but for a whole week, the old warrior exploded with, 'A week! Then the British people are starving. It must be remedied.' [49]

Rationing was finally abolished in July 1954, with meat and other food rationing being the last to go.

In world affairs, Churchill attempted to resist the tide of de-colonisation that had begun in earnest at the end of World War Two. Although Clement Attlee still believed in the empire as a force for good, he accepted Indian independence, which Churchill could never countenance. In 1942 he declared, 'I have not become the King's First Minister in order to preside over the liquidation of the British Empire!'[50] After all, he was the man who resigned from the Tory shadow cabinet in 1931, over Baldwin's support for the Labour government's decision to grant India Dominion status.

Churchill also wanted to keep British control of Egypt and the Suez Canal as it would give Britain great strategic leverage over the Middle East, as well as access to commercial shipping. However, revolution in Egypt in 1952, led by Colonel Nasser resulted in Britain reluctantly having to agree to withdraw from the Suez Canal two years later, thus losing her strategic advantage. Britain also had to give up rule of Anglo-Egyptian Sudan in 1956. Although the agreement to withdraw from Suez led to backbench rumblings and private regret by Churchill, this fell short of the threshold for turning the Foreign Policy Failure key.

Britain was now having to contend with significant rebellion in her colonies. In Kenya, the Mau Mau insurgency had been a thorn in the empire's side since 1952. Here, the Kenya Land and Freedom Army (KLFA) known as the Mau Mau, were carrying out guerrilla-style attacks on white settlers and also blacks who refused to take the Mau Mau oath of allegiance. The troubles led to a state of emergency being declared in October 1952, and British troops being sent out to maintain order. The Kenyan and British authorities carried out a counter-insurgency operation which involved the mass round-up and internment of suspects in camps. Many atrocities were committed by both sides. At the time of the 1955 UK general election, the outcome of the conflict remained unclear.

Britain faced more trouble in Cyprus. In 1955, protests, strikes and terrorism were unleashed by EOKA, who wanted the end of British rule and union with Greece. The British were also fighting a counter-insurgency campaign in Malaysia against communist forces. The conflict was similar to that of Kenya, with the widespread use of internment camps and scorched earth policies to deprive the communist insurgents of resources.

Britain still faced a serious situation in Malya. Following the assassination of High Commissioner

Gurney in October 1951, General Gerald Templer was chosen as his successor. Templer's approach was more aggressive, and resulted in two thirds of the guerrillas being wiped out over the following two years. He also reduced the rate of insurgent incidents and colonial/civilian casualties by eighty percent.

Overall, the outcome of these conflicts was generally inconclusive at the time of the 1955 election. Hence the two Foreign Policy keys were split.

European integration continued apace, however many Conservatives still wished to continue instead with the old policy of 'Imperial preference,' a system of mutual tariff reductions between parts of the British Empire, established in the Ottawa Conference of 1932. However, since the end of the Second World War, this idea was rapidly becoming obsolete due to the crumbling of the empire and liberalisation of global trade. Despite this, some Conservatives supported it as a kind of rearguard action to save the dying empire.

Faced with the choice between increased engagement with Europe and hanging on to the setting sun of colonialism, the Churchill government was instinctively predisposed towards the latter. Churchill told De Gaule that, 'Each time we have to choose between Europe and the open sea, we shall always choose the open sea.'[51] This ambivalence towards Europe, as we have seen is still very much with us.

There were a few foreign policy successes, but not unequivocally impressive. In October 1952, Britain detonated her first atomic bomb. The plutonium device was detonated inside the Hull of the Royal Navy Frigate HMS Plym, in Main Bay, Trimouille Island, part of the Montebello Islands, Western Australia. Churchill believed that this would keep the peace, claiming that. 'Safety will be the sturdy child of terror.' [52]

However, this achievement was soon undercut by the American detonation of the first Hydrogen bomb a month later on November 1st 1952 in the Marshall Islands. Since the new H-bomb was a thousand times more powerful than the A-bomb, the British bomb was no longer sufficient to win Foreign Policy Success Key nine. Although sometimes portrayed as gung-ho, Churchill was in fact horrified by nuclear weapons and deeply worried about the prospects of them being used.

One consequence of this fear was Churchill's desire to hold a bi-lateral summit with Soviet Leader Malenkov, by-passing the United States. This idea provoked serious division in the cabinet, and came close to triggering resignations, including that of Foreign Secretary Anthony Eden. Churchill also authorised the development of the British H-bomb without cabinet consultation. These conflicts came close to costing the Conservatives the Party Unity key. The summit never materialised, though Churchill was stubbornly holding out for it until near the very end of his tenure as Prime Minister.

The end of the Korean War in June 1953 was effectively a stalemate, with the earlier goal of regime change in the north, now unattainable. Britain had relatively little to do with the ending of the conflict, being junior partners in it, and were never anywhere near as heavily involved as the US, so this too fell short of securing the Foreign Policy success key.

Economically, the period was more successful, with GDP growth well above the average of the two Attlee terms. With no recessionary clouds on the horizon during the spring campaign of 1955, both economic keys remained true.

The months leading up to the coronation saw significant disasters strike the United Kingdom. In

December 1952, a five-day London smog caused around four thousand deaths and made an estimated 100,000 people ill. This paved the way for the clean air act of 1956. In February 1953, severe storms and high tides combined to cause devastating flooding along England's East coast from Canvey Island off the Kent coast up to Yorkshire. Over three hundred people were drowned and tens of millions of pounds of damage caused. This disaster led to the creation of the Thames flood barrier thirty years later.

The coronation of Queen Elizabeth II in June 1953 ushered in a more positive feeling that the days of post-war austerity and national crisis were coming to an end, and Britain could look forward to a better future. Street parties were held up and down the country and people began talking romantically about a new Elizabethan age. It did seem to be an important collective psychological marker, drawing a line under the early post-war years of struggle, privation and sacrifice. Sir Edmund Hillary's conquest of Mount Everest that same year also symbolised the vision that Britain was still at the cutting edge of progress and achievement.

The government had avoided serious political scandal and there was also an absence of serious social unrest sweeping the country. Some Britons no doubt felt unsettled by the immigration coming from the West Indies and Indian sub-continent, but there were few signs of major unrest brewing. The political keys were mostly favourable for the conservatives. They had not lost any by-election seats during the term, and the party was broadly unified.

Churchill, now at eighty and already struggling to remember the names of new people, was finally persuaded to relinquish power by his cabinet. King George VI was in fact so anxious about the decline in

Churchill's health that he had planned on asking him to stand down earlier, in favour of Anthony Eden. Unfortunately, Eden also suffered from serious illness himself during the term, and had this not been the case, it is highly probable that Churchill would have been replaced in 1953 at the latest - when he was paralysed down one side following a stroke. In fact, in February 1952, the Principal Private Secretary Jock Colville said to Churchill's Doctor that: 'I hate to be disloyal, but the Prime Minister is not doing his work. A document of five sheets has to be submitted to him as one paragraph, so that many of the points of the argument are lost.' [53]

The style of Churchill's governance is now almost unbelievable, making even Joe Biden look like a paragon of youthful energy. He would govern from his bed until noon, accompanied by a cat, a poodle and a budgerigar, which was often perched on his head. A garden girl (Number Ten secretary) was on hand to provide him with papers and take notes. In one absurd incident, the budgie relieved itself upon the bald head of Chancellor Rab Butler, who wiped his pate with a silk handkerchief, whilst muttering, 'The things I do for England.'[54]

After getting up and travelling to the Commons, Churchill would retire to his room, take a few sleeping pills and sleep for much of the afternoon.

Churchill was also becoming so deaf, that according to Sir Alec Douglas Home, a system of speakers and microphones was set up on the cabinet table. Unfortunately, the conversations were being picked up by a London taxi driver on his radio, and the idea had to be abandoned. [55]

Churchill was finally succeeded by the dapper and imposing figure of Anthony Eden, who thought that a snap election would serve to give him a personal mandate from the British people, and exploit a strong economy and relatively peaceful international scene. Churchill assured the public that 'No two men will ever change guard more smoothly.'[56]

Eden at that time was a popular and presentable figure - even having a bowler hat named after him. However, he called the election only sixteen days after being appointed PM and therefore had not established himself as a strong and credible national leader. He was charming rather than charismatic. His speeches were competent but not quite mesmeric, not really inspiring and influencing the public with soaring oratory. Therefore, despite high approval ratings, he failed to secure the Incumbent Leadership key for the Conservatives.

Labour were still led by the now rather tired and elderly Clement Attlee, who was struggling to hold the right and left wings of his fractious party together. Therefore, the Opposition Charisma key stayed firmly on the government's side. The Labour party was in fact in the grip of an ideological civil war between the left-wing Nye Bevan and his *Keep Left* group and the right-wing Gaitskellites. Gaitskell himself attacked, 'Communist - inspired' [57]speeches at the 1952 Labour conference, which Hugh Dalton described as, 'the worst Labour party conference for bad temper and general hatred since 1926.' [58]

The ideological divisions manifested strongly in foreign policy, with Bevan resigning from the shadow cabinet over Attlee's support for an American initiative to create a NATO-like organisation for south-east Asia, in order to contain communist China. The issue of German re-armament also divided the party. Despite Labour voting to disband the Keep Left grouping, Bevan's influenced continued. However, with the moderate, experienced and respectable Clement Attlee still at the helm, the opposition avoided yielding the Tories any bonus keys.

The continuing alliance between the Conservatives and the National Liberals gave the Tory government the Third Party Bonus key, thus reducing the balance of negative keys by one. The mainstream Liberals were showing no sign of a renaissance either, thus securing Third Party key five.

One issue that threatened the government during the months leading up to the poll was industrial unrest. During the spring, a strike by technicians led to newspapers not being printed. This accelerated the trend towards Television becoming the main medium of news distribution. Four days before the election seamen went on strike, resulting in a state of emergency being declared immediately after the election. The previous autumn, a similar strike had cut Britain's imports by half, so the panicky government reaction was understandable. With a rail strike also announced in the closing days of the campaign, the level of industrial unrest was sufficient to effect a half-turn of Civil Unrest key twelve.

Therefore, the Conservatives entered the 1955 general election with a net balance of two and a half negative keys; the Foreign Policy success key, the Policy Change key and Incumbent Leadership keys were lost, the Civil Unrest key half-turned, but the Third Party Bonus Key was still true. The Tories, led by the telegenic Anthony Eden had the edge over the reserved and ageing Clement Attlee, but the campaign that year was low-key and failed to stir much public interest. Most people were rather more interested in the romance between Princess Margaret and Captain Peter Townshend.

The Conservatives won re-election with a majority of fifty-eight.

May 1955 UK general election:

1) *By-election key*	true
2) *Unity Key*	true
3) *Incumbent Leadership Key*	false
4) *Opposition Charisma Key*	true
5) *Third Party Key*	true
6) *Cyclical Incumbency Key*	true
7) *Short-Term Economy Key*	true
8) *Long-Term Economy Key*	true
9) *Foreign Policy/Military Success Key*	false
10) *Foreign Policy/Military Failure Key*	true
11) *Policy Change Key*	false
12) *Civil Unrest Key*	half-turned
13) *Scandal Key*	true

Special Keys

5A *Third Party Bonus*   *true*

balance of negative keys: 2½

Campaign differential: nil

forecast: Conservative majority of 60

tally: Conservative 346   Labour c. 275

actual result: Conservative majority of 58

Conservatives 345 seats. Labour 277 seats

1955-59:
'You've Never Had It So Good.' Harold Macmillan 1957

Following their second election victory in 1955, things seemed rosy for the Conservative government of Anthony Eden. The Tories had achieved the highest percentage of the popular vote of any single party government in modern times. (49.7%) With their popular leader, a growing economy and relative peace, it seemed that Eden might be in power for a very long time.

History had other plans. The seeds of the next crisis were planted by Nasser's Egyptian revolution of 1952. Within two years the British were forced to relinquish the Suez Canal, much to Churchill's dismay. That canal, built by the French and then purchased by Disraeli, was a godsend to international shipping. It circumvented the necessity of having to sail round the coast of South Africa. It also provided an important strategic base for British power in the Middle East.

Psychologically incapable of accepting the imminent demise of the British Empire, successive UK governments continually tried to convince themselves that they were still top dog. The decline was precipitous. Going from being one of the 'Big Three' at the end of World War Two in 1945, to a world with only two superpowers in less than a decade, to a world with no British Empire at all, save a few fragments here and there within another decade, was a major change to absorb. It was a change that was not widely anticipated until it was actually happening. For example, as late as 1948, Sir Philip Mitchell, governor of Kenya, stated that the chances of his colony becoming an independent African state were as remote as those of a Native American republic being declared in the USA. [59]

The British developed nuclear weapons of course, but it was soon clear that the main players were the USA and USSR, and that the UK was only a satellite orbiting America and no longer the mighty planet herself.

It was this refusal to accept her status sliding down the international dominance hierarchy that led to Britain's biggest military misadventure since the war of 1812. The occasion that precipitated the crisis was Colonel Nasser's nationalisation of the Suez Canal in July 1956. Although this was perfectly legal and did not violate the Constantinople Convention of 1888, this action was not accepted by the British or the French. 'A man with Colonel Nasser's record' cannot be allowed 'to have his thumb on our windpipe'[60], asserted Anthony Eden.

Eden publicly compared Nasser to the fascist dictators of the last world war, likening non-intervention to the appeasement at Munich. 'The pattern is familiar to many of us my friends...we all know this is how fascist governments behave and we all remember, only too well, what the cost is in giving in to fascism.' [61]

Nasser's decision to nationalise the canal was triggered by the cancellation of an Anglo-American offer to fund the Aswan dam project. This offer fell through, following Nasser's recognition of the People's Republic of China and an arms deal with the USSR, which was followed by a Soviet counter-offer for the dam.

The British were worried on at least two levels. Firstly, they feared that Nasser could cut off or restrict shipping through the canal, which would clearly be a major blow to the British economy as well as in strategic terms. They were also highly concerned about the growing Soviet influence in the Middle East, and the attendant spread of communism there.

Eden is reported to have barked to Nutting the Foreign Minister, 'What's all this nonsense about isolating Nasser or "Neutralising" him as you call it? I want him murdered, can't you understand?' [62]

Although Eden's reaction was extreme, he was certainly not alone in his paranoia. The then Secretary of State for Commonwealth Relations and future Prime Minister, Sir Alec Douglas Home expressed similar sentiment: 'I am convinced that we are finished if the Middle East goes, and Russia and China rule from Africa to the Pacific.' [63]

As talks in London aimed at the internationalisation of the canal, through the setting up of a canal users association failed, Britain and France sent forces towards the Middle East. A proposal for internationalisation was put to the UN but was vetoed by the USSR.

The Americans meanwhile remained highly sceptical and concerned about the prospect of western military intervention. In a letter to Anthony Eden, President Eisenhower warned the British premier bluntly: 'I must tell you frankly that American public opinion flatly rejects the thought of using force.' [64] When the Anglo-French taskforce reached Port Said in late October, it was harassed by the US sixth Fleet, which was permanently based there. They shone their searchlights on the vessels and jammed their radar. [65]

Here is where the plot thickens. The conspiracy for Britain, France and Israel to collude against Egypt was first put to Eden on October 14th 1956 at Chequers by two French Emissaries: Major General Maurice Challe, the Deputy Chief of the French General Staff and Albert Gazier, the Minister of Social Affairs. The idea was that

Israel would attack Egypt, and then Britain and France would invade Egypt under the pretence of separating the attacking forces. They would then seize control of the Suez Canal and topple Colonel Nasser from power.

The timing of this proposal was most unfortunate because the Foreign Secretary Selwyn Lloyd was currently in the UN HQ in New York, having discussions with his opposite number from Egypt. They were apparently getting quite close to reaching a diplomatic solution. Lloyd was summoned back before a deal could be brokered.

The collusion was finally agreed to on October 24th in an old Resistance safe house in Sevres, Paris. It has become known as the Sevres Protocol.

In strong parallels with the ill-fated Anglo-American invasion of Iraq nearly half a century later, Eden's cabinet were supine in the face of this dangerous drift into unjustified, ill-thought-out military intervention. As with Iraq, the government's own legal advisors were sidelined. The legal case for war was opposed by the two law officers in the Foreign Office. Sir Gerald Fitzmaurice, the Chief Legal advisor was of the opinion that Nasser had not breached the terms of the Convention of Constantinople and so there was no legal basis for war. When it was suggested to Eden by Foreign Minister Anthony Nutting that Fitzmaurice should be brought into the circle, Eden's reply was extraordinary: 'Fitz is the last person I want consulted. The lawyers are always against our doing anything. For God's sake keep him out!'[66]

Sir Reginald Manningham-Buller, the Attorney-General, also complained about being left out of the loop. In fact, the only people who were told about the Sevres Protocol besides Eden, were the Foreign Secretary Selwyn Lloyd, the Foreign Minister Anthony Nutting, the

Chancellor Harold Macmillan and the Chief Whip Ted Heath. Even senior military commanders had to find out the plans from their French counterparts.

Matters came to a head at the end of October, when Israel invaded the Sinai Peninsula. Britain and France responded by demanding that both sides withdraw to a distance of ten miles from the canal. However, Israeli forces were still some seventy-five miles away from the canal at this point, so were in effect being invited to advance sixty-five miles toward it. A few days later, Anglo-French forces attacked Egypt under the pretext of stopping the ongoing Israeli invasion and pulling the two sides apart.

On November 5th the Anglo-French invasion force landed near Port Said. Militarily, the air attacks and sea landings were ineffectually opposed, but international opinion was strongly against it, leaving the British and French isolated on the world stage. The Americans were furious, believing that their lack of advance knowledge of the offensive was proof that the British, French and Israelis had colluded to stage the whole enterprise, when meetings were held in Paris and in 10 Downing Street.

With the pound plummeting, the US Treasury made it clear to Chancellor Harold Macmillan, that the only way to prevent a major run on the pound would be for Britain to declare a ceasefire and begin to withdraw her forces. The US Treasury Secretary George Humphries told Macmillan that, 'You'll not get a dime from the US government until you've gotten out of Suez.' [67]

There were also threats of intervention from the USSR, which was also trying to distract from its simultaneous invasion of Hungary. Bulganin the Soviet Premier declared that, 'We are fully determined to crush the aggressors by the use of force in order to restore peace in the East.' [68] These threats were clearly to be taken seriously when General Knightley sent a flash signal to the effect that, 'Information has been received that Russia may intervene in the Middle East with force.' [69]

On the 6th November cabinet support for the war collapsed, with Macmillan saying; 'We have played every card in our hand, and we have none left. If it came to World War Three the Americans would win it, but we should all be killed.' [70]

The United Nations decided to create a UN force for the Middle East, and the Anglo-French forces reluctantly agreed to withdraw from Suez on November 8th 1956. On 21st November the British agreed to pull out of Egypt altogether.

Within a few weeks it transpired that the Americans had forced the British pull-out by threatening to end financial help to the UK, which was still paying off debts from World War Two. The UK also suffered a serious run on the pound as a result of the crisis, with the Americans threatening to let the Pound crash if co-operation on Suez were not forthcoming.

Eden suffered another bout of ill-health following the crisis and flew out to the Bahamas to recuperate. He had suffered episodic attacks of fever and lassitude following a botched operation to remove a bile duct blockage a few years earlier, and the crisis had brought him under greater strain than almost any other British Prime Minister. His wife Clarissa said that she felt as if, 'the Suez Canal was flowing through the drawing room,' [71]

On Eden's return to Britain, he compounded his already damaged political reputation by flatly denying the collusion in the House of Commons. On 20th December, he answered a query from Labour's Dennis Healey with the lines; 'There were no plans got together to attack Egypt... to say it quite bluntly to the house, there was not foreknowledge that Israel would attack Egypt – there was not.'[72] Ted Heath later recalled his feelings: 'As I sat and watched him deny any "foreknowledge" of Israel's invasion of Egypt, I felt like burying my head in the sands at the sight of this man I so much admired, maintaining this fiction.' [73]

Eden resigned as Prime Minister in January 1957, ostensibly on health grounds. Like Blair after him, he never apologised for his war of aggression.

This debacle turned the Foreign Policy/Military Failure key decidedly against the Conservative government. The bitter irony of this was that Eden had been a highly experienced minister in foreign affairs under both Chamberlain and Churchill. When he became Prime Minister in 1955, John Boyd-Carpenter opined that, 'It's a pity he knows nothing about economics or social security or finance, but at least we shall be all right with foreign affairs.'[74]

Eden's replacement was the former Chancellor Harold Macmillan. Tory leaders were still selected by the so-called 'Magic Circle' of party

grandees who advised the monarch on the appointment of a new Prime Minister when the party was in office. Elizabeth II was the last monarch to have any say at all on the appointment of a Prime Minister. She was also the first British monarch to become entirely a constitutional one - that is a figurehead with no political power at all. For example, King George V prevented Ramsay MacDonald from resigning during the 1931 financial crisis, advising him to form a coalition government instead.

Macmillan had swayed the 1922 committee with a speech in the aftermath of Suez, which according to his biographer Anthony Sampson, 'had managed to give the impression that the war had been a kind of victory and that nothing much had happened.' 75 He suggested a new national direction in which the British should be, 'Greeks in the Roman Empire.' Enoch Powell described how Macmillan, 'with all the skill of the old actor manager, succeeded in false-footing Rab. The sheer devilry of it verged upon the disgusting.' 76

Apparently, Macmillan almost knocked Rab Butler off his chair with his expansive arm gestures. 77 This gave him the upper hand over his rival. The swift defenestration of the damaged Anthony Eden and replacement with the popular and experienced Harold Macmillan, salvaged Party Unity Key two for the Tories.

Macmillan proved to be one of the more successful of post-war Prime Ministers. He was generally perceived as a strong patrician figure, unflappable in difficult situations, with a ready wit and authoritative manner. His cabinet colleagues found him a little too authoritarian, With Selwyn Lloyd describing him as treating his ministers like 'subordinates, not colleagues' and talking about them, 'as though they were junior officers in a unit he commanded.'78 However, he was also seen as more competent and psychologically stable than his immediate predecessor.

He became highly popular. The attempt by cartoonist Vicky to lampoon him as 'Supermac' backfired, and became a generally positive or at least neutral epithet. Thus, Incumbent Leadership Key four was also rescued.

Macmillan's initial main priority was repairing the damage to Anglo-American relations that had been wrought by the Suez fiasco. This he achieved through developing a good working relationship with US President Dwight Eisenhower, who rated Macmillan highly.

This cooperation came to fruition in July 1958 when a sudden coup in Iraq led to the murder of the pro-Western King Feisal and his Prime Minister; thus, putting other pro-Western regimes in immediate jeopardy. King Hussein of Jordan and President Chamoun of Lebanon both requested Western help in the face of the Nasser-led United Arab Republic. The US responded by sending Marines ashore in Lebanon, and the British contribution took the form of landing 2000 paratroopers at Amman airport in Jordan.

Although Egypt and the Soviet Union protested this Anglo-American intervention in the Middle East, the danger from Pro-Nasser forces was deflected. This intervention succeeded in two ways for Macmillan. Firstly, it re-asserted British military power after the humiliation of Suez, whilst simultaneously reviving Anglo-American co-operation. This turned the Foreign Policy/Military Success key in the Conservatives' favour.

The British government could also look to some success in three of the long-running conflicts in its colonies. In Kenya, the conflict with the Mau Mau was effectively won after the capture of rebel leader Dedan Kimathi in October 1956. This broke the power of the Mau Mau, and although they did not entirely vanish, the guerrilla war was effectively over.

In troubled Cyprus, the escalation of EOKA terrorism led to the deployment of British paratroopers in January 1956. After three years of further violence, EOKA accepted the London agreement in March 1959 that authorised the independence of Cyprus from the British Empire. This was achieved later that year.

Malaya also became independent in 1957. Although peace talks with the communist rebels had broken down, their power was in steady decline, and the achievement of independence destroyed part of their Casus belli. The last significant stand by the communists resulted in their defeat, with many insurgents fleeing over the Thai border. All this helped to keep key nine in the Tory's favour.

Macmillan could boast of a few more foreign policy achievements. In 1957, Britain tested her first hydrogen bomb. It was a 1.8 megaton device detonated on November 8th 1957 off Christmas Island. Unfortunately, this was not without a cost. The increased production necessitated for the project was a contributory factor in the Windscale nuclear disaster in 1957. In October of that year, a fire broke out in a plutonium pile at the Cumbrian reactor, leading to radioactivity escaping through the 500-foot chimney before the fire was extinguished with water. Milk from some local farms was banned and radiation travelled as far as southern England and mainland Europe. Until Chernobyl, it was the world's most serious nuclear accident. The subsequent inquiry blamed the incident on 'An error of judgement'. [79]

This period also saw the rise of CND - the Campaign for Nuclear Disarmament, formed in late 1957. This was followed by a march from Trafalgar Square to the MOD base at Aldermaston early in 1958, and then a march of 2000 women dressed in funereal black sashes from Hyde Park to Trafalgar Square the same year.

CND believed in unilateral nuclear disarmament; that is if Britain voluntarily gave up her nuclear arms, then other countries would follow suit. However, the campaigners were over-estimating Britain's already shrunken global clout in a bi-polar world now dominated by the two superpowers. A.J. P. Taylor remarked that, 'Ironically, we're the last imperialists.' [80]

The issue of nuclear disarmament was now a bigger problem for the Labour party, splitting it in two. During the 1957 Labour conference Nye Bevan rebuked CND hecklers with the words; 'If you carry this (unilateral disarmament) you'll send the British Foreign Secretary naked into the conference chamber.'[81] (Not really an appealing prospect.)

On the cold war front, this period was one of rising tensions with the Soviet Sputnik satellite beating the Americans into space in 1957. This caused a significant crisis of confidence in the United States, which Macmillan compared in his diary to the impact of Pearl Harbour sixteen years earlier. [82]

Attempts to improve east-west relations with diplomacy were undermined by the diplomatic disaster of the 1956 summit held in Britain. Things went seriously awry when the British frogman 'Buster' Crabb disappeared in Portsmouth Harbour. It soon transpired that he had been spying on Soviet warships there – his headless body was washed up on the beach a few months later. The summit was also marred by a relief interpreter being hopelessly drunk and causing needless embarrassment.

Europe was about to take rapid steps towards political and economic union. In 1957 'the six' signed the Treaty of Rome, promising, 'an ever-closer union among the peoples of Europe.' This idea was alarming to most British politicians - on both sides of the great divide. Anthony Eden had opined that joining a federal Europe, 'is something which we know in our bones, we cannot do.'[83] However, the new leader of the Labour Party, Hugh Gaitskell also said that joining a federal Europe would mean, 'the end of Britain as an independent European state, the end of a thousand years of history. You may say, "alright let it end!" But my goodness, it's a decision that needs a little care and thought!'[84]

In November 1955 the cabinet's Economic Policy Committee decided that, 'It was against the interests of the UK to join a European Common Market.' [85] Many members of the government and civil service were quietly hoping for the new EEC's failure. Their policy was to push for a free trade area for the seven European countries not yet in the EEC. This failed to bear fruit this side of the next election.

The economy remained strong with growth being generally quite good, albeit somewhat erratic. Macmillan saw himself as a 'One-Nation Conservative' in the Disraeli mould, and as a Keynesian, considered it an economic imperative to keep unemployment low. This brought him into conflict with certain members of his cabinet who favoured reduced spending and control of the money-supply.

The political result was the resignation of three cabinet ministers, including the Chancellor of the Exchequer Peter Thornycroft. (The others being Nigel Birch and Enoch Powell.) This was dismissed by the Prime Minister as, 'a little local difficulty'[86]- and caused no serious long-term rupture in the party; with two of the ministers being brought back into cabinet within a year.

In 1957, Macmillan famously said that the British people had 'never had it so good.'[87] There was some justification in this, as living standards were rising steadily and unemployment remained very low. The quote is rarely given in full however, often giving it a boastful air of complacency. However, Macmillan finished the quote on a note of uncertainty, saying, 'Is it too good to be true? Or perhaps I should say, is it too good to last?' [88] At the time of the October 1959 election however, things were more or less going smoothly, thus securing the Short-Term Economy key.

The Long-Term Economic key was technically false for Macmillan's government, as growth lagged behind the previous two terms of rapid post-war recovery. One of the issues was the trade imbalance, due to strong imports and relatively weak exports. There was also a shortage of gold reserves and there were fears over the possibility of another devaluation of the pound. This was understandable since memories of the last two devaluations during the Attlee years were still fresh, and there was further volatility during the Suez crisis.

Chancellor Rab Butler moved to damp down what he perceived to be an overheating economy with his autumn budget of 1955. Here, he raised purchase tax, and included kitchenware in that tax; hence the budget being labelled as 'the pots and pans budget.' This budget reversed nearly all the tax cuts of the pre-election budget in the spring, leaving him open to charges of cynically trying to bribe the electorate with their own money. Very soon after this he was moved from the Treasury (though not from the cabinet.)

There were numerous quarters of GDP contraction during the term, with the worst being quarter three of 1958, which saw a contraction of -2.4. (Equalling the worst single quarters in the 1973-74, 1979-81 and 2008-09 recessions.)

However, as there had been no really serious economic crises during the term, and unemployment and inflation were low, this key is to be considered half-turned. This is a similar scenario to what was to happen in the next decade under Harold Wilson. The key's partial loss is only a reflection of moderate economic difficulties following periods of strong growth, and not indicative of major discontent.

Macmillan and most of his party had at least tacitly accepted the 'Post-War settlement' of the Attlee years, and there was no serious attempt to reverse it. There were a few pieces of significant reform. In 1958 a bill was passed allowing for the creation of female peers and also life peers. The latter enabled people to become peers for life, but removed their ability to pass the title down to their descendants.

One other significant reform was the Clean Air Act of 1956. This aimed at improving air quality, especially in major cities and to prevent deadly smogs like the one in London during the winter of 1952-53. These measures are notable as being among the first environmental policies. They encouraged smokeless fuels and discouraged black smoke.

There were also faint hints of the social liberalism of the next decade. In 1957, the Wolfenden report recommended the decriminalisation of male homosexuality, arguing that although many regarded it as immoral, that did not automatically entail criminalisation. Liberal Home Secretary Rab Butler was sympathetic to the recommendations, but judged party and country opposition too great to proceed with it.

One reform that did make it to the statue books was the Obscene Publications Act 1959. This was a private members' bill put forward by future liberal Home Secretary Roy Jenkins. It created the defence of 'literary merit' for obscene publications. We would be hearing more from that bill and its originator in the coming decade.

However, these reforms fell somewhat short of the threshold for turning the Policy Change key, which as with the previous Conservative administration remained false.

Although racial violence flared in London's Notting Hill Gate district in September 1958, it fairly soon subsided and came nowhere near the level necessary to topple the Civil Unrest key. So Key twelve remained wholly true. It did however cast a cloud of pessimism over Britain's ability to successfully absorb and integrate immigrants from the commonwealth.

The nearest brush with scandal came with the raising of interest rates in 1957. Labour's shadow Chancellor Harold Wilson alleged on the basis of some newspaper reports that the Chancellor Peter Thornycroft had leaked the decision in advance, so that some financiers in the City could take unfair advance of it. However, the government was exonerated in the 1957 Bank Rate Tribunal, making Wilson look foolish.

The political keys were positive. Although the government had lost some by-elections, the losses were below the threshold needed to cost them key number one. Although there had been resignations over fiscal policy, the differences were well below the level of conflict required for the unity key to fall. Macmillan, at least at the time of the 1959 election was very popular and the commanding figure on the British political scene. His assured patrician manner resonated with the public, with two thirds approving of his leadership according to polls[89].

The generally strong economy and restored British standing on the global scene left little for Labour to attack. The situation was strong enough for Macmillan's claim that 'the class war is now obsolete' [90] to hold some water. Thus, the Incumbent Leadership key was secured.

The new Labour leader Hugh Gaitskell from the right wing of the party, was quite dynamic, and had done well to reign in the warring factions of his party. Yet he fell short of the mark when it came to Opposition Charisma, thus securing key four for the government. The Liberals remained very weak, managing to win only six seats in the 1959 election. Key five remained intact.

As in 1955 the National Liberals were still relatively strong, and so Third Party Bonus Key 5A remained in force for the government's advantage.

The election campaign of 1959 was seen as being well-fought by both parties. The Tories effectively campaigned on Macmillan's slogan 'You've never had it so good'. The official campaign slogan was but a slight variation on it; 'Life is better with the Conservatives, don't let Labour ruin it.' Labour's Tony Benn took advantage of new technology with a TV campaign utilising the slogan 'Britain belongs to you.' Labour leader Hugh Gaitskell unfortunately made the mistake of contradicting his own manifesto, by ruling out tax rises under a Labour government. This gaffe probably cost Labour two or three seats.

October 1959 UK general election:

1) *By-election key*   true
2) *Unity Key*   true
3) *Incumbent Leadership Key*   true
4) *Opposition Charisma Key*   true
5) *Third Party Key*   true
6) *Cyclical Incumbency Key*   true
7) *Short-Term Economy Key*   true
8) *Long-Term Economy Key*   half-turned
9) *Foreign Policy/Military Success Key* true
10) *Foreign Policy/Military Failure Key* false
11 *Policy Change Key*   false
12) *Civil Unrest Key*   True
13) *Scandal Key*   True

Special Keys

5A) *Third Party Bonus Key* true

campaign differential: Conservatives plus 2-3 seats

balance of negative keys: 1½

(Two negative keys; Bonus 5A negated one of them, and one half- turned Key.)

forecast: Conservative majority of 95

363 Conservative seats, Labour c. 275 seats

actual result: Conservative majority of 100

Conservatives 365 seats Labour 275 seats

1959-64
'Winds of Change.' Harold Macmillan, Parliament of South Africa speech, 1960

Following their hat trick victory in 1959, the Conservatives looked about to sail confidently into the 1960's. The economy was strong, unemployment was low, and although Britain was in the process of accepting her loss of empire and super-power status, there was no widespread discontent in the country. Things seemed to be going smoothly for the government, but it was not to last.

The economy remained in a generally expansive phase throughout the term. However, there was an ongoing balance of payments problem which resulted in a nine-month wage freeze during 1961. This proved unpopular and led to a series of by-election defeats in 1962, most notably in Orpington.

Macmillan responded to the deteriorating situation by sacking eight cabinet ministers, including loyal chancellor Selwyn Lloyd, in what is known as 'The Night of the Long Knives,' after Hitler's deadlier purge in 1934. As the future Liberal leader Jeremy Thorpe said, 'Greater love hath no man than this, than to lay down his friends for his life.'[91]

Macmillan countered economic concerns by setting up the National Economic Development Council, known as 'Neddy.' This was an essentially corporatist body, designed to encourage government, businesses and the trade unions to work together in order to manage the economy. Despite the Conservatives having been in power for the best part of a decade, the post-war consensus was still strong, with its belief in mixed-economy, corporatist government planning and the keynesian belief in the responsibility of government to maintain full employment.

Despite challenges however, the mean GDP during the term slightly exceeded that of the two terms between 1951 and 1959, so preserving the Long-Term Economy Key.

Although a number of by-elections were lost, the Conservatives still won more than two-thirds of them, thus securing By-Election key number one.

On foreign policy, the Macmillan government had to manage the rapid disintegration of the British Empire, with multiple African countries declaring independence. In 1960, Nigeria, the Southern Cameroons, and British Somalia were granted independence. In 1961 Tanganyika and Sierra Leone broke away from Britain.

In 1962 Trinidad and Tobacco and Uganda became independent states. In 1963 Kenya left the British Empire after years of Mau Mau insurgency. During this period the British had interned the Kikuyu in camps. This led to a scandal with the revelations of poor treatment and conditions in the camp; notably the beating to death of eleven prisoners in 1959.

Harold Macmillan acknowledged the rapidly changing world in 1960, with his famous 'Winds of Change' Speech, delivered at the parliament of South Africa. He said, 'The wind of change is blowing through this continent. Whether we like it or not, this growth of national consciousness is a political fact.'[92]

This clearly signalled that Britain would no longer stand in the way of national independence movements. Macmillan's view was now one of pragmatism, believing that if a territory yielded more problems than benefits to Britain, we should let it go.

In Asia, Malaya, Sabah, Sarawak and Singapore became independent in 1963 as one country - Malaysia. This was three years after the Malayan authorities had declared the Malayan Emergency over. This new union was resented by President Sukarno of Indonesia who wanted to subsume Malaysia into Indonesia. This was followed by several years of confrontation between Indonesia and the UK.

On the European front, Macmillan wanted Britain to join the newly formed Common Market or EEC (European Economic Community) as it was known then. He made a formal application in 1961, only for it to be vetoed by French President De Gaul two years later. One major stumbling block was Britain's insistence on having free trade with the Commonwealth, which was resented by many Europeans.

The rejection was a crushing disappointment to Harold Macmillan. Sir Michael Fraser, the Director of the Conservative Department said that; 'Europe was to be our dues ex machine; it was to create a new contemporary political argument with insular socialists; dish the Liberals by stealing their clothes; give us something new after twelve-thirteen years: act as a catalyst of modernisation; give us a new place in the international sun. It was Macmillan's ace, and De Gaulle trumped it.' [93]

However, although De Gaulle's rejection was a bitter blow, a failed initiative such as this, is not enough to topple the Foreign Policy/Military Failure key ten.

The compromise position was EFTA (European Free Trade Area) which was agreed at the end of 1959. This was to facilitate trade amongst the seven West European countries not yet in the EEC. This at least had the advantage of not being in conflict with Britain's trade with the commonwealth.

In 1960, hopes of an improvement in East-West relations were dashed by the disastrous Paris Summit. This event was fatally undermined by the shooting down of an American U2 spy plane, along with the capture of its pilot Gary Powers. Khruschev publicly lambasted US president Eisenhower and Macmillan regarded it as one of the saddest episodes of his professional life.

A year later, the Cold War grew frostier still with the construction of the Berlin wall, which divided East and West Berlin. This was in a bid to prevent the brain drain to the west, which had reduced East Berlin's population by nearly forty percent since the war.

In 1961, the Soviets also continued to outpace the west in the space race, with the launch of the first man in space, Yuri Gagarin.

The conflict reached a dangerous flash-point a year later with the Cuban Missiles Crisis. This situation was brought about by the American discovery of Soviet missile systems on Cuba by U2 spy planes. These were not yet ready to be operational, but would bring parts of the eastern seaboard within range. Macmillan struck up a very positive working relationship with President Kennedy, who sought the Prime Minister's advice every day of the crisis. On October 25th 1962, Kennedy asked Macmillan about the wisdom of military intervention. Macmillan replied, 'Events have gone too far... you must try to achieve your objectives by other means.' [94] A day later Macmillan advised the President thus: 'At this stage, any movement by you may produce a result in Berlin which would be very bad for us all. That's the danger now.' [95]

It is not clear how great an influence Macmillan had on the resolution of the crisis – in which Kennedy's naval blockade forced the Soviets to agree to dismantle the missiles; but his influence was certainly a moderating one, which supported the President's cautious approach.

Macmillan also played the leading role in the signing of the 1963 Partial Test Ban Treaty between the USA, UK and USSR, which prohibited nuclear weapons from being tested above ground or underwater. In his obituary, Vernon Bogdanor wrote that, 'Macmillan's greatest achievement in foreign policy lay in hastening the thaw in relations with the Soviet Union in the post-Stalin, post-Dulles world. The nuclear test-ban treaty of 1963 represented the culmination of his efforts, eliciting tributes from both Kennedy and Khrushchev to his skill and patience as a negotiator.' [96]

Apparently, Macmillan's motivation for this was at least partly to deprive CND of the propaganda value of film footage of H-bomb mushroom clouds. Nevertheless, the treaty marked a significant step away from the brink of nuclear Armageddon seen in the Cuban Missiles Crisis the previous autumn. This secured Foreign Policy/Military Success key nine.

Although Britain had joined the nuclear club, it was clear she could not really compete with the Americans. The Blue Streak British missile was abandoned in 1960 due to cost and vulnerability, in favour of the U.S. designed Skybolt. It was apparent that the arms race had become too expensive for Britain. Instead, Britain acquired the POLARIS missiles from America in 1960, and the Americans obtained the use of the nuclear base on the Clyde in return.

Additionally, the Conservative government moved troops to Kuwait to protect it from possible Iraqi invasion in 1961; therefore, staving off such aggression for another thirty years.

As with the previous two Conservative administrations, Macmillan's government did not really make any radical changes to government policy, thus forfeiting key eleven. Attempted suicide was decriminalised in 1961, and the Betting and Gaming Act of the same year decriminalised gambling. The Licensing Act of 1961 liberalised pub opening hours. The first two acts were pushed through by liberal Home Secretary Rab Butler, but were of little interest to the rather bemused Harold Macmillan, in a foreshadowing of the much greater liberalisation of the next government.

One policy that has stirred feelings ever since is the cutting back of the national railway network, a policy known as the Beeching Axe, after Richard Beeching, who was the author of the government report: *The Reshaping of Britain's Railways* 1963. The view at the time was that railways were expensive to maintain and becoming rather obsolete in the age of mass private car ownership.

This mass cut-back of a third of Britain's railways, left numerous small and not so small communities cut off from rail connections.

The period was relatively free of strikes and civil disturbances. There were some anti-nuclear protests by CND, but these came nowhere near the level needed to topple the Civil Unrest Key.

One key that was to turn with a vengeance was the Scandal Key, number thirteen. The key started to get shaky in late 1962 when the Admiralty clerk John Vassall was convicted of passing secrets to the Russians. Vassall, who was gay, was lured to a party in Moscow when he was working at the British embassy. He was photographed in a compromising position and blackmailed into leaking information to the Soviets. He was jailed for eighteen years in 1963. Although not directly the fault of the Prime Minister, the episode symbolised a loss of governmental grip. At around the same time, Macmillan was being turned into a figure of fun by new satire show, *That Was the Week That Was* (AKA TW3) which regularly portrayed him as a doddering old fool.

Things went from bad to much worse the following year, when the government - and the entire British establishment were rocked by the Profumo Scandal. This involved the Minister for War John Profumo having liaisons with the call-girl Christine Keeler, who also turned out to be sleeping with the Soviet Naval attaché Yevgeny Ivanov.

John Profumo persistently denied all allegations of impropriety with Miss Keeler, and Macmillan failed to discuss the matter with him face to face - finding it too distasteful and embarrassing. However, Steven Ward, the Osteopath, artist and procurer of prostitutes for powerful men - at whose home Profumo met Miss

Keeler, sent letters to both the Prime Minister and leader of the Opposition Harold Wilson, detailing the affair. Profumo's position was now completely untenable and he was forced to admit the affair, before resigning as a minister, an MP and Privy Council member.

This affair severely shook the complacency of the British establishment, rendering it open to attacks of moral decay from liberals, socialists and cultural conservatives alike. Harold Wilson attacked Profumo as 'a corrupted and poisoned excrescence' of a 'small and unrepresentative section of society,'[97] which the Tories represented in parliament. Macmillan, through his inept handling of the scandal, either looked complicit in Profumo's behaviour or else naïve and incompetent. His approval rating dropped to just twenty-five percent. [98]

Salacious gossip filled the pages of newspapers in a more blatant way than ever before, signalling the shift in zeitgeist from the restrained fifties to the permissive, liberal and individualist swinging sixties. It was reported that up to eight High Court judges had participated in a sex orgy and that at a recent diner party, a senior politician had been seen naked and masked, wearing a sign around his neck emblazoned with the legend; 'If my services don't please you, whip me.'[99]

Lord Denning's report on the scandal in September 1963 blamed Macmillan and his cabinet for failing to deal with it effectively. He stated that Profumo's conduct had created a 'reasonable belief that he had committed adultery' and that 'it was the responsibility of the Prime Minister and his colleagues, and of them only, to deal with this situation: and they did not succeed in doing so.' [100] Thus, public confidence in the government was seriously damaged and Scandal Key thirteen turned against the Tories.

Steven Ward committed suicide in August 1963 after being convicted of living off immoral earnings. Christine Keeler was jailed for nine months for perjury and conspiracy to pervert the course of justice in December that year - in connection with an unrelated criminal case.

Pressure was steadily mounting on Macmillan, who was now seen as a 'failing representative of a decadent elite' [101] to go. The author Philip Norman wrote that in the wake of the scandal, Harold Macmillan was 'examined in a new and searching light. What it revealed was scarcely credible as a twentieth century politician. A dusty old man in a walrus moustache hummed and hawed in the accent which had ruled Britain for a thousand years, but which now signified only complacency, crassness and the natural conspiracy between men who shared the same public school and club.' [102]

'Macmillan was now uncertain whether to stay on or to resign. He did not want to look as though he was being pushed out of office by Profumo – resigning under a cloud of scandal. He wrote to the Queen saying that he had not yet decided. [103]

The leadership crisis reached a conclusion at the Conservative Party conference in October 1963. A few days before the conference, Macmillan was suddenly taken ill and hospitalised with prostate disease. Although the condition was known not to be terminal - and Macmillan lived for more than twenty years, it provided a dignified escape route, and he took it.

Macmillan resigned in his hospital bed, and his successor would be the last Tory leader to be chosen by the mysterious 'Magic Circle' of senior party figures, rather than to be elected by MPs.

In 1963 there were multiple possible contenders for the Tory leadership. One factor that widened the field was the bill that allowed Peers to renounce their peerages, and thus stand for election in the Commons. This situation had been brought about by the Labour MP Tony Benn, whose father, the 1st Viscount Stansgate had died - therefore automatically elevating Benn to the Lords and disqualifying him as an MP. Benn wanted to remain an MP and so campaigned for the right to renounce his peerage. This finally bore fruit in the summer of 1963, and became law as soon as the bill received the Royal ascent. This bill also permitted Tory lord Hailsham and the Viscount Alec Douglas Home to renounce their peerages as well; therefore, becoming eligible to become MPS and more importantly - run for the party leadership.

Although this was the last 'undemocratic' leadership contest, there was widespread consultation of Conservative MPS; who were asked for their top two preferences, as well as the candidate they most wanted to stop. Although Rab Butler was widely perceived as Macmillan's natural successor, it was Sir Alec Douglas Home who was to seize the crown; as he had the most first preferences amongst MPs, and perhaps more crucially, the fewest people against him becoming leader.

Home immediately renounced his peerage and was elected to parliament at the Kinross and Western Perthshire by-election on November 7th 1963. For twenty days he was Prime Minister without being a member of either House.

Although Douglas-Home's appointment helped to unify the party in the wake of the devastating Profumo scandal, salvaging the Party Unity Key, it could not hope to erase that scandal, and so Scandal Key thirteen would be turned against the Conservatives at the next election. Home was mild-mannered and unassuming, like Attlee and Major. When asked by Observer journalist Kenneth

Harris if he could one day be the next Prime Minister, Home replied with, 'I really don't think so, because I have to do my economics with matchsticks.' [104]

Additionally, the skullish-looking Home was a lacklustre debater and suffered from an out-of-touch, aristocratic image; thus costing

the Conservatives Incumbent Leadership Key three.

The next election would take place in October 1964. There had been a change of leadership in both main parties over the previous two years. Hugh Gaitskell, the right-leaning Labour leader, died in January 1963 after a brief battle against the immunological disease Lupus Erythematosos. His replacement was the centre-left Harold Wilson, who had unsuccessfully challenged Gaitskell for the leadership in 1960 and before that served in the Attlee administration as President of the Board of Trade at the young age of thirty-one.

Wilson's rallying cry was one of modernisation, especially technological modernisation of industry. Hailing 'The white heat' of technology, Harold Wilson said that Britain would become 'a stagnant backwater,' if we failed to embrace automation in our factories.[105] Declaring that, 'Socialism must be harnessed to science and science to socialism.' [106]Harold Wilson promised, 'undreamed of living standards and the possibility of leisure on an unbelievable scale.' [107]He made modern virtues like progress and reform his platform, skilfully avoiding divisive and potentially off-putting concepts like class-war, ideology and even the word 'socialism' from his speeches, in order to broaden his appeal.

Harold Wilson also avoided being drawn into Gaitskell's divisive ideological battle to reform clause 4; the clause that constitutionally bound Labour to a pledge of nationalisation. Wilson described removing the clause as like, 'Taking Genesis out of the Bible.' [108]

Wilson also was effective at utilising television, with his use of jokes and quick recall of facts, mirroring John F Kennedy's mastery of the medium in the states. His publicists correspondingly built him up as Britain's Kennedy, and while his charisma fell somewhat short of that, he was a highly effective opposition leader. He was also a very modern one; grammar school educated with a regional accent, he made a sharp contrast to Home, Macmillan and most of the top Tories. Like Tony Blair a generation later, he seemed to visibly represent the future, whilst his opponents represented a tired and discredited past. As Anthony Seldon commented, Wilson was, 'the most formidable opposition leader of the century until Blair.' [109] This was therefore just about enough to topple Opposition Charisma key four.

In the 1964 campaign, Labour attacked Home's aristocratic pedigree whilst making a lot of Wilson's grammar school background. (This was ironic since his government would try to get rid of them all.) Home was labelled as 'a remote 14th earl,' who could not possibly relate to real people. However, Home hit back at his opponent by saying, 'Come to think of it, I suppose he's the 14th Mr Wilson.' [110] The campaign saw an advance in the use of modern media and both sides put up a strong fight. However, Labour were probably the most effective campaigners, so there was a small campaign differential giving Labour two or three seats.

During the campaign, Home asked a make-up lady why she could not make him look better on television. He was informed that it was due to him having a head like a skull. [111]

One bizarre incident in the campaign was a failed plot by two left-wing students to kidnap the Prime Minister. The students followed Home to a house where he was staying and announced their plan to kidnap him.

Home managed to defuse the threat by telling the students that, 'I suppose you realise if you do, the Conservatives will win the election by 200 or 300.' [112]After he gave them some beer, they thought wiser of the scheme. I will not draw up a counterfactual for this eventuality, but will opine that though Home's threat was an effective bluff, it would not likely have made any significant difference to the outcome of the election.

The Third Party Key fell, as the Liberal vote share increased from six points in 1959 to eleven points in 1964. This sharp up-tick in third party support was a clear indication of growing discontent in the country, and thus a bad omen for the government's chances.

The Liberal revival could have been predicted at the time. Not so much from the polls; the last five of these suggested a Liberal vote increase of only three and a half percent[113], but from their improving by-election performance. They gained one seat from the Tories and came very close in another four. One can also point to the increase in the number of Liberal candidates being fielded; up by more than a hundred since 1959. Additionally, Liberal leader Jo Grimond was considered to be more effective at connecting with the public than his immediate predecessors.

Unfortunately for the Tories, the National Liberal vote was fading, with none of them left in the cabinet after the 'Night of the long knives.' As former heavyweights died or retired from public life, several of their MPs decided to stand as Conservatives in 1964. All this had the effect of erasing the Third Party Bonus key that had helped the Conservatives since 1947. After suffering a further decline in the 1966 election, the remaining National Liberals decided to merge with the Conservatives completely in 1968.

October 1964 UK general election:

1) *By-election key* — true
2) *Unity Key* — true
3) *Incumbent Leadership Key* — false
4) *Opposition Charisma Key* — false
5) *Third Party Key* — false
6) *Cyclical Incumbency Key* — true
7) *Short-Term Economy Key* — true
8) *Long-Term Economy Key* — true
9) *Foreign Policy/Military Success Key* — true
10) *Foreign Policy/Military Failure Key* — true
11) *Policy Change Key* — false
12) *Civil Unrest Key* — true
13) *Scandal Key* — false

balance of negative keys 5.

campaign differential: Labour plus 2-3 seats.

forecast: Labour majority of 2

tally: Conservatives: 305 seats Labour: 316 seats

actual result: Labour majority of 4

Labour 317 seats Conservatives 304 seats

On October 16th Labour returned to power after thirteen years in opposition. New Prime Minister Harold Wilson promised '100 days of dynamic action,' echoing President Kennedy. It was the first election in which both main party leaders were men born in the 20th century. It coincided with the beginning of a period of great social and cultural upheaval in Britain and the Western world. This was the tipping point when the tide of liberal individualism began to overwhelm the collective Christian Conservative mores and traditions of the West.

This was accompanied by the final death-throes of the British Empire, and aided by technological transformations, such as the rise of television, the birth-control pill, LSD and more accessible air travel. The previous thirteen years of Conservative rule had not seen much radical reform, but they had not been uneventful. This period had witnessed the definitive end of Britain's colonial power, with the humiliation of Suez and rapid decolonisation in Africa.

Domestically, the economy had recovered from the immediate post-war austerity, with rationing now a thing of the past. Increasing immigration from the Commonwealth was changing the ethnic and cultural make-up of parts of the country, especially the cities. Increasing affluence was helping to foster a new youth culture and generational identity, with the rise of Rock 'n' roll and the Beat generation.

However, the post-war consensus remained very strong with the Conservatives largely accepting Labour nationalisation and public healthcare. Things were outwardly very stable, but cracks were beginning to spread through the old establishments, most notably with the Profumo scandal. The furore over Lady Chatterley's Lover and the mockery of the establishment by satirical productions such as Beyond the Fringe, all signposted the permissive era that was starting to dawn.

Suddenly, the old-fashioned grandees like Macmillan, Home and Churchill seemed like yesterday's men.

Chapter 4 1964-1979:

CULTURAL REVOLUTION AND NATIONAL DECLINE

In these fifteen years, Labour and the Conservatives took it in turn to topple each other from power, yet Labour held office for eleven of them. In this period the country changed, yet many of the most profound changes were percolating up from below, rather than being implemented top down. Attitudes to sexual morality changed rapidly during the sixties and beyond with the 'permissive society.' Liberalising legislation was probably more following the tide of cultural change than directing it.

Church attendance plummeted as TV ownership sky-rocketed. Attitudes to fixed gender roles came under sustained feminist assault; and with it the taboos on divorce and abortion. Homosexuality was legalised and began its long march to cultural normalisation. The youth culture openly mocked and rejected the orderliness and politeness of the preceding generations. Rebellion and subversion became the order of the day. Pop music acted as a mouthpiece for the new youth movements and the drug culture influenced music and art, suggesting that the traditional cultural norms were straight-jackets of blinkered conformity waiting to be liberated. Immigration was increasing too, further eroding the monoculture of the mid-twentieth century.

Internationally, Britain had lost her empire, bar a few fragments here and there and could no longer call herself a world power. 'Managing national decline' became a new watchword. Membership of the European

Economic Community seemed the logical and attractive answer to fast fading super-power status. With industrial unrest on the rise, followed by inflation, the slow decline of heavy industry and the mid-seventies oil shock, Britain was feeling like a country sliding fast down the global pecking order.

The responses to this were the embrace of liberalism and pop culture in the sixties, with 'swinging London' acting as a kind of psychedelic re-invention of a changing nation. Left-wing radicals found meaning in their myriad anti-war, anti-colonialist, anti-nuclear and anti-capitalist movements and protests. At the end of this period an opposite kind of response was to emerge from the free-market disciples of Friedrich A. Hayek and Milton Friedman.

1964-66:

'Whichever party is in office, the treasury is in power.' [114]

Harold Wilson

Harold Wilson's first ministry only had a majority of four, so all but guaranteed that the term would be a short one. The new government believed in economic planning, and so upon coming to office, set up the Department of Economic Affairs (DEA) to promote economic growth and investment, thus taking considerable responsibilities off the treasury. The government also created a Ministry of Technology (Mintech) to update technology and technological practices in industry, building Wilson's, 'Britain that is going to be forged in the white heat of this revolution.' [115]

The Wilson administration however had to deal with an £800 million pound trade deficit which was partly as a result of the previous government's fiscal expansion. Harold Wilson was anxious to avoid any devaluation of the pound; with the memories of Labour-presided devaluations in the 1940s still fresh in the memory, he feared that Labour would be labelled as 'The Party of devaluation.'

So, Labour managed to avoid facing a devaluation crisis until the next parliament.

Overall GDP during the short first Wilson term was less than the two previous ones. However, there was mostly positive growth during the period and unemployment remained low. The question of whether to devalue the pound was kicked into the long grass, and so Long-Term Economy Key eight was half-turned. The government also managed to avoid recession, saving Short Term Economy key seven.

The main liberal legislative achievements during this short seventeen-month parliament were the suspension of the death penalty in 1964 and the Race Relations Act of 1965. The latter outlawed racial discrimination in public places and created the offence of Incitement to Racial Hatred. The need for this law had been highlighted at the 1964 general election, when the racist Tory candidate Peter Griffith won at Smethwick on a blatantly bigoted platform. He even displayed posters (not officially endorsed by Conservative central office) bearing the legend: 'If you want a n***** for a neighbour, vote Liberal or Labour.' Wilson denounced him in the commons as, 'a parliamentary leper.' [116] More was to come in the second term.

The government also significantly increased spending on education, making it the first government to spend more on education than defence. However, the full effect of increased Labour spending would not be felt until the second Wilson term.

Overall however, there was not enough innovation to turn the Policy Change Key in the election of March 1966. This however did not matter much, as a new government of less than two years is exempt from the loss of that key.

Internationally, the biggest crisis Labour faced was in Rhodesia. In November 1965 the white-minority government of Ian Smith declared itself independent of the British Empire. This was the first such mutinous succession of a British colony for nearly two centuries. Harold Wilson's government refused to recognise it, or to grant it official independence until the majority black population were allowed to vote. Smith remained intransigent on the issue and Wilson responded by cutting all ties with the former colony and going to the United Nations to get sanctions imposed on Rhodesia. Rather comically, the British governor Sir Humphrey Gibbs refused to resign, and clung on to office impotently for another four years.

There was no appetite for military intervention in Rhodesia, especially as many British people had relatives there. The civil service also advised Harold Wilson that such action was logistically almost impossible. Britain did the next best thing and began trying to throttle the Rhodesian economy: banning Rhodesian exports of sugar and tobacco to the UK, cutting off aid to Rhodesia, expelling the renegade country from the Sterling area and blocking Rhodesian access to the London capital market. Britain refused to recognise Rhodesian passports and blockaded the Rhodesian port of Beira with warships in a bid to bring about economic ruin.

The Labour government however, underestimated the regime of Ian Smith, with Harold Wilson telling the Commonwealth Prime Ministers' Conference in January 1966 that the Rhodesian economy would collapse in 'weeks rather than months.' The situation at the time of the 1966 general election was four-and-half months of sanctions without any success, plus the country's succession from what was left of the British Empire was a major humiliation; especially as Harold Wilson had expended so much energy in trying to persuade the Smith regime not to do so. Thus, Foreign Policy Key ten was lost to the Wilson government.

De-colonisation was to continue apace during Labour's six years in power, with Harold Wilson effectively the last Prime Minister to preside over any significant overseas territory. The British government presided over the independence of Botswana, Gambia, Guyana, Lesotho, Barbados, the Leeward Islands, the Windward Islands, Mauritius and Swaziland. This was essentially a continuation of British policy since at least Macmillan, so was not sufficient to secure Key eleven for Labour.

The Labour government created the Ministry for Overseas Development, appointing Barbara Castle as its first minister in charge. This innovation is still with us today, and has distributed considerable amounts of foreign aid overseas. These and other achievements still fell short of the threshold required to win the Foreign Policy/Military Success Key. Yet for a new government of less than two years, this did not matter much; to win the key would have acted as a bonus.

The domestic mood in early 1966 was generally optimistic, thus securing Civil Unrest key twelve. The administration had also managed to steer clear of any scandal, thus saving key thirteen.

Regarding the political keys, the Labour government had only lost one by-election, not enough to topple key one. The Labour party had also more or less stayed unified, thus saving key two.

The Conservatives had replaced their previous leader Sir Alec Douglas Home with the surprise choice of Edward Heath. Heath was a break with the past in at least two ways. Firstly, he was a grammar school boy not an old Etonian. Secondly, he was the first Tory leader to be elected by his fellow MPs, rather than be selected by the mysterious 'magic circle' as had previously been the custom. Heath had been leader of the opposition only since June 1965, and thus had had little time to connect with the public; ergo Opposition Charisma Key four stayed in the government's favour.

The Liberals slightly declined in support at the 1966 election. Their dip from 11.3 to 8.6% was foreshadowed by an average decline in opinion poll ratings in the months leading up to the election. They did not reach double figures in the polls after December 1965. Additionally, the number of candidates fielded by the party dropped from 365 in 1964 to 311 in 1966. [117] Thus, the Third Party Key was to remain in Labour's favour.

Harold Wilson, like Tony Blair thirty years later, was always very keen to court celebrity friends and associate himself with the fashionable and popular. This can be seen no more clearly than his pre-election gambit of awarding the MBE to the Beatles in October 1965. It was not without controversy however. No fewer than nine earlier recipients of the award sent their insignias back in disgust. Canadian MP Hector Dupuis claimed Mr Wilson's decision had placed him on the same level as 'vulgar nincompoops.' [118]

Ironically, John Lennon returned his insignia four years later; in 'protest of our support of the Nigeria-Biafra thing, against our support of America in Vietnam and Cold Turkey (his latest single) slipping down the charts.' [119] The band also attacked Wilson's tax policy in the song 'Taxman,' with the withering line: 'And my advice for those who die, declare the pennies on your eyes.' [120]

This underlined the phenomenon in the sixties called the 'brain-drain' wherein thousands of professional people in mid-sixties Britain with aspirations to high-earning, left the country for relative low tax havens such as the States, Canada and Australia. In 1963, The Royal Society reported that twelve percent of people awarded PhDs in Science and engineering were emigrating, with seven percent going to the United States. [121]

Labour went into the 1966 election campaign with the slogan 'You know Labour government works.' Overall, the campaign was not particularly eventful, save for Harold Wilson being hit in the eye by a stink bomb. He did however attack Heath for being too pro-European, accusing him of, 'Rolling on his back like a spaniel at any kind of gesture from the French.' The Prime Minister also suggested that the white supremacist Smith regime were hoping for a Tory win. [122] Overall, the Labour campaign seems to have been a little more effective.

Harold Wilson was at the peak of his popularity, being the dominant figure on the mid-sixties British political scene, enjoying approval ratings of at least sixty percent.[123] According to Nick Thomas-Symonds, 'throughout the campaign, Wilson had celebrity status with the public.'[124]Thus Incumbent Leadership key 3 was secured.

March 1966 UK general election:

1) *By-election key*   true
2) *Unity Key*   true

3) *Incumbent leadership Key*   true
4) *Opposition Charisma Key*   true
5) *Third Party Key*   true
6) *Cyclical Incumbency Key*   true
7) *Short-Term Economy Key*   true
8) *Long-Term Economy Key*   half-turned
9) *Foreign Policy/Military Success Key* false discounted
10) *Foreign Policy/Military Failure Key* false
11) *Policy Change Key*   false discounted
12) *Civil Unrest Key*   true
13) *Scandal Key*   true

<u>*balance of negative keys:*</u>   1½
(One false key and one half-turned key)

<u>*campaign differential:*</u> Labour plus 2-3 seats
<u>*forecast:*</u> Labour majority of 95

<u>*tally:*</u> Labour 363 seats Conservatives c. 250

<u>*actual result:*</u> Labour majority of 96

Labour 363 seats Conservatives 253 seats Liberals 12

Labour were returned to power in a widely expected near-landslide majority on March 31st 1966. This would be the first decisive Labour victory for twenty-one years and would be the last for thirty-one. Although the result was an excellent one for Labour, it did raise high expectations for their delivery in the coming term.

The win was especially a triumph for the wily and pragmatic Harold Wilson, who had mastered the modern era very effectively. With his trademark Gannex raincoat and pipe, Harold Wilson was an instantly recognisable figure, with a man of the people image. (Actually, the pipe was a prop and he preferred to smoke cigars in private.) Although often accused of lacking principle, it is also fair to say that moderates of either side of the political spectrum are frequently accused of amoral expediency by those on the more fanatical wings. Being a Prime Minister necessarily involves flexibility, calculation, persuasion and tact. As Barbara Castle put it: 'He had an eel-like quality; he could always wriggle his way out of difficulty.' [125]

1966-70:
'I'm an Optimist, But an Optimist Who Carries a Raincoat.' Harold Wilson [126]

As Mr Wilson returned triumphantly to Downing Street on April 1st 1966, he declared 'Now we have a clear mandate.'[127] His government increasingly ran into problems however, in the form of the continuing imbalance of trade, and mounting industrial action.

In July 1966 the government responded to the currency problem and consequent threat of run-away inflation by imposing a deflationary six-month wage freeze. This was followed by further pay restraint, spending cuts and increased surtax, Purchase Tax, (forerunner of VAT) fuel and alcohol duty.

Cuts included a £55 million cut in public spending for 1967-68, as well as a £100 million cut in overseas spending.[128] This prompted conflict within the cabinet, especially involving the Minister for Economic Affairs, the tempestuous George Brown, who threatened to resign several times within forty-eight hours.

Labour were also assisted by an American rescue-package.

The U.S. government was concerned that a devaluation of the pound would have a serious knock-on effect on the dollar.

The policy of wage constraint inevitably led to growing conflict with unions and strikes. The Labour government had to call a state of emergency in 1966 after a seamen's strike threatened to throttle vital supplies. Mr Wilson claimed that the strike was masterminded by communists, damning them as 'a tightly knit group of politically motivated men.' [129] Strikes however, were to be a thorn in the side of the Wilson administration.

There were other forms of unrest too. March 1968 witnessed the infamous Grosvenor Square, anti-Vietnam protest, in which thousands of protesters attempted to storm the American embassy. There was a second protest outside the embassy in October that year and outside Whitehall in January 1970. The period also saw anti-apartheid protests against sports teams from South Africa.

Additionally, there was unrest on the right after Enoch Powell, the Tory Shadow Defence Minister made his infamous 'Rivers of Blood' speech in April 1968. Powell launched an inflammatory tirade against immigration, claiming that Britain must be 'mad, literally mad as a nation'[130] to allow so many immigrants and their dependents into the country, adding that the nation was 'busily engaged in heaping up its own funeral pyre.'[131]

The remarks broke an unwritten agreement by the main parties not to talk heatedly immigration. This was at a time when colour bars had only recently been removed by the British army and not long after there had been a train drivers' strike against the employment of black drivers. This unease over immigration can also be seen reflected in TV sitcoms such as *Till Death Us Do Part,* and a few years later in *Love Thy Neighbour*. Powell's speech however, did influence future Conservative policy on immigration, but at the time badly inflamed racial tensions. It also ended Powell's front bench career: Edward Heath apparently never spoke to him again.

Industrial action continued to resurface in different industries during the remainder of the Labour term. In 1969 the government put forward a white paper designed to limit the power of the strikers. 'In Place of Strife,' was put forward by the Employment Secretary Barbara Castle, but plunged the Labour party into immediate turmoil, with around 100 MPs opposing it, including Home Secretary James Callaghan.

The recommendations were very modest in comparison with the restrictions brought in a decade or so later by Margaret Thatcher. This paper was mostly concerned with stopping unofficial strikes, effectively taking power away from factory floor rebels and centralising it with the official union leaders. It was also aimed at reducing internecine conflict between different unions. However, the opposition from the unions was such that most of the cabinet considered the plans as being too dangerous and difficult, and they were effectively shelved.

Harold Wilson retained a degree of public defiance against his internal critics, dismissing wild rumours concerning plots to oust him. In 1969 he delivered one of his best lines at a May Day rally in London: 'Let me say for the benefit of those who have been carried away by the gossip of the last two days, I know what is going on. I am going on.' [132] At least the Party Unity Key, which could otherwise have been lost had the government pursued *In Place of Strife*, was saved.

Overall, this level of unrest was not quite enough to topple the Civil Unrest Key, but was certainly enough to result in half of the value of the key being lost at the next election.

The government of Harold Wilson is perhaps best remembered for its record on liberalising reforms. These began in the first term, came to fruition in the second, and although some were private members bills, were all facilitated by Home Secretary Roy Jenkins. These included the decriminalisation of Male homosexuality in England and Wales, (gay men in Scotland and Northern Ireland had to wait until 1981 and 1982 respectively, and in the Isle of Man, until 1992.) It also included the decriminalisation of abortion - both bills passed in 1967. The latter was proposed by future Liberal party leader David Steel.

It is interesting to note how much unease and opposition there was to these two bills, especially to the one on male homosexuality - and not just from right-wing Tories. The Foreign Secretary George Brown polemicised against gay liberation in the Commons, saying, 'This is how Rome fell... we've gone too damn far on sex already!' [133] The times they were indeed a-changing.

In 1969 there were major reforms to the divorce laws, allowing 'irretrievable breakdown' of a marriage to be sole grounds for divorce. In 1970 they passed the Equal Pay act, ensuring that men and women would be paid equal amounts for the same work; although it did not come into force until 1976. In 1968 Labour brought in a second Race Relations Act, which was the immediate trigger for Enoch Powell's speech. This act extended the provisions of the first act to outlaw racial discrimination in education, employment and the provision of housing and public services.

Labour abolished theatre censorship, abolished birching in prisons and Borstals, and in 1969 suspended the death penalty indefinitely for murder; although technically it remained in force for Treason and setting fire to the Queen's docks, until Tony Blair officially abolished it thirty years later.

Attempts at reforming the House of Lords were not successful. The plans, which would have phased out hereditary peers, were blocked by an odd alliance between reactionaries like Enoch Powell, who were opposed to any change at all and radical leftists like Michael Foot, who thought the changes did not go far enough.

There were a few other reforms. One was the creation of a civil service department, headed by the Prime Minister. This was eventually abolished by Mrs Thatcher, but the Prime Minister's full title still includes the job description of 'Minister for the civil service.'

Another related reform was the creation of a parliamentary ombudsman to investigate civil service corruption and maladministration.

Labour also paved the way for the introduction of the decimalised currency in 1971 and the breathalyser to combat drink driving in 1967. Finally, the age of majority was lowered from twenty-one to eighteen in time for the 1970 election.

The Wilson government also made a significant change in the style of government itself. This was the first government to bring in paid political advisors who were neither civil servants nor MPs. This policy was to grow steadily over the next thirty years, but it really began here.

The most notable of these advisors was Wilson's political secretary Marcia Williams. Williams was often criticised for wielding too much power and influence and was often in conflict with other members of staff.

In terms of socialist policy, the Labour government's policy was rather restrained, nationalising only the steel industry.

There was however considerable reform in education. Labour significantly increased education spending and also instructed local authorities to convert selective grammar schools to non-selective comprehensive schools. By 1977, seventy nine percent of children were being educated in Comprehensive schools. [134] Labour felt that the grammar school system unfairly branded children and their parents as failures if they failed the eleven-plus exam. They believed that it perpetuated the class system. Harold Wilson said that he wanted a meritocratic society, in which 'brains will take precedence over blue blood.' [135] Education Secretary Toy Crossland said, 'I'm going to destroy every f****** grammar school in England, Wales and Northern Ireland.' [136] This policy has always been a controversial one, and is still lamented by many social conservatives today.

The other education policy most associated with the sixties Labour government, is the creation of the Open University, whereby people who missed out on a university education could study for a degree through part-time study and distance-learning. In addition to this, thirty new polytechnics were instituted. Overall spending on education rose from 4.8% in 1964 to 5.9% in 1968. The numbers of trainee teachers increased by a third. [137]

Labour also made reforms in welfare spending. National Assistance benefits were replaced by

Supplementary Benefits which were not means-tested. The government increased pensions, disability and sickness benefits. They also scrapped prescription charges, only to bring them back a few years later after the devaluation of 1967, as the alternative would have been to axe the building of new hospitals. Overall, the proportion of GDP spent on the NHS increased from 4.2% in 1964 to 5% in 1969. [138]

Labour set ambitious house-building targets of half a million a year. Although these were never met, they did build 400,000 in 1967 and '68. [139] Home ownership also increased during this period, reaching fifty percent by 1970. This was aided by policies such as exemptions from Capital Gains Tax, low-interest loans and provision of 100% mortgages for low-income home owners.

Labour did measurably reduce absolute and relative poverty, but a cloud of disappointment hung over their record for many on the left.

Overall, the Labour government made considerable changes to how Britain was governed, but was it enough to turn the Policy Change Key? Certainly, things were changing fast in the sixties but much of the change was from below, through the culture. Overall, the reforms of the Wilson administration were enough to achieve a half-turn in Key eleven.

The economy struggled with Balance of Trade problems, with the government delaying a devaluation of the pound that many economists believe should either have been carried as soon as Labour reached office in 1964, or very soon after their re-election in 1966. Several different events conspired however to weaken the pound in 1967. One was the Arab-Israeli Six Day War of June 1967 which disrupted oil supplies. The Nigeria-Biafra war from 1967-70 also did this, with left-wing critics accusing the Wilson government of siding with the likely winner, Nigeria in order to safeguard the oil. The dockers' strike of autumn 1967 put additional pressure on the pound and an appeal for further American assistance fell on deaf ears.

Finally, the government was forced to devalue the pound in November 1967 by fourteen percent against the dollar. This was accompanied by the rising of interest rates to eight percent and a slew of cuts. Other consequences of this were the unpopular return of prescription charges and postponement of raising the school leaving age to sixteen. (This was finally affected by the Heath government.)

The Prime Minister tried to reassure the public with a now famous broadcast claiming; 'that doesn't mean of course, that the pound here in Britain, or in your pocket or in your purse, or in your bank has been devalued.' He went on to attack the speculators, 'who sold sterling in a panic, and there were others who gambled against us in the hope of a quick gain.'[140]

The economic mood was so gloomy in early 1968 that five typists from Surrey made the headlines by deciding to work an extra half an hour a day for free, in a bid to help the ailing economy. They coined the slogan 'I'm backing Britain.' [141]Politicians and pundits praised the women, and TV personality Bruce Forsyth even released a single.

The Vietnam war also put further pressure on Sterling, vis-a-vis convertibility with the dollar and gold. The pound faced further pressure in March 1968 and one temporary solution was to close down the London gold market for the day. This action necessitated the creation of a bank holiday.

The volatile and often inebriated George Brown was unavailable when the decision was taken and resented being informed of the decision second hand. He retaliated by calling his own cabinet meeting which Harold Wilson understandably interpreted as an affront to his own authority and even as a potential coup against him. This led to Brown's resignation as Foreign Secretary the following day. He had been heard shouting, 'I'll never serve under that bloody little man again!' [142](though he stayed on as Deputy Leader.) Brown had in fact become something of an embarrassment for the government by this point. The previous November, he had insulted the newspaper magnate, Lord Thomson at a public dinner, before becoming involved in a drunken brawl with journalists.[143]

Labour were punished in the local elections of 1968 as the popularity of Harold Wilson and his government slumped badly. This was also reflected by the loss of many by-election seats during the term. The By-election key was therefore very easily toppled; this being the first administration since the war to lose that key. Only the Callaghan administration in the seventies and the Major administration in the nineties did comparably badly in by-elections.

Wilson's personal popularity had declined as well, thus depriving Labour of the incumbent leadership key. With Edward Heath still the Conservative leader in 1970, the opposition charisma was at least out of jeopardy. The dour and rather restrained Mr Heath was as far from charismatic as any modern party leader, having, in the words of Roy Jenkins, the demeanour of, 'an affronted penguin.'[144]

Things were going so badly for Labour that the chairman of International Publishing Corp Cecil King, publicly called for Wilson to go and even tried to involve Lord Mountbatten in a plot to remove him. This resulted in King's dismissal by the board, in May 1968.

Although the economic situation was better by the time of the next election in June 1970, unemployment had risen to around half a million. This was not very high by historic (or later) standards, but it was considered high by post-war standards. Overall GDP for the term was somewhat less than the average of the three previous administrations, thus losing Long Term Economy Key eight. However, the short-term economy was clearly not in any recession in 1970, and so at least key number seven was preserved.

On the overseas front, the scene was dominated by Vietnam, Biafra, Rhodesia, Czechoslovakia and the Arab-Israeli conflict. President Lyndon B Johnson of the USA had continually pressured Harold Wilson into supporting the American war effort, by sending British troops. Wilson consistently refused, knowing that such an act would lead to major street protests against his government as well as very serious rebellions in the Labour party, both at the parliamentary and grass roots level. His refusal to join the Vietnam War almost certainly preserved Unity Key two; although his compromise of lukewarm public support for the war, still led to protests in the UK and back bench rebellions.

In the view of many people on the left, Wilson's public ambivalence on Vietnam was both immoral and weak. The same criticism befell the abandonment of the Labour pledge to scrap Britain's independent nuclear deterrent, on the grounds that its purchase was too far advanced under the Conservatives to be cancelled without inordinate expense.

The other painful sore for the government was Rhodesia. While in March 1966 the government were refusing to call the British policy on the renegade former colony a failure, by June 1970 it could not really be described as anything else. The naval blockades and sanctions had failed to dislodge Ian Smith's racist regime from power and face-to-face meetings between the two national leaders had also reached an impasse, with both parties accusing the other of duplicity. Thus, the Foreign Policy/Military Failure Key was forfeited for a second time in a row.

Harold Wilson was struggling to find a foreign policy success. In 1967 he re-applied for Britain to join the Common Market, only to meet the same fate as his predecessor Harold Macmillan - a veto by De Gaule, who was wary of Britain becoming a Trojan Horse for American interference.

Labour recognised Britain's declining international status and the unaffordability of a global military presence. In November 1967 Britain withdrew troops from Aden, creating the Democratic Peoples' Republic of South Yemen. The following year it was announced that Britain would be bringing forward her withdrawal of forces East of Suez to 1971. This is seen by some as the official end date for the British Empire.

The other issue that contributed to the loss of key number ten was not foreign policy but could be described as military. It was Northern Ireland. In 1968 major protests were getting underway in Ulster, led by NICRA, (Northern Ireland Civil Rights Association), campaigning for the Catholic minority against discrimination in matters such as housing and employment rights. The Race Relations Acts of 1965 and 1968 had unfortunately not covered the religious groups in Northern Ireland.

The Catholics definitely had some legitimate grievances. The 1922 Civil Authorities (Special Powers) Act gave the Stormont parliament much power to curtail civil liberties, including the power of arrest and detention without due process. The Flags and Emblems

Act 1954, gave the police the power to remove flags and emblems likely to cause a breach of the peace - though the Unionist flag was excluded. Therefore, it was used to effectively ban the Catholic flag.

Labour responded to the protests by introducing some much-needed reforms. The Representation of the People Act 1969 removed the property qualification for voting which had disproportionately disadvantaged the Catholics. The UDR Act abolished the controversial reserve force the B specials, who were 100 per cent Protestant and seen by Catholics as an occupying Unionist army. It also created the Ulster Defence Regiment. The Housing Executive was tasked with the responsibility for fair allocation of social housing.

Unfortunately, these measures were not enough to prevent the province sliding into civil strife. The situation steadily deteriorated during 1969 and in August, British troops were sent into the troubled province. Although the intervention was initially supposed to be only temporary, troops from the mainland would be patrolling the streets for the next thirty-eight years.

In September 1969, troops erected the so-called 'Peace Wall', separating the warring communities of the Protestants in the Shankhill road district and the Catholic Falls Road district. By the time of the election the following June there were 7000 British troops in Northern Ireland, as violence continued unabated. This contributed further to the loss of the Foreign Policy/Military Failure Key.

Apart from some of the farcical antics of George Brown, the Labour administration had very largely managed to steer clear of scandal. One episode though was the 'D-Notice' affair. D-notices were a feature of voluntary arrangements between the government and the media, which gave guidance on what should or should not be published in the interests of national security. In February 1967 the *Daily Express* reported that the security services regularly scrutinised telegrams sent by the general public. Wilson accused them of breaching a D-notice. An inquiry subsequently vindicated the newspaper. This episode led to a marked deterioration in Wilson's relationship with the press.

In 1967 the pop group *The Move*, publicised their September single, 'Flowers in the rain,' with a cartoon postcard depicting Harold Wilson in bed with Marcia Williams. This touched on an ongoing rumour of a sexual relationship between the Prime Minister and his Political Secretary. Wilson sued and won. Yet none of this came anywhere near to toppling Scandal key thirteen, which remained true for the government.

Regarding Jeremy Thorpe's Liberals, the polls had not signalled any strong increase in their level of support and they had only managed to take one seat in a by-election. Therefore, the Third Party Key remained in the government's favour.

The Labour campaign was fought on the platform of defending Labour's record in office, and attacking the Conservatives as 'Yesterday's men.'[145] The Conservative line of attack focussed on the rising level of industrial strife in the country, and Labour's inability to counter it. Both campaigns focussed more on promoting their leaders individually than had been seen previously. Yet overall, neither party seemed to get any kind of tactical advance in the campaign.

The election result took the country by surprise, as most commentators believed that Labour was cruising towards an easy victory. This impression had been partly created by the improving economic picture over the twelve months leading up to the poll. Chancellor Roy

Jenkins' stewardship of the economy had led to a balance of trade surplus by the end of the parliament.

If a week is a long time in politics, four years had seen a polling rollercoaster for the Labour government. After initial Labour popularity, the strong Tory leads of 1968-69 were themselves wiped out with Labour getting ahead during the campaign. Wilson's approval rating led Heath's by over twenty points. [146] Ladbrokes were giving odds on of 20-1 for Labour. The false optimism is best summed up by Nora Beloff in the Observer who opined, 'Both party leaders are now recognising that only a bolt from the blue...can save Harold Wilson from becoming the first Prime Minister in British History to win three general elections in a row.'[147] Marcia Williams also admitted that, 'We were sure that we would win. We were quite unprepared for defeat.'[148]

One amusing anecdote from the campaign concerned Harold Wilson being heckled by a man over the issue of grammar schools. The man wanted to know how Wilson could move to abolish them after previously saying that their abolition would be 'over my dead body.' Wilson's repost was this; 'Friend, you're showing a morbid curiosity with my corpse.'[149]

June 1970 UK general election:

1) *By-election key*	false
2) *Unity Key*	true
3) *Incumbent Leadership Key*	false
4) *Opposition Charisma Key*	true
5) *Third Party Key*	true
6) *Cyclical Incumbency Key*	true
7) *Short-Term Economy Key*	true
8) *Long-Term Economy Key*	false

9) *Foreign Policy/Military Success Key* false
10) *Foreign Policy/Military Failure Key* false
11) *Policy Change Key* half-turn
12) *Civil Unrest Key* half-turn
13) *Scandal Key* true

<u>*balance of negative keys:*</u>   6
(5 keys plus two half-turns)

<u>*campaign differential:*</u> nil

<u>*forecast:*</u> Conservative majority of 28

<u>*tally:*</u> Labour Seats 288 Conservatives 330 seats

<u>*actual result:*</u> Conservative majority of 30

Conservative seats: 330 Labour seats: 287

With the pollsters and most of the commentariat expecting an easy win for Labour, the results came as something of a shock. One popular view was that Labour had lost through complacency. Another blamed negative economic news during the campaign.

Both of these views placed too much emphasis on the importance of the campaign and missed the essential truth; that the election is a referendum on the course of the whole term. As Lynton Crosby said, 'You can't fatten a pig on market day!'[150] One poll that did get it right was the very first BBC exit poll. It was carried out in the constituency of Gravesend Kent, because it was believed to be representative of the whole country. [151]

The result also confounded the majority of the public who had expected a Labour victory and provided strong evidence that general elections are not all about personality; Wilson was considerably more personally popular than Heath.

This election defeat would not be the end of Harold Wilson. He would continue to lead Labour for another six years – two of them as Prime Minister. Although the Labour era had been unexpectedly cut short, the very significant changes towards social liberalism would not be challenged by the Conservatives, and the anti-grammar school policy would be continued by Heath's Tory administration. Another policy that would continue and be brought to fruition was the quest to secure Britain's membership of the European Economic Community.

This shock election result is often seen as the marker for the end of the sixties era; together with the break-up of The Beatles and England's defeat in the World cup. The sometimes chaotic, but essentially optimistic sixties were giving way to something else. The unrest in 1968, particularly in the States suggested a turn towards a darker period ahead.

The escalating violence in Northern Ireland and the appearance of modern international terrorism, with events such as the blowing up of hijacked jets in the desert by the PLO, all signalled the end of notions of 'love & peace.' Whilst the economy was relatively healthy, a shadow of pessimism had been cast by the 1967 pound devaluation. Soon, rising unemployment and inflation would see this shadow lengthen, reaching a tipping point with the oil shock of 1973.

During the past six years a far bigger change had occurred in Britain, and indeed the western world as a whole, than that affected by changes to government policy. The Christian conservative glue that had held society together was crumbling in the face of a new tide of liberal individualism and with it, new configurations of collective interest. With church attendance plummeting and consumption of TV and pop music soaring, the old order, in the words of Bob Dylan was 'rapidly fading.'

Some of this was reflected by the liberal legislation of the 'permissive society' but much was changing beneath the politicians' feet, and in the air around them. The hippie movement offered one alternative to the declining collective order – that of sexual freedom, drugs and 'love'. The New Left offered a more confrontational approach. The latter also saw the adaptation of Marxian class struggle from economic class to identity politics.

The majority of Westminster politics remained focussed on more traditional matters such as the increasingly aggressive labour disputes, and the ever-difficult question of Britain's place in Europe. However, the socio-cultural changes wrought in the swinging sixties would continue to percolate down through the culture for the rest of the century – and beyond.

1970-74:

'Who governs Britain?' Edward Heath, February 1974 Election slogan.

The surprise Tory election victory of June 1970 brought the Tories back to power under Edward Heath. It also brought into the cabinet future Prime Minister Margaret Thatcher. Initially, the ideological agenda of the Heath ministry was to actually quite resemble that of Mrs Thatcher a decade later.

The Selsdon document, resulting from a conference in Selsdon Park Hotel in 1970, outlined Tory policies at the time of the 1970 general election; advocating tax cuts, shrinking the state, reducing union power and a crackdown on crime as the answers to the nation's problems. The ideas were mocked as 'Selsdon Man' by Harold Wilson, suggesting atavism, though of course this failed to prevent the election of a Tory government.

1970 however, proved to be a false dawn for proto-Thatcherites like Nicholas Ridley. This was due to a number of factors which blew the government off course. Initially though the early signs did point in a free market direction. In its first year, the government abolished the National Board for Prices & Incomes, the 2nd Reconstruction Corporation & Land Commission, repealed the Industrial Expansion Act and phased out the Regional Employment Premium. The administration also formed the Department of Trade & Industry, and its first Secretary of State John Davies publicly attacked the, 'soft, sodden morass of subsidised incompetence.' [152]

The first shattering blow to be delivered to the Tories was the sudden premature death of the Chancellor Ian Macleod, only a month into the new administration. His successor, Anthony Barber largely abandoned the earlier free-market course, partly in response to slowing growth and rising unemployment and instead increased spending on welfare and lowered taxes.

This essentially Keynesian policy triggered the so-called 'Barber Boom' in 1972, bringing a year and a half of strong growth. The policy was at least successful in reducing unemployment however. After hitting one million at the start of 1972, (the highest since 1940) the jobless total dropped to just over half a million by the end of the term.

It was perhaps the Heath government's anxiety about rising unemployment, (in contrast to Mrs Thatcher a decade later.) that led to much of the u-turning for which it is now famous. With heavy industry in decline for around a decade, there was growing concern that rising unemployment could result in worsening levels of crime and civil disorder. It was this thinking that led to the government rescue of Rolls Royce and Upper Clyde Shipbuilders in 1971. The government displayed further statist tendencies with the Gas Act 1972, which reorganised various regional gas boards into the British Gas Corporation.

Although the Conservatives had previously talked of privatisation, the only government sell-offs that they managed to accomplish were those of the travel agents Thomas Cook and Lunn-Poly, and the Carlisle pub chain.

The government also veered somewhat to the left with the Industry Act of 1972, which was designed to prepare the British economy for entry into the European Common Market. This act introduced regional development grants to help industry if it was seen to be in the interests of the wider economy.

One major problem the government struggled with was the need to control wages in order to fight inflation. This, as with the Wilson administration led to more conflict with the unions. It was on this topic that the Heath government anticipated the policies of its successor in the 1980s. The last Labour government had also produced a white paper aiming at bringing industrial action under greater control. 'In Place of Strife' was published and then abandoned in 1969 in the face of union and Labour party opposition.

The Heath government developed this line of attack a little further with the Industrial Relations act of 1971. This attempted to curb the problem of 'wildcat' strikes - industrial action without formal Union endorsement and votes. During the Selsdon conference, Heath had

Opined that, 'Employers have to be able to introduce new plant and get rid of men... the trouble at the moment is they cannot get rid of men.'[153]

One weakness of the act was the government's own dogged belief in Laissez-faire capitalism. The act was designed to uphold the principle of free collective bargaining. Therefore, no agreement between unions and employers could be legally binding if either said no. The act also required the unions to join a register, but again this was not legally binding, and so most unions boycotted it.

The bitter opposition to the bill and to the Heath government was reflected in a ferocious counter-attack by the unions in the form of a miners' work-to-rule overtime ban in late 1971. This developed into a full strike in 1972, leading to widespread black outs. The miners also picketed power stations and coal depots.

This was also the time when union firebrand Arthur Scargill came to national prominence. He initiated the then-novel strategy of flying pickets; whereby pickets were bussed in from far afield to shut down plants and stop strike-breakers, or 'scabs' from getting to work. Scargill wore his radicalism on his sleeve, exclaiming that, 'We were in a class war. We were not playing cricket on the village green...we were out to defeat Heath and Heath's policies. Anyone who thinks otherwise is living in cloud-cuckoo land.' [154]

The activism centred on the coke depot at Saltley in the West Midlands. Here, Scargill bussed in thousands of flying pickets in a bid to shut the plant, and thus starve Britain of coal. Eventually, the pickets won after tens of thousands of people converged on the site. This, plus widespread picketing across the country forced the Heath government's hand, and the dispute was ended with a generous offer for the miners. Heath's advisor and future cabinet heavyweight Douglas Hurd summed up the situation best, with the observation that the government was, 'wandering vainly over the battlefield looking for someone to surrender to – and being massacred all the time.'[155]

The paradox of all this, is that far from being hard-nosed and antagonistic towards the unions, Heath perhaps did more than any other modern Prime Minister to try and accommodate their needs. Jack Jones, the General Secretary of the TUC spoke warmly of him, saying,

No PM either before or since, could compare with Ted Heath in the efforts he made to establish a spirit of camaraderie with Trade Unionists and to offer an attractive package which might satisfy large numbers of working people...amazingly he gained more personal respect from union leaders than they seemed to have for Wilson or even Jim Callaghan. [156]

Union unrest had been rising since around 1966, and 1970 suffered the greatest number of days lost to strikes since 1926 - the year of the General Strike. All four years of the Heath government witnessed more than ten million days lost to strikes – the worst sustained period for industrial unrest since the early 1920s. Thus, the Civil Unrest Key was always going to be in jeopardy.

Following the government's defeat at the hands of the miners, Heath was forced to announce a ninety-day wage, price, dividends and rent freeze. This was followed by the imposition of a statutory prices and incomes policy, implemented through a Price Commission and Pay Board. Margaret Thatcher later attacked the U-turn as, 'precisely the policy we had ruled out in our 1970 general election manifesto.'[157]

The Heath government had also pledged to reduce the size of the state. The statistics flatly deny the fulfilment of that promise. During those four years state employment rose by ten per cent and social expenditure rose in real terms by 6.8%. [158]

With all the u-turning, it was quite fitting that Labour MP Edmund Dell said in the Commons that, 'Our pragmatic PM, having marched his troops up the hill to laissez-faire and disengagement, is marching them down to selective intervention on a massive scale.' [159]

The economy was further undermined by President Nixon's decision to end convertibility of the US dollar to gold and to introduce a ten per cent surcharge. This effectively brought to an end the global monetary regime of the 1944 Bretton Woods agreement and led to a new floating exchange rate system. The pound also was to float on the international exchange from now on - and as a result started to lose value.

One problem the Heath government had inherited from its immediate predecessor was Northern Ireland. Things went from bad to worse under the Tories. 1971 saw the first British soldier killed in Ulster in February. Within eighteen months there would be a hundred more. That year also saw the more militant Provisional IRA break away from the Official IRA. It also saw the first purely sectarian killings.

The British government responded with a policy of Internment from 1971-75, in which two thousand suspected IRA men were arrested. The policy was not a success however, as the RUC's files were out-of-date, and the policy simply increased resentment of the British. In August 1971, gunmen burned down 5000 Catholic homes and 20,00 Protestant homes. In January 1972, British troops fired on marchers in Derry killing thirteen.

This became known as 'Bloody Sunday' and led to the first significant IRA attacks on the mainland in revenge.

In February that year they bombed the Parachute brigade headquarters in Aldershot, but succeeded only in killing six civilians and a priest. Further escalation in street fighting led to Operation Motorman in the summer of 1972, when the British army smashed no-go areas, preventing a slide into all-out civil war. The Heath government's next response was to impose direct rule on Ulster, brushing aside the parliament at Stormont.

The following year, the government embarked on a potential game-changer. In December 1973, leaders from London, Dublin and Belfast signed the Sunningdale Agreement. This was a power-sharing deal that would set up a Ministerial Council and Consultative Assembly, drawn from both sides of the Irish border. This seemed like a breakthrough in the struggle for peace. However, it was not to be: just as a similar council in the 1920s was defeated by opposition from hard-line Unionists, so history repeated itself.

The following month the pro-agreement leader of the Ulster Unionists, Brian Faulkner resigned when the party narrowly rejected the power-sharing deal and was replaced by the anti-Sunningdale Harry West. The Party was torn apart by fighting, with the Reverend Ian Paisley having to be forcibly removed from the chamber by police. This resulted in the Ulster Unionists withdrawing themselves from the Conservative Whip permanently.

The anti-Sunningdale elements organised and mobilised themselves against the agreement. Loyalist paramilitaries formed the Ulster Army Council. In the forthcoming Ulster elections, the anti-Sunningdale loyalists formed the United Ulster Unionist Council (UUUC) to field candidates opposed to power sharing. Their Pro-Sunningdale opponents however were disunited and fielded candidates against one another. The result was that the UUUC won eleven of the twelve constituencies and declared the result a democratic rejection of the agreement.

The power-sharing deal finally collapsed early in the next parliament, but even at the time of the February 1974 UK general election, it was clear that the deal was in serious trouble, and could not rescue the Heath government's miserable record of failure in Northern Ireland. Therefore, Foreign Policy/Military Failure key ten was lost.

In foreign policy, the Heath government fared better. Unperturbed by the failure of the Wilson and Macmillan governments to gain entry into the Common Market, Edward Heath re-applied for membership. One stumbling block that had been removed was General De Gaulle of France who had died in 1970. De Gaulle had successfully blocked Macmillan's and Wilson's applications for British EEC membership, fearing that Britain could become a cipher for American sabotage.

Now with a post-De Gaulle France no longer engaged in obstructionism, the terms of Britain's membership were agreed upon in June 1971. Heath steered the European Communities Act through Parliament in October 1972 and Britain formally joined the European Economic Community on 1st January 1973; where she would stay for a further forty-seven years.

The Act only passed the House of Commons fairly narrowly and gave European law primacy over British law, allowing Britain full participation in the Customs Union, as well as bringing Britain into the Common Agricultural Policy and Common Fishing Policy.

This achievement by the Heath government successfully turned two keys in their favour. Entry into the Common Market was both a foreign policy success and a major policy change.

Although there was some internal opposition to EEC membership, most notably from Enoch Powell who feared an irrecoverable loss of sovereignty, the issue did not divide the Tories as much as it did Labour. In 1971 the Tory conference voted to join Europe by 2,474 to 324 votes. When European membership became a confidence vote early in 1972, only fifteen Tory MPs voted against the government. No cabinet minister resigned over the issue, and with Enoch Powell's departure to Northern Ireland at the subsequent election, the most vociferous Conservative Euro - rebel had been at least partially sidelined.

Therefore, the internal conflict over EEC membership proved insufficient to topple Party Unity Key two. Stuart Ball in *The Heath Government 1970-74* summarised thus: 'Under strong attack from without and in difficult circumstances, the party remained loyal. The paradox is not that there was so much unrest, but that it was so little and so late.'[160]

The Labour opposition was undergoing a swing to the left, and faced growing division over the European question. Although Harold Wilson had unsuccessfully applied to join the EEC in the late sixties, he supported rebel Tory calls for a referendum on the issue, and pledged to renegotiate the terms of Britain's membership, in order to accommodate the Euro-sceptics on his own benches. This provoked the resignation of several frontbench Europhile MPs, including future SDP leaders Roy Jenkins, and David Owen.

On the domestic front, the government made some changes to education. They raised the school leaving age to sixteen and provided free nursery education. Although they removed Labour's requirement for local authorities to convert grammar schools into comprehensive ones, Margaret Thatcher presided over the abolition of more grammar schools than any other Education Secretary - rejecting fewer than a tenth of applications to convert. She was however more widely known for the abolition of free school milk – with the soubriquet 'Margaret Thatcher, Milk Snatcher!'

The government also reorganised local government with a major shake-up of county names and boundaries. However, as Stuart Ball pointed out; 'Any gain in efficiency was at the price of adding to the impression of remote and faceless government.' [161]

Another minor success for the Conservative government was with Rhodesia. In November 1971 an agreement was signed between Britain and Rhodesia to restore diplomatic links and to work towards a legal independence. It would take nearly a decade for this to be fully realised, but it was nevertheless a step in the right direction.

Although Enoch Powell's 'Rivers of blood' speech in 1968 had ended his government career, it did exert a significant influence on government immigration policy, by bringing the issue of immigration into the national conversation. In 1971 an immigration bill passed through parliament, restricting immigration from Commonwealth countries to people who held work permits or had parents or grandparents in the UK.

Powell's intervention was therefore at least a partial success on his own terms, albeit at high personal cost. The issue of immigration was inflamed further that year by the expulsion of Asians from Ida Amin's Uganda. These included 57,000 British passport holders who had a right to live in the UK.

In the autumn of 1973 Britain was to witness a global crisis that would have profound effects on her economy and political fortunes. On October 6th Egypt and Syria attacked Israel on two fronts on the holiest day of the Jewish calendar, Yom Kippur. The war was a bid by the Arabs to re-take the territory that had been lost to them in the 1967 Six Days War, when an Israeli surprise attack had snatched the Sinai Dessert, Golan Heights, Gaza Strip and Jerusalem from Arab control. Within days the Arabs were making major advances and Israel was beginning to fear for her very existence. But then, the Syrians made the mistake of not pushing their advantage, allowing the Israelis to regroup and push back into Syria proper.

The Egyptians however made the opposite error of pushing too far across the Sinai Peninsula. The Israelis soon had the Egyptian Third army stranded in the dessert, and there was briefly a serious risk of a third world war, after the Soviets threatened to send troops to aid the beleaguered Egyptian forces. Fortunately, a ceasefire was agreed upon to end the fighting.

The economic after-shocks would be more long-lasting however. The Gulf States increased oil prices to the West by seventy percent in retaliation for American support for Israel. The conflict also split NATO, with many European members unwilling to allow the Americans to cross their airspace or use their territories in fear of Arab economic reprisals.

The oil crisis soon hit the UK with the speed limit on British motorways reduced to fifty mph. The Unions soon took advantage of the situation with the miners demanding a thirty-one percent pay rise. They said to the government; 'Why can't you pay us for coal? What are you willing to pay the Arabs for oil?' [162] Mr Heath had no answer. Although the National union of Miners (NUM) voted against strike action, they instead imposed an overtime ban, severely limiting production of coal for Britain's power stations.

This significantly impacted the production of electricity, and in response, the government were forced to produce an emergency budget in December 1973. Chancellor Anthony Barber described the situation as, 'The gravest situation by far since the end of the war.' [163] As a consequence, government spending was to be slashed by £1.2 billion, including the cancellation of a fifth of the new schools and colleges that had been scheduled to be built. [164]

In January 1974, British industry was put on a three-day week to conserve power. Householders were asked to only light one room at a time and TV stations had to shut down at 10:30 in the evening. Even sport was not immune to the privations and football matches were played on Sundays. The Tory Energy Minister Peter Jenkin even advised people to brush their teeth in the dark, and boasted that he did not need electric light to get ready for work. Predictably, journalists from The Observer took a picture of his house, which was sporting multiple lights.

Over the winter, the situation grew even worse. The NUM voted for renewed strike action early in February, and they were joined by power station workers and railwaymen. Edward Heath decided to go to the country in a bid to gain a fresh mandate from the British people. Heath's now famous slogan, 'Who governs Britain?' was aimed at highlighting the anti-democratic character of the strikers. In a television address, Mr Heath declared, 'This time the strike has got to stop. Only you can stop it... It is time for you to say to the extremists, the militants and the plain and simply misguided: we've had enough.' [165]

However, the fact that he had to ask the question was simply taken as confirmation that he had lost control.

The IRA too, stepped up their attacks on the mainland, with a bus bomb killing eleven soldiers on the M62. It was however the industrial strife though that had clearly cost the Conservatives Civil Unrest Key eleven.

The situation in Britain was becoming so desperate that Idi Amin mockingly started a 'Save Britain' fund. [166]

The crisis was all too much for Heath's Cabinet Secretary William Armstrong, who suffered a nervous breakdown and had to leave government. He was apparently found under a table muttering, 'moving the red army from here and the blue army from there.' [167]

The Tories had lost more than a third of the by-election seats that they had been defending over the course of the term, thus toppling key one. The Tory party was more or less unified, with the vast majority of MPs supporting Britain's entry to the EEC. Thus, Unity Key two was saved. The dour, humourless Heath was never going to be charismatic or any kind of a hero, being perceived as 'a rigid, humourless, Easter Island statue of a politician;'[168] and so Incumbent Leadership Key three was lost. Harold Wilson was not especially popular at this stage and appeared to have lost some of his old resilience and energy. Therefore at least the Opposition Charisma Key remained true for the Conservatives.

One key that had most definitely turned was the Third Party Key five. The opinion poll rating of Jeremy Thorpe's Liberals had been in double figures since the spring of 1972, and had frequently hit twenty percent since the previous autumn's crises. They had taken four by-election seats from the Conservatives during the term, and one from Labour. They were also fielding over 500 candidates for the February 1974 election - over 200 more than in 1970. [169]This turned the Third Party Key against the government.

The Scandal Key had been rattled a couple of times. In 1972, the Home Secretary Reginald Maudling resigned over his involvement with the bankrupt architect John Poulson. The police involvement into Mr Poulson's affairs led to the Home Secretary's resignation as members of his family had benefited from the company.

In May 1973, the government was rocked by the resignation of two ministers after they admitted to associating with prostitutes. Earl Jellicoe, the Lord Privy Seal and Tory leader in the Lords, and Lord Lambton, a Defence Under-Secretary were reported by the secret service. Unlike Profumo a decade earlier, there had been no compromise of national security and the scandals did not cause comparable damage to the government. These scandals though embarrassing, did not significantly taint the whole government, nor involve Edward Heath personally- so falling short of the threshold necessary to topple the Scandal Key.

The shift of government policy towards the centre is perhaps best summed up by a speech to the 1973 party conference by Peter Walker, the first Secretary of State for the new department of the Environment. 'The objective of the "new capitalism" is the harnessing of economic growth to the creation of a civilised society.' [170] This is a one-nation Tory piece of rhetoric that would not look out of place coming from Tony Blair. The 'failure' of the Heath government to do 'proper conservative things' is perhaps not so much of a surprise given that Heath was never really an ideologue like his titanic successor. As Enoch Powell once put it; 'If you showed (Heath) an idea, he immediately became angry and would go red in the face.' [171]

As election-day loomed, it was very apparent that the country was in recession, thus forfeiting Short Term Economy Key seven. However, because of the 'Barber Boom' earlier in the term, the long-term GDP was equal to the GDP of the Wilson years, and so narrowly saving key eight.

The campaign itself was notable for Heath's famous 'Who governs Britain?' gambit, and for the shortness of the Labour manifesto. The Tory campaign suffered a few big set-backs. Firstly, the latest set of balance of trade figures, published during the early stages of the campaign were the worst in history. Secondly, right-wing renegade Enoch Powell urged the electorate to vote Labour because of the Conservative's pro-European policy. He accused Heath of allowing Britain, 'to become one province in a European super-state.' [172]However, Powell was not representative of many Conservatives at the time, and by now was running as a UUUP candidate in Northern Ireland. This therefore did not jeopardise the Party Unity Key.

The Tories were fortunate also that the Labour campaign and in particular Harold Wilson were rather lacklustre, with Mr Wilson appearing to many as tired and old before his time. Overall, the campaign itself did very little to alter the fortunes of the parties; ergo, the Heath administration went to the polls with six negative keys.

This election illustrates the keys system beautifully. Edward Heath tried to turn the election into a single-issue referendum on trade union power. Elections are indeed referenda, but always on the performance of the government as a whole. That there was such a grave problem regarding the relationship between trade unions and government surely highlighted the poor performance of this Conservative administration.

Yet most of the pollsters and the media were expecting a Tory win. The famous psephologist David Butler predicted a Tory landslide to Tony Benn. 'He was afraid that the Labour party wouldn't survive,' recounted Benn.[173] *The Daily Mail* even ran their polling day headline with, 'A handsome win for Heath,' on the strength of the polls. [174] The Labour team did not really expect to win, with advisor Bernard Donoughue admitting that, 'many of them (leading party figures) saw little point in participating...as they believed we were going to lose.' [175]

The wisdom of making a general election into a single-issue referendum had been questioned the previous year in a strategy paper to the leader's steering committee. In February 1973, the paper had the following to say on the matter.

Ever since World War One, no general election has been confined to a single issue. There is no guarantee the electorate or significant parts of it will not decide to vote about something else with possibly disturbing results. [176]

The Tory failure in 1974 clearly illustrates the value of the Keys forecasting method. The public took – as they always do, a holistic approach. When Heath asked them, 'Who rules?' the British public replied, 'Not you.'

<u>*February 1974 UK general election:*</u>

1) *By-election key*   false
2) *Unity Key*   true
3) *Incumbent Leadership Key* false
4) *Opposition Charisma Key*   true

5) *Third Party Key* false
6) *Cyclical Incumbency Key* true
6) *Short-Term Economy Key* false
7) *Long-Term Economy Key* true
8) *Foreign Policy/Military Success Key* true
9) *Foreign Policy/Military Failure Key* false
10) *Policy Change Key* true
11) *Civil Unrest Key* false
12) *Scandal Key* true

<u>*balance of negative keys:*</u>   6

<u>*campaign differential:*</u> nil

<u>*forecast:*</u> loss of Conservative majority: Labour as largest party: either hung parliament or narrow Labour majority

<u>*tally:*</u> Conservative seats 291 Labour c 310 seats

<u>*actual result:*</u> hung Parliament. Labour as largest party

Labour seats: 301 Conservatives seats: 297 Liberals 14

1974:
'All I can say is my prayers.' Harold Wilson. [177]

The February 28th election had resulted in a hung parliament with Labour slightly ahead of the Conservatives by 301 to 297 seats. This was in spite of the Conservatives narrowly winning the popular vote. Despite the Liberals reaching their highest share of the vote for half a century at nineteen percent, they had only managed to secure fourteen parliamentary seats. The Liberals had obviously taken many votes from both the main parties. The Conservative vote share had declined by eight-and-a-half percent, but Labour's vote share had also dropped by nearly six points.

For several days, Edward Heath attempted to strike a deal with Liberal leader Jeremy Thorpe, who allegedly demanded the post of Home Secretary in return for cooperation with the Tories. It was all to no avail. On March 6th Harold Wilson became Prime Minister for the third time, but as leader of a minority government. When Ted Heath's colleagues tried to console him after the defeat, telling him not to blame himself, Heath replied, 'It was my fault for taking your advice.' [178] As he reflected on the paralysed state of the body politic, Jeremy Thorpe commented, 'We are all minorities now.' [179]

Although Labour were back in power, a second election was always highly probable and Wilson's skills of wheeling-and-dealing and art of the possible were more needed than ever. The Cabinet Secretary Sir John Hunt quoted the Prime Minister as saying; 'I've buried all the hatchets in the Number 10 garden, but I know where I've buried them and I can dig them up if necessary.'[180] His first action was to end the miners' strike by granting them a thirty-five percent pay rise. This action secured the Civil Unrest Key for his government.

The next most pressing problem for Mr Wilson's administration was Northern Ireland. At the end of 1973 the Heath government had reached an agreement at Sunningdale to begin power-sharing between Northern Ireland and the republic. This however, ran into serious difficulties almost immediately, with the Ulster

Unionists rejecting the plan as unification through the backdoor.

The situation deteriorated further in the spring with a general strike organised by militant unionists. The seven-day strike had brought Ulster to the brink of complete collapse with shortages of food, fuel, and power, all enforced by the intimidation of workers. Despite the severity of the crisis, Harold Wilson had declined to use the army as strike breakers. Harold Wilson condemned the strikers in a broadcast, attacking, 'people who spend their lives sponging on Westminster and British democracy, and then systematically assault democratic methods.' [181]

On the 28th May the chief executive of the power-sharing executive Brian Faulkner resigned along with the other members of the executive. Direct rule from Westminster resumed. This unfortunately cost Labour the Foreign/Military Failure key, since although the policy was already in serious trouble before the election, the total failure of power-sharing was not inevitable whilst the Conservatives were still in office.

IRA attacks on the mainland were to continue during this short term with a bomb attack in Westminster Hall in June, and an unclaimed bombing of the Tower of London. This relatively new and escalating development was not sufficient to topple Civil Unrest key twelve though. The further deterioration of the Northern Ireland situation certainly offered no hope of a foreign policy/military success for Mr Wilson. However, due to the shortness of the term, the lack of a foreign policy success did not result in a false key.

The Labour government had returned to office after the Conservatives had successfully brought Britain into the European Economic Community. This issue split the Labour cabinet and wider party, with the Labour left suspicious that the EEC was too much of a club for capitalists to be allowed to have control over Britain's government and economic policy. Tony Benn for example, believed the EEC to be a deeply undemocratic institution, attacking the European commission with the words, 'I can think of no body of men outside the Kremlin who have so much power without a shred of accountability.'[182]

This put Harold Wilson in something of a quandary. He was generally pro-European, though not at any cost, so his official policy was that Labour would re-negotiate the terms of Britain's membership of the Common Market, and then ask the British public to approve or disapprove the deal in a national referendum.

One concession the government did manage to contain was the setting up of the European Regional Development Fund, of which Britain would be a significant beneficiary. However, the split within the party and cabinet was still sufficient to cost Labour the Party Unity Key.

The economy was of course a major headache for Labour during this short seven-month term. Although GDP grew during the second and third quarters, unemployment was rising, shares had taken a severe pasting and the general mood was one of recession and instability. Thus, the Short-Term Economy Key remained negative for Labour in October 1974. As the term was under a year, the Long-Term Economy Key was rendered void.

The Wilson administration suffered a brush with scandal when it had transpired that Marcia Williams' brother had made a lot of money from buying, re-developing and re-selling land. There was brief excitement when a letter appeared, signed by Harold Wilson, implicating him in the deals. However, it was soon found that the signature had been forged by Wolverhampton insurance broker Ronald Millhench, who was subsequently jailed.

Wilson still faced the charge of hypocrisy after publicly attacking land speculation in the past and calling for public ownership of such land. He made matters worse by trying to draw a false distinction between property speculation and land reclamation. However, he had done nothing seriously wrong and the non-scandal passed.

Wilson did create a stir by promoting Marcia Williams to the Lords, as Lady Falkender. This was effectively a middle finger to the press who had continually attacked her and her influence over the Prime Minister. Yet the Scandal key did not turn.

As there was only one by-election in that brief term, the by-election key was effectively rendered void.

Wilson was not especially popular by this time, so the Incumbent Leadership Key was lost. His opponent Edward Heath was of course very obliging by having no charisma, thus preserving key number four.

The Liberals were still polling very strongly during the autumn campaign. Should the Third Party key be automatically turned against the new minority government of Harold Wilson?

The very strong Liberal performance in the polls and then in the result itself was mostly a reflection of the economic and industrial difficulties experienced under the old Heath government. The minority Wilson government had not been in power long enough for those influences to be expected to fade away. Additionally, the evidence from the February election showed that the Liberals reduced the vote of both main parties, but especially that of the Conservatives. Therefore, I decided not to turn the key for the election of October 1974.

The election campaign of autumn 1974 was not especially eventful. Wilson attacked Heath's, 'Dark age of frozen, broken-backed Britain, ruled under a state of emergency.' [183] Heath meanwhile argued for a national coalition to lead Britain through the crisis. Wilson hit back with the witty line attacking, 'Con policies, Con leadership by a Con party for a con trick.'[184]

October 1974 UK general election:

1) *By-election key*   n/a
2) *Unity Key*   false
3) *Incumbent Leadership Key*   false
4) *Opposition Charisma Key*   true
5) *Third Party Key*   true
6) *Cyclical Incumbency Key*   true
7) *Short-Term Economy Key*   false
8) *Long-Term Economy Key*   n/a
9) *Foreign Policy/Military Success Key* discounted loss
10) *Foreign Policy/Military Failure Key* false
11) *Policy Change Key*   discounted loss
12) *Civil Unrest Key*   true
13) *Scandal Key*   true

balance of negative keys: 4

forecast: Labour majority of 15

campaign differential: nil

tally: Labour 317 seats Conservative seats c 285

actual result: Labour majority of 3

Labour seats: 319 Conservatives seats: 276 Liberals 13

The second election result of 1974 was if anything, a bigger shock than the first. Most polls suggested a large majority for Labour, and the BBC exit poll predicted a triple digit landslide. [185] When it came, the small majority of the fourth Wilson ministry led to major falls on the British stock markets; investors and shareholders were obviously hoping for and expecting the stability of a much bigger Labour majority. The Liberals still won eighteen percent of the vote but achieved no breakthrough. One party that did perform well was the Scottish National Party. (SNP) They had gone from having just two seats in 1970 to eleven in October 1974.

1974 -1979:
'The crisis consists precisely in the fact that the old is dying and the new cannot be born; in this interregnum a great variety of morbid symptoms appear.' Antonio Gramsci [186]

The quote that introduces the last 'Old Labour' government is a rather ironic one. It comes from Antonio Gramsci, one of the founders of the left-wing Frankfurt school, which tried to explain the failure of socialism to triumph across Europe following World War One. For in the 1970s, there was a definite feeling of national malaise and decline; the old Keynesian system was failing with poor growth, high inflation and union unrest. Much of heavy industry was sinking into seemingly terminal decline and politicians appeared to be pursuing dead end streets. There was however a sea change on the distant horizon, but its revolutionaries would come from the right.

Harold Wilson's fourth administration began in the most uncertain of climates. With a majority of only three, it would be only a matter of time before by-election defeats reduced it to a minority government; thereby necessitating some sort of working arrangement with the Liberals.

The economic picture was gloomy indeed, and that was the one thing that both party leaders could agree on. Although GDP was growing during the second and third quarters of 1974, it would become sharply negative again at the end of the year, and would remain in recession through most of 1975. Unemployment was now rising steeply and would reach a million in the spring of 1975. During the seventies the percentage of shares in UK businesses owned by foreigners almost halved. The FTSE 100 plunged from 544 in May 1972 to 146 in December 1974. House prices fell steadily – by more than a quarter during 1974-76. [187]

The other major problem was inflation, in fact stagflation, since prices were rising in a stagnant economy. Inflation reached 16.7% in 1974 and 26% in 1975. It would remain in double digits for all years but one until 1982.

This problem of rising prices led to rising demands for wage increases and subsequent industrial strife. If wages rise too fast then unemployment results, compounding the problem of low growth. Wilson's solution was the so-called 'Social Contract' between government and the Unions. In return for the repeal of Heath's Industrial Relations Act, and a freeze on rents, the Unions would have to cooperate with the Labour government by accepting a policy of voluntary wage restraint. Additionally, there would have to be a year-long gap between pay settlements to provide some kind of stability. This would break down in 1978, after several years of high inflation, leading ultimately to the strikes now known as the 'Winter of Discontent'.

The major international issue that the Labour government had to face was Europe. The promised referendum on continued membership, which was first suggested by Tony Benn, was held in June 1975. The 'Yes' position was supported by the Prime Minister, the majority of the Labour cabinet, the Conservative party and the Liberals. The 'NO' position was supported by Labour rebels, the Scottish and Welsh nationalist parties and the Ulster Unionists.

Labour's official position was neutral as there was major opposition to EEC membership right across the party. At the 1975 spring conference, the Labour membership opposed EEC membership by almost two to one, and therefore official party policy would have to remain one of neutrality.

The most vocal 'No' campaigners in parliament were from the Labour side, with the exception of Enoch Powell. Cabinet nay-sayers from the Labour left included Tony Benn, Barbara Castle, Peter Shore and Michael Foot, who accused the pro-EEC cabinet ministers as, 'Conniving at the dismemberment of parliament.' Eurosceptics from the right of the Labour party included Eric Varley and Douglas Jay. The majority of the Wilson cabinet did support staying in the common market, including the Chancellor Dennis Healey, Foreign Secretary James Callaghan and Home Secretary Roy Jenkins (who had returned to the fold.) Labour was therefore badly split.

However, as a way of avoiding a party civil war, the normal policy of collective cabinet responsibility would be suspended, and individual Labour MPs, including cabinet ministers would be allowed to campaign according to personal conscience. This approach prevented a split from turning into a bitter schism.

The referendum result saw sixty-seven percent of the British public support continued membership of the EEC. In terms of the keys, it was neither a foreign policy success, nor a failure as it confirmed an existing state of affairs and the result was widely expected. After the referendum, the issue was generally regarded as settled, and hence Unity Key two fell back into the government's favour.

Northern Ireland remained a thorn in the government's side for the remainder of the term. In 1974, the Labour government introduced the Prevention of Terrorism act, which enabled the police to detain terror suspects for four to seven days without trial; and also to permanently expel suspected terrorists from Britain. This was brought in rather reluctantly by the liberal Home Secretary Roy Jenkins.

Although there was no real breakthrough, the level of violence did at least diminish somewhat by 1979. Notable developments in the conflict included the Women's peace movement which peaked around 1976-77. Yet, despite winning a Nobel prize, it failed to end the sectarian conflict.

There were of course many terrible outrages, including the Birmingham and Guildford pub bombings, the Balcombe Street siege of 1975, and the murders of TV personality and libertarian campaigner Ross McWhirter and Thatcher mentor Airey Neaves.

Opinion polling showed that public concern about Northern Ireland peaked in 1971, when poll respondents ranked it the second most important issue facing Britain, after the economy. However, it ceased to rank very prominently after 1974, as people had simply become inured to it. [188] Therefore, I do not count the Ulster troubles as easily capable of turning Military Failure key eleven after this date.

In March 1976, without any prior warning, Harold Wilson resigned as Prime Minister. The decision caused widespread bafflement but Mr Wilson simply said that he had always planned to retire about now. His advisor Bernard Donoughue, who supports Wilson's claims, quoted him as saying, 'I have been round this racetrack so often that I cannot generate any more enthusiasm for jumping any more hurdles.' [189]

Wilson's sudden resignation still set the political world reeling with conspiracy theories. Had Wilson been blackmailed? Had he received a terrible diagnosis? Did he know about some impending disaster and was jumping ship? However, the near-certain answer was the mundane explanation that he had simply had enough.

Wilson had certainly had his fair share of conspiracy theories. One of the silliest was he was really a KGB agent. The evidence for this chiefly revolved around his numerous trips to the USSR earlier in his career as President of the Board of Trade. The fact that he had not even tried to impose anything remotely resembling Marxism on the country was not allowed to spoil a good conspiracy theory.

Another idea was that a band of elderly, right-wing former secret service men were poised to stage a coup and remove Labour from power.

However, Wilson did seem to become increasingly paranoid about the secret service and his bizarre comments to the journalists Penrose and Courtiour following his retirement, underscored that impression.

Although not generally regarded as a great Prime Minister, Harold Wilson still won some impressive accolades. Joe Rogaly of the Financial Times, remarked that his tenure in office had witnessed, 'an almost total abolition of deference.' [190] Bernard Levin described Wilson as an, 'Incomparable political stuntman (who had ridden) the two bareback horses of Labour's left and right simultaneously.' [191]

His honours list led to a political row over some of the people he nominated for awards. These included a life peerage for Sir Joseph Kagan, maker of the Gannex raincoats worn by Harold Wilson, who would later be convicted of fraud. Others included businessman Sir Eric Miller who committed suicide the following year while under investigation for fraud, and a knighthood for future Referendum Party leader James Goldsmith.

An original list drawn up by his political secretary Marcia Williams was said to be even more controversial; though no evidence for this was ever found. The list was allegedly written on lavender paper and hence became known as 'The Lavender List.' This list of nominations poisoned Wilson's legacy. However, it fell well short of the threshold required to topple the Scandal Key.

Labour was plunged into an immediate leadership contest, with the Foreign Secretary James Callaghan, beating Dennis Healey and Michael foot to take the top post. Callaghan was distinguished for being the only person to hold all the great offices of state: Chancellor of the Exchequer, Home Secretary, Foreign Secretary, and Prime Minister. The avuncular Callaghan was a moderate, and fairly popular within the Labour party. He was also generally liked by the wider public, being nicknamed 'Sunny Jim'. However, he was not sufficiently strong to win the Incumbent Leadership Key, as he also became increasingly beleaguered.

The decision not to call an early election in September 1978 has been considered a major mistake on the part of James Callaghan. He had allowed expectations of an autumn election to build up, only to confound them. (A mistake repeated by his successor Gordon Brown thirty years later.) At the annual Trades Union Congress, he even sang the Edwardian music hall number, 'Waiting at the Church' to mock his opponents. However, it failed to unambiguously convey his change of plan regarding the election, looking like an exercise in pure whimsy. In retrospect, this was seen as hubristic. I shall consider the counterfactual situation of an autumn 1978 election in the corresponding chapter towards the end of this book.

By this point the Conservatives had also undergone a change of leadership. Edward Heath vowed to fight on after his defeat in the October 1974 elections. However, in February 1975 he faced a challenge from former Education Secretary Margaret Thatcher. Thatcher's candidacy was widely seen as a stalking horse for such male establishment figures as William Whitelaw, but she shocked her party and the commentariat by beating Edward Heath 130 -119. Heath immediately resigned following this blow and Thatcher beat four male rivals, winning the support of 146 Tory MPs.

Thatcher's influence was a polarising one form the start, drawing most of her support from the right of the party, from MPs from the South of England, from state schools and the non-Oxbridge educated; even though Thatcher herself was an Oxford graduate.

Thatcher was an opponent of the expansionist welfare state and Keynesian economics, favouring free-market neo-liberalism. In an interview with the *Daily Telegraph,* she made her position clear: 'If a Tory does not believe that private property is one of the main bulwarks of individual freedom, then he had better become a socialist and have done with it...why should anyone support a party that seems to have the courage of no convictions.' [192]

Suddenly, the ideological gap between the two main parties was widening.

Although the economy was growing again by 1976, inflation continued to be a major problem for the government, as were unemployment and industrial unrest.

Another serious problem was the weakening of the currency. In 1972 the pound stood at $2.60. By January 1976 it had declined to $2.0. That year the British government borrowed £3 billion from the central banks of multiple countries, including the USA, France, Germany, Switzerland and Japan. However, in September 1976 the Bank of England announced that it could no longer support the pound on foreign exchanges. The pound sank further to $1.68.

In a highly memorable and totemic incident, the Chancellor Dennis Healey, who was on his way to an IMF summit, ordered his chauffer to turn around at Heathrow airport and head back to Whitehall, as he was so concerned that the pound could crash whilst he was incommunicado for seventeen hours whilst on the plane. This happened during the Labour Party conference. In the conference hall, the Prime Minister made the following, highly significant speech:

We used to think that you could spend your way out of a recession and increase employment by cutting taxes and increasing government spending. I tell you in all candour that that option no longer exists and that insofar as it ever did exist, it only worked by injecting a bigger dose of inflation into the economy... higher inflation, followed by higher unemployment. That is the history of the last twenty years.[193]

This moment, marked the end of the dominance of Keynesian economics that had reigned since the Great Depression. A few days later, Dennis Healey announced that Britain would apply for a loan from the International Monetary Fund (IMF) of nearly four trillion dollars, the largest loan in the IMF's history at that point. The loan was so great in fact that the IMF had to source money from other lenders.

In return, the Labour government had to agree to deep cuts in public spending. Labour cut public spending by eight percent over the next three years – more than was ever cut by Mrs Thatcher. In the event, the government only needed to draw on about half of the loan, since the projected government spending proved to be an over-estimate. The pound began a modest recovery, reaching $1.90 in 1977.

The Callaghan government fought inflationary pressures with a policy of pay restraint. As with his predecessor Harold Wilson, this brought him into conflict with the unions. The Social Contract system held until 1978, and thereafter direct conflict with the unions soon embroiled the government in fresh crisis.

Industrial conflict had been growing since the start of Callaghan's premiership. In 1976-77, the focus of union confrontation was the Grunwick strikes in Willesden London. This dispute centred on union recognition at the photographic development company Grunwick. This strike was notable in that it was the first in which a mostly Asian workforce gained support from the wider trade union movement, with thousands of flying pickets being bussed in to the site. The dispute saw over 500 arrests, which was the most since 1926 for a single dispute.

However, the employers prevailed with assistance from the right- wing organisation NAFF (National Association for Freedom) which helped to break the Union of Post Office Workers boycott of Grunwick mail. The ultimate defeat of the strikers did not seriously deter new unrest. During that year the government had to employ thousands of troops to relieve a fire fighters' strike, manning 'green goddesses.' However, the defeat of the Grunswick strikers was a straw in the wind for the next decade's game-changing developments.

Other crises faced by the Callaghan government include the famous drought summer of 1976. With rivers and reservoirs running dry, the government was forced to introduce water rationing and even the deployment of standpipes in some areas. In August, a hapless minister of drought, Denis Howell was appointed; a week later heavy rain broke the drought and continued well into the autumn.

The patriotic Callaghan at least enjoyed taking part in the Queen's Silver Jubilee in June 1977. This was a big national event in a country that had changed a great deal since the coronation in 1953. Most people were still very pro-monarchy, and deference towards the royals was still very much the order of the day; with the exception of punkish anarchy from the Sex Pistols.

One scandalous allegation that did hit the headlines in this period was the one that enveloped and prematurely ended the career of Liberal leader Jeremy Thorpe. Thorpe had been accused of plotting the murder of Norman Scott, a model with whom he had had an alleged affair. The contention was that Thorpe was afraid that Scott would expose the affair, and thus ruin him politically. (Male homosexuality was still widely regarded as sleazy and taboo, even in the Liberal party.)

The story broke after a bungled attempt on Scott's life in 1975 led to Scott making the allegation against Jeremy Thorpe in court. Thorpe decided to quit the leadership of his party in May 1976 and was replaced by David Steel. The matter finally went to a high court trial in 1979, and although Thorpe was acquitted, his credibility could not recover. The fact that he had personally refused to give evidence at the trial probably did not help in this regard.

The Liberals were already losing support well before the allegations hit the headlines though, with February 1974 being the peak of Thorpe's career.

The Liberals would however prove vital to the Callaghan administration in early 1977, after by-election defeats wiped out their shoe-string majority; leaving Labour vulnerable to losing a no-confidence vote in the Commons. This cost the Wilson-Callaghan government key number one. The Lib-Lab pact lasted until September 1978, the date at which Callaghan had been expected to call a general election. The pact involved the Liberal party voting with the government, provided that a least some Liberal policies were considered.

Although the Liberals had been damaged by the Thorpe affair, they were still very strong by earlier standards in the run-up to the 1979 election, with the party consistently reaching double digits in the polls and fielding well over 500 candidates.

The sharply increased Conservative showing in the polls highlighted the exodus of ex-Conservative Liberal voters back to their mother party. This was a fairly predictable outcome of the Liberal party's role in propping up the failing Callaghan administration. This, combined with the poor Labour polling figures suggested that the Liberals were now a bigger threat to the Labour party than to the resurgent Conservatives; therefore, the Third Party key turned false for Labour.

By the late autumn of 1978, although the economy was growing and inflation was the least bad it had been since Labour had come to power, the relationship with the unions was deteriorating. The Social Contract had effectively been torn up after Labour delegates at the 1978 party conference voted against it, and now fresh conflict with the unions was looming.

A strike by Ford workers resulted in a seventeen percent pay increase, well above the five percent cap demanded by the government. The situation had also been aggravated by a shift towards devolved union management. Power was moving from the union high commands to factory floor activists; shop stewards were now making the pay claims. The Social Contract was now truly dead and buried.

With the simultaneous demise of the Lib-Lab pact, the political weather had suddenly turned chilly for Labour. The Ford strike was soon followed by a hauliers' strike at the end of the year. Other public sector workers soon joined in the disputes, including refuse collectors, NHS workers, school dinner ladies and caretakers, and even some grave diggers. NHS ancillary workers picketed hospitals, so that in many cases only emergency patients could be treated. BBC 1 and 2 were taken off air by technicians' strikes, as would ITV a year later.

At its peak, the 'Winter of Discontent' involved one-and-a-half million public sector workers. A vast pile of rat-infested rubbish built up at Leicester Square and Clapham Common, London. The city of Hull was effectively blockaded by hauliers who dictated what supplies could be allowed in and which could not. All this was compounded by the coldest winter since 1963, with many places cut off by snowdrifts. [194]

Perhaps the most potent story of the strike was the refusal by Liverpool gravediggers to bury the dead. The situation got so bad that corpses were stacking up in a disused factory, and the newspapers were mooting the possibility of mass burials at sea. Maj-General Michael Tillotson of the Civil Contingencies Unit, recounted a moment of unintentional black comedy when the Environment Secretary Peter Shore was asked what could be done about the situation in the graveyards. He replied with, 'Oh dear, surely we could provide a skeleton service.' [195] We also cannot be quite sure what the Chancellor of the Duchy of Lancaster, Baron Lever had in mind when he said, 'Let the dead bury the dead.'[196]

The famous 'quotation' which millions of British people still believe was uttered by James Callaghan, was in fact largely invented by a Sun reporter. What happened was that a reporter from the Evening Standard asked the Prime Minister, who was on his way back from a perhaps ill-timed visit to Barbados, following a summit in Guadeloupe: 'What is your general approach, in view of the mounting chaos in the country at the moment?' Mr Callaghan replied: 'Well, that's a judgment that you are making. I promise you that if you look at it from outside, and perhaps you're taking rather a parochial view at the moment, I don't think that other people in the world would share the view that there is mounting chaos.' [197]*The Sun* reduced that to 'Crisis! What crisis?' This proved the old adage that, 'A lie can get half way round the world before the truth can even get its boots on.'

Nevertheless, lasting damage was done to the government by this episode. The Environment Secretary Peter Shore described the situation as, 'Occupational tribal warfare...every separate group in the country had no feeling and no sense of being part of a community, but was simply out to get for itself what it could.' [198] Years later, Jim Callaghan in an interview with the journalist Michael Cockerell, condemned the more extreme elements of the strikes in stark terms: 'Some of the things that went on were quite disgraceful. Well, there was the refusal to bury people

.... there were the hospital workers who immediately put in a claim and turned off the heating boilers in the hospitals. I was disgusted with the behaviour of Trade Unionists who did that sort of thing.' [199]

The strikers had no respect for Labour, but were contemptuously bullish in their attitude to a potential Thatcher Government. Sid Weighell, the General Secretary of the National Union of Railwaymen was notably blunt in his assessment on working with Mrs Thatcher: 'I don't see how we can talk to Mrs Thatcher... I will say to the lads, "Come on, get your snouts in the trough." [200]

When the Social Services Secretary David Ennals was admitted to hospital during the strikes, firebrand union shop steward Jamie Morris even led a campaign to deny him such luxuries as soup, tea, newspapers, the tidying of his bed, and even the sight of human smiles. (Actually, Ennals was very well looked after in hospital, in the event.) [201]

On February 14th, Labour and the unions struck a deal, which was inevitably dubbed 'The Valentine's Day Deal' by the press. The government effectively abandoned their failed policy of pay-restraint, and instead sought to replace it with other means for combating inflation.

The deal ended the strikes, by which point had cost around thirty million working days – the greatest industrial action since the General Strike of 1926. The government hoped that it could hang on till the autumn with the chance that the strikes might fade from memory, or at least drop out of the national conversation. However, fate would not be quite so kind.

The Labour government was not entirely lacking in legislative innovation. In the current term, The Sex Discrimination Act 1975 and Race Relations Act 1976 came into force: the latter incorporating and expanding upon the Race Relations acts of the sixties, and the former building on earlier liberal legislation such as the Equal Pay Act.

The Race Relations Act prohibited discrimination on grounds of colour, ethnicity and national origin, in terms of employment, provision of goods and services, education and all public forums. The Sex Discrimination Act providing similar protection, but also including protection from harassment and the disposal of properties. These changes were also accompanied by the introduction of paid maternity leave. The Race Relations Act also established the Equal Opportunities Commission and the Commission for Racial Equality.

Another piece of reform was to extend child benefit entitlement to first-born children. This was introduced in 1977, facilitating the birth of this author in the same year: an exceedingly good piece of legislation.

Labour also set up ACAS in order to mediate in industrial disputes, and passed the Health & Safety at Work Act.

In the field of education, Callaghan anticipated the GCSEs and other educational reforms that were to come from Kenneth Baker, a decade in advance. In his 1976 Ruskin speech, he called for a core curriculum and a return to more traditional forms of learning. However, his lack of a majority and civil service opposition stymied the initiative.

These achievements still fell somewhat short of securing the Policy Change Key eleven. Had Labour succeeded in the next venture, they might just have managed to turn it.

Because Mr Callaghan was leading a minority government from early 1977 onwards, he needed the support of minor parties. This included the nationalist parties in Wales and Scotland. Therefore, the government pursued the cause of Welsh and Scottish Devolution. This culminated in two referenda in early March 1979.

However, the Welsh overwhelmingly rejected the idea with only twelve percent of the Welsh electorate endorsing the devolution. In Scotland, thirty-three percent supported a devolved Scottish assembly, as opposed to thirty-one percent who were against the idea. However, the legislation demanded that at least forty percent of the electorate would have to endorse the proposal in order for it to be implemented.

These failures robbed the government of the Policy Change Key, but did much more besides. The failure of Welsh and Scottish home rule, led to the nationalists turning against the government, and now that the Lib-Lab pact was finished, Mr Callaghan was in serious trouble. The Conservatives tabled a motion of no-confidence in the government and the Labour administration fell by a single vote on March 28th 1979. It was the first government to be brought down in such a fashion since that of Ramsay McDonald in 1924.

The following day, James Callaghan called a general election. With the vote in May coming so soon after the winter of industrial unrest and civic chaos, the Civil Unrest Key would be turned against the government. Although the economy was well out of recession by this point, the earlier recession during 1974-76 was easily sufficient to cost Labour the Long-term Economy Key. With no major foreign policy success or failure, the foreign policy keys were split. Party unity was just about good enough to avoid the loss of key two, but with the Liberals now in double digits in most polls, the Third Party Key was now false.

In the election battle itself, both parties fought a competent campaign. The Tories employed the services of Saatchi & Saatchi, who utilised the modern media to the full. The most memorable ad in the campaign was the now very famous poster, depicting an endless dole queue with the legend: 'Labour isn't Working.' It was a brilliant piece of propaganda, but highly ironic with the hindsight of knowing that unemployment would more than double within three years of the Tories coming to power.

When it was first unveiled in the summer of 1978, Dennis Healey publicly attacked it – and in so doing, foolishly attracted vastly more attention to it, than would otherwise have been the case. It re-appeared during the spring campaign the following year, under the banner, 'Labour still isn't working.'

Interestingly, the Conservatives turned down an offer from Jim Callaghan to take part in a live TV debate. This underlined how little confidence they had in Margaret Thatcher at this stage. We would have to wait over thirty years for a televised debate to feature in a British general election campaign.

Although Margaret Thatcher is today remembered as a titanic political figure who overcame all resistance like a political ice-breaker, she was not yet perceived in that light. That transformation of outer perception and inner self-confidence would be more fully realised by victory in the Falklands war three years later.

She was already taking elocution lessons for her voice which was deemed to be too high-pitched and condescending. TV personality Clive James likened it to, 'a cat sliding down a blackboard.' [202] All in all, although having a woman lead a major party was a novelty, she was not yet formidable enough to topple the Opposition Charisma Key.

The polls in the campaign paint an interesting picture. The Tory lead in the polls shrank throughout the campaign, whilst their lead on being the best party to deal with inflation, taxation and law & order grew. Callaghan's personal lead over Thatcher also grew considerably during the campaign from 39-33 to 44-25.[203] This undermines the popular belief that Tory campaigning was significantly superior to Labour's, as does the narrowing of the headline Tory numbers from around fifty to forty-three percent, during the course of the campaign. Research by MORI also suggested that people believed the Labour campaign to be superior. Therefore, I have not awarded the Conservatives a campaign advantage.

During the campaign, the Labour advisor Bernard Donoughue attempted to cheer up Jim Callaghan with a little optimism about the impending election. Yet the Prime Minister was not fooled. He turned to his advisor and said; 'It then does not matter what you say or do. There is a shift in what the public wants and what it approves. I suspect there is now such a sea change – and it is for Mrs Thatcher.'[204]

<u>May 1979 UK general election:</u>

1) *By-election key*   false
2) *Unity Key*   true
3) *Incumbent Leadership Key*   false

4) *Opposition Charisma Key*   true
5) *Third Party Key*   false
6) *Cyclical Incumbency Key*   true
7) *Short-Term Economy Key*   true
8) *Long-Term Economy Key*   false
9) *Foreign Policy/Military Success Key* false
10) *Foreign Policy/Military Failure Key* true
11) *Policy Change Key*   false
12) *Civil Unrest Key*   false
13) *Scandal Key*   true

balance of negative keys: 7

campaign differential: no advantage

forecast: Conservative majority c. 50

Conservatives C. 340-350 seats Labour 266 seats

actual result: Conservative majority of 43

Conservatives 339 seats Labour 269 seats Liberals 11 seats

As the seventies came to a close, the change of government seemed to reflect a change of zeitgeist. The economic crises, shortages and labour conflicts of the old decade had reached a nadir with nation-wide strikes that were dubbed 'the Winter of Discontent' after Shakespeare's Richard the Third. As the Times had put it in 1976, 'Britain is a country that resents being poor, but is not prepared to make the effort to be rich.' [205]The corporatist policy of one Conservative and two Labour

Prime Ministers, of working with unions to control wage rises in order to control inflation, had broken down.

The battle between different unions to secure higher wages for their members had brought the country to the brink of chaos. Margaret Thatcher described the mood of the time as one of 'snarling envy and motiveless hostility.'[206] The Callaghan government had come close to declaring a state of emergency and sending in the army. In turning their backs on co-operation with the Labour government, the trade unions had helped to drive them from office, and enable the electoral success of their future nemesis.

The British general election of May 1979 was a watershed moment in British politics. It ended the period of the post-war consensus; the decades in which both parties believed in a mixed-economy, full-employment and corporatist cooperation between government, business and the unions. This approach had finally been driven to destruction in the strikes of 1978-79. It marked the beginning of the end of the era of trade union power and high inflation. It also marked the beginning of a period of damaging internecine conflict within the Labour party, the division of the left and a more polarised society.

The election, which saw the biggest swing since 1945, also resulted in the election of Britain's first woman Prime Minister – in fact the first democratically elected female leader in the western world.

This year also dashed the hopes for Scottish and Welsh devolution - at least for the next eighteen years; the SNP dropped from eleven to two seats in parliament.

Although the Labour party would eventually return as a party of government, the old party of Wilson, Callaghan, Jenkins, Benn and Foot would never come back. The hard left would twice seize the high command of the Labour party over the next forty years, but on both occasions would be smashed at the polls. Like 1945, this election marked a new political settlement: this time the Thatcherite settlement.

Chapter 5: 1979-1997:
BREAKING THE POST-WAR CONSENSUS:
PRIVATISATION, WAR ON THE UNIONS, ARGENTINA,
AND INFLATION. DETONATING THE CITY

From May 1979 to May 1997, Britain experienced the longest period of one-party rule in living memory, initiated by a woman who was to become the longest serving Prime Minister in living memory. During these years the country was more thoroughly transformed by any twentieth century government bar Clement Atlee's. Margaret Thatcher came to office with the determination to tame the power of the Trade Unions, to reverse Britain's long-standing economic decline and cure the national crisis of confidence.

Thatcher saw the previous thirty-five years of the 'Post War Consensus,' as years of tolerated failure that withered national self-esteem and nourished a something for nothing culture and its attendant politics of envy. Coming to power after the debilitating strikes of the Winter of Discontent, her purpose was clear.

By the end of Thatcher's tenure in November 1990, trade union power had been effectively neutered, large swathes of the British economy had been privatised, the financial sector had experienced an explosion of wealth and power, and the old manufacturing base had been devastated. Many people had made large amounts of money, the business sector had innovated and progressed to an extraordinary degree; but millions of others had lost their livelihoods and their raison d'etre.

The Thatcher government had effectively resolved (in their favour) the twentieth century conflict between the trade unions and capitalism, and had to a large extent defeated the rampant inflation that had blighted the seventies. They had also significantly contributed to the defeat of Soviet Communism. However, they had also been the catalysts for the demise of British heavy industry, and had overseen a dramatic worsening of unemployment, urban decay, homelessness and crime. They also failed to resolve the bitter conflict in Northern Ireland, or the nature and extent of Britain's relationship with Europe. These were issues which would take future governments to tackle one way or another.

Britain had in many ways become far more prosperous, but at the same time more divided and polarised. During the last six and a half years of this period, the changes consolidated under the unassuming leadership of John Major. Although no radical change of direction was to come, by winning a fourth term for the Tories in 1992, he cemented one of his formidable predecessor's most notable achievements - by ensuring the creation of New Labour.

1979-1983: *THE FIRST THATCHER TERM*

'You turn if you want to. The lady's not for turning.' Margaret Thatcher Conference speech, 10th October 1980

Mrs Thatcher stood outside Downing Street on that late spring morning in 1979 and quoted a prayer, once attributed to Francis of Assisi.

Where there is discord, may we bring harmony. Where there is error, may we bring truth. Where there is doubt, may we bring faith. Where there is despair, may we bring hope. [207]

Margaret Thatcher, dubbed the 'Iron lady,' initially by the Soviet Tass news agency, saw her election as Prime Minister as the beginning of a mission to save Britain from socialism - and in particular from the radical trade unions whom had been at the forefront of the industrial disputes during the recent, tumultuous Winter of Discontent.

Her background was modest, being a grocer's daughter from Grantham, Lincolnshire, and grammar school educated. Therefore, she was different from most of her colleagues in several ways; being a woman, being from a lower middle-class background, being from outside the richer south east and in the degree of her ideological fervour.

She felt that many of the older Conservative politicians had simply given up being Conservatives and were happy to surrender to the left, and to the then pervasive idea of 'national decline.' She wrote in her autobiography; 'In the eyes of the "wet" Tory establishment, I was not only a woman but "that woman," someone not just of a different sex, but of a different class, a person with an alarming conviction that the values and virtues of middle England shall be brought to bear on the problems which the establishment consensus had created. I offended on many counts.' [208]

Thatcher never made much of being the first female Prime Minister, remarking; 'I was always asked how it felt to be a woman Prime Minister. I would reply; "I don't know, I've never experienced the alternative." [209]

Mrs Thatcher had been heavily influenced by her shopkeeper father, especially with his beliefs in thrift, ambition and personal responsibility. The following, highly illuminating quote sets out how Margaret Thatcher saw the functioning of the free market and the state.

I knew from my father's accounts that the free market was like a vast sensitive nervous system, responding to events and signals all over the world to meet the ever-changing needs of peoples in different countries, from different classes, of different religions with a kind of benign indifference to their status. Governments acted on a much smaller store of conscious information and by contrast were themselves blind forces blundering about in the dark. [210]

This is highly reminiscent of Sigmund Freud's comparisons between the characteristics of the conscious and unconscious minds; only here with the free market acting as a vast collective unconscious, and the state as the conscious tip of the iceberg.

The new government saw its most pressing concerns to be the battle to control inflation, and the need to reduce government spending and borrowing. Inflation was in double digits and rising, having been as high as twenty-six percent less than three years' earlier.

Thatcher quickly abandoned the corporatism of her three immediate predecessors and embraced the monetarism of Milton Friedman. In its first year, her government abolished the price commission and in its second, scrapped the Clegg Commission which regulated wages. The earlier corporatist body, NEDDY was allowed to continue for a dozen more years but was effectively sidelined.

Another, highly important reform introduced in 1979 was the abolition of exchange controls. These controls limited the amount of money that could be brought into or out of the country, and had been in place since the outbreak of World War Two in 1939. Their removal greatly facilitated international trade and boosted the British economy in the long run.

Thatcher and her chancellor Geoffrey Howe decided that the best approach to reducing inflationary pressures was to control the money supply. In the first budget of the new administration, interest rates were increased, peaking at seventeen percent, but taxation was shifted from tax on incomes to tax on spending. Therefore, the top rate of income tax was cut from eighty-three percent to sixty percent but VAT was increased from eight percent to fifteen percent in order to make up some of the shortfall in revenue. Unfortunately, this had the effect of increasing inflation in the short-to-medium term, pushing it to twenty percent in 1980, before falling back sharply.

The rate rises unfortunately had a detrimental effect on businesses struggling in what soon turned out to be the second recession in five years. The Iranian Revolution of early 1979, which installed the anti-Western Ayatollah Khomeini in Tehran, had had the unfortunate effect, (among others) of increasing oil prices. This in turn pushed the world economy into recession and hiked up inflation still further. Matters escalated some more in September 1980 when Iraq invaded Iran, leading to an eight-year bloody conflict.

These pressures were devastating on an economy that had not long before been bailed out by the IMF. Unemployment, which was already rising when the Tories took office, soared from 1.3 million in 1979 to two million in 1980, and then to three million in early 1982.

It was to remain above the three million mark for five years. Yet Thatcher stuck to her monetarist doctrine, in spite of worsening poll numbers (twenty-three percent approval rating in 1980 [211]) and even a letter signed by 364 economists, attacking her stance in 1981. Mrs Thatcher responded to the latter by insouciantly quipping that there were enough disgruntled economists to, 'provide me with bad advice for every day of the year except All Fools Day.'[212]

The downturn, which was roughly comparable to the 2008-09 recession in GDP terms; easily cost the Tories Long Term Economy Key eight, as GDP failed to grow at all during the entire term. It was the most dismal full government term for GDP since David Lloyd George's post World War One coalition government.

The deep recession and the highest unemployment since the Great Depression also cost the Tories multiple by-elections, thereby toppling Key one.

The dire economic situation combined with deteriorating polling data, was leading to growing dissent within the Conservative party. Opponents of Thatcher's hardline monetarist policies were known as 'wets,' implying weakness and timidity. Supporters of her ideology such as Sir Keith Joseph were correspondingly called 'dries.' During 1981, the Prime Minister had had to dismiss a number of ministers from her cabinet for being too 'wet.' First to go was Norman St John Stevens, the man who had coined the wryly ironic epithet of 'The blessed Margaret'. Thatcher roasted him in return, with the claim that he had 'turned indiscretion into a political principle.' [213]

Later that year a reshuffle saw a slew of ministers fired or moved. These included Jim Prior, Sir Ian Gilmour and Churchill's son-in-law Christopher Soames. Thatcher attacked Jim Prior in *The Downing Street*

Years, describing him as; 'an example of a political type that had dominated, and in my view damaged the post-war Tory party. I call such figures the "false squire." They have all the outward show of a John Bull – ruddy face, white hair, bluff manner - but inwardly they are political calculators who see the task of conservatives as retreating gracefully before the Left's inevitable advance.' [214]

Jim Prior was moved from Employment to Northern Ireland, and replaced by the saturnine Norman Tebbit, whose repost to complaints about unemployment was the now famous line; 'I grew up in the thirties with an unemployed father. He didn't riot. He got on his bike to look for work, and he didn't stop until he found it.'[215] This was often paraphrased as a command to the unemployed: 'Get on yer bike!'

Thatcher's impatience with the small c conservatism and over-caution of the political and Whitehall establishment is beautifully captured by an exchange between her and the civil servant Dr John Ashworth. The mandarin had presented Thatcher with a report on unemployment which stressed unpalatable facts. Thatcher replied with, 'The facts. The facts! I have been elected to change the facts.'[216]

However, the recession bottomed out early in 1981 and was followed by signs of a clear recovery by the spring of 1982, just enough to save Short Term Economy Key seven by the election in June 1983.

Although the great privatisation drive did not really get going until the second Thatcher term, there were smaller privatisations during the first. These included British Sugar, the National Freight Corporation and British Aerospace. Additionally, and even more significantly, the government's Housing Act 1980, allowed and facilitated council house tenants to buy their own homes from the council.

The next priority for the Thatcher government was to curtail the power of the unions, which they saw as dangerously out of control. The Employment Act 1980 sought to ban flying pickets, by removing the right to picket beyond a striker's own workplace and firm. It also gave the police powers of dispersal to deal with them. It also attempted to weaken the closed shop culture of unions, by demanding that eighty percent of workers had to support such a policy in a secret ballot.

The Social Security Act 1980 had also prevented strikers from claiming benefits. The 1982 Employment Act allowed Employers to sack striking workers, and also allowed firms to sue trades unions for damages, in the event of unlawful or unconstitutional industrial action. The government now also had the power to sequester union money if they broke the laws.

This was not yet the end of major union unrest however. In 1980, Britain experienced a two-month steel strike, and the following year a five-month long civil service strike. In that year, the government also backed off from confrontation with the miners over plans to close unproductive pits. There were not yet sufficient coal stocks to endure a major strike.

Together, the tax cuts, adoption of monetarism, the anti-union legislation, the removal of state controls on prices, wages and currency exchange, turned Policy Change Key eleven in the government's favour.

One problem that very nearly toppled Civil Unrest Key twelve was urban decay and unrest. The unemployment crisis hit inner city Britain hardest and in 1981 led to the most serious and widespread civil disorder in Britain during the twentieth century. The first serious violence erupted in Bristol in April 1981, triggered by a local police crackdown, and then exploded across the country during July. This time the worst hit areas were Brixton in South London and Toxteth in Liverpool, but affected many other urban areas. Around three thousand people were arrested and hundreds injured, with many properties looted or burned to the ground.

The left blamed the riots on heavy handed, racist policing, and the economic consequences of Thatcher's monetarist policies. The right laid the blame at the feet of immigration and the relaxation of discipline since the 1960s. A report into the riots by Lord Scarman blamed distrust and a 'them and us' culture between the police and ethnic minorities, as well as poverty, unemployment and poor housing; with its disproportionate effect on ethnic minorities. The riots however were not repeated during 1982 or '83, and so by the time of the June 1983 election, were no longer immediate enough to topple Civil Unrest Key twelve.

In terms of foreign policy, The Cold War had heated up, so to speak, following the Soviet invasion of Afghanistan at the end of 1979. The Thatcher government supported the deployment of American Cruise missiles to the UK, in order to counter the Soviet SS20's which were siloed in Eastern Europe. Debate raged as to whether these missiles were helping to protect Britain, or were making her a bigger target in the event of war, which to many, seemed to be coming ever closer.

The missile deployment was certainly controversial and protests against it made headline news in 1982 and '83. The Greenham Common Women's camp besieged the base, until most of them were cleared away by police and bailiffs early in 1984. There were protests at other bases and also action by the newly revitalised CND; with a march on Greenham Common and a vast rally in London.

These protests fell short of toppling Civil Unrest Key twelve, but showed the very sharp divisions within the country at the time. The ideological fight against Communism was made all the sharper, in the light of the turn towards monetarism and supply-side economics on both sides of the Atlantic. The Conservative position would eventually be vindicated by events, but not in this term.

The government enjoyed a clear success with the resolution of the fifteen-year-old Rhodesia crisis. With the rebel armies gaining ground, the white leadership of Rhodesia allowed for elections in 1979 which led to a black majority government led by Bishop Abel Muzorewa. This still failed to result in full international recognition and the lifting of all sanctions, due to the continuing exclusion of the externally-based Patriot Front from the political process.

This led to the Lancaster House negotiations in late 1979 between the governments of Britain and the now re-named Zimbabwe. This resulted in a ceasefire ending the fifteen-year-long bush war, and Zimbabwe briefly returning to direct British rule under the governorship of Lord Soames. A new election followed in early 1980, resulting in a new black majority government led by Robert Mugabe. Though not quite enough to secure the Foreign Policy/Military Success Key nine, it certainly contributed towards it.

Northern Ireland continued to be a thorn in the side of this government, as it had been for the previous four. Thatcher's first term saw the assassination of Lord Mountbatten in his boat off the Irish coast and the Hyde Park bombings which killed twelve Horse Guards and numerous horses in the summer of 1982.

It also saw multiple IRA prisoners go on hunger strike in support of demands for more prison rights. The Conservative government refused to give in, and ten hunger strikers died, after which the strike was called off. The most famous of the dead strikers was Bobby Sands, who was briefly elected to parliament as a Sinn Fein MP before his death.

Terrorism of a different creed was to strike London in May 1980. Iranian gunmen took nineteen people hostage in the Iranian embassy, and threatened to kill them unless political prisoners were released in Iran. The siege was broken by the SAS, in the first offensive use of the army on mainland Britain for seventy years. This episode highlighted the tough stance of the new government in the face of political violence.

The most dramatic foreign policy event of Thatcher's first term was also the least anticipated. The events of the spring-early summer of 1982 were to have a transformative effect on the fortunes and perceptions of Margaret Thatcher and her government.

On 2nd Aril 1982, Argentina invaded the British colony in the Falkland Islands and Mrs Thatcher's response to this event was the pivot that turned an unpopular Prime Minister, into a formidable national leader who embodied a whole decade and re-defined the premiership in Britain. Before this conflict, her party was at serious risk of losing Unity Key two, as the 'wets' were threatening to derail her agenda.

Thatcher accepted the resignation of Lord Carrington the Foreign Secretary, who became the last British politician to resign on the principle of ministerial honour. However, with British territory now invaded, Mrs Thatcher was able to play the role of national war chief, and decided to raise a task-force to re-take the islands. The force set sail from Portsmouth for the South

Atlantic, while diplomatic efforts to find a peaceful solution were given a chance.

Thatcher gained the support of the United Nations, in contrast to the Suez debacle a quarter-century earlier, claiming the right to self-defence and citing the rights of the 1800 Falkland islanders to national self-determination. America was also supportive, imposing sanctions on Argentina as well as supplying Britain with arms, as was France. The government also managed to achieve cross-party support for the war in the House of Commons.

Peace negotiations foundered on the requirement that Britain's taskforce be dispersed and removed from striking distance of the islands – thus leaving them vulnerable should Argentina renege on her part of the bargain. The Argentine promise to have its forces at least seven days away from operational readiness was also distrusted as unverifiable.

Additionally, Argentine demands included the appointment of two of their representatives on the Falklands' council, and the right to effectively overwhelm the islands with their own citizens, in order to win any referendum on their future Sovereignty. At one point, the Foreign Secretary Francis Pym and some of the Cabinet were prepared to accept one of the peace proposals brokered by the US Secretary of State Al Haig. Mrs Thatcher has stated that she would have resigned had both the Argentinians and a majority of her cabinet accepted this. Mrs Thatcher later said, in relation to this period that, 'When I'm out of politics, I'm going to run a business called "Rent-a-Spine." [217]

The diplomatic process continued even after the British capture of South Georgia, on April 25th. Mrs Thatcher batted away questions from journalists with the now-famous response; 'Let us congratulate our armed forces and the marines. Rejoice, rejoice.' [218]Nevertheless, the crisis soon became a shooting war with British airstrikes against the Falklands' capital Port Stanley on the 1st May and the sinking of the Argentine cruiser, the General Belgrano on May 2nd. The latter event caused controversy as the ship was outside the British exclusion zone. However, Admiral Woodward had concluded that the Belgrano group was engaged in a pincer movement against the British taskforce. This sinking, though controversial, did have the effect of scaring the rest of the Argentine navy away.

On 4th May, HMS Sheffield was lost to Argentine Exocet missiles; a new form of attack launched from aircraft at great distance. The Sheffield was the first major British warship to be lost in combat since 1945.

On the 21st May, British forces had established a Beachhead at San Carlos, allowing 5000 men to land. A week later victory was achieved by paratroopers in the battle of Goose Green, despite the loss of their commanding officer Lieutenant-Colonel Jones. This was despite devastating Argentine air attacks on British landing craft with HMS Coventry, the Atlantic Conveyor, HMS Ardent and HMS Antelope sunk. Although the losses were serious, they could have been still worse. The Atlantic Conveyor was believed to have been mistaken for the aircraft carrier HMS Hermes. If Hermes had been lost, the outcome of the war might have been very different.

Over the following fortnight, British forces closed in on Port Stanley, despite further devastating Argentine air attacks on ships at Fitzroy in which Sir Galahad and Sir Tristram were both hit, with over fifty fatalities and many more sustaining terrible burns. Within a month of the landings, the British had successfully recaptured the Falkland Islands - 'yomping' across the island to encircle the capital Port Stanley, forcing the Argentine surrender on June 14th. British naval losses were the heaviest since World War Two, 255 British servicemen were dead and many more wounded. Although the diplomatic process was clearly overtaken by events after the landing at San Carlos, a last-minute UN resolution tabled by the Japanese, calling for a ceasefire had to be vetoed by Britain.

Mrs Thatcher reacted to the victory with the following words; 'We have ceased to be a nation in retreat...Britain found herself again in the South Atlantic and will not look back from the victory she has won.'[219] The Prime Minister also won a memorable accolade from veteran Tory parliamentarian Enoch Powell, who referring to her 'Iron Lady' soubriquet on the eve of the war, predicted that we should find out soon what metal she was made of. After the victory he said:

Is the right honourable lady aware that the report has now been received from the public analyst on a certain substance recently subjected to analysis and that I have obtained a copy of the report? It shows that the substance under test consisted of ferrous matter of the highest quality, and that it is of exceptional tensile strength, is highly resistant to wear and tear and to stress, and may be used to the advantage of all national purposes. [220]

Overall, the victory in the war was a colossal boost for what had been a troubled and precarious administration, and easily won for the government Foreign Policy/Military Success Key nine, and secured Foreign Policy/Military Failure Key ten. It also secured Party Unity Key two, as well as Incumbent Leadership Key three. Had the war been lost, which had been a very real possibility, then the outcome of the 1983 election would have been rather different. I will consider that counterfactual scenario later on in this book.

With the Falklands won, Thatcher was now in command of her party, and was infinitely better placed to pursue her agenda and contest the next election.

The main opposition party had also undergone something of a transformation since the previous election. With left-winger Michael Foot becoming leader in late 1980, the party lurched further from the centre, promising nationalisation of the British economy, abolition of the House of Lords, unilateral nuclear disarmament and withdrawal from the Common Market. It is often now forgotten that Labour used to be the more Euro-sceptic party in the 70's and early 80's. The reason for this was that the EEC was against the nationalisation of the economy, and the Labour left felt that the European Economic Community, (as it was then called) was too capitalistic for comfort.

This move to the left was accompanied by drastic changes in the party electoral system, from an MPs only electorate to one that was shared between the unions (forty percent), MPs (thirty percent and members (thirty percent) They had also decided to give more powers to the National Executive Committee (NEC) to direct policy, and to extend the right of local parties to remove MPs.

All these changes led to a rupture between the party's left and right wings. This led to the famous gang of four breaking away from Labour and forming their own party the SDP. (Social Democratic Party.) They were all Labour right-wingers; Roy Jenkins, the former liberal Home Secretary and Chancellor, David Owen, the former Foreign Secretary, Shirley Williams the former Education Secretary and Bill Rodgers the former

Transport Secretary. This new party had essentially centre-left views and briefly even toyed with calling themselves New Labour.

They formed an alliance with the existing Liberal Party, and for a brief period the SDP-Alliance looked like it really might 'break the mould of British politics.' In 1981 David Steel even advised delegates at the Liberal assembly to 'Go back to your constituencies and prepare for government.' [221]

The combination of a left-wing Labour party with a leader who was frequently the object of mockery, and a centre-left party vying for power, had the effect of splitting the left-wing vote. The First Past the Post system effectively excluded the SDP-Alliance from winning many seats, but at the same time, they took crucial votes off Labour. This activated the Third Party Bonus Key 5 A.

The 1983 campaign was a professional one from the Conservatives, but Labour's performance left a lot to be desired. The dishevelled, elderly Foot was unkindly likened to the children's TV character Worzel Gummidge - a scarecrow who came to life. Foot was a strong public speaker, but did not really grasp the Television era, and in fact did not even own a TV. This was almost the equivalent of not being online in the early 21st century. The Times columnist Bernard Levin described him as, 'Lurching between disaster and calamity with all the skill and aplomb of a one-legged tightrope-walker' and a man, 'unable to blow his own nose in public without his trousers falling down.' [222]

Like that of Corbyn thirty-six years later, the actual Labour manifesto proved popular in itself, but this was not reflected in any way in the election result. Labour's Gerald Kaufmann described it as 'the longest suicide note in history.' [223] Also, like Corbyn, he suffered from appalling poll ratings, with a net disapproval rating of minus sixty shortly before the election. [224] Even the Shadow Home Secretary Roy Hattersley had to admit that, 'It was difficult to find anyone who regarded him as a credible candidate for the office of Prime Minister.' [225] All this ensured that the Opposition Implausibility Special Key 4A was turned in the government's favour.

June 1983 UK general election:

1) *By-election key*	false
2) *Unity Key*	true
3) *Incumbent Leadership Key*	true
4) *Opposition Charisma Key*	true
5) *Third Party Key*	true
6) *Cyclical Incumbency Key*	true
7) *Short-Term Economy Key*	true
8) *Long-Term Economy Key*	false
9) *Foreign Policy/Military Success Key*	true
10) *Foreign Policy/Military Failure Key*	true
11) *Policy Change Key*	true
12) *Civil Unrest Key*	true
13) *Scandal Key*	true

Special keys

4A *Opposition Implausibility Key*	True
5A *Third Party Bonus Key*	True

balance of negative keys: 0

campaign differential: Conservatives + 5 seats

forecast: Conservative majority 145

tally: Conservatives 398 seats Labour 200-220 seats

actual result: Conservative majority of 143

Conservatives 397 seats Labour 209 seats Alliance 23 seats

The election of 1983 was another very significant one. The Conservatives achieved a landslide majority of 144, just one seat short of Clement Attlee's historic win in 1945. It was Labour's worst result since 1935, and would not be worsted again until 2019. It proved a tremendous boost to the standing of Mrs Thatcher and brought a swift end to Michael Foot's leadership of the Labour Party. The SDP-Liberal Alliance would survive to fight another day, but the result was a bitter blow to their hopes of reshaping the mould of British politics.

However, interestingly, the Conservative vote share was marginally below that of 1979, and when the slightly lower turnout is factored in, saw a significant drop in the Tory vote. The SDP splitting the opposition is of course partly responsible for this, but the key system succeeds magnificently in forecasting this result.

The Labour campaign was closed memorably by leader-to-be Neil Kinnock in an iconic speech in Bridgend during the closing days of the campaign.

If Margaret Thatcher wins on Thursday, I warn you not to be ordinary, I warn you not to be young, I warn you not to fall ill and I warn you not to grow old.
226

1983-87:
'I am extraordinarily patient, providing I get my own way in the end.' Thatcher 1983 [227]

Following their landslide win in June 1983, the Conservatives commanded all that they surveyed. The opposition parties were shattered, the economy was on the mend, and the previous year's victory in the Falklands War had boosted national confidence. Inflation had dropped below five percent to the lowest point since the late sixties, and even though unemployment was above three million and still rising, GDP was recovering.

The Labour party elected a new leader in the autumn conference of 1983, and plumped for red-haired Welshman Neil Kinnock. Kinnock had courted controversy in the election campaign with some ill-judged comments on the Falklands. When a member of the public in a TV debate said that Mrs Thatcher had 'guts,' Kinnock responded with, 'And it's a pity that people had to leave theirs on Goose Green in order to prove it.'[228]

Although Kinnock had been something of a firebrand, he did learn the lessons of the 1983 disaster, and began the painful process of dragging his party towards the political centre. With the moderate Roy Hattersley as his deputy, the so-called 'dream ticket' also began to take campaigning and image-building more seriously. However, Kinnock could be accident-prone, famously slipping up on Brighton beach during the autumn conference. 'Bet it wouldn't happen to Maggie,' he quipped. [229]

The main priorities of the Thatcher government were in continuing to tackle trade union power and 'modernising' the economy. The latter involved a major privatisation programme, deregulation of financial services and the further pruning back of uncompetitive and highly subsidised industries such as coal mining. This set the scene for the greatest internal confrontation of the Thatcher years; the 1984-85 miners' strike.

Mining had been in long decline, with the numbers of miners declining by three quarters in the thirty-eight years between nationalisation by the Atlee government in 1946, and the last great strike in 1984. Around thirty pits had been closed by the Wilson-Callaghan government in the seventies. Many more had gone in the sixties.

However, a few things were different this time. Firstly, we had an ideologically motivated government, determined to clip the wings of the powerful unions and shift the economy towards financial services and banking. We also had an equally ideologically motivated Labour party and union movement, epitomised by the militant NUM (National Union of Miners) president, Arthur Scargill, who had said in 1983 that he could not, 'accept that we are landed for the next four years with this government.' [230]

We also had a grim employment climate in the eighties with three million on the dole. Being made redundant in the eighties was certainly not the same as losing your job in the sixties, when barely half a million were out of work. Unemployment was such a pervasive problem in Thatcher's decade that The Smiths could describe their era as 'The dole age.'

The National Coal Board (NCB) and government had backed away from a confrontation with the miner's union in 1981. However, matters came to a head for the mines in early 1984, when the coal board announced twenty new pit closures. This announcement was met by a strike at Cortonwood in South Yorkshire, the first pit earmarked for closure. Other pits soon joined in solidarity and a strike rapidly spread.

Arthur Scargill decided not to call a nationwide ballot as it was doubtful whether he would get the fifty-five percent support that the NUM constitution demanded. However, he decided instead to exploit a constitutional loophole that allowed the National Executive to call a national strike if a majority of their constituencies went on strike independently. In order to fulfil these conditions, flying pickets were despatched to 'persuade' recalcitrant areas to comply. This allowed the coal board and government to portray the strike as anti-democratic.

This created a very difficult situation for the Labour party of having to support the strike but also not be seen as a party in favour of lawlessness. Thatcher mocked Neil Kinnock's late public condemnation of picket violence, which only came after the General Secretary of the TUC had condemned it. She taunted him in the Commons as 'Little Sir Echo.'[231]

The strategy also brought the NUM into direct conflict with the law. As the strike was not democratic, the union relied on flying pickets being bussed in to pits, in order to coerce miners into supporting it. The problem with this strategy, was that secondary action had been outlawed by the 1980 Employment Act, and the government now had the powers to sequester, or seize funds from the unions if they broke the law.

The police were deployed in full riot gear to keep pits from being closed and violent confrontations between police and pickets were a staple feature of British TV news for a whole year. The conflict reached a climax when the pickets tried to shut down a coking plant at Orgreave, South Yorkshire in May 1984. This was an attempt to starve the steel industry of coke and therefore shut down the economy. Violence was severe, but the police prevailed. Due to the enormous number of arrests, stipendiary magistrates had to be employed to get through the backlog of court cases.

Next, the TGWU (Transport and General Workers union) called a national dock strike in support of the miners. This failed due to patchy support. If they had shut down all the ports, there would have a very good chance of victory; and quite possibly the resignation of Mrs Thatcher, and the defeat of her programme.

Late in 1984 the tide turned against the miners. Following a civil case brought about by two non-striking miners, the NUM was found guilty of breaking its own constitution by having an unofficial strike. The NUM refused to pay the fines, and so the courts attempted to sequester their assets. However, in practice, the NUM had already deposited its money in overseas bank accounts. Even so, by the end of January 1985 £5 million was recovered from overseas accounts.

Furthermore, revelations were soon afoot that the NUM were being funded by the Soviet Union and even Colonel Gaddafi. This further undermined their cause, especially since a policewoman had been killed by machine gun fire coming from the Libyan embassy earlier that year.

Support was further eroded by a horrific incident in which pickets in South Wales, dropped a concrete slab off a motorway bridge in a bid to murder 'scabs'- strike-breakers, who were being driven to work in a taxi. They killed the taxi driver instead, and were jailed for manslaughter.

In another revealing incident, when Norman Willis, the moderate General Secretary of the TUC condemned violence at a televised rally in South Wales, he was barracked by the audience and more ominously, a noose was lowered from the ceiling and dangled over his head.

In February 1985, the number of miners returning to work had now reached a majority, and with the NUM having rejected various offers of settlement, the strike was officially called off on March 3rd that year.

The strikers had made at least two major mistakes. The first was to start a strike in the spring when demand for coal would be decreasing, and secondly by the failure to call a full ballot, thus throwing away legitimacy. Part of the reason for going on strike early, was a clause from the 1982 Employment Act, mandating that union-wide secret ballots be held in order to authorise a strike. This came into force on November 1st 1984.

The Thatcher government had played their cards cleverly. Firstly, by building up stocks of coal and securing foreign supplies in anticipation of what was likely to happen. Memories of the Heath government's humiliation at the hands of strikers a decade earlier were still fresh. The legislation on picketing also proved decisive, as was the policy of increasing police wages and officer numbers in what was arguably a soft civil war.

The Conservative victory in the strike was a huge milestone, effectively smashing the unions' grip on power. There has not been any strike of comparable gravity in the thirty-eight years since. Employment secretary Norman Tebbit described it as breaking, 'not just a strike, but a spell.'[232] Margaret Thatcher said in her memoirs that, 'from 1972 to 1985 the conventional wisdom was that Britain could only be governed with the consent of the trade unions. No government could really resist, still less defeat a major strike, in particular a strike by the miners' union.'[233] A note of delusional optimism in the Labour party was sounded by Tony Benn, who said at the end of the strike: 'we're only halfway between Dunkirk and D-Day.'[234]

Victory in the bitter miners' strike therefore saved Civil Unrest Key twelve, Unity Key two, Incumbent Leadership Key three and possibly Policy Change Key eleven from being lost. If the miners had won, it is highly probable that Mrs Thatcher would have resigned, and the Tory party plunged into internecine conflict and recriminations. Thatcherism would have lost its momentum, and any successor would almost certainly not have equalled Mrs Thatcher in stature.

With victory over Scargill and the NUM assured, the Conservatives could increase their focus on other aspects of the British economy. In 1983 a deal was struck between Cecil Parkinson, the Secretary of State for Trade & Industry and the City of London, on a programme of de-regulation, in which the city would open up fully to competition on an international basis; allowing international membership of the stock exchange, the abolition of Fixed Commission Charges, and the computerisation of its trading centre.

These changes had been prompted by the need to settle an anti-trust case dating from the '70s. The reforms included the exclusion of the Stock Exchange from the Restrictive Trade Practices, and finally the Financial Services Act (1986.) The changes culminated in October 1986 with a dramatic transition to the modern age dubbed 'The Big Bang.' Its consequences were to vastly raise the importance of London as a global financial centre, and lead to the take-over of many established companies by larger entities, plus the redevelopment of the nearby Isle of Dogs and canary Wharf.

Another major plank of the Thatcher government was privatisation. This had been started on a relatively small scale in the first term, though really came to fruition in the second. In November 1984, the government privatised British Telecom (BT). This was by far the biggest privatisation the world had ever seen. An unprecedented number of people bought shares in BT, prompting Thatcher's Chancellor Nigel Lawson to hail it as, 'The birth of People's capitalism,' [235] as so many had bought a share in it. This huge privatisation was followed up two years' later with the sell-off of British Gas, for an even more gargantuan sum of money – to the tune of £5.4 billion. In the competitive world of free Market neo-liberal economics, everything counts in large amounts.

Thus, with the city deregulation and privatisation of major utilities, the Thatcher government secured Policy Change Key eleven for a second consecutive term.

Although the miners' strike was a game-changer, it was not quite the end of the struggle between Thatcherism and the unions. In 1986 Rupert Murdoch set up a new modern printing hall in Wapping, and wanted to transfer production of *The Sun* and *News of the World* from their antiquated premises in the old Fleet Street district of London. The printing business was one of the last bastions of union control, with unions successfully resisting the deployment of computerisation and being able to shut down newspaper production for months at a time. They refused to relocate to Wapping. Murdoch's plan was to hire non-union staff to work there, and to leave behind his old staff at Fleet Street, thus fatally undermining the union control of his business.

As with the miners, the print unions deployed flying pickets to try to prevent workers reaching the site, or newspapers being sent out. Again, as with the miners, a year-long strike ensued, and again, as with the miners, the strong arm of the police and the power of the courts finally broke the strike early in 1987. Despite the burning down of a news international depot, (London's biggest fire since the blitz) and sympathy action by railwaymen and the TGWU, the forces of unionism met a second crushing defeat in two years. Again, the Thatcherite laws curtailing union power proved decisive.

One development of this period that can be viewed in two different ways is Live Aid. In November 1984, Boomtown Rats singer Bob Geldof and Midge Ure of Ultravox teamed up to record the charity single 'Do they know it's Christmas Time?' in order to raise money for the Ethiopian famine, which was graphically depicted by reporter Michael Burke on the BBC news. The single was one of the biggest-selling records of all time, and was followed up by the sixteen-hour extravaganza at Wembley stadium the following July.

Left-wingers regarded this as the antithesis of Thatcherism, which they saw as mean-spirited, Scrooge-like and selfish. Those naïve enough to see it as marking a sea-change towards socialism were to be crushingly disabused by the result of the next general election, and the ascendancy of Yuppy culture.

However, from a free-market perspective it was also an example of individual initiative using the apparatus of the free-market and an example of charity activism in place of an ever-more interventionist state. In short, the sort of thing that Thatcher had also espoused. Nevertheless, Geldof did need to persuade the Prime Minister to waive the VAT for the single. Afterwards, he compared her iconoclastic belligerence towards the post-war settlement, to the spirit of the punks. [236]

In terms of foreign policy, the second Thatcher term was less dramatic than the first. However, the government did enjoy considerable success with its dealings with Europe. The battle over Britain's EC budget contributions finally reached a kind of a resolution at the 1984 Fountainebleau summit. The EC agreed to refund two thirds of the difference between the amount of money Britain paid into the E.C. and the amount she got back in return.

This success was followed in February 1986 with the Single European Act, which paved the way for the single European Market from 1992 onwards. Certainly, the British government could claim a considerable amount of credit for this achievement as the original white paper for this act was drafted by Britain's Lord Cockfield. However, concessions necessary for the passing of the act, put Europe firmly on the path to further integration, including an extension of qualified majority voting and a pledge to, 'ensure the convergence of economic and monetary policies within the EU.'[237] Thus Mrs Thatcher unwittingly stored up further conflict for her Conservative party.

The steadfast support of America in the Cold War was beginning to yield fruit with the appointment of the relatively youthful and reformist Mikhail Gorbachev to Chairman of The Soviet Communist Party in March 1985, following a series of elderly and decrepit leaders. Mrs Thatcher had met with Gorbachev at Chequers in late 1984 and declared that he was 'someone we can do business with.' [238]She also later remarked that, 'His personality could not have been more different from the wooden ventriloquism of the average Soviet apparatchik.'[239] She therefore deserved some credit in fostering good relations with such an important world leader.

It was becoming clear that the American re-armament under President Ronald Reagan was forcing the USSR into an arms-race it could not afford, and thus preparing the way for a more moderate leader. Certainly, the Cold War had not ended by the close of Thatcher's Second Term; but two summits between Reagan and Gorbachev had shown considerable promise.

The relationship between Thatcher and Reagan was not always as smooth and harmonious as has been portrayed. A temporary rift opened between the two leaders in October 1983 after America invaded the former British colony of Grenada. This was in order to remove the Marxist regime that had recently seized power in a coup, before murdering the former Prime Minister Maurice Bishop. The US intervention had been done without British approval. However, the operation was militarily successful in only sixty hours, and no long-term damage was inflicted upon Anglo-American relations.

In April 1986 the US launched air strikes against Colonel Gadaffi's Libya, in retaliation for state-sponsored terrorist atrocities in Europe. Some of the war planes were using British bases, and this led to controversy in the UK, since Mrs Thatcher had agreed to this usage without consulting parliament. However, nothing that happened in this term came anywhere near to toppling the Foreign Policy/Military Failure Key ten.

In October 1984, Margaret Thatcher had come perilously close to being the first British Prime Minister to be assassinated since Spencer Percival in 1812, when the IRA bombed the Tory conference at Brighton. Five people died, including the Deputy Chief Whip Sir Anthony Berry. Others were badly injured including Margaret Tebbit, the wife of Norman, who was paralysed for life. A statement from the IRA said, 'We only have to be lucky once. You will have to be lucky always.' [240]

Despite the outrage at Brighton, the following year the Conservative government sparked controversy by signing the Anglo-Irish agreement, which gave the

Republic of Ireland a say in the affairs of the North. While showing a strong resemblance to the failed Sunngingdale power-sharing deal a decade earlier, it was seen as a tentative step in the direction of peace. It did not go down well with the Ulster Unionists however, many of whom resigned from the House of Commons in protest. The Reverent Ian Paisley succinctly summed up his party's attitude to power sharing with the South; 'Never, never, never, never!'[241]

Although the level of violence in the troubled province dropped slightly during the term as a whole, peace also seemed no nearer. Overall, the agreement failed to turn either of the Foreign Policy Keys, and by the 1987 election, the keys were split; Foreign Policy/Military Success Key nine was lost, whilst Foreign Policy/Military Failure Key ten was true.

The UK economy improved steadily after 1983, and a major housing and stock market boom was underway from 1986. By the time of the election in 1987, both economic keys were true. However, unemployment was a continuing bane for the country, officially peaking in 1984 and not dropping below three million until early 1987.

Crime also rose steadily and violent disorder again returned to Britain's cities in the early autumn of 1985. The most horrific violence occurred at the Broad Water Farm estate in north London, in which PC Keith Blakelock was hacked to death by a mob, and several other officers and journalists were injured by gunfire from tenement blocks. However, this violence was not widespread in the eighteen months leading up to the next election, so fell short of turning the Civil Unrest Key twelve.

Britain was also shocked and embarrassed by a different sort of violence when British football hooligans rampaged at the Heysel Stadium in Belgium, leading to the deaths of nearly forty Juventas fans. British teams were banned from the continent and it seemed uncertain whether the game could continue in its current form. Eventually, reforms would improve the reputation of English football, though it would take the Hillsborough tragedy of 1989 to fully spur the changes.

Other areas of reform included local government. In 1984, the Conservatives introduced capping of local government expenditure in a bid to restrict what they believed to be out of control spending by profligate Labour councils. This led to some left-wing councils refusing to set taxes at all - effectively refusing to govern, and even firing all employees. Some Conservatives were afraid that the councils planned to create chaos and then spearhead the unrest into an anti-Conservative insurrection. The worst offender was Liverpool council, under the control of Militant leader Derrick Hatton. The Militant tendency was roundly condemned however by Labour leader Neil Kinnock at the 1985 Labour Party conference.

I'll tell you what happens with impossible promises. You start with far-fetched resolutions. They are then pickled into a rigid dogma, a code, and you go through the years sticking to that, outdated, misplaced, irrelevant to the real needs, and you end in the grotesque chaos of a Labour council – a Labour council – hiring taxis to scuttle round a city handing out redundancy notices to its own workers ... I am telling you, no matter how entertaining, how fulfilling to short-term egos – you can't play politics with people's jobs and with people's services or with their homes. [242]

Kinnock was tentatively trying to steer Labour back to the respectable centre after the disastrous electoral drubbing they had received in 1983, and so had to create some clear blue water between him and the far-left. The Militant operatives were consequently expelled from the party.

Eventually, the recalcitrant councils were defeated. The rebel councillors were barred from standing for office for five years by the district auditor. The following year, the government abolished the Greater London Council - fiefdom of left-wing icon Ken Livingstone, and arch Thatcher opponent. Additionally, the six metropolitan councils also faced the axe. Non-elected boards took over their administrative functions, and thus the Thatcher government had won another victory over its internal opponents.

Scandal would touch this administration on two occasions. In October 1983, the perhaps rather appropriately appointed Secretary of State for Trade & Industry Cecil Parkinson, was forced to resign after he got his secretary pregnant. Parkinson, whom had been Party Chairman at the previous election, was to return to front bench politics eventually; but the scandal was certainly a shock to the British government. However, one man's sexual behaviour, without the dangerous security implications of the Profumo Affair, was not sufficient to turn Scandal Key thirteen.

In January 1986 the Conservative government was hit by quite a different kind of scandal. The Westland Affair was about the future of Britain's last helicopter manufacturer Westland Helicopters. A split had developed in cabinet between the Defence Secretary and Thatcher's future nemesis, Michael Heseltine, who wanted Westland to be integrated into a European Consortium, and Thatcher and Leon Brittan, the Trade and Industry Secretary, who wanted it to go with an American firm. Heseltine walked out of the cabinet in protest that the Prime Minister was ignoring the principle of Cabinet Collective responsibility.

Brittan was forced to resign as well, after admitting to leaking a legal letter critical of Heseltine. Three years later, Brittan claimed in a TV interview that he had been pressured to leak the letter by Thatcher's senior advisor Charles Powell. These scandals were damaging and Westland briefly raised rumours of Thatcher's impending resignation; yet ultimately fell short of the threshold of turning the Scandal Key against the Thatcher government.

At the end of 1986 the government was forced to react to the growing public health menace of AIDS. The disease had been identified in 1981, with the first known British case reported that year. Although initially attracting only limited attention, serious concern about contamination of the blood transfusion service led to the Department of Health barring gay men and IV drug users from giving blood in November 1984. (Blood stocks could not be tested until the following year.) The illness then attracted major publicity with the revealed shock diagnosis of Hollywood star Rock Hudson in the summer of 1985, followed a few months later by his death.

At the end of 1986 a massive campaign was launched in the UK with the slogan, 'AIDS - Don't die of ignorance.' A TV advertising campaign also hit hard with images of tombstones and ice bergs - chiselled with those four dreaded capital letters; and narrated by John Hurt, with a dry voice like a talking skull. Although Britain's rate of cases was well below America's, there were fears and projections of vast numbers of deaths in the coming years. In the words of writer Graham Stewart, 'The combined threats to human life on earth from AIDS and nuclear Armageddon made the mid-eighties a period disfigured by fear.'[243]

In the final months of the administration, the government achieved one more privatisation spectacular, with the selling off of British Airways. With a strong economy, two major victories over the trade unions, and the Prime Minister's authority still intact, the government headed confidently into the general election of June 1987.

Labour meanwhile had begun to move back towards the political centre under Neil Kinnock. The biggest visible transformation however would be the campaign. Roundly mocked for their clumsy and dated campaigning four years' earlier, Labour had hired Peter Mandelson as their campaign director, and fully utilised modern technology in a campaign that was a world away from that of 1983.

Many still found it hard to visualise Labour in power, but Kinnock and co had definitely done enough to snatch back the Opposition Implausibility Key 4A from the government. However, Labour still managed to shoot themselves in the foot with the issue of nuclear weapons. Pledging unilateral disarmament, Kinnock claimed that he would not allow the Americans to fire cruise missiles from British bases – effectively removing Britain from the NATO nuclear umbrella. He also suggested that Britain's response to Soviet aggression should be guerrilla warfare from the hills; therefore, apparently admitting that his government would be unable to stop an invasion in the first place.

The Alliance continued, with David's Owen and Steele in charge of their two parties respectively. Although not quite matching the enthusiasm of four years before, the Alliance still narrowly gifted the Third Party Bonus Key 5A to the Conservatives.

Overall, I will not award any campaign advantage to either of the two parties.

June 1987 UK general election:

1) *By-election key*	false
2) *Unity Key*	true
3) *Incumbent Leadership Key*	true
4) Opposition Charisma Key	true
5) *Third Party Key*	true
6) *Cyclical Incumbency Key*	true
7) *Short-Term Economy Key*	true
8) *Long-Term Economy Key*	true
9) *Foreign Policy/Military Success Key*	false
10) *Foreign Policy/Military Failure Key*	true
11) *Policy Change Key*	true
12) *Civil Unrest Key*	true
13) *Scandal Key*	true

Special Keys
5A *Third Party Bonus Key*   true

balance of negative keys: 1

campaign differential: nil

forecast: Conservative majority 105

Conservatives 378 seats Labour 223-243 seats

actual result: Conservative majority of 102

Conservatives 376 seats Labour 229 seats Alliance 22 seats

1987-92:
'There is no such thing as society.'
Margaret Thatcher, interview in Woman's Own, September 1987.

With a landslide majority of 102 – the second three-figure win a row, the Thatcherites were emboldened, with this election marking their high-water mark. Mrs Thatcher was now the first Prime Minister in living memory to face the prospect of a full third term.

The 1987 election proved yet another bitter blow for opponents of Thatcherism. The SDP-Liberal Alliance began to disintegrate almost before all the results were declared. Labour were bitterly disappointed but decided to stick with Neil Kinnock, who would accelerate their march to the centre ground.

It was also instructive in illustrating the very limited power of campaigning and marketing. That the Labour party could make such paltry gains despite such a radically transformed style of presentation was a lesson lost on most at the time. It was especially lost on the Labour party, who would become increasingly obsessed with image-building and media manipulation over the next couple of decades.

This was the year when Margaret Thatcher made her infamous quote about society not existing, or so it seemed to many. Here is the full quote, taken from her interview with *Woman's own* magazine:

There is no such thing as society. There are individual men and women, and there are families. And no government can do anything except through people, and people must look to themselves. It's our duty to look after ourselves and then to look after our neighbour. [244]

Thatcher is not strictly speaking, denying the existence of society, rather attacking the notion of society as an abstract, divorced from the individual people who comprise it. In her memoirs she elaborates further:

The error to which I was objecting was the confusion of society with the state as the helper of first resort. Whenever I heard people complain that "society" should not permit some particular misfortune, I would retort, "And what are you doing about it, then?" Society for me was not an excuse, it was a source of obligation [245]

It was a message that future Tory leader David Cameron was to repackage twenty years later. Unfortunately, the distinction between a protective, all-powerful state and a society with grass roots participation and a limited state was lost, as only the first seven words of the quote were oft repeated by critics.

However, as the philosopher John Gray has pointed out, Thatcher's two big ideas, the liberation of enterprise through privatisation, tax cutting, deregulation and union control on the one hand, and the return to a pre-sixties social conservatism of family and local community on the other hand, are mutually incompatible. Although what they both have in common is a distrust of the state, they are still in conflict with each other because economic neo-liberalism is an individualist creed, whilst social conservatism is collectivist. The first will always act as a solvent on the second. [246] As Milton Freedman pointed out, Thatcher was really more of a nineteenth century Liberal than a normal Conservative. [247]

The Tories followed up their electoral hat trick with the privatisation of Rolls Royce and British Petroleum (BP). The sell-off of the latter was unfortunately timed however, as it was in the month of the stock market crash, known as Black Monday. The heady optimism in the City came to a dramatic end on Monday 19th October 1987, when a wave of panic selling on both sides of the Atlantic led to twenty-five percent of the value of the FTSE 100 being wiped out. Explanations for this varied from too rapid computerisation, to the basic instability of modern capitalism. Perhaps the most likely explanation was good old-fashioned hubris, greed, and over optimism.

The losses for British investors were made all the sharper due to the exact timing of the crash. The previous Friday had seen south-eastern England battered by the surprise hurricane, or Great Storm. This event led to London and the stock exchange being blacked out for several hours, and road and rail links in and out of the capital severed by thousands of uprooted trees and other debris. This prevented many investors from being able to sell their shares until it was too late.

The Chancellor Nigel Lawson pumped liquidities into the market and by mid-November things had stabilised. Fortunately, recession did not immediately follow as in 1929 or 2008, and by the following spring the Chancellor cut the top rate of income tax to forty percent and the bottom rate to twenty-five percent in a bid to stimulate growth. Thus, the two economic keys were saved - for now.

One piece of legislation that has had lasting consequences was the Education Act (1988). This is now regarded as the most important piece of education legislation since the Butler Act of 1944. This time, the Education Secretary was Kenneth Baker, and his act established the National Curriculum, GCSE and Key Stage framework which is still very much with us. It also established the concept of grant-maintained schools and City Colleges, which were allowed to opt out of local authority funding altogether. These were the direct precursors of the Academy Schools of the New Labour era.

There was also some bold reform of the health service. In 1989 the government set up the internal market in the NHS. This led to hospitals becoming self-managing trusts and GPs controlling their own budgets. District Health Authorities could purchase care from either the public or private sector, with hospitals left to compete for patients. The hope was that such competition would force the NHS to give greater value for money.

The government also continued to press ahead with its privatisation agenda, selling off British steel in 1988, the Water Board in 1989, and the electricity Board in 1990. One effect of the latter was to free-up the electricity companies to buy cheap imported coal, accelerating the already terminal decline of the British coal industry. These privatisations however would not turn the Policy Change Key, as they were a continuation of the policy that had begun in earnest during the second term.

The Conservatives also continued to pursue their anti-union agenda with a law preventing workers for being sacked due to non-membership of unions in 1988.

The act also introduced the auditing of union accounts, and greater help for union members who were being bullied or harassed by their union bosses. These measures were followed up by the 1990 Employment Act, which finally outlawed all closed shop practices, together with sympathy strikes.

Another major blow against the already weakened trade unions came in 1989, when the government repealed the 1947 National Dock Labour scheme which guaranteed permanent employment to the nation's dockers. The Thatcher government rushed the legislation through parliament so quickly, that by the time the TGWU had carried out the by- now compulsory secret ballots, and fought off legal action by employers, the NDLS had already been removed from the statute books. They were striking for a scheme that no longer existed. In the wake of this government victory, casual labour returned to Britain's docks.

However, these anti-union victories, like the privatisations and tax cuts, were still a continuation of existing government policy, and so Policy change Key eleven was lost to the Conservatives.

One attempt at radical innovation that most definitely backfired was the Poll Tax. The Poll Tax, or as Margaret Thatcher euphemistically put it, 'The Community Charge,' was born out of the desire to cut Labour councils down to size. Despite considerable victories against them during her second term, she still wanted to find a way to make the alleged over-spending and consequent over-taxing by local councils visible to their electorates. Taxing all individual adults equally, bar the disabled, might be the way to do it. The previous local tax called the Rates, had been tied to property valuation, like the council tax that replaced Thatcher's endeavour in 1993.

The Conservatives felt that this kind of tax penalised property ownership and enterprise, and that taxing all individuals equally was the answer. Scotland was used as a guinea pig for the new tax in 1989, and it was introduced in England & Wales on April Fool's Day (perhaps appropriately) the following year.

The tax was widely perceived to be unfair, and polls showed that around three quarters of voters were opposed to it.[248] On 31st March 1990, a day before its implementation, crowds a quarter-of-a-million strong protested the tax in Trafalgar Square. Although initially peaceful, a hard core of three thousand or so turned violent and pitched battles with the police ensued. Several hundred people were injured or arrested. Civil Unrest Key twelve was now threatened.

It was clear that by spring 1990, the tide was turning against Mrs Thatcher.

The Previous autumn, her Chancellor Nigel Lawson resigned after a battle of influence with the Prime Minister's economics advisor Allan Walters. The first bone of contention had been whether to join the European Exchange Rate Mechanism (ERM) which was the fore-runner of the Euro. Lawson supported the idea, whilst Walters did not.

The second bone of contention was Lawson's shadowing of the Deutschmark in preparation for British entry into the ERM. This entailed using interest rates to make the pound's exchange rate mirror that of the German currency. The problem here was that keeping the pound very strong with low interest rates, compounded by further rate cuts in the aftermath of the 1987 crash, was causing an inflationary bubble.

In a bid to reduce inflation, Lawson raised interest rates just as the economy was heading towards recession. The policy – initially concealed from the Prime Minister, led to conflict between them from 1988 onwards, with Mrs Thatcher famously saying that, 'There is no way in which you one can buck the market.' [249]Tensions came to a head in October 1989, when Nigel Lawson offered the Prime Minister an ultimatum: To choose between him or Walters. Thatcher refused to fire Walters and Lawson resigned on October 26th. This proved a devastating blow for Mrs Thatcher's authority from which she never fully recovered.

A few months later, Thatcher faced a leadership challenge from the backbencher Sir Anthony Meyer. Although having no serious chance of becoming Prime Minister, he hoped that his challenge would open the door for others. The attempt failed, and Meyer was dubbed 'Sir Nobody'[250] by the tabloid press. Nevertheless, it was a sign of growing unease and discontent within the party.

It was ironic that Thatcher's fortunes were sinking just at the moment when free-market capitalism had won the historic fight against communism. The late autumn and winter of 1989 had witnessed the downfall of Communist power in the Warsaw Pact countries and the demolition of that hated symbol of Cold War division: the Berlin Wall.

Yet it was the issue of Europe that had been becoming increasingly problematic for the Thatcher government. Tensions within the cabinet had been rising since Mrs Thatcher's speech to the College of Europe at Bruges, in which she contrasted European Centralisation with the movements against state control in the by-then crumbling communist bloc. She also implied that the moves to ever-closer union were incompatible with her own government's deregulatory agenda.

It is ironic that just when those countries such as the Soviet Union, which have tried to run everything from the centre, are learning that success depends on dispersing power and decisions away from the centre, some in the Community seem to want to move in the opposite direction.

We have not successfully rolled back the frontiers of the state in Britain, only to see them re-imposed at a European level, with a European super-state exercising a new dominance from Brussels... Europe will be stronger precisely because it has France as France, Spain as Spain, Britain as Britain, each with its own customs, traditions and identity. It would be folly to try to fit them into some sort of identikit European personality. [251]

This moment marked the real beginning of the Tory party's long civil war over Europe. It was so significant, that a right-wing Euro-sceptic group even named itself after this speech - The Bruges Group. It is an internal conflict which is still playing out as I write this in 2023.

Thatcher was increasingly at loggerheads with the EC's three stage plan for European Monetary and Economic Union, unveiled by European President Jacques Delors in April 1989. This plan would culminate in full monetary union - the creation of a single currency by the end of the century. Thatcher was also worried about the reunification of Germany, which she saw as a threat to European stability.

Her Environment Secretary Nicholas Ridley expressed this sentiment in crude terms in an interview for *the Spectator*, in which he described the moves towards European Monetary Union (EMU) as, 'all a German racket designed to take over the whole of Europe.' He also opined on the desirability of giving up sovereignty to the EC: 'You might just as well give it to Adolf Hitler, frankly.' [252] This interview led to his resignation in July 1990, leaving the Prime Minister isolated in the cabinet. It looked like Unity Key two was now in serious jeopardy.

Mrs Thatcher had also faced down a direct rebellion the previous year, when Howe and Lawson had threatened to resign on the eve of the Madrid summit, unless she committed Britain to joining the ERM. She fudged the issue by appearing to commit to join – but without setting a date. However, it was clear the crisis would only continue to grow in the cabinet.

That Thatcher's authority within her party was weakening, was underlined by her eventual capitulation on Britain joining the ERM the following year. This it duly did in October 1990, at the behest of new Chancellor John Major. Mrs Thatcher's scepticism would be proved right two years later, but at the time she seemed an increasingly reactionary figure, trying Canute-like to stop the onward march of European integration. In her memoirs she explains her decision thus: 'I had too few allies to continue to resist and win the day.'[253]

The new chancellor also proposed the creation of a hard ECU

(European Currency Unit) which could be floated on the markets in competition with existing European currencies. EC members would be free to either opt in or out of it. This would be to allow market forces to determine whether monetary union happened or not. However, Europe saw this as a wrecking tactic to undermine EMU and nothing came of it.

The government was also running out of luck on the economy. The housing boom had peaked in 1989 and had begun to go into decline by the end of the year. By autumn 1990 it was clear that the UK economy as a whole was also heading into recession. The previous year Unemployment had been reduced to 1.6 million - close to the level that the Conservatives had inherited from Labour in 1979. It was rising steadily now, thus jeopardising both the economic keys.

In August 1990, the almost spring-like atmosphere of dawning world peace was shattered when Iraq invaded and conquered Kuwait within a few hours. It then started massing troops on the border with Saudi Arabia, threatening the vast oilfields of its southern neighbour. The response of US President George H W Bush was swift and decisive. Tens of thousands of American troops were pouring into Saudi Arabia in a bid to prevent Saddam Hussein seizing that vast reservoir of economic power. Margaret Thatcher was in complete agreement and Britain too was committed to the defence of the Arabian peninsula from Iraqi aggression.

This initial phase of the conflict was called 'Operation Desert Shield.' Now that the Cold War was effectively over, United Nations backing was received for a UN-authorised taskforce to go in and recapture Kuwait. With an ultimatum set for 15th January 1991 for Iraq to withdraw from Kuwait, a clear opportunity and danger presented itself to the Thatcher government. Would a swift and decisive victory in this war salvage the Foreign Policy/Military Success Key nine, or could a bloody disaster in the deserts cost the Tories Key ten?

It was during the long build up to war, but not because of it that Mrs Thatcher's fate was sealed. Her party turned against her over her views on Europe, the Poll Tax and because of the deteriorating economy.

The trigger for the leadership challenge came from the resignation of Deputy Prime Minister Geoffrey Howe, principally about differences over European policy. Howe had recently caused consternation when he had denied that the government was opposed to joining a single currency in a TV interview. By now, relations between him and the Prime Minister were at breaking point: 'In the cabinet he was now a force for obstruction, in the party a focus of resentment, in the country a source of division. On top of that, we found each other's company almost intolerable.' [254]

Mr Howe's resignation speech was devastating, especially because nobody thought that the mild-mannered politician, once dubbed 'Mogadon man' had it in him. The most memorable comment was about how Thatcher had undermined Howe as Foreign Secretary in his attempts to improve relations with Britain's European partners. 'Like sending your opening batsmen to the crease, only for them to find the moment the first balls are bowled, that their bats have been broken before the game by the team captain.' [255] Howe ended the speech with a veiled invitation for Michael Heseltine to launch a leadership bid to topple Thatcher: 'The time has come for others to consider their own response to this tragic conflict of loyalties with which I have wrestled for perhaps too long.' [256]

This resignation left Mrs Thatcher as the last remaining member of the cabinet she had appointed eleven years earlier, and proved the trigger for the former Defence Secretary, Michael Heseltine enter the fray.

In the ensuing leadership contest, the charismatic Heseltine managed to win 152 votes to Thatcher's 204. This left Thatcher two votes short of an outright victory. It would have to go to a second ballot. Thatcher initially decided to fight on, but soon found that she had lost the confidence of her cabinet who, 'Almost to a man they used the same formula. This was that they themselves would back me, of course, but that regretfully they did not believe I could win.' [257] She also found herself unable to get a campaign team together, as no one wanted to defend the fatally wounded leader.

Thatcher dropped out of the race, which went on to a second ballot, with Home Secretary Douglas Hurd and Chancellor John Major throwing their hats into the ring. The result saw Mr Major winning 185 votes, just short of the amount for an outright win, Mr Heseltine on 131 and Hurd on 56. With Hurd knocked out, Heseltine immediately conceded, and the Thatcher years were suddenly over. In the words of Anthony Seldon, Margaret Thatcher, 'fell because she failed to notice she had not carried her supporters with her.' [258]

Those eleven-and-a-half years were certainly ones that had changed Britain – probably forever. The union unrest, which had dominated the 1970s had been effectively subdued. After the final employment act of the Thatcher years, days lost to industrial action were only a small fraction of what they had been in the seventies and eighties. The privatisations and 'Big Bang' in the City, and move away from manufacturing to a service economy had also radically transformed the nation's economic life.

During her tenure, around two thirds of industrial assets that had been owned by the state were privatised. The government had also been effective at cutting the size of the state. Public spending fell from forty-four percent of GDP in 1979 to forty percent in 1990. The size of the civil service also shrank from 730,000 to 562,000 over the same period.

However, over a fifth of Britain's manufacturing base had been destroyed in the 1979-81 recession - a figure exacerbated by the purist monetarism of the time. Unemployment too, had risen to levels not seen since the

Depression of the thirties; and although it had been cut dramatically during the late eighties boom, was rising rapidly by the day of Thatcher's exit from Downing Street.

The period also saw a sixty percent increase in recorded crime and substantial worsening of income inequality. Homelessness too became a prominent feature of many of our cities. Despite considerable efforts, the conflict in Northern Ireland had yet to be resolved and the same could be said of our relationship with Europe.

On the world stage, Britain's close and productive relationship with President Reagan had played a significant role in the ending of the Cold War and the downfall of Eastern bloc communism. Thatcher's resolute handling of the Falkland's war had also greatly increased our standing on the world stage. However, her refusal to support sanctions against South Africa had alienated Britain from much of the commonwealth, though probably made little difference to the final outcome.

Although the great inflation battle had been largely won, it had come at a cost – the high unemployment aggravated by the high interest rates. It was also an incomplete victory, as inflation briefly hit ten percent again in the final weeks of Mrs Thatcher's premiership. It would take the final chapter of Tory rule under her successor to finally achieve that feat.

One more, and arguably greatest victory of the Thatcher years – the defeat of old Labour and the ascendancy of New Labour, would also be sealed under the stewardship of Mrs T's mild-mannered successor.

John Major went from being a relative unknown less than eighteen months earlier, to being the youngest

Prime Minister to date in the twentieth century. His unassuming, rather restrained manner made a noticeable contrast with his predecessor. At his first cabinet meeting on taking office, he broke the ice with the line, 'Well, who'd have thought it.' [259] He started office pledging to forge 'a country that is at ease with itself.' [260] His immediate priorities were the deteriorating economy, the hated Poll tax, splintering party unity over Europe and impending war in the Gulf.

The first real change in his style of administration was to reintroduce cabinet government. Mrs Thatcher generally had decided policy in advance of cabinet meetings, and simply used the meetings as a place to announce decisions that had already been made. The former party chairman Chris Pattern described the first cabinet meetings under Major as being so liberating that it made the 'ministers feel like the prisoners in Beethoven's Fidelio, released into the sun, blinking and singing of freedom.' [261]

Major's first real test of premiership was the Gulf War, which would witness the biggest commitment of British military strength since the Korean war, forty years' earlier. The deadline of 15th January 1991 for Saddam Hussein to withdraw from Kuwait came and went, and the next day the Allies struck with a six-week campaign of bombing and artillery. With three quarters of a million troops and fourteen hundred aircraft, operation Desert Storm proved irresistible. The desert landscape afforded nowhere for the Iraqi forces to hide, and when Iraqi attempts to bring Israel into the war failed, the writing was clearly on the wall for Saddam Hussein's pretensions of regional domination.

Thoroughly weakened and outgunned, the Iraqi forces were rapidly routed in the 100-hour ground campaign that came at the end of February. The one-sidedness of the campaign recalled Victorian imperial contests between European firepower and African tribesmen. Allied casualties were extraordinarily light, with more troops killed in accidents in the run up to war than in the war itself. Only one of the twenty-five British fatalities were due to land combat with enemy forces.

This almost embarrassing display of western military superiority was decisive in establishing what was then termed the 'New World Order'. Although it is now a term banded about cynically by conspiracy theorists; then, it symbolised the definitive victory, (or so it seemed) of western military might, western capitalism, combined with the soft-power of language and culture; all under the umbrella of western liberal-democratic philosophy. This was the time that Frances Fukuyama called the 'End of History,' meaning that the fall of Soviet Communism would lead to a gentle slide into universal liberal democracy. Such talk may sound naïve a generation later, but the victory in the deserts was certainly significant as the first major clear-cut military win for the United States since 1945. At the very least it helped the Conservatives to secure Foreign Policy/Military Success Key nine.

During the Gulf campaign, war of a different sort came to the Major war cabinet in a most unexpected fashion. They all had a lucky escape when the IRA mortar-bombed Downing Street in their second bid to assassinate the cabinet in seven years. On February 7th, three mortars were fired at the Headquarters of British government. One exploded in the Downing Street gardens, around a hundred feet away from the Cabinet rooms, shattering the windows, and leading to a senior civil servant pushing the Prime Minister to the floor, for his own protection. No one was hurt, but the cabinet decided to retreat to the underground COBRA rooms to continue.

With the war won, the next most pressing government priority was what to do about the Poll Tax. This detested tax was to be dealt with by new Environment Secretary Michael Heseltine, who had long been one of its opponents. He was brought back into the cabinet by Major, in part at least, so as to avoid him being the skulking backbench rebel for the new Prime Minister that he was to Mrs Thatcher. Heseltine was determined to abolish the Poll tax. One unnamed government minister was quoted as saying that Heseltine desperately wanted, 'to obtain the scalp of the Poll tax to place on Mrs Thatcher's grave.' [262]

The announced abolition of the Community charge was announced in the Commons in March 1991 to loud cheers. The resultant bill received the Royal Ascent shortly before the 1992 general election, and the new Council tax – similar to the original 'Rates' was introduced in 1993. This did much to boost the government's standing, and possibly also avoided the loss of Civil Unrest key twelve.

Moving into the spring of 1991 and beyond, the main focus shifted to the deteriorating British economy. Major's chancellor Norman Lamont was mocked for his overly optimistic talk of the 'green shoots of recovery'[263]. He attracted even more adverse criticism for his callous statement that unemployment is, 'a price worth paying' for reducing inflation. [264]Business failures soared, house prices crashed and the dole queues steadily lengthened. The problem with the house price crash was severe, as many people were left with negative equity - meaning that their outstanding mortgages were worth more than the remaining value of their homes. Re-possession rates surged as optimism evaporated.

In the late summer of 1991, Britain faced a recurrence of the problem of urban unrest which had plagued the eighties. This time, rioting, looting and arson centred on the north east, with Tyneside bearing the brunt of the violence. Predictably, the government blamed criminality, whilst the church and the left blamed urban deprivation and unemployment. As in the previous two outbreaks of trouble, the violence subsided, falling short of the threshold necessary to turn Civil Unrest Key twelve.

Perhaps the most important and contentious issue that the new Major administration had to grapple with was Britain's role in Europe. Major's Europhile leanings had already become apparent as Chancellor, when he brought Britain into the ERM. These were to be confirmed in a speech he delivered in Bonn in March 1991: 'I want us to be where we belong; at the heart of Europe, working with our partners in building the future.' [265]

In December 1991, John Major signed Britain up to the Maastricht treaty, which led to the formal establishment of the European Union, which was to replace the European Community in 1993, confirming Europe's path to 'an ever-closer union of peoples.'

However, Mr Major managed to extract three concessions to satisfy the vocal Euro-sceptic wing of his party. Firstly, he had the word 'federation' removed from the documents, and replaced with the word, 'subsidiarity.' This established the idea that foreign, defence and security policy remained under sovereign control of the member states, with Community intervention to be used only when necessary.

Secondly, he secured agreement for Britain to make her own arrangements for joining the single European currency, and in her own time. (The rest of Europe was still committed to monetary union in 1999.)

Thirdly, he secured an opt-out of the Social Chapter, which was concerned with employment rights. The remaining EU countries still signed up to it in a separate treaty, as Britain would eventually do under Tony Blair.)

These concessions were absolutely vital if he was to have any hope of keeping his party united. Employment Secretary Michael Howard and Home Secretary Kenneth Baker were strongly opposed to elements of the treaty, with the latter threatening to resign if Britain signed up to the Social Chapter. The Tory old guard of Thatcher, Tebbit and Ridley decried the treaty, calling for a national referendum to be held. However, the balancing act proved just enough to buy off most of the Eurosceptic right of the party - at least for the time being. However, the treaty contributed to Foreign Policy/Military Success Key nine, preventing the loss of Foreign Policy/Military Failure Key ten, and also secured Party Unity Key two.

Despite the change of party leadership, the Tories continued to be pummelled in by-elections and local elections, thus toppling Key one, for the third term in a row.

On the domestic front, Mr Major wanted to improve the quality, choice, user-friendliness and accountability of public services. This he attempted to do in his Citizen's Charter. This established targets that government departments would need to meet in order to secure their Charter Mark. Although this scheme was met with a mixture of apathy, cynicism and derision from both within government and in the media, with the hotline for cones becoming a favourite comedy target - at least some improvements in public services were eventually achieved. The scheme would last twenty years before being replaced by the coalition in 2011.

Major can also boast some modest reforms on increasing government transparency and accountability. He published the hitherto secret Ministerial code in 1992, and then the Civil Service code four years later. His 1991 'Competing for quality' initiative resulted in the civil service having to compete with the private sector in a 'market testing' process that eventually led to a considerable amount of Whitehall work being outsourced to the free market.

In March 1992, the Prime Minister called a general election. Things did not look good for the Conservative government. The economy was still mired in recession, with unemployment over two and a half million and rising. GDP figures for the first quarter of 1992 came out days before the election and showed continuing negative growth, thus costing Short Term Economy Key seven. Interestingly, the mean GDP of the 1987-1992 term was almost exactly equal to the two previous terms, 1979-87. This was due to the very severe recession of 1979-81 which reduced overall growth in the first Thatcher term to nil. So Long Term Economy Key eight was saved - just!

Major was certainly no charismatic figure, with his grey appearance and wooden performances, so Incumbent Leadership Key three was forfeited. Labour's Neil Kinnock was more spirited than Mr Major, but was also more irritating to a lot of people, thus securing Opposition Charisma Key four for the government. The SDP had decided on a merger with the Liberals in the aftermath of their second disastrous election defeat in 1987. Dr David Owen refused to join them and tried to soldier on with his own SDP; finally disbanding the party after winning fewer votes than the Monster Raving Loony Party at the Bootle By-election in 1990.

The new merged party called itself the Liberal Democrats and was led by former army officer Paddy Ashdown. They were several points behind where the Alliance had been in the previous election, and Labour was up correspondingly. Labour had moved further to the centre since 1987 and many moderate socialists who had abandoned the party for the Alliance had now drifted back. Polling evidence showed that Liberal Democrat voters were equally hostile to both Labour and Conservatives [266], and so the Third Party Bonus Key 5A disappeared this time around. Yet the Third Party Key itself remained True for the Tories.

The campaign was a highly professional one for all three main parties. John Major utilised a soap box to appeal directly to the people. He effectively stood on a platform of creating a 'classless society' affording opportunity for all, whilst painting Labour as the party of resentment of wealth and cynicism about aspiration. 'I want to bring into being a different kind of country, to bury forever the old divisions in Britain between North and South, blue collar and white collar, polytechnic and universities. They're old-style, old-hat.' [267]

He also skilfully mocked Kinnock's 'Don't be old' speech that was delivered in on the eve of his drubbing at the previous election. 'I warn you not to be qualified. I warn you not to be successful. I warn you not to buy shares. I warn you not to be self-employed. I warn you not to accept promotion. I warn you not to save. I warn you not to buy a pension. I warn you not to buy your own home.' [268]

Neil Kinnock also effectively conveyed a Prime Ministerial demeanour and Paddy Ashdown fought a highly energetic campaign, though in both cases courted disappointment by raising overly optimistic expectations. One way in which Labour slipped up in this particular vein and gave away seats to the Conservatives, was in the now infamous Sheffield Rally. In this American-convention-styled event, Labour appeared to be taking the electorate for granted in a pre-emptive victory rally. Kinnock was seen shouting 'We're alright! We're alright,' and the crowd shouted it back at him.[269] Unfortunately, the electorate decided otherwise. This was covered on the evening news, and was even mocked by ITV's *Spitting Image*. It probably did not lose Labour many votes, but gave maybe two or three seats to the Conservatives.

April 1992 UK general election:

1) *By-election key* — false
2) *Unity Key* — true
3) *Incumbent Leadership Key* — false
4) *Opposition Charisma Key* — true
5) *Third Party Key* — true
6) *Cyclical Incumbency Key* — true
7) *Short-Term Economy Key* — false
8) *Long-Term Economy Key* — true
9) *Foreign Policy/Military Success Key* — true
10) *Foreign Policy/Military Failure Key* — true
11) *Policy Change Key* — false
12) *Civil Unrest Key* — true
13) *Scandal Key* — true

balance of negative keys: 4

campaign differential: + 2-3 to the Conservatives

forecast: Conservative majority 20

Conservatives 335 seats Labour 265-275 seats

actual result: Conservative majority of 21

Conservatives 336 seats Labour 270 seats Liberal Democrats 20

1992-97:
'We give the impression of being a party in office, but not in power.'
Norman Lamont, resignation speech, May 1993.

On the 10th April 1992, the Conservatives celebrated their fourth election victory in a row, with John Major being dubbed 'The Comeback Kid.' The IRA also celebrated the win, by detonating a large truck bomb outside the Baltic Exchange in London, killing three and causing £800,000,000 worth of damage - more than all the previous twenty years of bomb attacks in Northern Ireland combined.

However, with the win, which astonished most commentators and much of the public, the Conservatives seemed to be in an almost unassailable position. Many commentators voiced the opinion that if Labour could not even win during a recession, when could they win? Speculation grew as to whether Britain was now effectively a one-party state.

A devastated Labour Party turned to Scotsman John Smith to bring it further towards the political centre - this after all, was the only place they could win, claimed the prevailing wisdom. Much focus was on the campaigns and whether Labour's promise to raise income tax was the decisive factor. However, the keys show otherwise.

Despite the Conservative ebullience, the economic climate stubbornly refused to show signs of recovery. Unemployment continued to creep towards the three million mark and the housing market continued its miserable implosion. The economic situation was to come to a crisis point in September, with the infamous episode known as 'Black Wednesday.'

Britain's membership of the European Exchange Rate Mechanism (ERM) was contributing to the depth and prolongation of the recession by preventing the pound from devaluing naturally against other currencies; thus, choking off British exports. John Major was openly dismissive of the growing calls for devaluation, labelling them as, 'quack doctors peddling their wares. Miracle cures simply don't work – never have, never will.' [270] A crisis point was reached however on September 16th, when the pound was forced out of the ERM altogether and lost around ten percent of its value. The Major government tried to prop up the failing pound in a bid to keep it in the ERM. The Bank of England (which was not yet independent of the government.) started buying pounds in a bid to raise the value of the currency.

When this failed, John Major called a meeting of the Chancellor Norman Lamont, Foreign Secretary Douglas Hurd, President of the Board of Trade Michael Heseltine and Home Secretary Kenneth Clarke, to the indignation of Lamont. Clarke later said that, 'It meant that there were the senior members of the government – all of us with our hands dipped in the blood.' [271] Presumably

Major was trying to widen the field of responsibility, plus the field of likely media targets for blame.

The government raised interest rates to twelve percent and then pre-announced a further raise to fifteen percent for the following day. It was all to no avail, and in the evening, Lamont was forced to announce that Britain would indeed be leaving the ERM, after he had publicly ruled out such a decision only a few weeks earlier.

The interest rate rises were immediately cancelled, but the damage had been done to the government's reputation for economic competency. Labour leader John Smith taunted Major in the Commons, calling him, 'a devalued Prime Minister of a devalued government.' [272] Within a few weeks, the Labour party established a solid lead in the polls that would last for over thirteen years, with only one very brief interruption. Immediately, Major and Lamont were pilloried in the press and their post-election honeymoon was brought to an abrupt end. On taking the post of Chancellor, Lamont had apparently been warned that it would make him the most unpopular man in Britain. He ruefully remarked later that the prediction was, 'The only Treasury forecast in my time that was ever correct.' [273]

Major and Lamont defied calls for their resignation, with the Prime Minister apparently telling Lamont that, 'You are a lightning conductor for me.'

The disastrous events of 'Black Wednesday' cost the Major administration the Foreign Policy/Military Failure Key straight away. It also led to an almost immediate breakdown in party discipline, with the so-called 'Euro-rebels' scenting government weakness and deciding to exploit it to the full. Peter Hennessey graphically captured the Prime Minister's bleak predicament from Black Wednesday 1992 onwards:

'Major's memoirs are written on scar tissue, not paper.' [274]

The rebels had been emboldened a few months earlier by Denmark's vote against accepting the Maastricht Treaty. They were viscerally opposed to Britain's entry and especially against entry into the looming single currency.

In 1993, the government suffered a Commons defeat on the Maastricht treaty, as a hard core of vocal rebels were now openly opposing them and they only salvaged their European policy by turning it into a confidence vote. The Labour party also voted against the treaty, as they were then demanding a national referendum to settle the matter. This cost the Tories Party Unity Key two.

Yet another key would soon be threatened by the fall-out from 'Black Wednesday.' At the end of September 1992, the Culture Secretary David Mellor was forced to resign after revelations appeared, first about his affair with the actress Antonia de Sancha, which was followed by fresh revelations that he had accepted a month-long holiday from Mona Bauwens, the daughter of Jaweed-al-Ghussein, the financial director of the Palestine Liberation Organisation.

In a libel action by Bauwens against The People, George Carmen QC said that Mellor had acted like the proverbial ostrich, 'exposing all his thinking parts.' [275] The cumulative effect of these revelations proved irresistible and Mellor resigned in disgrace. Mellor had earlier talked publicly about the need to reign in the irresponsible excesses of the tabloid press. It appeared to some that the press could now sense governmental weakness and were taking advantage of the situation.

Scandal would increasingly plague the Major administration, with multiple scandals involving many different individuals. Some of the worst embarrassment for the government came in 1994, after Mr Major announced a 'Back to Basics' initiative. This was a culturally conservative agenda that many interpreted as a crusade for family values.

From this point onwards there were myriad scandals involving MP's extra-marital affairs and financial shenanigans. The individual cases sometimes blended tragedy and farce; for example, Stephen Milligan, who was found dead on his kitchen table, wearing stockings and suspenders, covered head, and an orange in his mouth. His friend, the MP and TV personality Gyles Brandreth, believed that he died celebrating his promotion to a ministerial job. [276]

Another high-profile case was that of Environment & Countryside Minister Tim Yeo, who resigned due to fathering an illegitimate child, after he had publicly attacked single mothers and broken families.

One even more damaging revelation was that of two MPs taking bribes from Harrods owner Mohamed Al-Fayed to answer questions. The 'Cash for Questions' scandal embroiled Northern Ireland Minister Tim Smith and the Minister for Regulation & Corporate Affairs, Neil Hamilton.

Other high-profile scandals included the conduct of Chief Secretary to the Treasury Jonathan Aitken, over claims that he had a hotel room paid for by a Saudi Businessman, had inappropriate commercial dealings with arms traders and had procured prostitutes for a Saudi Prince. Aitken sued the Guardian Newspaper and Granada TV for making the allegations. However, he was convicted of committing perjury during his own trial and was later sentenced to prison.

Another casualty of the sleaze epidemic was Northern Ireland Minister, Michael Mates. Mates had befriended the corrupt Cypriot businessman Asil Nadir, who had fled the country following charges of massive fraud. Mates had gifted Nadir a watch, which was inscribed with the legend: 'Don't let the buggers get you down.' [277] Mates was later forced to resign after a letter from him to the attorney general interceding on behalf of Asil Nadir got leaked to the press.

In 1996, it was found that Westminster council, in the 'Homes for Votes Scandal' had carried out a policy of removing homeless people from the borough and replacing them with likely Tory supporters.

The Arms-to-Iraq scandal was a different kind of scandal that began with four directors of the British arms company Matrix-Churchill being tried for selling weapons to Iraq. The trial collapsed when it transpired that government ministers had advised them about how to do so. Defence Minister Alan Clarke coined a cynical catchphrase when he admitted in the Commons to being 'economical with the actualité.' This led to the Scott report of 1996 which criticised the lack of ministerial accountability. The government again turned the Commons vote on this matter into a confidence vote, which they narrowly won.

While none of the scandals individually had a devastating impact on the government, the drip, drip, drip of sexual and financial impropriety created the impression of a Conservative Parliamentary party mired in scandal. So much so, that a new word 'Sleaze' entered the political lexicon; and indeed, has stayed there ever since. According to a poll carried out in October 1994, two thirds of the public thought the Conservatives gave the impression of being 'sleazy and disreputable.' '

[278]One particularly ferocious take down of the floundering Major administration came from Paul Johnson in *The Spectator*: 'This is a government born in

treachery, surviving by subterfuge, double-dealing and fraud, Janus-faced and brazen, slippery and underhand, a dismaying blend of incompetence and low cunning, doomed to end in shame and recriminations.' [279]

The cumulative effect of these scandals and Mr Major's ineffectual response to them - often trying to defend a clearly tarnished minister for too long, (notably in the case of Neil Hamilton.) before giving in to the inevitable; clearly cost the Major administration Scandal Key thirteen. It also gave the impression of a weak administration, lacking grip.

One legacy of the sleaze was the setting up of the Nolan Commission to uphold standards in public life. Although many of its recommendations were watered down in the face of backbench Tory hostility, the committee on Standards in Public Life, as it is now known is a positive legacy of the scandals of the 1990's. Though as we have seen, its efficacy is rather limited.

[280] Chancellor Norman Lamont was finally sacked in May 1993 after the government's position was further eroded after breaking their election promise not to raise VAT, and by their drubbing in the 1993 local elections and Newbury by-election. When asked if he regretted his claims about 'the green shoots of recovery,' he responded insouciantly by quoting the Edif Piaf song, 'Je ne regrette rien.' [281] Not long after, Lamont was dismissed from the cabinet in June 1993. His resignation speech contained the following devastating lines:

There is too much short-termism, too much reacting to events, not enough shaping of events. We give the impression of being a party in office, but not in power.
[282]

The international scene during this period was characterised by the changed world order that ensued following the collapse of the Soviet Union at the end of 1991; leading to a uni-polar world of one super-power, namely the United States. Although Britain and the west were no longer threatened with nuclear Armageddon, there was an increase in small wars in the chaotic vacuum created by the implosion of the Soviet Empire.

The greatest anxiety focussed on Yugoslavia, which was plunged into civil war in the summer of 1991. Although the initial conflict resulted in international recognition of Croatia, the spotlight soon moved to Bosnia-Hercegovina in the spring of 1992. Here, a vicious ethnic civil war developed with the Serbs being the main aggressors, putting the capital Sarajevo under siege for three years and carrying out genocide; euphemistically referred to as 'ethnic cleansing.'

The Major administration was the driving force behind the London conference in 1992, which resulted in the policy of creating UN 'safe havens' in Bosnia, which actually were not very safe at all. (Some were overrun by Serb forces in 1995.) Britain contributed a considerable number of peacekeepers and admittedly had to labour against American standoffishness due to fears of being embroiled in 'another Vietnam'.

Finally, in September 1995 NATO intervened, launching air and artillery attacks on Serb positions throughout Bosnia. This led to a change of fortunes in the conflict, and a ceasefire in October that year. This was followed by the Dayton-Ohio Agreement authorising a NATO peacekeeping force that has prevented a recurrence of war for the past twenty-five years. Although Britain played a significant role in the 1995 intervention, it fell well short of the requirements to win the Foreign Policy/Military Success Key nine.

Nearer to home, the Major government did have some real success in taking the first steps to resolve the Northern Ireland conflict. In early 1993 the British public recoiled in horror at the IRA bombing of Warrington, in which two children were killed. This increased the demands for an end to the troubles, spurring talks between the different parties. The outcome of this was the Downing Street Declaration in December 1993. This was a joint statement issued by the British Prime Minister John Major and Irish Taoiseach Albert Reynolds. This statement affirmed the right of the people of Northern Ireland to decide their own destiny democratically, and the imperative of achieving this peacefully, and with peace being the end result.

The following August the IRA declared a ceasefire. This was followed by a Loyalist ceasefire a few months later, and seventeen months of peace in the troubled province. However, a major stumbling block to the peace process was the refusal of the British government to admit Sinn Fein into the talks, due to the refusal of the IRA to decommission its arms.

A potential solution was proposed by the three-man commission set up by Senator George Mitchell in January 1996. It suggested that disarmament could take place alongside talks, and not as a pre-requisite to them as the British wanted, nor only as a consequence to them as Sin Fein wanted.

However, the proposal was overtaken by events in February 1996, when the IRA detonated a truck bomb beneath the Canary Wharf Tower in London's Docklands, killing two and causing massive damage. This attack was followed by the bombing of the centre of Manchester in June that year, and by a final campaign of false alarms during the 1997 general election, which resulted in the disruption of the Grand National and chaos on the motorway network.

In Ulster itself, there was serious rioting in the summer of 1996, when a standoff developed between Loyalist marchers and the Royal Ulster Constabulary (RUC) who were trying to re-route the march away from Catholic streets near Drumcree Church. The government over-ruled the police in the face of Unionist pressure. However, the volte-face was followed by days of serious Catholic rioting.

Ultimately, the peace process remained stalled until after the 1997 general election, thus costing the Major administration the Foreign Policy/Military Success Key nine.

One crisis that added to the loss of key eight was the BSE Crisis of 1996. In March of that year, it was announced that twelve people in Britain had died from the human form of BSE, or Mad Cow Disease as it was referred to popularly. This followed eight years of government denials of even the remotest possibility of the dread disease being passed onto humans via the consumption of beef.

Immediately, the European Union banned the export of British beef (the USA had banned it in 1989) and the government found a public health and international trade and relations crisis on its hands. The government's response was the mass slaughter of a million cows that were born before the ban on feed made from animal remains had come into effect. Fortunately, the human epidemic was mercifully small-scale, with fewer than two hundred cases reported. However, the European Union maintained the ban on British beef for ten years.

One major change in the political landscape resulted from the Labour party's long march back to the centre.

Leader John Smith consolidated the moderation policy of his predecessor Neil Kinnock, and was enjoying solid leads in the opinion polls.

Tragically, he died suddenly of a heart attack in May 1994, after years battling against heart disease. His successor was the young and charismatic Tony Blair from the right of the party, who effortlessly beat John Prescott for the leadership. Blair, together with Gordon Brown and Peter Mandelson are generally regarded as the architects of New Labour.

The project essentially created a hybrid movement, with its economic policy combining the Thatcherite anti-union, tax-cutting, deregulating agenda, with a social-democratic devotion to public sector spending. Its domestic policy combined Conservative toughness on law and order and anti-welfare dependency with a liberal, Roy Jenkinsesque view on permissiveness and minority rights. Its foreign policy combined right-wing patriotism and a hawkish pro-Americanism, with increased spending on international aid. The movement also represented a decisive break from the Euro-scepticism of Labour's recent past, being unapologetically pro-European; though not without divisions on the question of the single currency.

One major reform that Blair brought about whilst in opposition, was the abolition of Clause Four. This was the rule in the Labour party constitution that bound the party to re-nationalisation of the British economy. This change, enacted in 1995 was seen as a watershed moment for New Labour. With his relative youth, good looks, public speaking skills, energy and charm, Tony Blair robbed the Conservative government of Opposition Charisma Key four.

At the same time, John Major's image of a colourless and indecisive Prime Minister robbed the party of Key three. In 1995 Blair taunted Major in the commons, saying, 'There is one big difference. I lead my party, he follows his.' [283]

The schism over Europe would dog the Major administration for the remainder of its time in office. The majority of Major's cabinet were pro-European, especially Ken Clarke, Douglas Hurd and Michael Heseltine. However, senior Euro-sceptic voices would include Michael Portillo, Michael Howard and John Redwood.

In the summer of 1993, in the wake of the close Maastricht vote, John Major was being interviewed by Michael Brunson of ITV. He removed his lapel mic, but did not realise that one of the camera mics was still on. His comments were rather revealing. He turned to Brunson and said: 'What I don't understand Michael, is why such a complete wimp like me keeps winning everything,' He also referred to the Tories as, 'a party that is harking back to a golden age that never was, and is now invented.' When Brunson suggested a major reshuffle, the Prime Minister had this to say.

I could bring in other people. But where do you think most of this poison is coming from? From the dispossessed and the never-possessed. You can think of ex-ministers who are going to cause all sorts of trouble. We don't want another three more of the bastards out there. [284]

The final sentence was widely interpreted to be a reference to John Redwood, Michael Portillo and Peter Lilley. Portillo in fact suggested to Major that he solve the problem by firing either the Euro-sceptic half of the cabinet or the pro-European half, and that if he were fired as a result, he would not hold it against Major.[285]

The Prime Minister declined to take this advice, as its repercussions would have been too explosive.

The following autumn Major was caught out in similar fashion yet again. This time in Japan when a hidden tape-recorder caught him attacking his Euro-sceptic critics: saying that he could hear the, 'flapping of white coats' when his 'barmy' right-wing opponents criticised him. [286]

These unguarded comments did little to endear Mr Major to his Euro-sceptic right.

In 1994, the government withdrew the whip from several Tory Euro-rebels for voting against the EC Finance Bill. The effect of this action was to wipe out their own slender majority for several months until the whip was finally restored.

This disastrous combination of internal division, sleaze and lost reputation for economic competence, resulted in the Conservatives losing every single by-election seat that they contested during the term; hence key one was easily toppled. These by-elections witnessed dramatic gains for the Liberal Democrats as well as Labour; for example, the huge swing at Christchurch in 1993.

The Lib Dems also fared very well in the local and European elections during this period. With the ideological convergence now taking place between Labour and the Liberals, the prospect of Lib-Lab tactical voting was becoming widely anticipated. This was all the more so because of the publicity generated by GROT, (Get Rid of Them) an anti-Tory tactical voting movement led by the CND campaigner Bruce Kent. Research by Curtis and Stead estimate that between twenty-five and thirty-five Tory seats were lost to the Liberal Democrats as the result of tactical voting. Norris, using different methodology suggests a loss of twenty-four seats.

In New Labour, New Tactical Voting, [287]1998, Curtis, Stead and Norris show that the change in voting patterns was caused by changed perceptions of the parties. In 1992, Liberal Democrat supporters were marginally more sceptical of Labour than they were towards the Conservatives. However, five years later, they were considerably more favourable towards Tony Blair's New Labour. The research also showed that Conservatives were significantly less hostile to Labour in 1997 than in 1992; suggesting that the drop in turnout that year was disproportionately affecting the Conservative party.

Yet another headache for the Major government appeared in the form of the Referendum Party, led by the financier Sir James Goldsmith. This party campaigned for a national referendum on continued EU membership. Although the party only reached around two or three percent in the national polls, it was clearly having a disproportionate effect upon the Tory vote. Polling revealed that two-thirds of its supporters were disaffected Conservative voters, and hardly any had voted Labour.

Psephologists have argued over the impact of this party. John Curtice and Michael Stead claimed that four Tory seats were lost as a result of the Referendum Party. [288] Ian McAlister and Donley T Studler disagree, claiming that at least sixteen seats were lost due to Sir James Goldsmith's party.[289] The exact number will be never known, but at the time of the 1997 election, the strong Liberal Democrat performance plus the rise of the Referendum party would be sufficient to turn the Third Party Key against the government.

The government of John Major continued to pursue Thatcherite policies during the remainder of Tory rule, with the privatisations of Coal (1994) and the railways

(1996) both causing considerable controversy. The Criminal Justice Act (1994) brought about some significant changes, such as increased police powers to stop illegal raves, to stop and search suspects, to infer from suspects' silence and also the reduction of the age of consent for gay men from twenty-one to eighteen.

The hard-line position of Home Secretary Michael Howard was in response to the growing public concern about crime. This period saw a number of high-profile murders, including the murder of Liverpool toddler James Bulger by two boys in 1993, the racially motivated murder of Stephen Lawrence the same year, the stabbing to death of Head Teacher Philip Lawrence in 1995 and the Dunblane massacre of sixteen school children and their teacher in 1996. The latter atrocity resulted in the banning of handguns in the United Kingdom.

Another significant reform included the Disability Discrimination Act 1995, which outlawed discrimination against people with disabilities.

Regarding European policy, Major was now effectively caught between the two wings of his party, and found it impossible to satisfy them both. The rebels too, were afraid of mounting a leadership challenge in case it resulted in the election of their opponents.

In June 1995, John Major tried a desperate gambit. He resigned the leadership of the Tory party in order to force a contest, telling his opponents that, 'It is time to put up or shut up,' [290]thus flushing out the rebels. The Right-wing Welsh Secretary John Redwood resigned from the cabinet to stand against Major. His campaign used the slogan, 'No change, no chance,' - calculated to play on backbenchers' fears of losing their seats. The Tory press were divided, with the once loyal *Sun* kicking the Prime Minister with the headline: 'Redwood or Deadwood.'

Yet Major won with a two-thirds majority. In one of his best lines Major told the House of Commons that, 'I understand that he (Redwood) resigned from the Cabinet because he was devastated that I had resigned as leader of the Conservative party.' [291] This contest pre-empted the rebels in the last year in which they could have reasonably launched a challenge against him. However, nothing was substantially changed by this exercise.

One more key that was about to turn against the government was the Cyclical Incumbency Key. This turns when a government has been in power for four terms or more, as was the case for the Tories in 1997. The 'time for a change' refrain was growing stronger and the government were seen as stale and tired.

Despite the disaster of Black Wednesday in 1992, Britain's ejection from the ERM had actually been a blessing in disguise for the economy - if not for the government's fortunes. Leaving the ERM had resulted in a weakening of the pound which helped British exports recover from the doldrums of the early nineties. GDP started growing consistently from the time of the pound's departure from the ERM and started a remarkable fifteen-year period of growth. Interest rates and inflation would be very low by the end of the term, and in fact for the following quarter-century.

Unemployment had briefly peaked at three million early in 1993, before beginning a steady descent to less than two million by the following election. The net result of this is that both economic keys were true for the Conservatives at the 1997 election. The only other key to stay true was Civil Unrest Key twelve. There was plenty of crime, peaking at a post-war high in 1995, but major riots, strikes and mass protests there were not.

John Major decided on an unusually long seven-week campaign, presumably in the hope that Tony Blair would be rumbled by the public. However, the polished Blair campaign easily out-dazzled grey Major, who resorted to his soap box again, but to little effect this time. The superior New Labour campaign added two or three seats to Labour's total, boosting their majority by ten.

Europe would continue to dog the Conservatives during the campaign, as it became clear that quite large numbers of Tory candidates were rejecting Major's 'wait and see' line on the Euro. In a desperate plea to his fractious party, Major, in lines reminiscent of Nye Bevan said, 'Like me or loathe me, do not bind my hands when I am negotiating on behalf of the British nation.' [292] In a final desperate move, Major announced in a press conference that he would offer Tory MPs a free vote on the single currency if he won the election.

It soon transpired that he had neglected to tell Chancellor Kenneth Clarke, or Deputy Prime Minister Michael Heseltine. Major compounded the oversight with a gaffe; saying that he did not need to consult, 'Ken Clarke or Joe Bloggs.'[293]

During the campaign, Mr Blair made a speech in which he set himself and his party on the side of modernity, painting the Tories as fuddy-duddies, trapped in a black and white world

I am a modern man. I am part of the rock and roll generation - the Beatles, colour TV, that's the generation I come from. [294]

May 1997 UK general election:

1) *By-election key*	false
2) *Unity Key*	false
3) *Incumbent Leadership Key*	false
4) *Opposition Charisma Key*	false
5) *Third Party Key*	false
6) *Cyclical Incumbency Key*	false
7) *Short-Term Economy Key*	true
8) *Long-Term Economy Key*	true
9) *Foreign Policy/Military Success Key*	false
10) *Foreign Policy/Military Failure Key*	false
11) *Policy Change Key*	false
12) *Civil Unrest Key*	true
13) *Scandal Key*	false

balance of negative keys: 10

campaign differential: Labour + 5 seats

forecast: Labour majority 150-200

Conservatives 163 seats Labour 420-440 seats

actual result: Labour majority of 179

Conservatives 165 seats Labour 419 seats Liberal Democrats 46

The election of 1997 witnessed the biggest swing between the major parties since 1945, and delivered the Labour party's best result ever, and the Conservatives' worst since 1906. The Tories lost half their seats, being entirely wiped out in Wales and Scotland, and becoming largely a rural and suburban party outside of London. The defeat also claimed the scalp of the Tory right's hero Michael Portillo, whom many had considered the next leader.

The Liberal democrats had more than doubled their parliamentary strength to reach their best result since 1923. The election was also notable for the victory of TV journalist and war reporter Martin Bell against the corrupt Tory MP Neil Hamilton in Tatton.

After eighteen years, Tory rule had finally come to a shattering end. The Conservatives could boast of effectively ending the labour disputes that had so dominated the 1970s. They had privatised the public utilities and could claim to have made them more efficient. They had modernised and turbo-charged the City and shifted the economy away from manufacturing and towards services. They had finally won the great inflation battle, and had supported America in the final victorious chapter in the Cold War.

However, they had also presided over enormous levels of wealth inequality, and regional inequality to go with it. They had finally brought unemployment down to an extent, but after years of it being above three million, and with it still being higher than when they took office. The Big Bang in the city had ushered in a culture of greed and materialism, and the last term of Toryism had seen sleaze become endemic in parliament.

John Major's contribution had essentially been one of consolidation. The radical work had been more or less concluded by the time Mrs Thatcher had left office. His softer stance and milder leadership style, in the words of Ken Clarke, amounted to, 'Thatcherism with a human face.'[295] Perhaps Major's three most important achievements were bringing Britain into the Maastricht treaty, which would determine Britain's relationship with Europe for the next twenty-five years, beginning the Northern Ireland peace process, which would bear fruit under Tony Blair, and for winning a fourth Conservative term, which led directly to the creation of New Labour.

Standing on the steps of Downing Street for one final time as Prime Minister, John Major declared, 'When the curtain falls, it is time to get off the stage.' [296] He then made good on his promise, and a new era in British political life had begun.

Chapter 6: 1997-2010

THE NEW LABOUR YEARS: RECONCILING THATCHERISM WITH SOCIAL DEMOCRACY AND LAW & ORDER WITH LIBERALISM

'Our task is not to fight old battles, but to show there is a third way, a way of marrying together an open competitive society and successful economy with a just and decent society.' Tony Blair [297]

From 1997 to 2010 Labour governed Britain again. Yet it was a very different kind of Labour government to the ones seen previously. Out was the commitment to nationalisation, and in was the befriending of big business. Essentially, it was a hybrid movement that sought to reconcile opposites to create a 'Third Way.'

It sought to reconcile free market Thatcherism with the social democratic big state, tough-on-crime authoritarianism with social liberalism, and minority rights. It married patriotism with internationalism, pro-Americanism with pro-Europeanism. New Labour also wanted to clean up the sleaze of politics and renew public trust after the erosion it had undergone during the last term of the Tories.

Did it succeed? Well, to a point yes, but the New Labourites had to struggle with the reality of a party composed largely of tribally socialist and anti-capitalist members. For a long time it was a success story, but in the end, did New Labour transform Britain to the extent that Thatcher and Attlee did? Not quite. The huge increase in public service investment and improvement has been progressively undone by Conservative austerity since 2010.

Rather than clean up politics, New Labour departed from government with the House of Commons just as mired in scandal as it had been when they took office. The questions over our relationship with Europe remained unresolved, and our international standing had taken a hit from our involvement in the war in Iraq. Although the fusion of Thatcherism and the Social Democratic state had worked well for a long time, the financial crisis of 2008 had tarnished the former and robbed the latter of its source of funding.

One way in which all the promise of 1997, and not just concerning New Labour, has sadly failed to materialise, is in a simple thought experiment. How would a well-informed person in that heady year have reacted if they could have seen the news from twenty to twenty-five years' hence? Most of their expectations would have been totally upended. Back then, at the grinning zenith of the Blair years, one would have imagined that future Britain would have become fully enmeshed into a European super-state, almost certainly in fact a member of the single currency. Few would have imagined that we would still be spending pounds and pence. The idea of us actually leaving the EU would have been a remote possibility indeed.

Looking at the wider world, most would have expected a much more peaceful international scene, with Russia probably a liberal-capitalist ally. It was still the time of the 'End of History,' with the world perhaps not quite becoming a living realisation of John Lennon's 'Imagine,' but at least heading in that general direction. *The Guardian* in December 1995 asking; 'Whatever Happened to War? All over the world peace is breaking out and it's more than just a trend.' [298]The current

(2023) situation in the Ukraine would certainly have come as a shock, and when combined with Brexit would be the antithesis of all New Labour utopian speechifying. The COVID-19 pandemic and attendant lockdowns, would have seemed like something out of a dystopian novel.

After the death of Princess Diana towards the end of that summer, many were predicting the demise of the British Royal family, perhaps with its abolition on the death of Elizabeth II. A time traveller from Diana's funeral, jumping exactly twenty-five years later to that of the Queen, would have been struck by the contrast in the public mood between the two events, and how the public anger and disaffection with the royals in the 1990s had seemingly vanished. They would also be surprised by the positive public reception given to King Charles; the villain of September 1997. However, the ongoing media circus surrounding Harry and Meghan would not have seemed out of place from a nineties' perspective.

Our time traveller would also contrast the mighty, presidential standing of Blair in their time, with the shrunken, degraded stature of British political leaders a quarter-century later; with Prime Ministers now almost literally here today, gone tomorrow. Our visitor would also be shocked to see a grey-bearded old lefty regain control of the Labour party in 2015, and find that a generation after the Blair landslide, that the party is once again being dragged kicking and squally towards the centre ground after a disastrous defeat. The return of double-digit inflation and their attendant strikes in 2022 would also seem like history was running backwards instead of forwards. The orange populist across the pond would look like a character from a satire show, maybe an invention of Chris Morris.

Although our time traveller would probably not be too surprised by gay marriage, they would probably feel that with the current 'woke' politics and cancel culture, the liberal-left movements from their own time were evolving into something more sinister. The cultural division and polarisation within the country would also be disquieting to someone from a more laid-back and libertarian era.

Not all of this of course is due to the failings of New Labour, but it is quite a shocking illustration of the illusory nature of our cultural and political world. Feelings about issues, for example, that the Euro was 'the way things are going' can prove very wrong indeed. Some of the New Labour transformations are indeed still with us; most visibly in the form of the devolved parliaments and Supreme Court. However, even there, someone from 1997 would be taken aback at the strength of the demands for Scottish Independence. Devolution was supposed to neuter such impulses.

As with Thatcher before, New Labour forced their opponents to change, adapt and even emulate them. David Cameron was sometimes dubbed 'Tory Blair' and his promotion of social liberalism and faux environmentalism was a sincere form of flattery to Tony Blair's New Labour. Less positive parts of the legacy include the politicisation of the civil service and the obsession with spin and media manipulation. Although in fairness it was already developing before Tony Blair came to office. However, some positive achievements are still with us, for now at least: the minimum wage, the Human Rights act and the historic achievement in Northern Ireland.

1997-2001:
"We are intensely relaxed about people getting filthy rich, provided that they pay their taxes" Peter Mandelson, Silicon Valley speech, October 1998

In May 1997 Labour stood higher than any British party in modern times. Their majority was overwhelming, the Tories were crushed and smitten, and the media lay adoring at their feet. Tony Blair, who became Britain's youngest Prime Minister since Lord Liverpool in 1812, was master of all he surveyed. Yet, New Labour seemed almost stunned by their own success. This was a party that had grown afraid to be optimistic after four election defeats in a row, and had simply refused to believe the landslide widely signalled in the polls. Standing outside Downing Street Mr Blair promised to lead 'a government that seeks to restore trust in politics' and 'a government of practical measures in pursuit of noble causes.' [299]

The first major change brought about by New Labour was Independence for the Bank of England. This policy change, made only a few weeks after taking power, allowed the Bank of England to set interest rates. It would, as Ed Balls put it, 'create space for us to get rid of the debilitating meetings on monetary policy.'[300] The move was widely praised, and well received by the City.

However, this policy was coupled with another that almost led to the resignation of the Governor of the Bank of England Eddie George. Chancellor Gordon Brown had sprung upon George the idea of removing the bank's regulatory powers and transferring them to a Securities & Investment Board. Disaster was only averted through Blair's intervention and a compromise solution.

On the economic and financial side of government, there was relatively little other major reform during this term. To show that they were really new Labour, Gordon Brown cut Corporation tax to its lowest level ever. Their windfall tax on the privatised public utilities shored up left-wing support, while the abolition of married couples' tax allowance and mortgage tax relief created controversy.

More significantly though, Labour stuck to the Conservatives' restrictive spending plans for the first two years of the term. Labour were still very frightened of the charge that they were essentially still old Labour in yuppie clothing, believing (The keys say wrongly) that their pledges to raise income tax in 1992 lost them the election. Apparently, John Major bumped into Labour Home Secretary Jack Straw in the Commons and asked him: 'Why on earth are you sticking to our spending plans? We would never have!' Straw replied: 'Yes, but you have more latitude than us.' [301]

Brown raised money by indirect taxation, but even so, Government spending as a percentage of GDP fell to a near post-war low of 36.3% in 1999-2000. After major public criticism of increasing NHS waiting lists in the winter of 2000, Brown reluctantly agreed to an increase in government spending on health. However, the real spending increases would not materialise until Labour's second term.

Nevertheless, the economy grew very strongly during Blair's first term, securing both the economic keys for Labour.

One of the significant changes brought about by New Labour include changes to the style of government itself. Following John Major's more democratic, cabinet government, the Blair years saw a return to something similar to Thatcher. Cabinet meetings were now relatively short, generally under forty-five minutes, and mostly consisted of the Prime Minister or the Chancellor informing the rest of the cabinet of decisions that had already been made by very small groups of key political figures. The cabinet were there simply to listen. The cabinet was not consulted about Bank of England Independence, nor the decision to go ahead with the Millennium Dome for example.

Alastair Campbell, Blair's abrasive and combative Press Secretary was the first to be present at cabinet meetings, acting as a restraint on dissent. Blair was often criticised for his preference for 'sofa government' - that is governing with a very small group of advisors and ministers. The civil servant Sir Robin Butler said that the cabinet under Blair had returned to its eighteenth-century origins, as 'a weekly meeting of political friends.'[302]

Blair further politicised the civil service by giving political advisors the power to give order to civil servants for the first time. Special orders in council empowered Press Secretary Alistair Campbell and Chief of Staff, Jonathan Powell in a major departure from normal protocols. At a pre-election seminar Powell warned Whitehall mandarins to expect, 'a change from a feudal system of barons to a more Napoleonic system.'[303]

New Labour in fact, acted as a duopoly between Blair and Brown. These two, together with Peter Mandelson were the architects of the movement in 1994. Enmity and fierce rivalry had developed between Blair and Brown since the 1994 leadership contest. Blair had persuaded Brown not to stand against him. Mandelson, originally a Brown supporter had switched allegiances to support Blair. Brown took a decade and a half to forgive him and thus New Labour were split into a Brown camp and a Blair-Mandelson camp thereafter. This division at the top of the party was initially a source of creative friction, but increasingly as time went on, a source of paralysis and instability.

New Labour brought about many constitutional changes during its first term. One of these was the removal of all but ninety-one of the hereditary peers in the House of Lords. The arbitrary number of surviving peers was the result of haggling between Labour Lord Chancellor Derry Irvine and the Tory Viscount Cranborne. The deal was for 650 hereditary peers to go quietly and not disrupt the government's legislative programme.

An even bigger piece of constitutional reform was the creation of the devolved parliaments for Scotland, Wales and Northern Ireland. Referenda on the question were held in 1997 and the parliaments were set up in 1999. The MPs are elected by the Additional Member System, and have significant powers, including partial powers to raise taxes. However, foreign policy remains in the hands of the national government in Westminster.

Labour also established the London Assembly and the first directly elected Mayor. It was assumed that these new devolved governments would be easily controllable Labour fiefdoms, though things did not quite work out that way. In Wales, Blair's favoured candidate for First Minister, the Welsh Secretary Ron Davis, was forced to resign after being attacked on Clapham Common after agreeing to go for a meal with a male stranger.

This embarrassment led the Labour MP Rodri Morgan, whom Blair strongly opposed to become the favourite. Labour used the Trade Union block vote as well as a whipped vote of MPS and delegates to stop him and foisted Alun Michael on Wales as First Minister. It was a hollow victory, as Michael was forced out in a no-confidence vote a year later and replaced by Morgan.

This contradictory New Labour behaviour, of devolving powers, and at the same time trying to control the outcome of the process, was to lead to even greater problems in London. Here, left-wing renegade Ken Livingstone was eager to run for the job of mayor. After all, he had effectively been mayor when he led the Greater London Council in the eighties.

The Labour high command instead backed Health Secretary Frank Dobson. Brown said to Blair that 'Red Ken' had to be stopped 'at any cost...whatever it takes,' [304] Again, as in Wales, the Blair placeman won the nomination with the aid of whipped votes, but this victory was not even a pyrrhic one. Livingstone decided to run as an independent and won; pushing Dobson into third place.

More significant Labour reforms came with a European flavour. In 1998 Labour introduced the Human Rights Act which incorporated the European Convention on Human Rights into British Law. Another policy change was the decision to opt back into the Social Chapter of the Maastricht Treaty. John Major had secured an opt-out when he signed Britain into the treaty in 1991. However, Tony Blair, and his progressive Foreign Secretary Robin Cook, brought Britain back into it in 1997. This treaty provided protection to workers from exploitation and harassment in the workplace.

This change also reflected a change of foreign policy from that of the Major years, when pro-Europeanism had to be awkwardly balanced against Euro-scepticism. However, we would not see the end of conflict on that particular issue.

Labour also introduced the National Minimum Wage in 1999, which although initially fiercely opposed by the Tories, has proved an enduring and accepted success. Another significant reform was the Freedom of

Information Act 2000, which allows ordinary citizens to request information from the government and other authorities. There was the Data Protection act 1998, which gave individuals some control and protection, over what information could be held about them, its accuracy and utilisation.

New Labour continued the socially liberal tradition of the Wilson governments of the sixties and seventies. Indeed, the former Home Secretary Roy Jenkins was a mentor to Tony Blair when he reached office. One of the first things Labour did was to equalise the age of consent for gay men with that of heterosexuals, to sixteen. In 2000, they overturned the traditional ban on homosexuals serving in the armed forces. (Servicemen had been going to military prisons for being gay as recently as 1990.)

Blair also championed multiculturalism and allowed immigration to increase. It was during this term that immigration began to be talked about by mainstream politicians, notably the Tory leader William Hague. As late as 1997, very few people rated immigration as being one of their top priorities, However, from 2000 onwards, the numbers citing it as a major concern, steadily increased. [305]

One of Labour's most controversial policy changes during this term was the abolition of the student grant and the introduction of Tuition fees. These would steadily increase over the coming years.

All in all, this enormous list of policy innovations surely won New Labour the Policy Change Key.

The hybrid nature of New Labour was often summed up in the much-ridiculed phrase, 'the Third Way.' Although the idea itself was not entirely new, it had not been fully embraced before by the major parties. Essentially taking and combining the elements from free-market conservatism, social conservatism, liberalism and socialism that worked and discarding the rest was not necessarily woolly-minded, confused or mendacious. Blair did have trouble selling it though as a serious idea.

Labour suffered from being out of office for so long, and developed a fear that the British people were afraid of ideology. By recognising that the right had to care more for the poor and needy and that the left had to get over its animus with ambition, New Labour had actually found a rational winning economic formula. By demanding that social reactionaries had to accept that freedoms and rights enjoyed by the majority should be extended to minorities, whilst simultaneously demanding that liberals had to accept the importance of security and law & order, they found a social position that now represented the majority of the population.

By asking little Englanders to get over their Europhobia, whilst asking the left to get over its knee-jerk anti-Americanism, Labour was developing a sensible foreign policy; or so it seemed. Personal freedom, economic freedom, strong public services and social justice were not necessarily in conflict with one another. Combining ideas from apparently irreconcilable opposites, amounted to what Andrew Rawnsley dubbed a 'unified field theory of politics.' [306]Blair added that 'State power is only one means to achieve our goals, but not the only one and emphatically not an end in itself.'[307]

The Third Way of course had many critics. The problems in it included the claim that it made choices redundant, and therefore ultimately made democracy redundant. Roy Hattersley described it as being, 'little more than a benign version of the one-party state. Taking the politics out of politics is not only absurd, it is democratically dangerous.'[308] David Marquand in *The Progressive Dilemma*, said the Third Way was simply 'wallpaper over the unresolved contradictions within New Labour.'[309]

Although Blair soon dropped the label 'Third Way' the basic philosophy would remain in control of Labour policy until Corbyn.

One of the strangest episodes in recent British history followed the tragic death of Diana Princess of Wales in a Paris car crash on August 31st 1997. The country was stricken by a kind of collective grief never known before in modern times, or seen since. Blair rose to the occasion with all his communicative brilliance, articulating real emotion, whilst remaining Prime Ministerial. 'She was ... the People's Princess and that is how she will stay, how she will remain in our hearts and our memories for ever.'[310] This raised Blair to a new level of popularity, whilst the House of Windsor was hit by its worst crisis since the abdication of Edward VIII.

Diana's death, soon after her divorce from Prince Charles had been finalised, and after so much public bad blood between her and the House of Windsor, was highly difficult for the royals to handle. Any public display of grief would be labelled as crocodile tears, while the absence of such reaction would be seen as heartless and cold. Wild conspiracies were circulating that the accident had been no accident at all. (They are still very much alive online.) Charles was viewed with the utmost suspicion.

As days passed by, the royal flag was not flown at half-mast and no public appearances or broadcasts from senior royals followed. The newspapers began to circle the imperilled House of Windsor. 'Where is our Queen?

Where is her flag?' screamed *The Sun*. The *Daily Mail* enquired: 'Has the House of Windsor got a heart?'

It was here that the New Labour spin machine provided some real help to someone outside their own ranks. Blair managed to persuade Buckingham Palace to lower the flag to half-mast and for the Queen to do a live broadcast on the *Six O' Clock News*. This reduced the temperature of the national fever. The funeral of Diana was a very modern and populist affair, befitting the New Labour style. Elton John sang his re-worked 'Candle in the Wind' at Westminster Abbey, and crowds thronged the streets.

In time, the monarchy at least partially recovered its badly tarnished standing and Blair, the already popular and charismatic Prime Minister, saw his status expand to that of a president as the monarchy was badly eclipsed. In the autumn of 1997, his poll ratings hit a stratospheric ninety-three per cent, a figure never seen before or since by any Prime Minister. [311]

On the foreign policy front, Labour was considerably more pre-European than the Tories, though there was still internal division. The brooding, truculent chancellor Gordon Brown was much more of a Euro-sceptic than Tony Blair, insisting that the United Kingdom had to pass five economic tests before membership of the Single Currency could be countenanced. Roy Jenkins and Liberal Democrat leader Paddy Ashdown urged Blair to seize the day and commit Britain to the Euro, but Brown ruled out entry for the duration of the parliament.

One of the most important achievements of the Labour government was in Northern Ireland. The peace process had begun in earnest with the Downing Street Declaration of 1993 and had appeared to be making real progress before the Canary Wharf bombing of 1996. With the change of government, dialogue between the different factions resumed. The IRA renewed their ceasefire in July 1997 and in December of that year Sinn Fein's Gerry Adams and Martin McGuiness were invited to Downing Street. Progress was assisted by the spontaneous and likeable Northern Ireland Secretary Mo Mowlam, who connected with the people of Ulster in a way not matched by any of her predecessors and even managed to have talks with the prisoners in the notorious Maze prison.

The talks came to a climax at Hillsborough castle in April 1998. There, Tony Blair's brilliant use of rhetoric and acting was on full display, if tellingly a little undermined by New Labour falsity.

Now is not the time for soundbites, we can leave those at home... I feel the hand of history upon our shoulders.[312]

Eventually, the long and gruelling negotiations came to fruition in the form of the now famous Good Friday Agreement. The Easter connection provided the highly encouraging symbolism of rebirth and renewal. At the end of the talks Mr Blair exclaimed: 'Today is only the beginning. It is not the end. Today we have the sense of the prize before us. The work to win that prize goes on.'[313]

The agreement itself involved both Catholic and Protestant parties in Ulster, as well as the governments of the United Kingdom and the Republic of Ireland, recognising that Northern Ireland was part of the United Kingdom, and could not become part of a united Ireland without the majority popular consent of both North and South. It also recognised equal rights of all citizens irrespective of religion. It authorised the establishment of a Northern Ireland Assembly, which would reflect all the political parties, as well as power-sharing organisations involving cooperation between the Republic and Northern Ireland and between Northern Ireland and mainland United Kingdom.

The agreement also involved all parties to commit themselves to peaceful means and the decommissioning of all weapons. The British agreed to restore 'normal' civilian policing to the province and both sides agreed an early release programme for terrorist prisoners.

The agreement was ratified by referenda in both the North and South the following month. Although the issue of arms decommissioning proved a stumbling block, the agreement did bring about the end of sectarian violence in Northern Ireland, though not immediately.

It took the vast Omagh bomb, planted by the splinter group The Real IRA in August, to fully cement the agreement through almost universal public revulsion to the single worst atrocity of the troubles. This enormous achievement of the Good Friday Agreement, which only five years earlier, would have seemed highly improbable, easily secured Foreign Policy/Military Success Key nine.

The Foreign Policy Keys were also jangled by Britain's major role in the Kosovo war of 1999. The situation had been deteriorating since the previous spring, when armed conflict broke out between Serbia and the separatists of the Kosovo province. The Serbs burned villages, slaughtered livestock and carried out a scorched-earth policy to defeat the rebels. There were numerous reports of ethnic killings.

Following the break-down of the NATO-brokered Rambouillet agreement in March 1999, NATO launched air-strikes against Serb targets in a bid to bring them back to the conference table. When the Serbs failed to back down, the bombing escalated into a major air war.

The range of targets now being extended to the economy and infrastructure and the state TV broadcasting centre.

Although over half the military hardware and personnel were provided by America, Blair was highly influential in driving the conflict, especially in forcing Milosevic to finally back down in June. Blair, while originally believing that the war could be won by air power alone (along with all the other leaders) proposed a coalition of the willing, to invade Kosovo with ground troops. Britain would be providing fifty thousand - virtually the entire combat force at the time. This convinced the Serb leader that NATO would put its money where its mouth was, and that he could not simply tough out the air campaign. Without Mr Blair's resolve and leadership, it is not at all certain how or when the Kosovo war would have ended.

With the surrender of Milosevic, NATO troops moved into Kosovo unopposed and the province became a NATO protectorate. Within eighteen months Milosevic was overthrown in a popular revolt. This eleven-week conflict had the potential of costing Labour Foreign Policy/Military Failure Key ten, but ultimately strengthened Blair's position at home and abroad.

One foreign policy imbroglio that tested Britain's pursuit of global justice was the surreal drama of the arrest and detention of former Chilean dictator General Augusto Pinochet. Pinochet had come to England in 1998 for back surgery, only to find himself placed under house arrest. The impetus to arrest and initially to try Pinochet came from Spain, seeking redress for its citizens murdered by the right-wing Chilean regime. Although the High Court ruled that he could be tried, he was eventually sent back to Chile on the grounds that he was unfit to stand trial. This was a typical New Labour triangulated compromise; making the gestures against a bogey man of the right, whilst not quite following through with it in practice.

New Labour had been elected on a platform of restoring trust and integrity to politics. However, the reality was to fall far short of this promise. One of the worst scandals happened relatively early in the first term. In November 1997 it was claimed that Tony Blair had accepted a hefty donation from the Formula One boss Bernie Ecclestone. It was also alleged that the government had exempted Formula one from the new ban on tobacco advertising. For several days the Labour party refused to confirm when or whether the donation had been made or how much. Then, Ecclestone himself revealed that it had, and that it had been to the tune of £1,000,000.

After denying any knowledge of the donation on radio, Gordon Brown shouted at his staff, 'I lied, I lied! My credibility will be in shreds. I lied. If this gets out, I'll be destroyed!'[314] Tony Blair went on Television to preserve his whiter-than-white image, telling John Humphreys. 'I'm a pretty straight sort of guy.'[315] Because Labour were still stratospherically popular that autumn, the affair blew over without causing serious damage.

The Foreign Secretary Robin Cook, fond of the phrase 'ethical foreign policy' was also hit by embarrassment after having an affair in which he left his wife for one of his staff, Gaynor Regan. Because the affair broke in 1997 when Labour were still in their pomp, the press went relatively easy on Cook and he kept his job. However, his ex-wife took her revenge with a book on her ex-husband, mockingly entitled, 'A Slight and Delicate Creature.' In it, she accused Cook of 'Selling his soul to New Labour.'[316]

Scandal, or the appearance of it, was to result in the double resignation of Peter Mandelson. He resigned as

President of the Board of Trade in December 1998, after failing to declare a loan for a house that he had borrowed from the Paymaster General Geoffrey Robinson. In January 2001 he had to resign again, this time as Northern Ireland Secretary after allegations that he improperly used his position to secure a passport for one of the Hinduja brothers, who had made a major contribution to the Millennium Dome. However, they were also being investigated for alleged corruption in India. Although Mandelson was exonerated by the Hammond inquiry two months later, he was cast into the political wilderness for years.

These episodes combined with the Ron Brown and Robin Cook affairs had done much to erode the government's once squeaky-clean image. A poll in January 2001 revealed that forty-seven percent of the public agreed that the government were 'Very sleazy and disreputable.' [317] However, this proportion was still just less than half, and the damage fell short of that inflicted by Profumo, or the nineties Tory sleaze, so Scandal Key thirteen suffered a half-turn.

Although this era is remembered as relatively peaceful and tranquil, with the labour disputes of the past apparently settled, it was shaken by a potentially disastrous episode of industrial action. In late summer 2000, lorry driver protests against high fuel prices had begun spreading across Europe. At the time, almost no one imagined that they would be replicated in the UK, at least not on any significant scale; that kind of thing was not very British.

However, a smallish group of farmers and hauliers began blockading oil refineries and fuel depots. The government did not initially take the protests very seriously, but they rapidly spread around the country in September 2000. Within days, fuel began rapidly drying up with panic buying commonplace across the United Kingdom. 'Go slow' protests brought additional chaos to motorways. It became very clear that Britain was in imminent danger of grinding to a complete halt. Tanker drivers refused to break the strikes, citing fear of attack by protesters. The army simply did not have enough trained tanker driver to cope; only sixty such drivers, when two thousand were needed. The government could not afford to openly back down, but they were also powerless to act effectively.

Fortunately, the protestors, who only numbered around 2,500, calculated that mass starvation and deaths due to ambulance shortages would lose them all public support, and so backed down. They gave the government a sixty-day ultimatum to reduce fuel costs. The Labour government successfully defused the crisis in November 2000 with a package of cuts for the protestors, equivalent to a cut of eight pence to the litre, and a general freeze in fuel duty for all motorists for the next eighteen months. The military had also been training troops as tanker drivers. Thus, Civil Unrest Key twelve had been saved.

One way in which the Blair government had been assisted during this period was by the risible ineptitude of the principal opposition. Following the meltdown election performance of 1997, the Conservatives choose the young, former Welsh Secretary William Hague as their new leader. They passed over the much more experienced and credible ex-Chancellor Ken Clarke, because the Euro-sceptic wing of the party was now in the majority, and Clarke's enthusiasm for joining the Single Currency was undisguised. The right's hero, the Defence Secretary Michael Portillo had unexpectedly lost his seat in the election, so was not eligible to stand for the leadership.

Hague was dogged from the start by the memories, reinforced by frequently aired clips, of him as a fifteen-year-old young conservative, speaking at the 1977 party conference. His early attempts to appear 'with it,' such as donning a baseball cap at the Notting Hill carnival were simply embarrassing; as was his suggestion in the wake of Diana's death that an airport be named after her. His attempt to slap down Viscount Cranbourne, over his deal to accept the axing of most of the hereditary peers was met with humiliation.

Hague's voice and manner were frequently mocked and although quite effective in the Commons, almost no one could imagine him ever becoming Prime Minister. In the words of Andrew Rawnsley, the Tories were 'ridiculed and marginalised' during this period. [318]Thus, the Opposition Charisma and Opposition Implausibility Bonus Key were both turned in the government's favour.

In the first half of the term, Tony Blair was having talks with the Liberal leader Paddy Ashdown on a possible coalition. In the run-up to the election, Blair had indicated his willingness to form an alliance with the Liberals, but this was mostly because he was not expecting such a big win. Blair also faced fierce resistance to working more closely with Ashdown from his Deputy John Prescott, who threatened to resign if Blair pursued this path. 'The day that man walks through the door is the day I walk out of it!' [319] Ultimately, the discussions came to nothing, and Ashdown quit the leadership, and front-line politics, early in 1999.

Ashdown was succeeded by Charles Kennedy who approached the 2001 election with a 'decapitation' strategy. This was not directed against the government but against the Conservatives, hoping to take the seats of the Tory high command, thus paving the way for the Liberal Democrats to become the principal opposition. This failed to happen either, but it ensured that the Third Party Key remained true for Labour.

Labour did not lose a single by-election during this term, so preserved Key one. Although there were battles over the elections of Rodri Morgan and Ken Livingston, and conflict between Blair and Brown, party discipline remained largely intact. Thus, Key two was still true. Blair's popularity remained high and his personal authority strong; salvaging the Incumbent Leadership Key three. Labour was cruising to an easy re-election in the spring of 2001, and almost everyone knew it. Still, there were a few more hiccups along the way. After all we don't want life to be boring, do we?

In the spring of 2001, rural Britain was hit by the return of a disease not seen since the late sixties; Foot & Mouth. After the first case in February, the disease spread rapidly through the nation's farms. Although unlike BSE, Foot & Mouth was not a deadly or terrible disease for farm animals, and could not be spread to humans, it was met with a similar response. Vaccination had been used abroad, but the Ministry of Agriculture and the farming communities were dead against it. The latter claimed that people would not want to eat the meat from vaccinated animals. So, a massive slaughter policy was put into effect. Day after day the news showed medieval funeral pyres of burning carcasses. Large areas of the countryside were made out of bounds and the London march of the Countryside Alliance was cancelled, for fear of spreading infection.

The election had been scheduled for early May, but after some equivocation, Blair postponed it by a month; he did not want it to be dubbed 'the dead cow election.' The army were called in to support the huge anti-Foot &

Mouth operation, which involved the slaughter of two million cows, sheep and pigs - many of them healthy. Fortunately for Labour, by the time the election campaign started in earnest in early May, the number of new cases had passed its peak and had begun falling rapidly.

The election campaign itself was conducted in the face of unprecedented public apathy. Some newspapers rightly pointed out that this was effectively a referendum on the government. This is of course always true, but its truth was made more obvious by the inevitability of its result, and by the lack of a credible opposition. It was not all plain sailing though. Blair found himself publicly harangued by a woman in Birmingham over the poor hospital treatment of her partner, and John Prescott found himself embroiled in a fracas in North Wales. He punched a man who egged him.

Ugly incidents made no real difference however, and Labour were well-served by the uselessness of the 'alternative.' The Tories pledged tax cuts, but found themselves on the defensive over their commitment to public services; a reversal of the way of things a decade earlier. Later in the campaign they adopted the slogan, 'Ten days to save the pound.' This backfired in at least three ways.

Firstly, the categorical nature of the mantra was undermined by the limited nature of the actual promise; Euro-membership was to be ruled out for the next term only.

Secondly, by making the election into a referendum on the single currency, the Tories risked being seen to lose the argument if Labour, or rather when Labour won.

Thirdly, it reinforced their image as the 'pub bores' on Europe.

The choice was between a successful and still united Labour party, and in the words of Andrew Rawnsley: 'A party seen as reactionary and irrelevant, with a leader seen as implausible and repellent.'[320]

With no negative keys and one bonus, Labour cruised to an inevitable second landslide victory.

June 2001 UK general election:

1) *By-election key*   true
2) *Unity Key*   true
3) *Incumbent Leadership Key*   true
4) *Opposition Charisma Key*   true
5) *Third Party Key*   true
6) *Cyclical Incumbency Key*   true
7) *Short-Term Economy Key*   true
8) *Long-Term Economy Key*   true
9) *Foreign Policy/Military Success Key* true
10) *Foreign Policy/Military Failure Key* true
11) *Policy Change Key*   true
12) *Civil Unrest Key*   true
13) *Scandal Key*   half-turn

Special Keys
4A *Opposition Implausibility Key*
    true

balance of negative keys: 0. 5

Overall balance: 0.5 positive Keys

campaign differential: Labour + 5 seats

forecast: Labour majority 160
(150, plus 10 for campaign differential)

Conservatives 165-170 seats Labour 410 seats

actual result: Labour majority of 167

Conservatives 166 seats Labour 412 seats Liberal Democrats 52

The result witnessed an unprecedented second Labour landside, with Tony Blair becoming the first Labour Prime Minister to face the prospect of a second full term of office. The Tories were smitten again. The only consolation they could draw was that they had not regressed into third place. The Liberal Democrats consolidated their 1997 sensation. However, the turnout at only fifty-nine percent was the lowest since 1918. The government of the day had been elected by the lowest share of the electorate since October 1974. It was a massive victory to be sure, but not really a vote of enthusiasm for Tony Blair or New Labour.

2001-2005:
'Let us re-order the world around us.' Tony Blair, Labour Conference 2001

Following their enormous election victory, the second biggest single party majority in modern times, Labour were masters of all they surveyed. Although there was no repeat of the euphoria that greeted their initial triumph, they were in some ways freer. Now, they had made significant inroads into the Tory orthodoxy of the past two decades. Now, it was the Tories who were on the back foot over spending plans, and now, not spending enough on public services was more worrying to people than rumours of tax rises. The Tories had been forced to accept the minimum wage and the Social Chapter.

Now, no longer bound to the Conservative spending plans, the Chancellor could really increase public spending. This he did. Public spending as a percentage of GDP rose from a measly 36.3% of GDP in 1999-2000 to 41.3% in 2005/06. The NHS saw the longest continuous funding increase in its history, with maximum wait times for operations, reduced from eighteen months to eighteen weeks.

Public satisfaction improved markedly as well. The government also set up Foundation hospitals and Academy schools, which were allowed considerable financial independence, though the former faced opposition from Brown.

Labour also enacted more constitutional reforms, passing a bill to replace the Law Lords with a Supreme Court and reforming the office of the Lord Chancellor. These received the Royal Ascent just before the 2005 general election. The idea behind this was to try and bring the UK nearer to Montesquieu's principle of the separation of powers; the system as used in the United States whereby the executive, legislative and judiciary are separate entities.

Originally, it was decided that the Lord Chancellor could not simultaneously be part of all three facets of government, and therefore should be abolished. However, it soon transpired that it would be very difficult to abolish the Lord Chancellor, since it would require numerous different acts of parliament to do so.

Thus, the title itself survived, but some of its functions were devolved to the Lord Chief Justice and others to the Speaker of the House of Lords. The Lord Chancellor's department was originally renamed the Department of Constitutional Affairs, and later the Ministry of Justice. The role could also now be held by MPs, and not only by Peers as had previously been the case.

However, it is foreign policy that the second Blair ministry is most remembered for. The relatively peaceful post-cold war decade, the 'long nineties' era came to an abrupt and shocking end on 11th September 2001.

The 911 attacks on the World Trade Centre and Pentagon shook the complacency of the previous decade and brought a new enemy into sharp focus. Tony Blair immediately rallied round President George W. Bush and pledged to support the Americans in everything they thought was necessary to defeat terror.

This is not a battle between the United States of America and terrorism, but between the free and democratic world and terrorism. We, therefore, here in Britain stand shoulder to shoulder with our American friends in this hour of tragedy, and we, like them, will not rest until this evil is driven from our world. [321]

Britain's first major role was supporting the American-led invasion of Afghanistan. Following the refusal of the Taliban to hand over Osama Bin Laden and his Al-Qaeda followers to the Americans, the allies attacked Afghanistan by air and special forces, spearheading the rebel Northern Alliance to strike southwards at the capital Kabul. Britain's role was second only to the United States, and Blair's role as global advocate and diplomat were second to none. During the build-up to war, Tony Blair visited many countries, in order to build a coalition of the willing.

The outcome of the initial phase of the conflict was a swift victory for the allies, as Taliban forces crumbled with city after city falling to the US-led forces during November 2001. The allies also destroyed the Tora Bora cave network, the main base of Al-Qaeda. This early success, with very few allied casualties would be followed however, by twenty years of counter insurgency against the Taliban, ending in ignominious failure.

Tony Blair seized the moment with a kind of messianic zeal. At the 2001 Labour Party conference at Brighton, he had this to say.

This is the moment to seize. The kaleidoscope has been shaken. The Pieces are in flux. Soon they will settle again. Before they do, let us re-order the world around us. [322]

This crisis brought into play the crusading, messianic dimension of Tony Blair that had been first seen during the Kosovo war two-and-half years previously. Here again he was fighting evil. But was his visionary rhetoric, the path to the realisation of dreams or nightmares?

At the start of 2002, President Bush gave a speech in which he spoke of an 'Axis of evil,' which consisted of a list of countries that he deemed dangerous and antagonistic to the United States and her way of life.

Among them was Iraq, and soon the drums of war were beating for intervention here as well.

However, the early phase of the 'War on Terror' was perceived as a major success for Britain. Blair was seen as a charismatic and decisive player in the fight against terrorism. Britain's involvement in, and advocacy of the War on Terror was sufficient to turn Foreign Policy/Military Success Key nine in the government's favour.

Bush formally made his case for the invasion of Iraq in his address to the UN Security Council in September 2002. The British government continued to back him to the hilt, despite reservations by the French and Germans. The UN Security council passed Resolution 1441 which authorised the return of weapons inspectors to Iraq, promising 'serious consequences' if they were to be obstructed by the regime. All the time, sections of the British media promoted the case for war, with scare stories of WMDs able to strike Britain within forty-five minutes.

The inspectors set to work, but in February 2003 the IAEA (International Atomic Energy Agency) 'found no evidence or plausible indication of a revival of a nuclear weapons programme in Iraq.'[323] A month later Hans Blix, leader the UN weapons inspectors said that no evidence of WMDs had been found.

Meanwhile, anti-war protests were building across the western world, with more than a million protesters marching against the war in London in February; the UK's biggest ever political demonstration at the time.

When America and Britain failed to persuade the UN Security Council to vote for a second resolution, explicitly authorising war, they decided to go it alone. President Bush gave Saddam Hussein a final ultimatum; to leave power or face invasion.

In the UK, International Development Secretary Claire Short threatened to resign from the government, branding Blair 'reckless' in a BBC radio interview. However, she was soon persuaded to stay by Mr Blair, only to resign a few months later; and consigned to political oblivion.

Labour won the vote in the House of Commons to authorise war, though with considerable Labour dissent. The support of the Conservatives under Ian Duncan Smith saved the government from defeat. Had the vote been lost then Tony Blair himself would have resigned along with many others. That is a counterfactual situation that we shall come to later on.

The only Labour cabinet minister to resign was Leader of the Commons Robin Cook, who made a passionate speech in condemnation of the government's decision.

Days later the allies attacked Iraq from the south. Within three weeks they had taken over Baghdad and statues of Saddam were toppling for the cameras. As with Operation Desert Storm, twelve years earlier, the allied casualties were light. On May 1st, President Bush proclaimed 'Mission Accomplished.' He spoke rather prematurely.

The successful initial stage of the invasion was soon followed by a growing nationalist insurgency. Even after the capture of Saddam Hussein in December 2003, the insurgency grew stronger, not weaker. Catastrophic mistakes were made by the American de facto viceroy Paul Bremer early on. In the immediate aftermath of the invasion, Bremer fired all members of Saddam's Bath party from administrative posts; effectively disbanding most of the Iraqi civil service.

Equally disastrous was the decision to disband the Iraqi army; effectively putting hundreds of thousands of armed men onto the streets with no jobs. It did not require a military genius to predict that this would help foster an armed insurgency.

The allies did not have the manpower or the organisational competency to impose law and order. Widespread looting followed the fall of the Bathist regime. Western troops stood by as mobs ransacked Iraq's national museum. There was no adequate control of the country's borders, allowing foreign fighters to pour in.

General Sir Mike Jackson believes that an invading army has 100 days to impose law & order and deliver basic supplies and establish basic governing competence for the civilian population, before any goodwill is irrevocably lost. Foreign Secretary Jack Straw described this as, 'A tragically lost opportunity.' [324]As the situation worsened, he said to a junior minister; 'I long for Iraq to go away. Every morning I get up and it is still there.' [325]

After August 2003 the United Nations were effectively bombed out of Iraq after their headquarters were repeatedly attacked by suicide bombers.

Almost as bad politically was the failure to find even one solitary weapon of mass destruction. This was less of an issue in the States, where the war was emotionally justified as revenge for 911. In the UK however it was a grievous blow to the government's casus belli. Matters escalated to fever pitch in July after the government came to loggerheads with the BBC. This resulted from a programme by the corporation arguing that the claim that Iraq's weapons of mass destruction could be deployable in forty-five minutes was included at Alistair Campbell's insistence, and was not backed up by credible evidence.

After Biological weapons expert, Dr David Kelly identified himself to his superiors as the documentary's source, his name was given to the press. Number ten deliberately released enough biographical information to the press that his identity became guessable. The MOD had a policy of confirming the name of the source to any journalist who could guess it. Kelly was hauled before a Commons select committee and interrogated. A few days later, Kelly was found dead in the woods near his home. The cause: apparent suicide. The BBC revealed that he had been the source for journalist Andrew Gilligan's report. Kelly's death was met by headlines such as 'Spun to death.' [326]

Certainly, the legal case for war was highly dubious. All twenty-seven lawyers at the Foreign Office thought it was illegal, as did top law lord, Lord Bingham.

The matter finally went before the auspices of the Hutton Committee, which ruled in the government's favour in January 2004, heavily criticising the BBC. It led to the resignation of the Director-General of the BBC Greg Dyke.

However, by now, the clear public perception had been created that the government had knowingly lied about the existence of WMDs in Iraq, in order to facilitate the American plans for invasion. The Hutton inquiry was widely dismissed as a 'whitewash' (as was the Butler inquiry later that same year.) According to polls, fifty-four percent of people agreed that the dossier had been 'sexed up' and fifty-five percent thought the Hutton inquiry was a whitewash. [327]

Protestors now commonly carried placards attacking 'Bliar.' The Press Secretary Alistair Campbell who was accused of spinning or 'sexing up' the 'dodgy dossier' became the only senior figure to resign over the affair. In spring 2005, sixty-three percent of people thought that the government were' dishonest and untrustworthy.'[328]

All the while the insurgency continued in Iraq, broadening into a Sunni-Shiite civil war, and the British death toll would finally reach 179.

Apart for a very brief period during the invasion phase of the war, the conflict only enjoyed the support of a minority of the British public. From early 2005 onwards, just over fifty percent of British adults thought that the war was wrong, compared with barely thirty percent who agreed with the decision to invade. [329] The appalling images of torture and abuse that surfaced from the infamous Abu Ghraib prison in spring 2004 destroyed what shreds of moral authority the west still had.

Blair's silence on Guantanamo and extraordinary rendition further darkened his own reputation. Thus, the Iraq war cost Labour the Foreign Policy/Military Failure Key ten, Party Unity key two, Incumbent Leadership Key three and Scandal Key thirteen. Labour won exactly two thirds of the by-elections they had to face this term, so narrowly salvaged Key One.

On the European front, Blair accepted the freedom of movement of people from the newly expanded EU in 2004. A large influx of migrant workers from Eastern Europe arrived to the UK. While this had very considerable benefits, it did stoke the growing unease and resentment towards both immigration and the EU that would eventually pave the way for Brexit.

In spring 2003, the Treasury organised a series of seminars for senior ministers, debunking the case for joining the Euro. This led to a serious spat between Blair and Brown. Blair turned on his chancellor saying, 'If you are not going to give me what I want, then you will have to consider your position.' Brown replied with, 'I'll do just that.' [330] This incident had the potential to derail Blair's administration, and effectively led to Blair's abandonment of his ambition to take Britain into the single currency.

One other area of European policy that made the headlines a year later was the ratification of the Lisbon treaty. Blair capitulated to Europhobe foes in the Tory party, the press and sections of his own party, by pledging to hold a referendum on it. He attempted to make it sound defiant and heroic with the rallying cry, 'Let the issue be put and let the battle be joined.'[331]

In one respect, the tenor of the government's tone was becoming very authoritarian following 911, with various acts of parliament allowing police and security forces more and more power. The 2001 Anti-Terrorism, crime & Security Act allowed MOD police to operate outside of their bases, and the indefinite detention of foreign suspects without trial. This was followed by the Criminal Justice Act 2003, which permitted the detention of UK citizens for fourteen days without charge. The 2005 Prevention of Terrorism Act established the 'control order,' a form of house arrest after the High Court ruled against the indefinite detention of foreigners at Belmarsh prison in London.

The socially liberal policies also continued to advance however. In 2004, the government abolished Section 28, which prohibited the promotion of homosexuality by local councils. It also introduced the Civil Partnerships Act 2004, which allowed same-sex couples to have their relationships legally recognised, and with comparable rights to a married heterosexual couple. They also legalised gay adoption, by removing the necessity that adopting parents had to be married.

Fox hunting was outlawed in 2004. Pro-hunting protesters battled police outside parliament and there were also protests during the term from Fathers 4 Justice, who dressed up as superheroes to campaign for better access to their children. (To no great effect.) Blair was also heckled at the 2004 party conference. These and the much greater anti-war protests during 2003 were ultimately insufficient to topple the Civil Unrest key.

Were the changes brought about by Labour enough to keep Policy Change Key eleven? I find this term as difficult to judge as the second Wilson term of the sixties. I would say not quite, but the increases in public spending, public sector reform, creation of tax credits, constitutional reform and anti-terror legislation in the wake of 911 were significant changes. The changes lead to a half-turn of the key. They still did a lot.

The economy remained strong during this term, although growth proved a little sluggish compared to the 1990s. Overall, long-term GDP was less than the average growth of the first Blair term, and final Major term. However, even more so than the election of 1959, the loss is a relative one. Growth was consistent throughout this term and there was never a recession, or even widespread fear or expectation of one during this period. Polling just before the 2005 election revealed that sixty-three percent of people though the economy would either stay the same or improve. [332] Unemployment, inflation and interest rates remained low, and house prices climbed higher.

Although the stock market remained mired in the doldrums during the first half of the term, it was recovering strongly during the second.

Furthermore, the economy had performed so well that the Chancellor Gordon Brown was able to boast of, 'The longest period of sustained growth since records began in 1701.'[333]

Therefore, key eight remained true for the government in 2005.

At the time of the 2005 election, there was no sign of any recession or economic meltdown, and so Short-Term Economy Key seven was also true for Labour.

As with their first term, the Labour government was blessed with an ineffectual opposition. Following the 2001 election, the Tories plumped for Ian Duncan Smith as leader. His two far more charismatic rivals, Ken Clarke, the former Chancellor and Michael Portillo, the former Defence Secretary were cast aside in favour of the earnest but rather wooden Duncan-Smith. He was widely seen as one of the least effective main party leaders in modern times. The final straw for Duncan-Smith came during the 2003 party conference when he delivered the line, 'The quiet man is turning up the volume.' He managed to get the delivery so badly wrong that it simply drew fresh mockery and ridicule. Within weeks a no-confidence vote was held and he was defeated.

Duncan Smith, or IDS as he was often known, was succeeded by the former hard line Home Secretary Michael Howard. Howard's ascension to the leadership was unopposed, being effectively a coronation.

Howard had formidable experience, and certainly managed to instil greater discipline into the Tory party, but he was no leader. Unpopular with the liberal-left for his authoritarian leanings, and being labelled by Anne Widdecombe as 'having something of the night about his character,' [334]Howard failed to connect with the public, and therefore Opposition Implausibility Bonus Key 4A was still the albatross around the Tory neck.

IDS had achieved something else as well. By enabling the government's victory in the Iraq war vote, Duncan-Smith had therefore thrown away the possibility of gaining any votes resulting from the war's unpopularity. Michael Howard kept that second albatross dead and heavy round his neck by re-affirming his support during the 2005 general election campaign. His accusations that the Blair government had lied about intelligence were consequently blunted. Thus, a unique key: Opposition Complicity Bonus Key 4B, was minted for this occasion!

In addition to the policy division provoked by the decision to go to war in Iraq, there was growing conflict between Blair and Brown. The latter was becoming increasingly resentful over Blair's refusal to make way for him. Apparently, Blair had agreed to step aside for Brown in late 2003, before announcing a year later that he would fight the forthcoming election, but not the one after that. Brown raged, 'There is nothing that you could ever say to me now that I could ever believe!' [335] This further contributed to the loss of Party Unity key two.

Blair's announcement that the 2005 election would be his last as Prime Minister was the typically New Labourish tactical wheeze that backfired in the long-run. In the words of the former Cabinet Secretary Sir Andrew Turnbull; 'If you announce you are going to devalue the currency in three and a half years, the devaluation happens now.' [336]

This foolish decision further contributed to the loss of Incumbent Leadership key three.

Scandal key thirteen was further trashed by 'Cheriegate' in which the Prime Minister's wife had involved a convicted conman in arranging the sale of a flat. Another scandal involved the Home Secretary David Blunkett. The congenitally blind, no-nonsense minister had had an affair with Kimberly Fortier, the publisher of the Tory Spectator and wife of the managing director of Vogue magazine.

He fathered a child with her and was caught up in a battle to prove his paternity. (It makes a change for a politician to be the one trying to prove a baby is his.) The scandal deepened when it transpired that Blunkett had accelerated the Visa application for a nanny and spent public money on his lover's travel arrangements.

He foolishly demanded an inquiry to clear his name. The investigation rather inconsiderately proved the allegations were true, providing the smoking gun which fired him from the cabinet. He shot himself in the other foot by dissing many members of the cabinet in a biography - just when he most needed their help. Blunkett became the first Home Secretary to be brought down by scandal for thirty years.

Brown was replaced as Campaign Manager in the 2005 election by Allan Milburn, before being re-instated as joint manager. This re-instatement was known as the 'ice cream pact' after Blair and Brown were seen eating ice cream together on the campaign trail.

The campaign of 2005 saw Labour more effective and organised than the Tories both locally and nationally. Although Blair was a tarnished figure, he was considerably more charismatic than Michael Howard, and the Tories failed to project the appearance of either a Prime Minister-in-waiting, or even a credible team.

The topic of the war flared up strongly after extracts from Attorney General Goldsmith's legal advice were published by the Mail on Sunday. Blair, Brown and Howard all re-affirmed their support for it. Blair saying on live TV that, 'I'm not going to stand here and beg for my own character. People can make up their minds whether they trust me or not.'[337]

The Liberal Democrats failed to capitalise on the anti-war sentiment to the extent that they might perhaps have done. Their leader Charles Kennedy was generally well-liked, but was perhaps too laid-back to be the galvanising voice for protest. The anti-war vote consequently was fragmented, splitting between the Liberals, the Greens, the nationalists and George Galloway's Respect party. Therefore, Third Party key five remained in the government's favour. Overall, the campaign differential favoured Labour by a nominal 2.5 seats, or enlarged their majority by five.

May 2005 UK general election:

1) *By-election key* — true
2) *Unity Key* — false
3) *Incumbent Leadership Key* — false
4) *Opposition Charisma Key* — true
5) *Third Party Key* — true
6) *Cyclical Incumbency Key* — true
7) *Short-Term Economy Key* — true
8) *Long-Term Economy Key* — true
9) *Foreign Policy/Military Success Key* — true
10) *Foreign Policy/Military Failure Key* — false
11) *Policy Change Key* — half-turn
12) *Civil Unrest Key* — true
13) *Scandal Key* — false

Special Keys
4A Opposition Implausibility Key
4B Opposition Complicity Key

balance of negative keys: 2½.

campaign differential: Labour + 2.5 seats

forecast: Labour majority 65

tally: Conservatives 200-220 seats   Labour 354 seats

actual result: Labour majority of 66

Conservatives 198 seats Labour 355 seats Liberal Democrats 62

The 2005 election was a historic and unprecedented hat trick win for Tony Blair. No Labour party leader had one three majorities in a row, nor had one secured even two workable majorities at all, let alone three. It was a modest improvement for the Tories and the best result for the Liberals for eighty years. However, Labour had now been re-elected by the lowest share of the electorate of any British government. Despite the controversies of the term, turnout was only a whisker above that of 2001.

More people had voted for Neil Kinnock in 1987 and for John Major in 1997 than had voted for Blair in 2005. The previous election had seen northern working-class voters turn to apathy. This time, more southern middle-class voters had deserted Labour over the war. They had lost four million votes and yet still won handsomely.

An uglier side of the election had been the comparative success of BNP candidates in a number of Labour districts. It was no longer bold, confident morning for New Labour.

2005-2010:
'I began hoping to please all of the people all of the time and ended wondering if I was pleasing any of the people any of the time.' Tony Blair Speech to

Communication and Liberation conference, Rimini, Italy, 27/08/09

Following re-election in May 2005, British politics had entered a curious period of limbo. Blair had announced that he would not stand for a third term, and with Brown snapping at his heels, his exit would be sooner rather than later. Although Blair's personal ratings had declined, he still managed to pull off a bit more of the old Blair magic.

July 2005 was one of the most extraordinary months in recent times. In the first week, the G8 summit at Gleneagles in Scotland had been an especially high-profile occasion. Activists under the banner 'Make poverty history' had pressured governments to do more to combat Third World poverty. Bob Geldof was holding a major charity concert at Wembley Stadium exactly twenty years after Live Aid rocked the world for the Ethiopian famine. This time it was not simply to raise money for a specific disaster, but to pressure the leaders of the G8 to do something to help the world's poor. The three main areas were debt relief for third world countries, fair trade and better aid.

That same week, Tony Blair had used his charm to secure Britain's role in hosting the 2012 Olympics. A day after this, Al-Qaeda terrorists attacked London in the form of four co-ordinated suicide bombings, killing fifty-six people, including the four terrorists. The effect of this atrocity was for terrorism and counter-terrorism to dominate the news headlines for the best part of a month.

The G8 summit made some achievements, but these were much less than had been hoped for. However, the shift in focus to terrorism meant that the politicians could not be adequately held to account and the moment was lost.

In retrospect the summit yielded paltry returns. Much of the aid money announced consisted of money that had already been pledged, but was presented as being new. (A tactic sometimes used by Gordon Brown when Chancellor.) The debt relief was often conditional on countries allowing western firms to run their infrastructure. There was also backsliding on even the amounts of aid that were pledged. All in all, these events were not sufficient to turn any keys.

The situation in Iraq remained a difficult one with a continued anti-western insurgency. The American 'surge' strategy of 2007, increased force levels and fought more of an offensive rather than a defensive war, did turn the tide by the latter part of the year: western casualty figures dropped sharply. However, the British forces in the south had been progressively cut and British troops largely retreated to the airport base at Basra - effectively abandoning the south to the militias.

When asked how the decision to invade Iraq fitted in with the major policy decisions since 1945, the BBC foreign affairs correspondent John Simpson replied that; 'I'm afraid it fits in with some of the worst... Britain's reputation has suffered simply because it is obvious we played no serious part in the planning and organisation, and the whole idea of a follow-through.' [338] The occupation of Iraq remained highly unpopular with the British public, keeping Key number ten turned against the Labour government. Tony Blair however, continued and still continues to refuse to apologise for the decision to go to war itself. In the words of Andrew Rawnsley, Blair was, 'good at apologising for things that were not his fault, and about which he could do nothing, such as the Trans-Atlantic slave-trade and the Irish potato famine. His stubborn streak rarely allowed him to admit his own mistakes.' [339]

In Afghanistan, British troops replaced Americans in the Helmund province. Here, they encountered fierce resistance from the Taliban, and a period of intense fighting and higher British casualties ensued.

During late 2005 and 2006, The Blair government needed to be rescued by the Conservatives on a vote for the renewal of Trident. In 2006 the government lost a vote on extending the maximum detention of terror suspects to ninety days. (They had to make do with twenty-eight.) The Terrorism Act 2006 also criminalised the 'glorification' of terrorism. Later that year an act was passed allowing the government to seize the assets of suspected terrorists.

Government fortunes were to hit a new low in May 2006, with the resignation of Home Secretary Charles Clarke, over the release of more than a thousand foreign prisoners without consideration for deportation.

Party tensions reached a crisis point in September 2006, when a Labour rebellion was triggered by opposition to Blair's support for Israel during the Lebanon war that summer. Seventeen Labour MPS signed a letter calling for Blair to resign and seven of them resigned as Parliamentary Private Secretaries. Blair announced that the upcoming party conference would be his last, thus avoiding imminent political defenestration.

It was not only Brown and the Labour rebels who were posing a threat to Blair's premiership. At the end of 2005, the Tories elected a new leader following their third consecutive electoral drubbing. They chose the young and telegenic David Cameron, who had only been an MP since 2001. Cameron immediately seized the initiative and gave Blair a run for his money in the

Commons. In December 2005 he taunted Blair, with the quip, 'He was the future once.' [340]

Almost immediately, the Tories drew level with Labour in the polls and within a few months had established a small lead. Apart from a brief blip after the Fuel Crisis of 2000, the Tories had been consistently behind Labour since the aftermath of Black Wednesday in the autumn of 1992. Cameron was sometimes dubbed 'Tory Blair' and with good reason. He was youngish, a good public speaker and with a full head of hair. His approach was to repackage the Conservative party as socially liberal, environmentally conscious and modern. Critics argued that much of this was phoney. A good example was of him cycling to work, whilst a chauffeur drove his car with all of his stuff in it, some minutes behind him. [341]

The final months of Blair's premiership were to be dogged once more by scandal. In 2006, his deputy John Prescott, was exposed as having an affair with a member of staff, and of using Whitehall rooms for that purpose. A series of hugely embarrassing newspaper articles reduced Prescott to a laughing stock, but he did not resign. He was allowed to carry on until Blair went.

Impropriety of a more financial kind was the subject of the Cash for Honours scandal during 2006-07. Because of a regulatory loophole, loans made to the Labour Party did not have to be declared. When several nominations for peerages were turned down by the House of Lords Appointments Commission, suspicions were aroused that the loans were part of a quid pro quo arrangement. A major police investigation was launched and involved the Labour Chief Fundraiser Lord Levy, (dubbed Lord Cash point by the press,) being arrested and interrogated by police.

The Prime Minister was also interviewed by the police. It was the first time that a serving Prime Minister had been questioned as part of a police investigation. (It would not be the last.) Ultimately, the case was dropped for lack of definitive evidence that such a quid pro quo arrangement had been made in advance. However, Levy had to step down from his role in 2007 and the party would be seriously struggling for campaign funds at the next election. Blair drove the New Labour Chevy to Lord Levy, but the levy was dry. At the end of Blair's tenure, the Scandal Key was already turned against the government. Turning it back would be a tall order.

One positive development during Blair's final days in office occurred in Northern Ireland. Although the Good Friday Agreement in 1998 had halted most of the political violence, serious divisions continued to plague the province, with the Northern Ireland Assembly being suspended for five years between 2002 and 2007; with direct rule being re-instated from Westminster. This was due to arguments over weapons decommissioning.

Following the decommissioning of IRA weapons during 2005 and the St Andrews Agreement of 2006, which was endorsed the following year in the elections, the Democratic Unionist Party and Sin Fein formed a government in May 2007. Old foes Ian Paisley and Martin McGuinness became First Minister and Deputy First Minister respectively. The British army ended Operation Banner, which had been deployed to control the streets since 1969. This remarkable achievement; the definitive end of the Northern Ireland Troubles, secured Foreign Policy/Military Success key nine for the Labour Government.

Tony Blair served as Prime Minister for just over ten years, the longest modern tenure after Margaret Thatcher. The Blairite settlement fused Thatcherite free-market and anti-union reforms with the social democratic ideals of the Labour party. It also combined social liberalism with increasing authoritarianism against crime and terrorism.

Internationally, it tried to be pro-American and Pro-European; although the former came at a terrible cost, and the latter was not fully realised. Overall, the much-mocked 'Third Way' philosophy was not too far off the mark. The politicisation of the civil service and obsessive focus on spin and government by media, were unfortunate aspects of this period. Looking back from the troubled vantage point of 2023, New Labour still did much to be admired.

Gordon Brown became Prime Minister on June 27th 2007 in a wholly uncontested coronation. Having served as Chancellor of the Exchequer for ten long years, he seemed to have ample experience for taking on the top job. Standing outside 10 Downing Street, he invoked his boy scout pledge to, 'do my utmost.'[342] Brown initially enjoyed an unexpected honeymoon of public support. Although the new Prime Minister was not charismatic and was often described as being dour, his poll ratings soared to a net positive of twenty points[343].

A combination of positive publicity and the nagging insecurity about political legitimacy, due to taking the top job unopposed, led Brown and his inner circle to seriously consider an autumn election. Expectation became stronger and stronger until reaching the point when Brown wobbled. The Tories enjoyed a slight post-conference bounce and Brown bottled out of the early election. He appeared on TV on Saturday 6th October to rule out an early election on the grounds that he wanted more time to set out his vision for change. This did not seem convincing to most people and the day became dubbed 'chicken Saturday.' From this moment on,

Brown's poll ratings collapsed and he became a target of near-universal mockery.

What had happened here was that Brown had temporarily secured the Incumbent Leadership Key during his honeymoon period, and then abruptly squandered it by allowing expectations of a snap election to build up before abruptly dropping the idea with a disingenuous and unconvincing justification. This situation of temporary popularity as a result of novelty in the post was to occur a decade later with Theresa May. In that later instance, the situation was reversed, with the decision to call the election and the way it was conducted being the cause of the lost key. We shall examine what would have happened if Brown had gone for that early election in the counterfactuals.

Gordon Brown was hit by a deluge of embarrassments over the ensuing two months. The next disaster to strike was the loss of data discs containing the personal information of millions of people. The mishap was almost certainly not Brown's fault, but it furthered the impression of a terminally accident-prone administration.

In November, suspicions were raised about businessman David Abrahams, who was donating money to the Labour party via proxies - against party rules. The donations were linked to a rather controversial planning application for a business park. Although, like the previous cash for honours scandal, no Labour Minister was convicted, this affair snuffed out any hopes that the party could move on from sleaze any time soon.

Gordon Brown had suffered such a colossal reversal of political fortunes in the course of one autumn that Vince Cable roasted him in the Commons with the line:

'The House has noticed the remarkable transformation in the last few weeks: from Stalin to Mr Bean!' [344]

A worrying straw in the economic wind was the collapse of Northern Rock bank in September 2007. This prompted the first run on a British bank in a century and a half. The bank was nationalised by the government, but this episode was a warning that the Prime Minister would soon find his words about 'the end of boom and bust' coming back to haunt him.

With Brown's popularity dented, the Blair-Brown factional fighting in the Labour party began to resume. Brown himself became increasingly stressed and difficult to work with. He was finding it incredibly difficult to make decisions. He also suffered from a difficulty in trusting colleagues, and thus an inability to delegate. These two problems intersected disastrously. Cabinet minister Tessa Jowell said that 'He (Brown) chaired the cabinet but he didn't lead the cabinet. That was the big difference with Tony.' [345]

Brown was also notoriously bad-tempered, becoming obsessed with micro-managing everything himself. A civil servant who applied for a job in the cabinet was asked in the interview if he could tolerate 'extreme verbal abuse and violence done to objects.' He decided to decline the position. [346] Another unnamed civil servant said that 'Gordon's mood was absolutely black the whole time. He was in a permanent state of rage.' [347]

When advisor Stephen Wood attempted to brief Brown on which delegates he should speak to at a meeting of the European Council, Brown exploded; shouting 'Why have I got to meet these fucking people? Why are you making me meet these fucking people? I don't want to meet these fucking people!' He then rudely shoved the advisor aside as he went in. [348] His behaviour was so bad that he received an unprecedented reprimand from Cabinet Secretary Gus O'Donnell. Never a frown with Gordon Brown.

Gordon Brown disappointed supporters, mainly as a result of them projected their false expectations onto him. For years, people had seen Brown as more left-wing than Blair, as well as more substantial and less-focussed on spin. The truth was that he was neither. It is true though that Brown cultivated the image that he was nearer to real socialism. It was noted that during some of his conference speeches towards the end of the Blair era, that he avoided using the phrase 'New Labour' - opting to miss out the novel adjective: as if to say 'I will give you real Labour.'

Brown suffered more odium after abolishing the 10p starting rate of income tax in his final budget as Chancellor. There was a delayed reaction, but saw many Labour supporters angry that Brown was making the poor pay more, and in a time of recession. New Chancellor Alistair Darling eventually increased the threshold for the starting rate, and correspondingly lowered the threshold for the top rate in an act of recompense. Yet Brown's socialist credentials were tarnished.

The disillusionment felt by Labour supporters towards Brown was aptly summed up by the Guardian columnist Polly Toynbee.

The emperor has no clothes, the box of secrets is empty. In one iconic error Brown has blown away his most admirable reputation; a ten-year record of directing money to the poorest. This does inestimable harm. [349]

In May 2008 Labour suffered a painful blow with the loss of the Crewe & Nantwich by-election to the Tories. This was a brutal turnaround in the party's fortunes. For years, Labour had been doing well in by-elections, only losing to the Liberals in the post-Iraq era. The loss of Crewe & Nantwich was the first Labour by-election loss to the Conservatives for thirty years. Labour MPs and activists now started to express the view that Brown's position was irretrievable. With this and other by-election defeats, Key one turned against the Labour government.

Just as Brown had reached such a low ebb that people were despairing as to whether he was capable of tying his own shoelaces, something happened that at last allowed him to play to his strengths. The stock markets had been falling for a year, when the situation reached a crisis point with the downfall of Lehman Brothers in September 2008. This started a domino collapse of the American banking sector that had to be stopped by massive intervention. This included bail-out packages for the US mortgage lenders Fannie Mae and Freddie Mac. The crisis soon spread to Britain. HBOS lost a third of its share value in twenty-four hours. The government brokered a private sector takeover of HBOS by Lloyd's Bank.

However, the contagion soon spread to other banks. By the end of September 2008, the problem facing the financial sector was now two-fold. A liquidity crisis had been combined with a deadly lack of capital. The only source of emergency capital was the state. Chancellor Alistair Darling began planning a major recapitalisation plan to be financed by the sale of government bonds. The markets continued to plunge drastically during early October, and on the 8th, the Bank Rescue Package was announced.

The government was to spend £137 billion pounds by buying shares in the failing banks. The Treasury would eventually aim to recoup its losses through dividends, and eventually by selling the shares. (At the time of writing, the government loss is still £33 billion.)

This policy was coupled with the Credit Guarantee Scheme, which saw the Treasury underwrite debt, with the hope of encouraging greater bank lending to customers. This followed the Special Liquidity Scheme which had been announced the previous spring. This allowed banks to swap mortgage-back securities and others for UK Treasury bills. Thus, UK Treasury securities became collateral at a time when lending, even between banks had frozen up.

The government also had to nationalise Bradford & Bingley and buy £20 billion worth of shares in the failing Royal Bank of Scotland. A year later they bought another £25 billion, resulting in the government holding over eighty percent of the bank's shares.

The Bank of England set interest rates at their lowest level in history, and early in 2009 began the policy of Quantitative Easing; whereby the banks buy government bonds in order to raise their value and lower the yield. This is effectively the electronic printing of money.

All these measures prevented the complete meltdown of the UK banking system - and therefore of the entire economy. Chancellor Alistair Darling said later in an interview that had the government not intervened the way it did, the Royal Bank of Scotland would have simply shut its doors and cash points, leading to 'complete panic.' He added 'There was a grave risk of going from an economic crisis to a political crisis, where you have a breakdown of law and order. We were that close to the brink.' [350] Brown's handling of the Global Financial Crisis won him plaudits from around the world. The American Nobel Prize-winning economist Paul Krugman praised Brown claiming that, 'Mr Brown and Alistair Darling, the Chancellor of the Exchequer have defined the character of the worldwide rescue effort, with other wealthy nations playing catch-up,... And they may have shown us the way through this crisis.' [351]

Brown's rescue package was certainly emulated by the USA and much of Europe. Suddenly, Gordon Brown had been given a chance to demonstrate his competence. This, together with earlier progress in Northern Ireland won Labour Foreign Policy/Military Success Key nine.

Brown also moved to shore up his threatened position by bringing back Peter Mandelson into the cabinet. Mandelson, who had recently served as an EU commissioner was made a peer and appointed Business Secretary in October 2008. The following year he was also bestowed with the grand titles of First Secretary of State and Lord President of the Council. Although Brown and Mandelson had been bitter enemies since the 1994 leadership election, they had managed to patch up their differences sufficiently to join forces to steady the listing Labour ship.

On the overseas front, Britain's involvement in the war in Iraq finally came to an ignominious close in 2009, when all British troops were withdrawn from the troubled land; apart from the 179 who had been lost there. The Afghan war was by now the most problematic with higher casualties than had been experienced in Iraq. The TV coverage of military coffins arriving at Royal-Wooton Basset was a continual reminder of the unresolved conflict.

In the autumn of 2009 Brown faced further embarrassment when The Sun featured Jacqui Janes, a mother who had lost her son in the conflict, feeling angry and insulted by the untidiness of the handwritten letter that she had received from the Prime Minister. She described it as 'a disgraceful, hastily scrawled insult.' [352] Although many people realised this might be due to Brown's poor eyesight (He had lost one eye, and damaged another during a rugby match as a teenager.) the continuing losses, (457 killed by the end) which were getting harder and harder to justify to the general public, cost Labour Foreign Policy/Military Failure Key ten.

Although the bank rescue plan saved the economy from implosion, it did not prevent a lengthy recession. The UK economy contracted by more than six percent between 2008 and 2009, roughly equal to the 1979-81 recession. Unemployment rose less steeply than in that slump, or the early nineties downturn, reaching almost 2.7 million, or 8.4 % in 2011. [353]

Many companies had learnt from past experience that if you lose skilled worker, you will not get them back. Therefore, many older more experienced workers were kept on, but the young were hit hardest by unemployment.

The economy took five years to recover from the recession in GDP terms and many economists speak of a lost decade of growth following the crash. Wages in 2023 are still below the pre-crash level in real terms. House prices fell by sixteen percent compared with twenty-one percent in the early nineties crash, but have still yet to recover the 2008 value. All this decline and slow recovery easily cost Labour both economic keys for the 2010 election.

As the term wore on, any hope that the government's fortunes could be salvaged by the bank rescue were soon dashed, along with any hope that Labour would be able to shake off the miasma of sleaze that had hung over it for so long. In 2008 Peter Hain was forced to resign as

Work & Pensions and Welsh Secretary after a late declaration of £100,000 of donations for his failed Deputy Leadership campaign. More was to come. In 2009, two Labour Lords were the first to be suspended since the seventeenth century, after an undercover journalist recorded them offering to change legislation for donations.[354]

Then in April 2009, the government advisor Damian McBride was forced to resign after emails discussing a smear campaign against leading Conservatives was leaked to a political blogger and made public. The plan was to circulate false and obscene claims about David Cameron, George Osborne and Nadine Dorries. [355]

This unfortunate episode highlighted how Brown was as equally preoccupied with spin as his predecessor, but just not very good at it.

An unnamed civil servant said of Brown: That's all he cared about - doing a clip for TV every two hours. I'd always bought the line that Gordon was the great strategist, the thinker, and Tony was the one obsessed with the media. The scales fell from my eyes. With Gordon, it was all about the headlines.[356]

The reliance on spin was one of the most destructive and counter-productive aspects of New Labour. As this book hopefully shows, elections are won and lost on the basis of government performance, not on marketing and spin. Alistair Campbell's endless battles to control the news agenda were a self-defeating waste of energy. It was basically a modus operandi suited to a totalitarian state. It could only work if governmental control of the media was complete and absolute.

There was very little Campbell & co could do to silence Labour's critics in the popular press. They were powerless to stop the endless leaking to the media from government departments. They were unable to stop backbench rebellions. They could not stifle all the media mocking birds, such as *Bremner, Bird & Fortune*, John Culshaw, *Have I Got News for You* and *the News Quiz*; and thank heavens for that.

In fact, the reputation Labour gained from their spin and propagandising, undermined the credibility of the very real achievements that they had accomplished. Every bit of positive news was soon dismissed as yet more spin and hot air. As this book demonstrates, the path to winning the keys to Downing Street is that of good governance.

The Worst was to come in May. The Daily Telegraph began publishing in instalments, details of how MPs from different parties had abused their expenses allowance and had claimed outrageously from the public purse. Typical cases included claiming on second homes, renovating second homes, renting them out, over-claiming on Council Tax, and various luxuries. Especially egregious examples included the Conservative MPs Peter Viggers who claimed £1400 for a 'floating duck island,' and Douglas Hogg who claimed for the cleaning out of his moat.

The consequences of this were especially corrosive given that it was being revealed during a recession. Both main parties were hit hard, but the general feeling was that David Cameron handled the affair better than Gordon Brown. There were resignations aplenty, with numerous MPs deciding to stand down at the next election. Probably the most high- profile casualty was the Speaker of the House of Commons Michael Martin. He was ousted for approving the allowances system in the first place, and for attacking MPs who supported the Daily Telegraph's decision to leak. He appeared to be more concerned about the leak itself than the corruption it exposed. He was the first Speaker to resign for more than three hundred years.

The cabinet also saw the resignation of Home Secretary Jacqui Smith, the Secretary of State for Communities and Local Government Hazel Blears, and the Exchequer Secretary to the Treasury, who was caught out avoiding Capital Gains Tax. The Conservative Shadow Cabinet lost Alan Duncan. Six MPs, (all Labour) and two Tory Peers were prosecuted for fraud and false accounting. All but one of them were sent to prison.

Although the scandal damaged the standing of both main parties (less so the Liberal Democrats) it had happened after twelve years of majority Labour government - the first eight of them with a landslide majority. It had been Labour who had control over the system and the rules, and it had been Labour who had been elected at least in part on an anti-sleaze ticket.

A Populous survey found that over sixty percent of people thought that Gordon Brown was the leader most damaged by the scandal, compared with just five percent who thought it was Cameron. Even before the scandal broke, just nineteen percent of respondents believed that MPs worked for them. [357] The effect of all of this was to turn the Scandal Key against the government.

Gordon Brown tried to counter the wave of negativity against his government and against politicians in general, by appearing in a video, on the then still-novel YouTube platform. Unfortunately, all it proved was that he was not much of a Youtuber. His intermittent, inappropriate forced smiling and swaying from side to side, turned the video into an international comic hit. [358]He was mocked by the Communities and Local Government Secretary Hazel Blears, who said 'YouTube if you want to,' in a newspaper article. [359]Alas, underlining the fact that he lacked his predecessor's easy charm and charisma. Incumbent Leadership key three was firmly against the Labour government.

From Summer 2008 onwards, Labour suffered from episodic rumblings about the leadership. In September 2008, the Junior Whip Siobhain McDonagh was sacked after openly expressing doubts about Brown's leadership of the party. She was supported by a string of other MPs, mostly ex-ministers. The rebellion was effectively soon buried by the financial crisis, which putting Brown in a better light, shored up his position.

The following summer the Foreign Secretary, David Miliband wrote an article in the Guardian, setting out Labour's future. However, the article entirely ignored Gordon Brown. That summer also saw the resignation of the Work & Pensions Secretary James Purnell, who openly called for Brown to step down as Prime Minister. The final attempt at regicide came in January 2010, when ex-ministers Patricia Hewitt and Geoff Hoon publicly called for a leadership ballot, but to little effect. The impact of all this however, was to ensure that Party Unity Key two remained false for the Brown administration.

One key that was not so easily called was Policy Change key eleven. The Bank Rescue Package, and the raising of the top rate of income tax to fifty percent, are certainly a change in direction, and fly in the face of the orthodoxy developed over the previous thirty years.

However, these policies are remedial and fire-fighting measures. They are not driven by any change in ideology, rather than by a desperate need to avoid disaster. The changes were also intended to be temporary ones, and to a large extent were. Most of the shares bought in the banks have since been sold off. Though Quantitative Easing continued until 2020, and was only reversed in 2022 with Quantitative Tightening.

Does it meet the threshold needed to turn key eleven in the government's favour? I think it merits a Half-Turn.

Although the term had seen an economic crisis and an unpopular government, there had been no widespread civil unrest; hence key twelve was to stay true for the Labour government.

The regeneration of the Tories under the politically effective, though ultimately vacuous David Cameron, robbed Labour of the Opposition Implausibility Bonus Key 4A. The UK withdrawal from Iraq and winding down of the conflict following the American 'Surge,' also robbed them of the Opposition Complicity Key 4B. Yet Cameron was not really charismatic, falling some way short of the Blair standard that he had been modelling himself upon. Thus, Opposition Charisma Key four remained in the government's favour.

One consequence of the 'election that never was' in the autumn of 2007, was the changing of guard in the Liberal Democrats. The leader at the time was Sir Menzies Campbell, who was unkindly and rather unfairly portrayed by the media as a silly old duffer who ought to retire to a care home. This resulted in his party languishing in the teens in opinion polls.

After the near-death experience of the election scare, Campbell was brow-beaten into resigning, and was replaced by Nick Clegg; a youngish man in the Blair-Cameron mould. Clegg steered the party a little to the right economically, abandoning their commitment to raise the top rate of income tax, just as it was about to go up anyway under Labour. Clegg was not initially especially popular or unpopular. Then during the campaign something strange happened.

During the election campaign of 2010, all three-party leaders had agreed to do a TV debate for the first time. The idea had been mooted occasionally for the past thirty years, but had never got very far. Now it was happening. The effect of the debate when it happened, was to make an overnight, but very fleeting star of the Liberal leader. Suddenly people began describing him as charismatic and the Liberal poll numbers began to surge. This strange phenomenon was dubbed 'Cleggmania,' and nothing quite like it had been seen before, or since.

This threatened to topple Third Party key five. As the final days of the campaign drew towards a close, the Liberals and Labour were roughly neck and neck with the Tories leading by about seven or eight points.

Would I have called the Third Party Key if I had been using this forecasting model back then? Well, for a change in third party support to be significant, it has to average at least five percentage points. The increase in Liberal support in the final week's polling was about five points- just enough. However, I would have to also take into account the rather unusual set of circumstances surrounding this development.

Normally, a sharp increase in third party support is reflective of growing discontent in the country. This is generally bad news for the party in power. However, this time it was resulting directly from the novel situation of a TV debate between the three main party leaders, which gave unprecedented equal exposure to Nick Clegg; a political figure whom most people had barely heard of. Therefore, the rise in third party support was not necessarily indicative of widespread discontent in the country.

Secondly, the rise in Liberal support seemed to be at the expense of both main parties. In the last ten polls before the election, the Labour vote share dropped by three points compared to the last ten polls pre-debate.

(The poll immediately before the debates saw the start of the Lib Dem surge, so I discounted it.) The Tories dropped 1.8%, the Lib Dems gained by 6.3% and the minor parties dropped by 1.5 %. [360] It was therefore only having a slight differential impact against Labour, and so, would likely give a small advantage to the Conservatives in the headline vote battle with Labour.

However, in terms of seats won directly by the Liberal Democrats, a generally rising Liberal tide of yellow would cost more Conservative seats as there were many more Con-Lib marginals than Lab-Lib marginals at that time. Overall, the impact of the 'Clegg-Mania' surge would probably make little to no difference regarding the number of Labour or Conservative seats. Ergo, it would not turn Third Party key five.

As Labour had been in power for only thirteen years, this would not be long enough to topple Cyclical Incumbency Key Six.

The campaign itself was not particularly inspiring with both main parties shooting themselves in the foot in different ways. The Tories were somewhat hobbled by Cameron's vacuous, 'Big Society' slogan, as canvassers could not sell it on the doorsteps; as they did not understand what, if anything it meant.

Gordon Brown seriously embarrassed himself with comments made while a live microphone was still attached to his lapel. He insulted an elderly woman he had been talking to in Cheshire, by referring to her as, 'some bigoted woman,' over her concerns about mass immigration.

He went back and apologised but the damage was done. He had insulted a large tranche of Labour supporters like her.

Since Brown was universally rated as having come last in all three debates it is safe to safe that there was still a small differential advantage to the Conservatives despite their rather lacklustre campaign.[361] Therefore

Labour lose three seats as a result of it. The only other notable event of the campaign was Nigel Farage's brush with death, after a light plane he had been hiring for the campaign crashed with him in it.

May 2010 UK general election:

1) *By-election key* — false
2) *Unity Key* — false
3) *Incumbent Leadership Key* — false
4) *Opposition Charisma Key* — true
5) *Third Party Key* — true
6) *Cyclical Incumbency Key* — true
7) *Short-Term Economy Key* — false
8) *Long-Term Economy Key* — false
9) *Foreign Policy/Military Success Key* — true
10) *Foreign Policy/Military Failure Key* — false
11) *Policy Change Key* — half-turn
12) *Civil Unrest Key* — true
13) *Scandal Key* — false

balance of negative keys: 7½

campaign differential: Labour minus 2-3 seats

forecast: hung parliament

Conservatives as the largest party

tally: Conservatives 300-320 Labour 260

Labour 255 seats Conservatives 300-320 seats

actual result: hung parliament

Conservatives 306 seats Labour 258 seats Liberal Democrats 57

The election of 2010 brought Labour's run of big wins to an abrupt end. It also led to Britain's first hung parliament since 1974. In the end, 'Clegg-mania' had not materialised in the results: The Liberals actually lost a few seats, with an only marginally higher vote share. In the immediate aftermath of this inconclusive result, Gordon Brown tried to hang on, but proved unable to strike a deal with the Liberals and nationalists - it just would not work. Nick Clegg seemed to have more personally in common with David Cameron and did not want to look like he was propping up a loser. Clegg's negotiations with Brown were essentially only for use as leverage in striking the right kind of deal with David Cameron's Conservatives.

On the evening of 11th May, David Cameron became Prime Minister after reaching an agreement with the Liberal Democrat leader to form a coalition government - the first since 1945.

The New Labour era was conclusively over. Overall, the Blair-Brown settlement had witnessed the acceptance and amalgamation of the value of ambition and the free market, with the equal need for strong public services and for giving a helping hand to the poor and disadvantaged. New Labour had perhaps achieved its greatest success with healthcare. Funding had increased from 6.6% to 9,6% of GDP. The number of people waiting longer than six months for non-urgent treatment dropped from 400,000 in 1998 to almost nil by 2010. Public satisfaction with the NHS, also rose from thirty-nine percent in 2001 to seventy-four percent in 2010. [362]

Internationally, the doctrine of liberal interventionism and pro-Americanism had gone tragically awry, whilst the complementary position of forging better relations with Europe, had somewhat stalled due to divisions within the cabinet, and in particular, the power-struggle between Blair and Brown.

The competing drives of enabling individual liberty and tough-minded security, did eventually lead to a contradictory mess, but not without real achievements, such as progress on gay rights. The aim of cleaning up politics and restoring faith in democracy fell embarrassingly short of the mark, though the devolved assemblies are a lasting legacy.

Overall, the basic idea of a synthesis of the workable aspects of right and left was a good one. It was also at least partially successful. However, the downfall of New Labour, apart from luck inevitably running out, were the personality flaws of the two men who ran the movement, and their dysfunctional relationship with one another.

Ultimately, the fact that Cameron's Tories broadly accepted the New Labour settlement, as Labour had accepted the Thatcherite settlement before it, was perhaps their greatest legacy.

Chapter 7: 2010-2024:
AUSTERITY BREXIT COVID & COST OF LIVING CRISIS

In May 2010 Conservative rule returned to Britain, after a New Labour era for the first two-thirds of which, it seemed like the Tories had been permanently consigned to the dustbin of history. However, just as Thatcher had indirectly re-made the Labour party, so had Tony Blair at least partially re-made, and certainly re-branded the Tories. In was gay marriage, and at least on the surface, greater concern for the environment.

The transformation would have been much more stark had not the financial crisis interceded to demolish Cameron's earlier pledge to match New Labour spending. This event blew the Cameron Conservatives off-course before they had even taken office, and so the first six years of Tory rule will always be primarily remembered as the time of austerity. With deep cuts in public spending and reform of the welfare system, a chilly breeze was perceptible in national life. This at least though, was a policy that was consistently implemented.

Other promises, such as cutting immigration to the tens of thousands were not implemented at all. Yet, it was in the area of greatest Tory factionalism – Europe that David Cameron's greatest headaches were to emerge. Unable to resist growing back-bench demands for a referendum on the terms of Britain's EU membership, compounded by the rising UKIP challenge, Cameron took a gamble and lost.

The second half of this period is the story of a rudderless government blown off-course by wholly unexpected defeat in a referendum of their own calling.

Whether David Cameron could have successfully faced down his own party and refused to hold the referendum is a question that will never be satisfactorily be answered. Yet, it is academic now. The government then faced itself in the predicament of losing many of its top players, including the Prime Minister and Chancellor, and having to implement a policy that it largely did not believe in.

During its last four years the storm clouds gathered some more, with the COVID pandemic, cost-of-living crisis and war in Ukraine. It seems that the administration will end its days as it began – in crisis.

2010-15: THE CAMERON-CLEGG COALITION: AUSTERITY AND THE RETURN OF EURO-SCEPTICISM

'There is such a thing as society, but it's not the same as the state.' [363]

In May 2010, Britain was to be led by its first coalition government since World War Two. A coalition agreement released on 20th May set out its programme, containing the bold statement: 'The government believes that our political system is broken.' It promised constitutional reform, including the staging of a referendum on AV (Single alternative vote.) It also listed six areas in which the Liberal Democrats were allowed to disagree with the Conservatives: 1) AV-2 2) Tuition fees, 3) Trident, 4) Nuclear Power, 5. Tax allowances for married couples.

Another document on the following day asserted that, 'There is no constitutional difference between a coalition government and a single party government.' It pledged to allocate posts to the Liberals on a roughly proportionate basis.

Many commentators expressed doubts as to whether the coalition would be able to last a full term. These concerns were to be addressed by the Fixed Term Parliament Act 2011, which effectively tried to lock in the coalition for a full term. The act stipulated that a term had to last for five years, and removed the Prime Minister's prerogative of calling an election at a time of their choosing. In order to go to the country earlier, either the consent of at least two-thirds of the House of Commons would be required, or the government would have to lose a no confidence motion, with at least fifty percent of MPs voting against it.

This act removed mutual suspicions that either the Prime Minister would be tempted to dissolve parliament early in order to secure a majority, or that Nick Clegg would be tempted to throw in the towel and trigger an early election for partisan reasons.

David Cameron was true to his word and appointed several leading Liberal Democrats to the cabinet and many more to junior posts. The Liberal leader Nick Clegg became Deputy Prime Minister, Vince Cable became Business Secretary and Chris Huhne became Secretary of State for Energy and Climate Change. David Laws was initially Chief Secretary to the Treasury and Danny Alexander Secretary for Scotland, but Laws was forced to resign a few weeks after taking up the post, due to his failure to declare expenses for a flat, and was replaced by Alexander, who in turn was replaced as Scottish Secretary by Michael Moore.

The coalition was effectively governed by what became known as 'The Quad', consisting of Prime Minister David Cameron, Chancellor George Osborne,

Deputy Prime Minister Nick Clegg and Chief Secretary Danny Alexander. Cameron and Clegg had much in common and were able to work very effectively together. Civil servants also noted how the calm, dignified and unflappable Cameron, with his relatively hands-off approach was a positive contrast to the control-freakish, tempestuous, Gordon Brown.

The coalition's overriding priority was the economy. Britain had suffered the deepest recession for thirty years and the banking sector suffered its greatest crisis since the 1930s. When new Chief Secretary David Laws took office, he found a note from his Labour predecessor, informing him simply that, 'I am afraid there is no money.' [364] This letter would eventually be used by David Cameron as a campaign prop at the 2015 election.

National debt was a serious problem and George Osborne pledged to eradicate it within one parliament. Until the 2008 crisis, the Tories had promised to stick with Labour's spending plans. The crash changed all of that. Now, the whole focus had shifted to austerity and the need for deep cuts in public spending. Health, education and international development were to be ring-fenced. The cuts were therefore to fall most heavily on local government, the home office, welfare and defence.

One of the areas most cut was the civil service, whose numbers were reduced from 470,000 to 400,000. Public sector pay was also frozen and pensions were reduced, with retirement age raised from sixty to sixty-five, pensions calculated on the basis of average life-time earnings, rather than final salary, and an increased employee contribution.

Local government spending was cut more sharply than in any period since 1945. Central government funding for local government was reduced by twenty-seven percent. [365] Local government employment fell by half a million and spending fell on average by fifteen-to-twenty percent, with big cities worst affected. [366]

Communities Secretary Eric Pickles introduced a Localism Act in 2011 - designed to empower people to take more control over the running of local amenities. This made less difference than hoped for, as most people were not particularly interested in doing this. There were some more reforms in local government and Home Office. Local referenda for elected mayors, created mayors in several cities.

In 2011 the Police Authorities were abolished and replaced by directly elected Police & Crime Commissioners. These elected figures had the powers to appoint and dismiss Chief Constables, determine the police budget and local policing priorities. However, these commissioners were elected on a miserably low turnout.

An area that faced both significant cuts and structural reform was welfare. Ian Duncan Smith was the steely and reforming Secretary for Work and Pensions. After his earlier, unsuccessful tenure as Conservative leader, Duncan Smith set up the think tank, 'The Centre for Social Justice'. This generated radical ideas for welfare reform. The centre-piece of this was the amalgamation of six different benefits into the new Universal Credit. This idea - though held up by ICT problems, finally started to come into effect in the autumn of 2014.

The new benefits regime also became far more rigorous than in the past. People claiming jobseekers' allowance would now face significant penalties, including the loss of several weeks' benefit for failure to attend job interview, apply for jobs, or attend signings.

They also lost payment for the first week of their claim, in a bid to deter short-term claims.

Disability too was affected. People claiming the disability allowance would now face rigorous medical assessments, and if deemed unfit to work were transferred to the new Personal Independence Payments (PIP)

There was also now a cap on the maximum benefits that people could claim: £350 per week for individuals and £500 per week for families at one address. In justification of the policy, David Cameron said, 'I've lost count of the number of people who've said, "I go to work early in the morning and on the way, I pass neighbours with their curtains closed, lying in, because they've chosen to live on benefits." The cap is going to help us crack welfare dependency.' [367]By March 2014, some 38,600 households had been capped. This had significant public support.

However, much less popular was the so-called bedroom tax, or Spare Room Subsidy, in which families living with a spare bedroom suffered a ten percent reduction in housing benefit. The idea was to nudge people into freeing up larger dwellings for big families. There was no real evidence that it achieved its stated objective.

Benefits were also craftily reduced further by the switching of the measure of inflation used to raise them – from that of the Retail Price Index to the Consumer Price Index, which is lower. Additionally, a number of benefits faced freezes and below-inflation rises for several years.

Pensions also faced considerable changes. One change, welcome to most pensioners, was the introduction of the 'triple lock,' which ensured that pensions would rise at the rate of either inflation, average wages or 2.5% - whichever was the higher. The return of this kind of linkage helped arrest the steady erosion of state pensions that had been happening for the past thirty years.

Another development, perhaps less welcome, was to keep and in fact accelerate the increase in retirement age that had been agreed by the last Labour government. The rise in retirement age to sixty-six, was to be brought forward to 2020 and sixty-seven in 2028.

Overall, there was to be major structural reform of the National Health Service, at least in England. Health Secretary Andrew Lansley piloted the reforms in 2011-12. These reforms essentially devolved the responsibility for the direct running of the NHS from the Health Secretary to a central commissioning board called Public Health England. The Strategic Health authorities and Primary Care Trusts would also be replaced by GP-led commissioners. Public health functions would pass back from central to local government, where they had been until 1974. Additionally, an economic regulator would oppose anti-competitive practices.

These reforms would prove highly controversial, with many critics on the left seeing them as a preparatory step towards privatisation. Others simply saw it as organisational change for the sake of it, that was a distraction from the real challenges, and one that we could ill afford to indulge.

Another key weakness is that whether control is devolved or not, the Health Secretary is still seen as responsible in the eyes of the public.

The Health Act 2012 was duly passed, albeit it with some House of Lords amendments and Lansley was replaced as Health Secretary by the more emollient Jeremy Hunt, who was deemed better at selling the changes to the NHS, public and media.

Although NHS spending was not strictly cut under the coalition, the pace of funding increase was so dramatically slowed down after 2010 that it certainly felt like a cut. During the New Labour years there had been a real terms funding increase of seventy percent, and mostly in the last two terms. This compares with a five percent increase during 2010-15. [368] One growing problem was of an ageing population. The first of the sixties baby boomers were reaching retirement age in the year the coalition came to power.

Additionally, there were growing numbers of younger people suffering from 'lifestyle'- related conditions such as diabetes. In practical terms, therefore, the NHS was effectively undergoing cuts. The NHS Chief Executive David Nicholson warned that the government would have to make, 'Major efficiency savings of £15-20 billion by 2014.' [369]

Therefore, savings had to be made. These came in the form of cutting the price paid by commissioners for treatment, wage freezes for staff and even redundancies for some clerical staff.

Education too had its reforming zealot, Michael Gove. Gove introduced the biggest shake-up in education policy since Kenneth Baker's introduction of the GCSE system in the late 1980s. Gove's main priority was to make educational standards more rigorous and objective and improve the calibre of teachers. This included tackling the growing perception of grade inflation, wherein exams were seen as becoming too easy. He also introduced the Academies act, which allowed any school the right to become an academy - carrying on from where New Labour left off. He also created 'free schools' which were independent schools set up by parents, teachers and charities.

David Cameron had immense faith in his friend Michael Gove, even describing him at the 2013 conference as having, 'a belief in excellence and massive energy, like a cross between Mr Chips and the Duracell Bunny.' [370] However, the education profession were rather less sanguine. His reforms became increasingly unpopular, with senior historians writing to the Observer to denounce his proposals for the new history curriculum in early 2013. This was followed by 100 academics attacking his ideas. Gove retorted that they were, 'enemies of promise,' and that he would, 'refuse to surrender to the Marxist teachers.' [371]

The National Union of Teachers, (NUT) passed a motion of no confidence in the Education Secretary, for the first time in 150 years. In 2014, the combative Gove, also got into a silly spat with Home Secretary Theresa May over which department was more responsible for failing to counter Islamic fundamentalist infiltration in a school. A civil service enquiry blamed the department of education.

In July 2014 David Cameron moved Gove to the post of Chief Whip, where he could impose much needed discipline on the fractious party.

Another area of education feeling the changes was higher education. In December 2010, the government decided to triple university tuition fees to £9,000. The issue saw twenty-one Liberal MPS vote against and was followed by major protest. In November, angry students even stormed Conservative Central office, causing damage inside. A month later there were many arrests at a rally in central London. This however was too fleeting to seriously threaten Civil Unrest Key twelve.

This issue though, resulted in huge unpopularity for Nick Clegg and his Liberals, as they had very publicly pledged not to do this at the last election. Their TV party election broadcast had even been called, 'Say Goodbye to broken promises' and even featured Clegg walking through a blizzard of 'broken promises' the first of which was tuition fees.[372] They also signed a pledge not to raise the fees for the National Union of Students. The effect of this policy was to turn Clegg into a hate figure, with many people viewing him as a traitor and a turncoat. The man who was briefly the object of 'Clegg-mania' in the spring had gone from hero to zero.

The Lib Dems poll rating collapsed into single figures, and their popularity took over a decade to even begin to seriously recover. Thus, the Tories had indirectly strengthened their own hand at the next election, by hobbling a rival. This collapse in Liberal support, highlighted by both polls and dire local election results, made the party's rout at the next election widely predictable. Thus, the Third Party Bonus key 5A was triggered early in the parliament, meaning that the Tories could still expect to get a majority with even five negative keys.

Despite the terrible cost exacted upon the Liberal Democrats, their role in the coalition was not entirely in vain. One policy introduced because of them, was the raising of personal tax allowances to £12,500 by the end of the parliament. This was both compassionate towards the poor and also helped to make work pay, thus promoting the work ethic.

One piece of liberal reform that united the leadership of all three main parties, but massively divided the Tories, was gay marriage. Cameron framed the policy in terms of promoting marriage in general, by offering the stability it can bring to homosexuals. However, it was neither in the Tory manifesto nor in the coalition agreement. Cameron wanted to build on New Labour's achievements with Civil Partnerships, but was unprepared for the gales of criticism that would blow up from both the backbenches and grass roots membership of his party.

According to polling, seventy-one percent of Conservative constituency chairmen were opposed to it.[373] Gay Tory MP Alan Duncan attacked it, saying, 'It is losing us twenty percent of our membership. It is just so badly explained. Why are we doing it? To purge accusations of Blimpism? It is poisonous to the party.'[374]

The issue came to a free vote in early 2013 and was passed with Labour support. However, Conservatives voted against it by 136-127. The Conservative MP Edward Leigh summed up the socially Conservative position which was seriously at odds with the party leadership, and would be increasingly a problem for the next decade and almost certainly well beyond, with these words: 'We should be in the business of protecting cherished institutions and cultural heritage. Otherwise, what, I ask is a Conservative party for?'[375]

Overall, the enormous scale of the cuts and public sector reforms was certainly sufficient to win the Conservatives Policy Change key eleven.

What is often now overlooked is how different the Conservative agenda was, at least on paper, in the early days of Cameron's leadership. Initially, Cameron and Osborne were committed to matching Labour's spending commitments. They were trying to outflank them on being green and on developing a fairer society. The crash of 2008 changed everything. The commitment to match Labour spending was dropped and upon taking office in the worst economic climate for any incoming government since Harold Wilson in 1974, the primary focus had to be on deficit reduction.

The biggest influence before the crash was Cameron's anarchic but creative, 'blue skies thinker'

Steve Hilton, described by top civil servant Gus O'Donnell as, 'brilliant but bonkers.' [376] Hilton was the man behind the 'Big Society' motif that was banded about in opposition and in the first half of the coalition. Although this was supposed to be about devolving responsibility away from the state towards families and communities, it lacked serious support in cabinet, was never properly fleshed-out, and failed to capture the public imagination. It was widely perceived as a cynical smokescreen for cuts.

Essentially Thatcherite but more libertarian, Hilton's ethos is perhaps best encapsulated by Cameron's re-working of an old Thatcher trope at the 2006 party conference. 'There is such a thing as society - but it's not the same as the state.' On face value this looks like a repudiation of Thatcherism, which played well to moderates.

However, on further examination, especially with the full original quote, it is not really the case. Mrs Thatcher, in her famous 1987 interview, was attacking the idea of society as an abstract used to dump blame and avoid personal responsibility. She was advocating that individuals, families and communities do a little more and rely on the state a little less. This fits closely with Hilton's ideas about localism and with the draconian cuts in welfare etc that were to come. It also perhaps reflects the fact that Hilton was the son of two Hungarian refugees, or as Mathew D'ancona put it; 'An angry young man breaking free from the shackles of Communism.'[377]

Hilton came into conflict with Whitehall mandarins over his plans to shrink the civil service until it could fit into one building. His elected mayors proposal failed to achieve the enthusiasm hoped for. Ultimately, facing increasing marginalisation in the cabinet and opposition from George Osborne and the mandarins, Hilton quit Cameron's inner circle and left for America in 2012.

Regarding foreign policy, the single most important question was increasingly Britain's relationship with the European Union. During his time as Leader of the Opposition, David Cameron was hopeful that his party had left its ideological schism over Europe behind. With the issue of whether or not to join the single currency fading during the late 00's, Cameron hoped that his party would simply stop 'banging on about Europe' and move on. He was to be sadly disabused upon assuming the office of Prime Minister of the not very United Kingdom.

During the course of the troubled fiver-year term, the greatest conflict was generally within the Conservative party, rather than between the Tories and their junior Lib Dem partners. This took the form of backbench rebellions by right-wing Euro-sceptic MPs, who had never really liked David Cameron and had only tolerated him because they thought he would win them power. When he failed to do so properly, their anger and contempt began to find itself expression.

In 2011, the coalition moved to forestall serious rebellions by passing the European Act. This stipulated that any further transfer of British sovereignty to the EU had to be approved by a referendum. However, the intention behind it was soon to meet disappointment.

In October 2011, the Tory Euro-rebels proposed a bill to bring about a referendum on continued EU membership. All major parties imposed a three-line whip against it, but eighty-one Tory MPs rebelled against their leadership with two junior ministers resigning.

A few months later, David Cameron blocked a prospective EU treaty, so that it had to be re-negotiated with the UK outside. This was another attempt to throw red meat to the rebels, but the result was simply to whet their appetite for more. As Seldon and Snowdon point out, 'by the spring of 2012, the pressure for Cameron to commit to a referendum is becoming virtually unstoppable.' [378] In June 2012, Cameron blocked the EU from extending the Eurozone banking union across the EU. This won him some applause. However, when he mounted a passionate defence of the European Union, the Tory outcry was so great that he felt compelled to write a newspaper article in the *Sunday Telegraph*, hinting at a future referendum.

In October 2012, fifty-three Conservative rebels joined forces with Labour to pass an amendment calling for a real-terms cut in the EU budget. By this point UKIP were reaching ten percent in the polls.

There were additional attempts by Tory MPs to bring in legislation that would force the government to hold an EU referendum. These were frustrated for now, but in the longer-term something would have to give.

The crucial decision came in January 2013, when David Cameron announced at the Bloomberg building in London, that the government would attempt a re-negotiated settlement of the terms of Britain's EU membership, followed by an in-out referendum to be held during the next parliament. 'I never want us to pull up the drawer-bridge and retreat from the world. I am not a British isolationist. I don't just want a better deal for Britain. I want a better deal for Europe to.' [379]

A month later, the Prime Minister secured a 3.3 % cut in the EU budget, to the tune of £32 billion. Even this failed to pacify the rebels or win Cameron many plaudits. The rebels now attempted to force the government's hand by introducing legislation demanding a referendum in the current parliament. Meanwhile any concessions that Cameron might be able to extract from the EU were dismissed by former chancellor Lord Lawson as, 'inconsequential.' in an article for *The Times*.

All of these battles cost the Conservatives Party Unity key number two.

Concurrent with this internal party conflict, was the rise of the UK Independence Party. (UKIP) This party, whilst relatively marginal in the 1990s and early 00's had become quite prominent since 2004. Initially they were aided by the brief endorsement of former TV host Robert Kilroy Silk, who helped them win a dozen seats in 2004. They were aided again five years later by the expenses scandal, which enabled them to position themselves favourably against the corrupt Westminster elites. With the apathy of the 90s and 00s now giving way to the anti-politics of the post-crash era, UKIP were well-positioned to become a major force.

With the ebullient Nigel Farage becoming official leader in 2010, after nearly dying in a plane crash during the election campaign, the party were rapidly on the up, far-outstripping the popularity of the Referendum party of the 1990s to become the most successful new party in living memory.

In the face of this kind of insurgency, Cameron's 2006 dismissal of them on LBC radio, as 'fruitcakes, loonies and closet racists,' made him look arrogant, out-of-touch with and dangerously contemptuous of a large swathe of his own party. The Chairman of the Conservative 1922 committee, Graham Brady summarised Cameron's failed efforts to get to grips with this new threat as, 'always behind the curve and never established consistency on how to deal with UKIP.'[380]

The strength of UKIP's rising support was illustrated at the Eastleigh by-election in February 2013. The Conservatives not only failed to re-take the seat from the Liberals but were pushed into third place by UKIP. In the run-up to the 2014 Euro elections, Nick Clegg took on Nigel Farage in a live TV debate on Europe - and lost. The days of Clegg-mania were long, long gone. In the election itself, UKIP came first, with the Tories pushed into third place - the first time that this had happened in a national election. At this time, Cameron suffered a foreign policy humiliation when he failed to prevent Claude Juncker from becoming EU President. London mayor Boris Johnson dismissed Cameron's efforts as, 'The quintessence of turd-polishing pointlessness.' [381]

Worse was to come for the government. In autumn 2014, two Tory MPs, Douglas Carswell and Mark Reckless defected to UKIP, triggering by-elections which they both won handsomely as UKIP candidates. The loss of these, and other by-elections, easily toppled key one for the Cameron administration. With UKIP now at around fifteen percent in the national polls and a general election looming, Third Party key five was also lost for the Tories.

One other issue that involved sovereignty and identity was Scottish independence. When the SNP won a majority of seats in the Scottish parliament in May 2011, the prospect of Scotland breaking away from the union suddenly became quite real. The response of David Cameron was bold and decisive: he decided to call a referendum, which was eventually scheduled for September 2014. At Scottish Widows, Cameron gave a passionate speech advocating the UK staying together.

I care far more about my country than I do about my party...I would be heartbroken if this family of nations we have put together... was torn apart...if you are fed up with the effing Tories give them a kick and maybe we'll think again. This is a totally different decision to a general election. This is not a decision about the next five years. It is a decision about the next century. [382]

In a bitterly polarised campaign, the 'Better Together' remain campaign was to triumph, with a fifty-five - forty-five margin, and on a turnout of eighty-five percent; the highest ever in the UK. This was in spite of its negativity; focussing on loss of EU membership and financial uncertainty, to the point of being dubbed 'Project Fear'; an epithet more commonly associated with the Brexit referendum two years later.

Although Cameron caused resentment by bringing up the West Lothian question in the days following the referendum, the victory in Scotland, in holding the United Kingdom together, was sufficient to win the Tories Foreign Policy Success key nine.

The electoral consequences of this vote were not immediately anticipated however. The psychological impact of millions of natural Labour supporters disobeying their party in the referendum, effectively broke the spell that Labour had cast over Scotland for decades. They now had moral permission to vote for something else. Well before the 2015 election results were called, all the polls predicted an SNP landslide in Scotland. Although this did not really threaten the Tories, as they were only defending one solitary seat north of the border, it was disastrous for Labour. However, since the election is predicted here from a Tory perspective, then no keys are changed by it.

Constitutional reform was the number one agenda of the Liberals when they entered into the coalition and they had high hopes.

The first item that had been agreed upon was a national referendum on the Alternative Vote. (AV) Although this idea had previously been described by

Nick Clegg as a 'miserable little compromise.' [383] it was nonetheless supported by the Liberals in the first nationwide referendum in Britain since 1975.

However, the lonely Liberals were badly undermined by the dramatic slump in their standing and particularly their leader's standing since the vote on tuition fees. Clegg was therefore no longer the best man to make the case for it and his advocacy now looked like self-interested opportunism. The problem was with both Labour and the Conservatives attacking the proposal, the 'Yes' campaign was severely hamstrung. Also, the slogan, 'Yes to Fairer Votes,' seemed compromised from the start.

The result: a rejection by sixty-eight percent of voters, on the same day that the Liberals lost over 700 councillors in the May local elections, was a devastating blow for Nick Clegg and his party. In the first year of the coalition, the party had also lost a quarter of their members. [384]

Unperturbed, the Liberals now began to focus on the next part of the constitutional agenda - Lords reform. The proposals were for a second chamber that was eighty percent elected and twenty percent appointed. However, opposition from Tory rebels and Labour effectively scuppered the bill through denying it a timetable. Clegg decided to withdraw it rather than see an unacceptable amount of parliamentary time wasted on the slow death of the bill. Clegg saw it as betrayal by his coalition partners. Speaking in the Commons, he said;

The Conservative Party is not honouring the commitment to Lords reform and as a result, part of our contract has now been broken... So I have told the Prime Minister that when, in due course, Parliament votes on boundary changes for the 2015 election, I will be instructing my party to oppose them. [385]

The piece of constitutional reform that the Conservatives had been after, was for the equalisation of all UK constituency boundaries, in a slightly smaller 600-seat House of Commons. This was because the system at that time was seen to strongly favour Labour. Clegg was true to his word, and so this proposed reform was scuppered too, in tit for tat style. However, there had been no such quid pro quo arrangement in the coalition agreement involving Lords reform for boundaries reform. There had only been an agreement to bring the motion to parliament - which had been honoured, and to stage the AV referendum - which had also been honoured.

Though constitutional reform had largely failed to be delivered, the very considerable changes made to public spending, welfare and public services were still easily sufficient to win the Conservatives Policy Change key eleven.

In terms of foreign affairs, the government found itself facing the prospect of military action on three occasions. The first was in the Libyan civil war, which began in the wake of the Arab Spring, which saw popular unrest spread throughout the Middle East and North Africa that year.

David Cameron had long held a deep personal antipathy for Libyan dictator Colonel Mumar Gaddafi. In particular in was deeply touched by the murder of policewoman Yvonne Fletcher outside the Libyan embassy and the Gaddafi-mandated Lockerbie bombing of his youth. He felt revulsion at Blair's attempts to rehabilitate Gaddafi in the mid 2000's and at the decision by the Scottish parliament to release the Lockerbie bomber Al-Megrahi on compassionate grounds in 2009. He disbelieved Gordon Brown's explanation that it was entirely the decision of the Scottish parliament, and in fact upon entering No 10, conducted an inquiry to prove that the Westminster government, 'did all it could to facilitate' Al-Megrahi's release. [386] This was concurrent with extensive lobbying by BP.

When in March 2011, Gadaffi's forces had crushed rebellions in the western, more loyal part of the country and were heading for the rebel-held city of Benghazi, Cameron decided to intervene. Faced with considerable opposition from Whitehall and an ambivalent Barack Obama, Cameron found a fellow traveller in French President Sarkozy. They also won support from the Gulf Cooperation Council, and finally achieved authorisation from the United Nations Security council. (Five abstained.)

After a convincing House of Commons win, Britain and France launched air strikes against Libyan forces on the 19th March 2011 under the NATO umbrella. The Americans only contributed to the earliest stages of the conflict, before taking a back seat. Although the prima facie justification of saving Benghazi was swiftly achieved, the mission was to continue for over half a year - with the real casus belli of regime change. Tripoli eventually fell in August, and in October, Gaddafi was lynched by the rebels after his convoy was hit by a NATO air strike. Following this, NATO decided to call an end to operations on the 31st October.

The long-term consequences of this war were to be regional instability, and it would not have turned Foreign Policy/Military key nine, since this was to be the first modern war in which there was never a majority of public support at any stage in the operations. [387]

The Middle East was to rear its war-torn head again in British politics two years later. In the summer of 2013, President Assad of Syria caused international outrage by using deadly nerve gas in a civilian area of Damascus - in clear breach of international law. Apart from Saddam Hussein's 1988 attack on the Kurds, this was the worst single WMD incident since 1945. It also crossed President Obama's 'red line in the sand' wherein American intervention would be justified. Obama initially decided to launch airstrikes, but Assad's decision to allow UN weapons inspectors into the country bought him time.

In Britain, Cameron recalled Parliament from its summer recess to discuss the crisis. Labour were very reluctant to authorise military action without UN authorisation. Obama was now prevaricating. Opinion polls showed that public opinion opposed intervention by two-to-one.[388] With the UN weapons inspectors asking for another week, the government began to retreat in the face of Labour opposition and tabled a motion condemning Assad and proposing military action as a possibility; requiring a second vote to actually authorise bombing. The government fell on the first vote: defeated by 322-220. Thirty Conservative MPs voted against and twenty-six abstained.

This was the first time that a British government had been defeated in the house on war since the American war of Independence in 1782. Obama backed off from intervention as opposition was strong in Congress too. It was summed up in *The Spectator* with the following line: 'From a sleepy summer recess, Cameron has conjured up one of the most spectacular parliamentary defeats in modern political history.'[389] This clearly forfeited

Foreign Policy/Military Failure key ten for the government.

Following this failure, Britain only played a fairly minimal role in the strikes against ISIS the following year, restricting military action to Iraq. Additionally, the government was to withdraw British troops from Afghanistan by the end of 2014. That conflict had become deeply unpopular during the Brown premiership, and was a thorn in the government's side, and one that they had been understandably eager to pull out. The cost of the war was high - 457 servicemen dead.

Despite, or perhaps because of the austerity, the economy effectively went sideways for the first three years of the coalition. Unemployment peaked at 8.5 percent in 2011 – still lower than in the 1979-81 and 1990-92 recessions, but the pattern of the recovery was the opposite of those earlier recessions. With the 80s recession, the aftermath was marked by strong GDP and wage growth, but persistently high unemployment. In the 2010s we saw relatively low and faster falling unemployment, but with very sluggish GDP and wage growth.

The harsh austerity measures drew criticism, not merely at home but also abroad, with the IMF's chief economist Oliver Blanchard accusing George Osborne of, 'playing with fire.' [390]

The grim situation was brought into sharp focus with an explosion of urban rioting that shook Britain's cities for five days in August 2011. The violence was triggered by the police shooting of a biracial man in Tottenham. Protests outside the police station then spread around the capital, and pretty soon around the country.

Outside London, the worst affected cities were Birmingham, Liverpool and Manchester. Five people were killed and around 3,000 arrested. Many buildings were set alight and police forces struggled to contain the worst rioting for exactly thirty years. This resulted in blame being apportioned to the government for the austerity and also the big cuts in police forces.

The government however, would not be swayed from its parsimonious course. Ultimately, the brevity of the disturbances, which were not repeated during the rest of the parliament, prevented them from turning Civil Unrest key twelve.

The period also saw a surge in the number of people having to rely on foodbanks. Oxfam spoke of, 'the shocking scale of destination, hardship and hunger in the UK. It is completely unacceptable that in the seventh richest nation on the planet, the number of people turning to food banks has tripled.' [391] In this period, the Red Cross began providing volunteers for the first time in the UK due to hunger, and in early 2014, twenty-seven bishops signed a letter attacking austerity and the inadequacies of the benefits system in addressing poverty.

The 2012 Olympics, staged in London for the first since 1948 (another time of austerity) were bequeathed to the coalition by Tony Blair. They provided a glimmer of light in this era of collective gloom, as the wettest summer for 100 years dried up sufficiently for the games. Britain did well, but the continuing unpopularity of the government was highlighted by the booing of Chancellor George Osborne as he presented awards.

2012 was also the year of the so-called 'Omnishambles' budget. This epithet was created by Labour leader Ed Miliband, and referenced the TV political comedy *In the Thick of it*. The budget proved especially unpopular as it saw Osborne cut the top rate of income tax from fifty to forty-five percent, whilst at the same time raising VAT on food served at above ambient temperature - such as Cornish pasties. This was seen as a giveaway for the rich at the expense of the poor. The 'pasties' tax was in fact abandoned, but ultimately the lower top rate of tax collected more revenue. [392]

The following year, Britain lost her triple A status, and there were strong indications that she had suffered a double-dip recession, and was even poised to enter a third. After the 2013 budget Miliband trolled Osborne, by mocking his fondness for using Twitter. In summing up the budget in under 144 characters: 'Growth down. Borrowing up. Families hit and millionaires laugh all the way to the bank. #downgradedchancellor.'

However, from the spring of 2013 the government's fortunes were about to change. Revised economic data showed that Britain had not suffered a double-dip recession after all and would easily avoid a third. Growth was now returning and unemployment falling. By the end of the term, the UK was enjoying the strongest growth-rate in Europe, although not the best productivity rate. This recovery therefore proved sufficient to salvage both economic keys for the government.

Osborne's 2014 budget was judged to be much more successful. Pensioners were now allowed to draw down as much of their savings as they liked, with restrictions on access to pension pots being lifted. Stocks and shares allowances were to be merged into a new £15,000 NISA. There was also a further attack on welfare, with a cap of £119.5 billion on government welfare spending per annum. Osborne declared that, 'Never again should we allow (welfare) costs to spiral out of control and its incentives to become so distorted that it pays not to work.' [393]

By the end of the term, the coalition had reduced public spending as a share of GDP, from forty-five percent in 2010 to forty percent by 2015. This is comparable to the cuts made by Thatcher over the course of her eleven-year tenure.394 The Office of Budget Responsibility (OBR) set up by the coalition in 2010, was also seen as a good innovation, and effective bulwark against profligate and irresponsible governments and government departments.

One key that nearly turned for the government was the Scandal key. In 2009 Cameron had appointed former Editor of *The News of the World*, Andy Coulson as his Director of Communications, after Coulson had been forced to resign from the *News of the world*, following a phone-hacking scandal. Coulson continued working for the Conservatives in office, until he was forced to resign from his post in January 2011, following further revelations about the phone hacking scandal, and in particular, what he knew about it. On his resignation, Coulson said, 'When the spokesman needs a spokesman, it's time to move on.' 395

Cameron came under heavy fire for appointing Coulson after the phone hacking scandal had been exposed and for keeping him on for so long. Was he naive? Or did he not care about Coulson's role in the scandal? This led to the resignation of Rebecca Brooks as director of News International, and the jailing of Coulson for five months.

The matter went to the Leveson inquiry, which exonerated the Prime Minister and Culture Secretary Jeremy Hunt of any wrongdoing.

Other scandals included the resignation of Chief Secretary David Laws for irregularities in his expense claims, just a few weeks into the government's life. 2011 saw the resignation of Defence Secretary Liam Fox over allegations that he gave a lobbyist friend, unauthorised access to the MOD. Then 2012 brought the resignation of Liberal Secretary for Energy and Climate Change, Chris Huhne, who was jailed for perverting the course of justice. In this case, Huhne arranged for his wife to admit responsibility for his own speeding offence in a bid to preserve his licence. However, as I am making the forecast from the perspective of the Conservatives, Huhne's and Law's downfall make no difference to the keys.

One bizarre scandal involved the Chief Whip Andrew Mitchell, who resigned after he was accused of swearing at police officers whilst being asked to dismount his bike when exiting Downing Street. He was accused of calling the officers 'plebs' which was politically toxic, especially because of the deep resentment towards the government over austerity and the perceived over-privileged nature of many government ministers. Mitchell however denied using the word 'pleb' and after several officers involved in the case were fired from the force for dishonesty connected to the case, Mitchel was offered a police apology.

Overall, however, none of these incidents and accusations were sufficient to taint the Prime Minister, or government as a whole, so failing to topple Scandal key thirteen.

Before we move on to take a look at the election campaign itself, we should examine the principal opposition party - Labour. After losing office in 2010, Labour elected Ed Miliband, who took the party in a slightly more leftish direction than it had known under Blair and Brown. He argued that the New Labour modus operandi of using capitalism to provide the tax receipts for social democracy was severely inadequate in the post-crash era, and was not even adequate before it. He argued that the link between GDP growth and real wage growth had long been withering on the vine, pointing to the decline in real wages for the poorest half of the population during the 00's - a decline masked by government tax credits and soaring personal debt.

Miliband argued for a 'responsible capitalism that gave workers a stake in their jobs. [396]However, Labour under Miliband did not inspire economic confidence, and Miliband failed to connect with the public. He was perceived as geeky and awkward, and somehow not comfortable in his own skin. He was mocked for looking like Wallace from *Wallace & Gromit*, (except for having more hair) and for looking odd whilst eating a bacon sandwich.[397] In September 2014, even Jonathan Freedland said in the Guardian that, 'With just eight months to go, he doesn't yet look the part.'[398]

Therefore, Miliband fell far short of turning the Opposition Charisma key against the government. Yet, at the same time he also avoided gifting the Conservatives the Opposition Implausibility Key 4A.

This was for several reasons. Firstly, he did have sound and interesting ideas. Secondly, although he shifted his party a little bit towards the left, he was still very moderate, and could not be credibly described as extremist or 'loony left.' Thirdly, he managed to keep his party broadly unified and disciplined; there was none of the bitter ideological divisions of the 1980s or indeed the bitter personality-based factionalism that had disfigured the latter two thirds of the New Labour era. Fourthly, he managed some effective moments, such as his call for a windfall tax on utilities and his cracks at Cameron and Osborne in the commons.

Fifthly and perhaps most tellingly, his party's prospects of winning power, if not a majority were taken seriously by the pundits.

Although Cameron was generally judged to be a more effective leader than Miliband, he too, fell well short of securing the Incumbent Leadership key for the Tories. He was not charismatic, and was not sufficiently in command of events, or respected by his own party to be the strong dominant leader needed to secure that key. The polling guru John Curtice opined that, 'People used to think that Cameron was charismatic. But he is proving to be a kind of average Prime Minister. His ratings are not terrible, but he's not Thatcher, he's not Blair. He is not a dominant figure. Nobody loves him.' [399]

The election of May 2015 was of course not a surprise in its announcement or timing, as it had been long pre-ordained by the Fixed Term Parliament Act. Yet despite this certainty of timing and long period available for preparation, neither party campaigned particularly well. Cameron was criticised for an apparent lack of drive, with the Daily Telegraph commenting on, 'his lack of obvious desire and passion to win.' [400]

His façade of falsity was embarrassingly exposed when he muddled up the name of the football team that he was supposed to be a supporter of.[401] Cameron responded by trying to go more OTT in his public appearances - for example when in praising small business entrepreneurs he said, 'taking a risk, having a go, having a punt, that pumps me up.' [402]

Ed Miliband also faced criticism and mockery, especially when answering Jeremy Paxman's query as to whether he was tough enough for the job. 'Hell yes, I'm tough enough.'[403] The problem faced by Miliband, was that it was almost impossible to project strength and leadership with the kind of voice he possessed. Additionally, he did himself no favours by agreeing to be interviewed by comedian Russell Brand, whose anti-politics narrative argued that since the introduction of universal suffrage, the elites have ensured that no meaningful change can be achieved by government and therefore people should refuse to vote.

The Tories though had another ace up their sleeves in the form of Lynton Crosby. Crosby decided to focus on the 'wedge issue' of the impending SNP landslide in Scotland. The idea he wanted to get across, was that an undemocratic SNP-Labour coalition would take power, with Ed Miliband propped up by Nicola Sturgeon's party; which voters outside of Scotland had no opportunity to vote for. A poster featuring a miniature Miliband, poking out of the breast pocket of Alex Salmond's suit, with an expression of a confused boy was rather effective.

At the end of the campaign, Miliband's last blunder was to unveil a limestone tablet, inscribed with Labour pledges. It simply looked like a man standing in the shadow of his own political tombstone. It was dubbed the 'Edstone' accordingly, and comically signposted where the election was heading.

Overall, neither party really achieved a decisive campaign advantage, so the effect of the campaign was probably nil.

May 2015 UK general election:

1) *By-election key*	false
2) *Unity Key*	false
3) *Incumbent Leadership Key*	false
4) *Opposition Charisma Key*	true
5) *Third Party Key*	false
6) *Cyclical Incumbency Key*	true
7) *Short-Term Economy Key*	true
8) *Long-Term Economy Key*	true
9) *Foreign Policy/Military Success Key*	true

10) *Foreign Policy/Military Failure Key* false
11) *Policy Change Key*   true
12) *Civil Unrest Key*   true
13) *Scandal Key*   true

<u>*Special Keys*</u>
Third Party Bonus Key 5A   true

<u>*balance of negative keys:*</u>   4

<u>*campaign differential:*</u> nil

<u>*forecast:*</u> Conservative majority of 15

<u>*tally:*</u> Conservatives 333 Labour c. 240

<u>*actual result:*</u> Conservative Majority of 10

Conservatives 330 seats Labour 232 seats Liberal Democrats 8
SNP 56

The election of 2015 came as a major surprise for most commentators, who widely expected another hung parliament. The pollsters had plainly got it wrong, with most of them showing the two main parties level pegging until the very end. It was the greatest polling failure since 1992, but it would not be the last. Subsequent research showed that the sampling was at fault, with left-leaning younger voters being over sampled.

The result also came as a surprise to the Prime Minister, who on the evening of polling day, expressed the view that, 'I can't construct a scenario in which we win over 300 seats...it's just not going to happen.[404]'

The result, which Cameron described as 'the sweetest victory' was important for several reasons. Firstly, it gave the Tories a clear, though slender majority, thus ending the coalition with the Liberals. Secondly, it devastated the Liberal Democrats, reducing them to their lowest parliamentary strength since 1970. They would not make any significant recovery at the next two elections. Thirdly, it led to the SNP landslide in Scotland, thus seriously hampering Labour's chances of securing a majority in the foreseeable future. Fourthly, the strong UKIP showing, combined with the Conservative majority, now made the Brexit referendum inevitable. Cameron could no longer blame the Liberals for tying his hands – he would have to do it.

Yet, there other lessons in this historic and far-reaching vote. Some big assumptions had been smashed overnight. It had been widely assumed that the collapse in Liberal Democrat support would disproportionately benefit the Labour party - as Liberal voters were perceived as being left-of-centre. This proved false. It was also assumed that the rise of UKIP would be disproportionately bad for the Tories, since they were right-wing. This also proved false, as UKIP votes were equally strong in old-Labour working class districts as they were in Tory ones. It seems that many working-class Labour supporters lean left on the economy, but right on culture, so felt alienated by both main parties.

The final comfortable myth that was punctured was that of the infallibility of polling and especially of exit polling. Although the BBC exit poll was much more accurate than the regular polls, it still did not predict a

Tory majority. Could voters have been ashamed of voting Tory at a time of food banks and austerity? It is impossible to be sure. But one thing is certain. The keys would have offered a vastly superior method of
electoral divination than any of the conventional tools on offer.

2015-17: BREXIT: A NATION POLARISES
'I think frankly when it comes to chaos you ain't seen nothing yet.' Nigel Farage, [405]

In the wake of the election victory, Cameron seemed to be in a position of strength and should have looked forward to several more years in Downing Street, despite his rather foolish pre-election announcement that he would not seek a third term. However, it was not to be. With the coalition over and Tory majority rule established, there was now no way to duck the promised referendum on EU membership. This resulted in the passing of the European Union Referendum Act in September 2015 which received Royal Ascent in December. The Act stipulated that a referendum on continued EU membership must be held before the end of 2017.

In early 2016 the campaigning began. 'Britain Stronger in Europe' was the Remain slogan, versus 'Vote Leave' on the Brexiteer side. Although the Tory party was officially neutral, Remain was endorsed by Prime Minister David Cameron and Chancellor George Osborne. It also found the endorsement off all other major parties, save UKIP, as well as big business, the trade unions, the IMF and President Obama, who warned that Britain would 'be at the back of the queue' if she left Europe. [406]The cabinet did not however, remain so united, with several leading Conservatives breaking ranks with the leadership to support Vote Leave.

The biggest name was London Mayor Boris Johnson, who announced his conversion to Leave in February. He became the official leader of Vote Leave, and his extroverted and idiosyncratic manner was effective at connecting with potential leave voters. By this point he had also returned to parliament and many felt was angling at replacing Cameron; who after all would be stepping down before the next election, then scheduled for either 2019 or 2020.

Many have questioned his integrity in supporting Leave, as it provided a terrific platform for his own political ambitions, even if Leave lost. This is particularly compelling when we realise that the Conservative leadership election process allows the membership to have the final say, after the MPs whittle the list of candidates down to just two. The membership is particularly right-wing and Euro-sceptic; choosing Ian Duncan Smith over the far more charismatic and experienced Ken Clarke for the sake of ideological purity in 2001.

Other big names joining the Leave camp included Justice Secretary Michael Gove, who also took a prominent role in the campaign. He dismissed expert pessimism about the impact of Brexit by memorably declaring that, 'People in this country have had enough of experts.' [407]

Ian Duncan Smith, who had resigned from the cabinet in March, in protest at cuts in disability allowance also threw his weight behind Vote Leave.

The Leave campaign was criticised for dishonesty with their repeated claim that Brexit would save Britain £350 million a week, a claim disproven though repeated anyway. Director of vote Leave and Johnson adviser Dominic Cummings cheerfully advised his boss, 'Don't worry Boris, everyone knows the real figure is not £350 million after rebates, but every time a journalist tells you that it's only £170 million, everyone thinks that £170 million is a f*** of a lot of money. The more they ask the better. It's great for vote leave.' [408]Their campaign shifted to a relentless focus on immigration; a simplistic approach, but the consistency of message effectively tapped into public anxieties.

These anxieties had been stoked significantly by the European migrant crisis of the previous summer, when millions of people fleeing the war in Syria came to Europe, with Germany in particular accepting huge numbers. The Cameron administration held firm in the face of European pressure to accept large numbers, even after the outcry caused by a picture of the dead toddler Aylan Kurdi washed up on a Turkish beach. An incident that proved Stalin's old observation, that one death is a tragedy, a million is a statistic. Anxiety over immigration and terrorism was also increased by the horrific ISIS atrocity at the Bataclan concert in Paris the previous winter.

Although the Leave campaign left something to be desired, the same could be said for Remain. Cameron and Osborne's campaign was criticised for its relentless negativity and scaremongering, dubbed 'Project Fear,' with the Tory leadership failing to make a positive case for Britain's continued membership.

Another problem facing the Remain campaign was the lacklustre advocacy of Labour's new leader Jeremy Corbyn. Corbyn, a veteran left-winger and anti-war campaigner was elected to the leadership in September 2015 on a wave of enthusiasm for change following the party's humiliation at the 2015 election under Ed

Miliband. Though initially dismissed a fringe candidate, Corbyn rapidly gained massive traction, and the party experienced a huge influx of new member - most thought to be Corbyn supporters, thus ensuring his victory, against the strong advice of party elders such as former leaders, Tony Blair, Gordon Brown and Neil Kinnock.

Corbyn however, had a long history of Euroscepticism and although he supported Remain, he was not very convincing or enthusiastic - therefore failing to communicate the message to Labour supporters. The Leave campaign meanwhile had two very effective, independent communicators in Boris Johnson and Nigel Farage. An additional handicap for Remain, is that they were scaremongering about hypothetical things that might happen in the future; whereas Farage and Johnson were scaremongering about immigration, which was present in the here and now.

A week before the vote came the shocking murder of Labour MP Jo Cox, gunned down by a man reportedly shouting a nationalistic trope. Whether this had any effect on the vote is debatable, but was almost certainly very minimal. Conspiracy theories abounded as to whether it was a set up job to scare people into voting Remain. If so, it failed.

In the final days of the campaign most polls and most commentators were predicting an easy win for Remain. As polling drew to a close and the public switched on the BBC's coverage, many were to get the shock of their lives. At 04:40 on the morning of June 24th 2016, the result was known: a 52-48 vote to leave the EU.

Later that day, David Cameron stood on the steps of Downing Street to make this announcement.

The British people have made a very clear decision to take a different path and as such I think the country requires fresh leadership to take it in this direction. I will do everything I can as Prime Minister to steady the ship over the coming weeks and months, but I do not think it would be right for me to try to be the captain that steers our country to its next destination.

Was Cameron guilty of jeopardising his country's future in order to try and save his own political skin? Or was the referendum inevitable? Historians will argue this one for decades and probably centuries. However, it can be said that the decision was not taken lightly and Cameron's complacency about the arguments and likely result were shared by a huge number of people. Anthony Seldon sums up his predicament rather well: 'His personal tragedy was to be cut off in his prime, and that the road on which he had embarked with such relish after the 2015 general election led nowhere.'[409]

The shock of the Brexit referendum result was an almost incalculable blow for millions of liberal-left people across the country. It was so unexpected as to trigger choruses of, 'How could this happen?' Labour MP David Lammy exclaimed, 'We can stop this madness'[410] Pop stars at the Glastonbury festival, which was ongoing at the time, were desperately telling the crowds and themselves that, 'We can stop this.'

What this seismic event showed is the huge values gap that had emerged between liberal-left, metropolitan Britain, and culturally conservative, rural and small-town Britain, between the white working class and lower middle class versus the upper middle class, between graduates and non- graduates and between London and the university towns versus the rest of the country. The feeling in the left-behind regions was that EU membership benefited others but not them.

Ultimately it was a conflict about identity, with more culturally conservative people believing strongly in nationalism and British cultural identity, with more liberal-left metropolitan types regarding this as old-fashioned, racist and backwards looking. Although this division had been brewing for several decades, Brexit was the issue that brought it out into the open for the first time.

The referendum result caused an even greater crisis for the Labour party than it did for the Conservatives. Many Labour supporters felt that Corbyn's advocacy of EU membership had been half-hearted, and that a more genuinely pre-European leader, could have won the referendum for remain, as the result had been so close. Corbyn faced a mutiny in the parliamentary party, with twenty-three of his thirty-one shadow cabinet resigning within days of the result. A confidence vote was triggered and Corbyn was heavily defeated by 170- 40. In the Commons, David Cameron said, 'For heaven's sake man, go.'[411] However, multiple trade unions rallied to save the embattled Corbyn, who knew that the union and grassroots membership would support him. A contest was held, with Corbyn being comfortably re-elected in September 2016, easily beating rival Owen Smith by sixty-two to thirty-eight percent.

Following David Cameron's resignation, the Conservative party began the process of electing a new leader for the first time in just over a decade. Cameron had been the longest-serving Tory leader since Mrs Thatcher and despite the difficulties during his tenure, had served for longer than Eden, Home, Heath, Callaghan or Brown.

The contest initially featured Home Secretary Theresa May, former London Mayor Boris Johnson, the Secretary for Work & Pensions Stephen Crabb, former

Defence Secretary Lima Fox and Energy minister Andrea Leadsom. The contest was initially fought to be a close call between Johnson and May, however Johnson pulled out after his hitherto supporter Michael Gove decided to run against him. Whether he could have won if he had decided to stay in the race and fight Gove will of course never be known, but Gove came only third in the first ballot, which saw the elimination of Fox and the withdrawal of Crabb's candidacy.

The second round jettisoned Gove, leaving Leadsom and May to fight it out - or so it seemed. Leadsom however, shot herself in the foot with an interview for The Times in which she claimed to be better-placed to be Prime Minister than Theresa May, because being a mother, gave Leadsom,' a very real stake' in the future, as opposed to the childless May. [412] Leadsom soon dropped out of the contest due to the controversy triggered by the article and May was sworn in as Prime Minister on the 13th July 2016.

Theresa May arrived at ten Downing Street with a radically different mission than that of her predecessor David Cameron; to take Britain out of the European Union. She also had a different domestic agenda, and one largely shaped by her two close advisors Nick Timothy and Fiona Hill. This was a somewhat left-leaning, One Nation conservatism; favouring state intervention in the markets to bring about stability, worker-representation on boards, cutting energy bills, investing in infrastructure, helping to reduce wealth inequality, especially forgotten communities and the JAMs (Just about managing). She was also concerned about gender equality, domestic violence, modern slavery and provision for mental health.

May resented the all-male, public school educated set of Cameron and co, finding them smug and elitist.

Although she was a Remainer, she was not a passionate one, and only identified as such late in the campaign, presumably to keep her options open for the leadership. She attacked Cameron's recently knighted director of communications, Craig Oliver at an awards ceremony in 2016. She referred to his reported attack of wretching and nausea upon hearing the referendum result: 'I have to say, I think we all know that feeling. Most of us experienced it too when we saw his name on the resignation honours list,' [413]

May certainly was a new broom, unceremoniously dumping George Osborne with the lines, 'I hope you understand if I give you some advice as an "older sister." You need to get to know the Conservative party better.' [414] Osborne resigned his seat immediately and became editor of the *Evening standard*, from where he would wreak revenge on May. Had he not done so, he might have been well placed to topple Mrs May after the election of 2017.

In Osborne's place was appointed Philip Hammond. This was an appointment that would cause endless friction for May, since the dry Thatcherite Hammond was not very sympathetic to May's centrist domestic and economic agenda.

David Davis was brought in to head a new and unique department, that of exiting the EU. (DEXEU) - generally known as the Brexit Secretary. Most of her defeated rivals eventually got jobs. Liam Fox was to return as Secretary for International Trade. Boris Johnson became Foreign Secretary, in what the Labour MP Kevin Brennan described as, 'The strangest move since Caligula appointed his horse a senator.' [415]. Michael Gove had made himself a persona non grata for his betrayal of Boris Johnson and so had to spend a year of penance on the backbenches; before coming back after the 2017 election as Secretary of State for the Environment.

Amber Rudd filled May's old shoes as Home Secretary and Justine Greening was appointed Education Secretary.

May's introversion and inability or unwillingness to network with other MPs was exposed by the admission from Chief Whip Gavin Williamson, that he had to make over half the junior ministerial appointments: 'I appointed most of them because she didn't know their names.' [416]Williamson also described how May could not see the point in making personal connections with her own MPs, even once she had become Prime Minister: 'I wanted her to go the House of Commons tea rooms after PMQs and chat to people, but she wouldn't do that. She preferred a Pret a Manger salad in her room in the House of Commons. She never got it.[417]

On the overriding concern of the day - Brexit and how to manage it, May and her team woefully underestimated the difficulties and complexities involved. Their initial strategy was to try and negotiate Britain's exit from Europe, and her post-Brexit relationship with Europe in parallel. The reasonable concern, was that if we delayed negotiating our post-exit relationship with the EU until we were out, then we could be left stranded; out of Europe but sans deal on future relationship.

However, the European Union saw things differently, and demanded that nothing could be discussed until Britain had triggered Article fifty: the process by which the United Kingdom formally handed in her notice for leaving. This created an unbridgeable impasse. May tried to negotiate with individual member states one by one, but the EU held firm and held together. Although May parroted the slogan, 'No deal is better than a bad deal,' she was just as guilty of failing to prepare for No deal and anticipate its likely consequences, as Cameron was for failing to prepare for a Leave vote. The EU's chief negotiator Michael Barnier said that, 'I never heard her (May) talk to me about no deal. Never.' [418]

The May government was also guilty of failing to anticipate how big a problem Northern Ireland would be; in particular the border between it and the republic to the south.

In fairness, Theresa May was hardly alone in this. Much hubris was spouted by the Brexiteers, with Michael Gove claiming that, 'Getting out of the EU can be quick and easy - the UK holds most of the cards.' [419] David Davis also opined on 10th October 2016 that, 'There will be no downside to Brexit, only a considerable upside.' [420]

Combined with a lack of realism and imagination, the May administration was also guilty of a failure to reach out to experts, elder statesmen, the Remainer factions of their own party and to potentially receptive members of the opposition. May failed to listen to differing viewpoints, choosing instead a tribal path, and retreating into the bunker of Downing Street and her special advisors. In Anthony Seldon's devastating words, 'It was one of the worst failures of imagination and opportunity by any Prime Minister since 1945.' [421]

The 2016 Tory conference threw more red meat to the hard Brexiteers, but further polarised the country and antagonised the EU. Home Secretary Amber Rudd caused offence by suggesting that companies should be forced by law to publish the percentage of foreign staff that they employed. The Prime Minister herself stirred the hornets' nest some more with the line that, 'If you are a citizen of the world, you are a citizen of nowhere.' [422]

On the home front, the government found a new challenger from the anti-Brexit campaigner Gina Miller, who launched a legal challenge against the government triggering Article fifty without a Commons vote. The argument was that because the referendum was not legally binding and technically only 'advisory,' it did not give the executive the authority to withdraw Britain from the European Union. The Supreme court found in Miller's favour, resulting in a Daily Mail headline attacking the judges as, 'Enemies of the people.' [423] This ruling resulted in the Commons repealing the 1972 European Communities Act, that had paved the way for Britain's entry to the then EEC under Ted Heath.

The European Union (notification of withdraw) bill passed the Commons on its second vote. Two House of Lords amendments to protect EU nationality and to demand a meaningful Commons vote were defeated by the government and the bill received the royal ascent on the 16th March 2017. A letter triggering Article fifty was submitted to EU President Donald Tusk on March 29th 2017. Britain now had two years to negotiate a Brexit deal - or so it seemed.

May's relationship with her Chancellor Philip Hammond became more and more problematic. At the 2016 conference, May had strongly signalled a left turn: 'Where Markets are dysfunctional, we should be prepared to intervene.' Hammond meanwhile tried to carry on from where Osborne had left off.

In early 2017 the conflict came out into the open when Hammond announced a rise in Class four National Insurance for the self-employed. This was severely problematic however, as the Conservative manifesto for the previous election in 2015 had ruled out tax rises for the duration of the parliament. The situation deteriorated further when Hammond's team briefed the press that May was 'economically illiterate.' [424] However, the outcry was so great that the Treasury were forced to abandon the policy.

With the government needing the support of the Commons for the difficult Brexit negotiations ahead, and Theresa May and her party ahead in the polls, the temptation for the Prime Minister to go for a snap election, to get both the mandate for Brexit and for her own premiership was very strong. Despite publicly ruling out an early election, telling Andrew Marr that; 'I don't think there's a need for an election, the next election will be in 2020,' [425] in April 2017 May announced that there would be one in June. It was to be a fateful decision.

The decision to go to the polls early was brought about by a number of factors. One was the polls, another was the apparent unelectability of Jeremy Corbyn. A third was the unexpected by-election win at Copeland and Stoke, which was the first time that a governing party had taken a seat off the opposition in a by-election since the Falklands war, thirty-five years earlier. Thus, By-election key one was secured. In the words of Dennis Kavanagh and Philip Cowley: 'No right-of-centre party across the world had ever had an electoral asset as strong as May. No left-of-centre party by contrast had ever had an electoral liability like Corbyn.' [426]

The Conservatives yet again hired Lynton Crosby to manage the campaign. He decided upon a presidential type of campaign that featured May very prominently. Unfortunately, he made this choice whilst hardly knowing the Prime Minister at all. It was this fateful focus on the personality of the leader that was to disastrously expose May's fatal shortcomings in communication skills and presentational self-confidence.

The manifesto was an interesting though controversial one, including the return of grammar schools and fox-hunting, more house-building, cutting net migration to below 100,000, replacing the triple lock on pensions with the double lock and the means-testing of winter fuel payments. It was so diverse and radical that even *The Guardian* praised it on the 21st May as, 'the most adventurous re-statement of Conservatism since Margaret Thatcher.'

However, there was one plank of the manifesto that drew enormous criticism and unpopularity: the reform of social care payments, dubbed, 'the dementia tax.' This policy consisted of raising the floor at which people would have to pay for domestic, as opposed to residential care from £23,000 to £100,000. However, the most controversial change was that wealth would now include property, and not simply savings, as had been the case before. This 'dementia tax' became so unpopular and controversial that it had to be dropped. May failed to acknowledge the U-turn however by declaring that, 'Nothing had changed,' whereas everything had changed. [427]

Meanwhile May's awkward persona was being relentlessly exposed by the presidential nature of the seven-week-long campaign. Her mantra of 'Strong and stable' was becoming derided as robotic. She drew more adverse criticism for ducking out of the leaders' TV debate and substituting Home Secretary Amber Rudd in her place. She drew mockery when asked what was the naughtiest thing she had ever done in a TV interview; replying, 'I must confess, that when me and my friends used to run through the fields of wheat, the farmers weren't too pleased about that.' [428]

Events during the campaign took a much darker turn when an ISIS suicide bomber attacked a concert by

American pop star Ariana Grande, killing twenty-two people. May's response seemed wooden and failed to connect with the public.

A week later, more terrorists killed eight people on and around London Bridge in a van and knife attack, before being shot by police. Here, Jeremy Corbyn successfully pivoted the debate to the effects of Tory police cuts whilst May was Home Secretary. Corbyn by this time had also proved far more effective than anyone had thought, with his traditional soapbox approach connecting with a large swathe of disaffected younger people. In particular, his proposals for rail re-nationalisation and abolition of tuition fees won many plaudits.

May's ability to campaign was so poor, that her advisor Fiona Hill became effectively her minder, accompanying her on her campaign bus. She had this to say: 'The journalists didn't like her. She was surly and not particularly pleasant. She was very quiet and seemed unhappy. I asked her, "Have you been down to talk to the journalists at the front of the bus?" She replied, "Why should I?" I said, "Because we're campaigning and you have to tell them the story?" [429]

Lynton Crosby was also scathing, saying that, 'She wasn't good. She would say that she liked general election campaigning but she didn't. What she liked was knocking on doors. She didn't like handling the national media and came over as a reluctant Leaver. As soon as she had anything off-piste to say, she came across poorly.'[430]

The election campaign itself is widely believed to be pivotal in 2017. What actually happened is that it simply exposed the weaknesses of Theresa May's leadership which were already there. Her inability to connect with the public, to network and build working relationships with colleagues or the press, her lack of strategic clarity, paucity of imagination and her tribalism.

At the outset of the campaign, May appeared strong enough to hold the Incumbent Leadership key three. This was not through charisma but through novelty in the post making her temporarily the dominant political figure at that time. In the words of Steve Richards, 'Her authority was so dominant before calling the election, that I think in some ways she had become the most powerful Prime Minister since Margaret Thatcher in the mid-to-late 1980s.'[431] The election campaign was thus the reality-revealer. It did not change anything in itself, just pulled away the curtain.

Even despite May's campaign implosion, division within the Conservative party over Brexit was enough to cost them Party Unity Key two. There was a significant number of Remainer rebels such as Ken Clarke and Anna Soubry, in addition to old guard figures such as Major and Heseltine. This was in addition to significant divisions between 'soft Brexiteers' like the Chancellor Phillip Hammond and the 'hard Brexiteers' such as Michael Gove and Jacob Rees Mogg.

Corbyn had performed a remarkable campaign turn-around, to the point where May's lead over him in satisfaction had collapsed from twenty-nine points before the election was called to just four points, immediately before the vote was held. [432] However, his appeal was too limited to a large minority of younger, left-leaning people to win him the Opposition Charisma key.

The minor parties were in complete disarray, with UKIP having collapsed following Nigel Farage's resignation as leader after the 2015 election, and the perception that their cause had already been won. The SNP also faced significant decline and the Liberal

Democrats had failed to make any significant progress under Vince Cable and then Tim Farron. Thus, at least Third Party Key number five was secure. The Conservatives had only been in power for seven years by this point, so Key six was true as well.

The economy had fared relatively well and so both economic keys remained true.

The defeat suffered by the government on the Brexit referendum was easily sufficient to cost the Foreign Policy Failure key ten. There had been no major success in foreign affairs, and so key nine was also lost.

Obviously, leaving the European Union would have been sufficient to topple Policy Change key eleven, but they had not done it yet; so that key too was lost.

Although Brexit had cause terrible division in the country, it had not manifested in real civil unrest and so key twelve remained true.

The government had not been mired in sleaze, so key thirteen also remained secured.

By the day of the election itself on 8th June 2017 the earlier wild but commonplace expectations of a landslide had receded, but, despite five negative keys, most commentators still expected the Tories to win a comfortable majority. The electorate decided otherwise.

June 2017 UK general election:

1) *By-election key* — true
2) *Unity Key* — false
3) *Incumbent Leadership Key* — false
4) *Opposition Charisma Key* — true
5) *Third Party Key* — true
6) *Cyclical Incumbency Key* — true
7) *Short-Term Economy Key* — true

8) *Long-Term Economy Key*   True
9) *Foreign Policy/Military Success Key* false
10) *Foreign Policy/Military Failure Key* false
11) *Policy Change Key*   false
12) *Civil Unrest Key*   true
13) *Scandal Key*   true

---

balance of negative keys: 5

campaign differential: accounted for already by loss of key 3

forecast: hung parliament

tally: Conservatives 318 seats Labour 250-260 seats

actual result: hung parliament

Conservatives 317 seats. Labour 262 seats

As the BBC exit poll was announced, the disbelief in Conservative Central Office was palpable. Yet, there had been no mistake, save theirs during the campaign. The result was extraordinary in a number of ways. Despite the loss of Conservative seats, the party had substantially increased its vote share from thirty-seven to forty-two percent. May had achieved the highest Tory vote share since the great Thatcher landslide of 1983, and only a whisker away from that.

Corbyn had achieved the highest Labour vote share - forty percent, since Tony Blair's second landslide in 2001; as well as the biggest gain in Labour support between elections since Attlee in 1945. It was also the first election since 1970 when the two main parties achieved more than eighty-percent of the vote between them. In terms of the actual percentage of the electorate voting for parties, Corbyn achieved the greatest show of public support since Blair in 1997.

It is hard to think of another election in which the assumptions that were so strong at its outset, were so upended in the result. Most pollsters steadfastly continued to predict a Tory majority - and a comfortable one at that until the very end. It transpired that the pollsters had overcompensated for their error in 2015. Then, they had over-sampled younger, left-leaning people, and so two years later they did the reverse and under-represented them. Unfortunately, the dynamics of the campaign with the older Conservative base simultaneously demoralised and complacent, and the younger Corbyn base fired up, led to the turnout dynamic pushing in the opposite direction of the pollsters' expectations.

The effect of this result was devastating for May, who probably only survived due to the lack of an obvious successor. Gone was her Thatcheresque air of authority with Jeremy Corbyn feeling buoyed and confident and almost like a winner. His raised status was signposted by his invitation to speak at Glastonbury festival and by the youthful chants of, 'Oh Jeremy Corbyn.'

The effect was to be paralysing for the Brexit process, leading to two and a half years of impasse. Gone was most of Theresa May's ambitious manifesto, the focus now was on political survival. For the Just about managings (JAMs), it would be an unfortunate case of

Jam tomorrow. In the words of Anthony Seldon: 'The biggest single indictment of Theresa May is that she blew all that goodwill and respect and within twelve months had become a figure of contempt across the political spectrum.'[433]

2017-19: THE BATTLE FOR BREXIT

'The Government cannot just be consumed by Brexit. There is so much more to do.' Theresa May [434]

In the wake of the electoral disappointment, May did herself no favours with a speech that sounded like it had been written in anticipation of a big victory. No one was impressed. She was forced to record a second message, later that day to make amends, saying that she was, 'particularly sorry for those colleagues who were MPs or ministers, who contributed so much to our country and who lost their seats and didn't deserve to lose their seats.' Nine junior ministers had in fact lost their seats that day.

May also responded to the electoral drubbing by firing her two closest aides Nick Timothy and Fiona Hill. They became the sacrificial offerings, though in fairness to them they had been opposed to the presidential style of the campaign that had been imposed on them by Lynton Crosby. None of this impressed ex-Chancellor George Osborne who attacked May on the Andrew Marr show as, 'a dead woman walking.'[435]

In such a weakened position, May was unable to effect dramatic changes in personnel, such as removing her recalcitrant Chancellor for example. She did though appoint Damian Green as First Secretary and bring back

Michael Gove into the fold as the new Secretary for DEFRA.

May's overriding priority though was to find a way to make the parliamentary arithmetic work. She approached the Democratic Ulster Party (DUP) and on the 15th June a confidence and Supply agreement was reached that would give the Conservatives a de facto majority of thirteen.

Very soon after the election, Britain was shocked by her worst national disaster since Hillsborough twenty-eight years earlier. Seventy- one people lost their lives when fire ripped through Grenfell Towers in North Kensington. May's awkward communication style was shown up badly here, as it had been throughout the election. This was compounded by bad advice from her officials to keep out of the way and not meet victims. Jeremy Corbyn ignored any such caution and was seen hugging residents and looking natural, relaxed and empathetic. May's absence only reinforced her new image of being cold and out-of-touch. An interview with the BBC's Emily Maitlis was a disaster. Some wondered how different the outcome of the election campaign could have been had the fire happened a few weeks earlier.

Brexit Secretary David Davis tried to continue with his earlier strategy of simultaneous negotiation of Britain's terms of EU exit and the terms of post-Brexit relationship with the EU. He said that getting his way would cause, 'the row of the summer.' In fact, he was forced to climb down in the face of EU intransigency. *The Financial Times* dubbed it, 'the row-back of the summer.' They expanded the critique further with the lines, 'The government is so used to improvisation and secrecy, that it is wrong-footed by the EU's diligence and candour.[436]

Theresa May was hit by more embarrassment at the 2017 Tory party conference when prankster Simon Brodkin handed her a comedy P45 form in the middle of her speech, triggering a fit of coughing. Then the letters on the wall behind her starting falling off, one by one. [437]

Although May managed to agree phase one of the negotiations with the EU in December 2017, which guaranteed rights for EU citizens still living in the UK, and British ex-pats in the EU, as well as a Brexit 'divorce bill' of around £35 billion, the biggest roadblock by far was Northern Ireland. This had not been properly anticipated or planned for, and with the DUP propping up the minority Conservative government, the issue was set to become a major problem.

The majority of Brexiteers did not want a no-deal Brexit, with all the economic damage and chaos at customs which that would entail. However, the 'hard' Brexiteers did not want Britain to remain in the Customs Union or Single Market.

A hard Brexit would therefore create problems for Northern Ireland, because the EU demanded a hard border between Northern Ireland, and the Republic, once Britain left the EU. The idea of a hard border between Northern and southern Ireland was anathema to the Catholics in Northern Ireland, and to those south of the border. The only alternative was a customs border down the Irish Sea, between Great Britain and Ulster. This of course was anathema to the Protestants. The option of keeping the whole of the United Kingdom in the Customs Union was anathema to the 'hard' Brexiteers, as represented by the European Research Group in Parliament (ERG.)

The Northern Ireland Protocol, later called the Irish backstop was a compromise proposal that would have kept Northern Ireland in both the Customs Union and the Single Market, with the rest of the United Kingdom also kept inside the Customs Union until a more permanent and satisfactory solution could be found. David Davis proposed a 'Max Fac' border in Ireland, with technology replacing physical infrastructure such as checkpoints and fences. However, the technological infrastructure would take too long to implement and would not in any case satisfy the EU. Moreover, Britain would be unable to exit the customs union without EU agreement and would risk being kept in a kind of backstop limbo.

In March 2018, a twenty-one-month transition period was agreed upon, wherein Britain could continue to have some benefits and responsibilities of EU membership after technically leaving. The UK was now set to leave the EU in practice on 31st December 2020.

In July 2018 a white paper was produced indicating the government's plans for Britain's post Brexit relationship with the EU. This was known as the Chequers plan, since it resulted from a cabinet meeting held at the Prime Minister's country residence. The plan was to keep the UK in the backstop, so as to avoid a customs border down the Irish Sea, and to keep British access to the Single Market for goods, but not for free movement of people, services or capital.

This deal was not popular amongst Conservative MPs, being dismissed by the ERG as 'BRINO' (Brexit in name only.) It prompted the resignations of Foreign Secretary Boris Johnson, who claimed it would make Britain, 'a vassal state' of the EU. [438] as well as Brexit Secretary David Davis, who told May that the deal was, 'incompatible with what you said in your conference speech and in our manifesto.'[439] Johnson and Davis were replaced by Jeremy Hunt and Dominic Raab respectively.

Theresa May's prospects were not helped by the extraordinarily undiplomatic language of Donald Trump while on his state visit to the UK in July 2018. The rambunctious president said, 'I actually told Theresa May how to do it but.. she didn't listen to me...and her deal will definitely affect trade with the United States, unfavourably.' He went on to praise May's rival Boris Johnson, saying. 'I think he would be a great Prime Minister. I think he's got what it takes.' [440]

Worse was to come in September when Nigel Farage announced his return to front-line politics, attacking the Chequers deal in typically pithy fashion: 'A betrayal of everything people voted for... she doesn't believe in Brexit, she doesn't believe in Britain, she doesn't believe we're good enough to run our own affairs.' [441] Boris Johnson weighed in with a colourful metaphor: 'We look like a seven-stone weakling, being comically bent out of shape by a 500lb gorilla.' [442]

In September, the Chequers deal was also rejected by the EU, for what Michael Barnier describes as, 'Cherry picking' with the four freedoms. [443]

The ugly mood was illustrated by an unnamed cabinet minister who said in The Times that May should, 'bring her own noose' to a meeting of the 1922 committee in October. [444] This too, in the month when three quarters of a million people marched for a second referendum.

Before returning to this all-consuming gorgon of Brexit, let's take a look at the other significant issues that impacted on Theresa May's time in office. There were a number of scandals. In the wake of the 'Me Too' movement, the autumn of 2017 saw the resignation from the government of Defence Secretary Michael Fallon. Fallon had been accused of touching the knee of journalist Julia Hartley Brewer over a decade earlier. He attempted to hang on to his job, but a further, more recent allegation surfaced that he had made sexually inappropriate comments to Leader of the Commons Andrea Leadsom, after she complained about having cold hands.

A month later, First Minister Damian Green was forced to resign after pornography was found on his office computer and over his subsequent lies about the matter to colleagues and officials.

The International Development Secretary Pritti Patel resigned in November 2017 after failing to be honest with the Prime Minister about ministerial meetings with Israel.

In spring 2018 the government was hit by a different kind of scandal when it transpired that thousands of immigrants from Caribbean countries who had come to the UK between 1948 and 1970 had been detained, discriminated against and in eighty-three cases, actually deported from the country because they had lacked documentation proving the legitimacy of their residency in the UK. This was due to the government's tougher line on immigration, even though in 1971, the Heath government had given the 'Windrush' generations indefinite leave to remain in the UK. The government had also destroyed the immigrants' landing cards in 2010.

The scandal led to the resignation of Home Secretary Amber Rudd in April 2018 and she was succeeded by Sajid Javid – the son of a Pakistani Muslim immigrant. Although a compensation scheme was eventually implemented, by June 2022 only seven percent of victims and one quarter of actual claimants had been compensated thus far. [445]

Although these scandals were damaging, they did not impugn the integrity of the Prime Minister herself, or establish a clear impression of a government rotten with corruption. The sexual scandals were about individual failings and the Windrush scandal was one of systemic failure, building up over a long period of time. Thus, Scandal key thirteen remained true for the government.

In terms of foreign affairs, apart from Brexit, the biggest crisis for the May government came unexpectedly from the streets of Salisbury. In March 2018, an elderly man Sergei Skripal and his daughter Yulia fell ill with suspected poisoning in the Wiltshire city. A police officer who attended the scene, also fell ill. It soon transpired that they had been poisoned with a Novichok nerve agent. Skripal was a retired Russian military officer and double agent, and Theresa May publicly accused Russia of the crime. Twenty-three Russian intelligence officers were expelled - the greatest number for over thirty years. May then lobbied the EU for support against Russia. This rare instance of successful statecraft resulted in an EU statement; 'We stand in unqualified solidarity with the UK in the face of this grave challenge to our shared security.' [446] The EU followed Britain's example by expelling over 100 Russian intelligence officers. Three months later, a woman in Amesbury died after being given what appeared to be a perfume bottle which she sprayed on her wrist. This was the same nerve agent that had been carelessly discarded by Russian agents. Although May's role in this case was successful - allowing her to draw on her experience as Home Secretary, much in the way that the 2008 financial crisis allowed Gordon Brown to draw on his time as Chancellor; overall it fell well short of securing Foreign Policy Success key nine.

The same can be said of Britain's limited intervention in Syria against the Assad regime in April

2018. This followed further use of chemical weapons by the regime in civilian areas. British jets joined forces with the Americans in a bombing mission against suspected chemical plants in Syria. May decided to undertake this action without a Commons vote due to opposition from Jeremy Corbyn. She had clearly learned the lessons from Cameron's debacle five years earlier.

The seventieth anniversary of the NHS founding was marked by the announcement of an increase in spending to 3.4%. Although this was less than the 3.7% average increase since its founding, this at least marked a move away from the grim austerity of the Cameron years. It also marked an abandonment of the policy of competition, announced in the 2012 Health Act. This change of policy, though significant, falls way short of turning Policy Change key eleven.

Although Jeremy Corbyn had seen an unexpected spike in popularity during the 2017 election, resulting in buzzwords such as 'youthquake,' his moment in the sun would prove short-lived. The explosion of controversy over the rise of anti-Semitism in the party, epitomised by Corbyn's approval of an antisemitic mural in 2012, effectively ended this period of 'Corbynmania' in the spring of 2018.

One third party development which perhaps had the potential to turn key five was Change UK, or the Independent Group for Change, set up in February 2019, after seven Labour MPs left the party in protest against Jeremy Corbyn's leftward lurch, failure to deal with anti-Semitism and apparent ambiguity over Brexit. They were joined soon by three Tories who were unhappy at their party's hardline approach to Brexit.

The grouping campaigned for a second referendum on Brexit and a return to a more centrist consensual politics. Yet the group never caught the public imagination. They made several key mistakes, including failure to become a proper party, just a grouping, which many people found a something and nothing movement. They failed to elect a leader and the name 'Change UK' sounded vague, shop-worn and tired. They also failed to field candidates in the 2019 Euro-elections. Therefore, they never stood a chance of tipping Third party key five against the government.

By the end of 2018, May's Chequer's deal was now in serious trouble, with the greatest difficulties being faced with her own MPs. Brexit Secretary Dominic Raab resigned in November, as did the Secretary for Work and Pensions Esther Mcvey. The latter declaring that, 'We have gone from "No deal is better than a bad deal" to any deal is better than no deal.' [447]

The Shadow Attorney Sir Keir Starmer used the 'Humble Address' procedure to force the government to release the legal advice of his counterpart Geoffrey Cox. After failing to produce the advice, the House of Commons found the government to be in contempt of parliament for the first time in history. The advice was then published, but was still deemed to be incomplete. However, what was released effectively confirmed that that Britain would indeed find itself permanently trapped in the backstop.

The first meaningful vote on Theresa May's deal was pulled at the last minute in December 2018, after facing the near-certain prospect of a crushing defeat.

This humiliation precipitated a vote of confidence being held on Theresa May by Conservative MPs. Although May survived - winning by 200 to 117, the scale of the victory was not quite decisive enough to shore up her increasingly precarious position. May then foolishly repeated the mistake of her two predecessors David Cameron and Tony Blair by pledging to stand down by the next election; thus, making her even more of a lame duck Prime Minister. The Financial Times summed up the situation on the 12th December with this assessment: 'The race for the Conservative Party leadership was underway whatever the outcome of Wednesday's confidence vote.'

The EU remained stone-faced and intransigent, with Juncker declaring that, 'We do not want the UK to think there can be any form of renegotiation whatsoever.' [448] The British public remained bitterly divided with thirty-six percent supporting a second referendum, thirty-one favouring a no deal Brexit and only eleven percent believing that May should simply force her deal through parliament. [449]

Theresa May now belatedly set up a cabinet committee to look at the prospect of a no-deal Brexit: EUXT (P) (European Exit and Trade) preparedness.) The Attorney General Geoffrey Cox lambasted his fellow politicians by saying that, 'If no deal happened - the public would say,

"What are you playing at? What are you doing? You are not children in the playground. You are legislators and this is your job." [450]

When the meaningful vote was finally held on 15th January, the result was the worst defeat in British Parliamentary history; 432-202 against. 140 Conservative MPs voted against the government, one more than rebelled against Tony Blair's war in Iraq. All ten DUP lawmakers voted against it. May's response was this: 'It is clear that the House does not support the deal...but tonight's vote tells us nothing about what it does support.'

The follow day a confidence vote was held in the government. Jeremy Corbyn delivered his verdict: 'This is a catastrophic deal...The Prime Minister's governing principle of delay and denial has reached the end of the line.' The government won by 325-306.

The House also voted against May going back to Europe for better terms.

The second vote on the deal was also lost – though not quite so catastrophically by 391-242. It was only the fourth worst defeat in UK parliamentary history. This was followed by an amendment by Tory MP, Caroline Spelman to rule out a no-deal Brexit. This passed despite government whipping against it. The BBC's Laura Kuenssberg pronounced that, 'This is now a crisis... the rules that traditionally have preserved governments are out of the window. The Prime Minister has been defeated again. Her authority - if not all gone, is in shreds.' [451]

Next, Parliament voted to ask the EU for an extension to Article fifty by 412-212, and Commons Speaker John Bercow ruled out the holding of a third meaningful vote, citing a precedence from 1604. With the deadline approaching there was an unprecedented atmosphere of paralysis and polarisation. A million people marched for a second referendum; equally the greatest ever protest in British history - against the Iraq war in 2003; this time under the banner of 'Put it to the People.' Meanwhile, a pro-Brexit march started in Sunderland and headed south.

In a bid to cut through the politicking and appeal straight to the people, Theresa May went on TV to attack her fellow parliamentarians, in a speech reminiscent of Ted Heath's appeal to the public in 1974.

The public have had enough. You are tired of the infighting. You are tired of the political games and arcane procedural rows. Tired of MPs talking about nothing else but Brexit. You want this stage of the Brexit process to be over and done with. I agree. I am on your side. It is now time for MPs to decide.

This riled up many parliamentarians but ultimately changed little. Immediately after this, a delegation from the ERG told May she had to go. Ian Duncan Smith told her, 'No one believes that you are capable of making the changes required. You've run out of road. You know what has to happen. You have to say that you're going to go and that you're not going to be part of the future process.' [452]

John Bercow eventually allowed a somewhat re-worked third meaningful vote - but alas, it met the same fate as its hapless predecessors, being defeated by 344 to 286. This finally prompted the Prime Minister to begin talks with Labour in a bid to resolve the impasse.

This failed to bring fruit, only further Tory scorn. However, the Commons did receive its request for an extension to Article Fifty; to October 31st 2019.

The May local elections were dire for the Conservatives who lost over 1300 councillors. May, who was simultaneously hit by the resignation of her Defence Secretary Gavin Williamson for leaking sensitive information from the National Security Council, appealed once more to her MPs. She warned them of the dangers of endless extensions to Article Fifty that would lead to, 'a nightmare future of permanently polarised politics.' [453]

May offered MPs a Commons vote on whether to hold a second referendum on the government's deal. This prompted the resignation of Leader of the House Andrea Leadsom, as May's offer conflicted with what had previously been agreed. So far, there had been thirty-six ministerial resignations under Theresa May - twenty of them over Brexit.

The Euro elections were the next broadside to batter this already badly-listing ship of state. The Conservatives came fifth on nine percent. The result was the Tories' worst ever in a national poll. Nigel Farage's new Brexit party topped the poll with thirty-two percent.

The following day, the 24th May, Theresa May stood outside Downing Street and made a fateful, though inevitable announcement.

It is and will always remain, a matter of deep regret to me that I have not been able to deliver Brexit. It will be for my successor to seek a way forward that honours the result of the referendum.

She confirmed that she would be standing down as Conservative leader on the seventh of June and would remain as Prime Minister until a successor was elected.

Britain's most disastrous Prime Minister since Anthony Eden received some further insults from her rival Boris Johnson. 'There are two people I credit for my emergence as front-runner: Theresa May for her failure to deliver, and Nigel Farage who exploited the position left by her failure to deliver.' [454]

President Trump also added a touch of derision in his characteristically blunt fashion: 'The good news for the wonderful United Kingdom is that they will soon have a new Prime Minister. While I thoroughly enjoyed the magnificent state visit last month, it was the Queen whom I was most impressed with.'[455]

The leadership challenge to replace Theresa May, saw an unprecedented thirteen MPs throw their hats into the ring. When asked if she was going to watch the televised leadership debates, May replied that, 'I know everything I need to know about these people. I don't need to know any more.' [456]

I will leave the last words to historian, Anthony Seldon.

May wasn't up to it. Never again. [457]

In the crowded field of the 2019 Conservative Leadership challenge, Boris Johnson won with a clear majority over the former Foreign Secretary Jeremy Hunt, after other heavyweights such as Sajid Javid, Michael Gove and Dominic Raab were knocked out during the five rounds with MPs.

The ebullient though anarchic Johnson cast himself as the only candidate who could 'Get Brexit done' and break the three-year old political impasse. His motivation for leading the leave campaign had been questioned by some. 'One thousand percent cynical,' [458] opined former Chancellor George Osborne. Johnson's right-hand man Oliver Lewis elaborated further: 'Come out for Brexit and we lose, I position myself as a hero Euro-sceptic, from which I can win the leadership at the next contest. If we win, then I'll be clear favourite for PM.'[459]

This conspiratorial view of Johnson's motivations is lent a bit of weight by his reaction to the shock result: 'Holy S***, f***, what have we done?' [460]

However, by summer 2019, with the May premiership ending in such dismal failure, the bar had been set quite low for her successor. Now, in Downing Street, Dominic Cummings effectively took charge and ruthlessly focussed minds on the one goal of achieving Brexit at any cost. 'Brexit is the sole objective for the next ninety-five days until the deadline on October 31st. We are leaving by any means necessary.' [461]

He threatened to fire anyone caught leaking cabinet papers in a bid to impose some order on the chaotic Downing Street of 2019.

Johnson's first big gambit was his decision to prorogue parliament on the 28th August. This arcane procedure was designed to effectively shut down parliament for six weeks until the Queen's speech in the middle of October - thus robbing it of time to obstruct Brexit ahead of the deadline. MPs were understandably furious that the executive had decided to silence them in this way, and used the six days before prorogation to pass what became known as the Benn Act, after Hillary Ben. This act stipulated that if no deal were to be agreed by the 19th October, then the Prime Minister was to request an extension to the 31st January - thus ruling out a no-deal Brexit.

The government's response was to withdraw the whip from the twenty-one Conservative MPs who voted for the Benn Act. These included some high-profile names. In addition to well-known remainer rebels such as Anna Soubry and Ken Clarke, there was another former Chancellor, Philip Hammond and the grandson of Sir Winston Churchill, Nicholas Soames. This act prompted the resignation from the cabinet of the Work and Pensions Secretary Amber Rudd and Boris Johnson's own brother Jo, the Science Minister. The Prime Minister reportedly told his aides; 'Those perfidious f******, I'll deal with anyone who goes against me.' [462]

Meanwhile, the Supreme Court ruled that the prorogation of parliament was unlawful and be immediately annulled. Their reasoning was that they could find no good reason why parliament should have been prorogued. This followed a ruling in the same vein by the Scottish Supreme court, which argued that the prorogation was intended for the, 'Improper purpose of stymieing parliament.'[463] Prior to this ruling, there had been some uncertainty as to whether the prorogation had actually been justiciable.

Johnson's complete loss of control of parliament was further underlined by Dominic Grieve's forcing of the government to publish its communications concerning the prorogation as well as 'Operation Yellowhammer' - the contingency planning for a no-deal Brexit, especially relating to anticipated shortages of food and medicine.

In October, the Prime Minister finally agreed a deal with the EU. The main difference between it and the failed deal of Theresa May was that Northern Ireland would remain in the Single market, whilst Great Britain would exit both the Single Market and the Customs Area. The bill passed the House of Commons on its first reading, but the Commons defeated the timetable for debating it, thus scuppering any chance of leaving the EU on October 31st. Additionally, Oliver Letwin tabled a motion withholding parliament's approval until the legislation had actually been passed.

With this intransigence, Johnson's next move was to try and call a general election to break the deadlock. However, with the Fixed Term Parliament Act still in force and with Labour opposed to the idea, this tactic too appeared blocked. However, it was decided that an election could be called using a simple Act of Parliament, which would only require a simple, rather than a two-thirds majority. With the SNP in favour of an election being held before Alex Salmond's trial for sexual assault in the new year, Labour decided to abstain, and the vote to go for a December election passed by 299 to 70 votes.

The necessity of going to the country was underpinned by an IPSOS-MORI poll showing that only fourteen percent of the public had confidence in the government. [464]

As the parliament - the longest since the seventeenth century drew to a close, the Attorney General Geoffrey Cox launched an excoriating attack on what he saw as a corrupt parliament, trying to obstruct the will of the people by using any ruse that came to hand.

This Parliament is a dead parliament. It should no longer sit. It has no moral right to sit on these green benches.... They could vote no confidence at any time. But they are too cowardly. [465]

As the election neared, the government also appeared to be drawing a line under the decade of austerity, with policies announced such as increasing the police force by 20,000 and more funding for health and education.

By this point Corbyn had long ceased to be popular or exciting and his party was being battered by continuing allegations of anti-Semitism. Boris Johnson campaigned heavily on the dominant theme of the day – Brexit. His memorable phrases included an 'oven-ready' deal and making Britain, 'Corbyn neutral.'

The Labour campaign was effectively hobbled by the party's torturous position on and relationship with Brexit. There was a split between the long-term Eurosceptic leader, whom many saw as a closet Brexiteer and the Europhile parliamentary party. There was also a divide between the mostly socially conservative white, working-class constituency of the party and the culturally left-wing, middle-class chunk of the party's electoral coalition.

This was placed under further strain by Boris Johnson's effectiveness at campaigning in working class areas. Although upper class, his bombastic and dishevelled style seemed to connect to Brexit voters. He was described by his 2016 leadership campaign manager Mark Fullbrook as 'The Heineken politician - able to reach and attract support that no other Conservative could dream of.'[466] Contemporary Historian Anthony Seldon described him as, 'an exceptional communicator with an inimitable ability to reach out beyond his party.'[467] Thus, Johnson secured Incumbent Leadership key three for the Tories.

Corbyn came under particular pressure following a car-crash interview with the forensic Andrew Neil. Neil probed the absurdity of Labour's Brexit policy. The policy was that they would annul Johnson's deal and agree their own deal. This would be followed by a referendum asking people to choose between Labour's deal and no Brexit. Corbyn though would not campaign for his own deal in the referendum, and nor in all probability would any other senior government figure. Most leavers simply saw this as a ruse to cancel Brexit altogether.

Corbyn's electoral position was also not helped by a terrorist incident in which two people were stabbed to death by a convicted terrorist on early release at London Bridge. This put Corbyn's association with terrorists such as the IRA and Hamas into sharp focus. Pictures had surfaced of him laying a wreath at the funeral of one of the terrorists of the 1972 Munich Olympics siege. Corbyn's defence was that he was, 'Present but not involved.'[468] This sounded all too much like a darker equivalent of Bill Clinton's defence of his youthful cannabis experiences. 'I smoked but I didn't inhale.'

As a result, Corbyn achieved the worst personal approval ratings of any opposition leader since MORI polling began on the topic in 1977, with a net approval rating of minus forty-four just before the election.[469] This disastrous performance gifted the Conservative government, Opposition Implausibility key four A, as well as securing Opposition Charisma key four.

The threatened Remainer alliance between the Liberal Democrats, Greens and Welsh nationalists was fatally undermined when Nigel Farage announced that he would stand down candidates in Tory-held seats. Thus, key five was saved for the government. Being in power for nine-and-half years was also way too short to threaten the Cyclical Incumbency key six. Few by-elections had been lost, so key one also remained true.

The short-term economy was stagnating but not in recession, so was narrowly saved. Long-term economy key eight did not fare so well, with growth being slowed down by Brexit uncertainty and the long malaise that still had not been shrugged off from the Global Financial Crisis over a decade before. Although there had been no recession or major devaluation during the term, the continuous anxiety and uncertainty caused by the political crisis and its visible symptoms in the stock market and currency trading were sufficient to topple key eight.

The newly-agreed Brexit deal, though not pleasing everyone was more than many had considered possible, and so succeeded in rescuing Foreign Policy Success key nine. It also had rescued Foreign Policy Failure key ten, which would have been lost had no deal been forthcoming. Although achieving Brexit would be enough to turn Policy Change key eleven in the government's favour, it had not yet been passed by parliament, and until the government got itself a reasonable majority might never be achieved. Thus, key eleven remained lost to the Johnson administration.

Although the country was bitterly divided, there was not really major civil unrest on the streets, and so Civil Unrest key twelve remained true.

Although there had been some government scandal, it had not been sufficient to taint the government as a whole or impugn the office of the Prime Minister. The Windrush scandal was more a systemic failure of policy implementation than an episode of vice or lawbreaking. Events like the resignation of Defence Secretary Michael Fallon, were isolated incidents of poor personal behaviour and fell somewhat short of the systemic sleaze that engulfed the Major administration. Thus, key thirteen remained true.

December 2019 UK general election:

1) *By-election key*	true
2) *Unity Key*	false
3) *Incumbent Leadership Key*	true
4) *Opposition Charisma Key*	true
5) *Third Party Key*	true
6) *Cyclical Incumbency Key*	true
7) *Short-Term Economy Key*	true
8) *Long-Term Economy Key*	false
9) *Foreign Policy/Military Success Key*	true
10) *Foreign Policy/Military Failure Key*	true
11) *Policy Change Key*	false
12) *Civil Unrest Key*	true
13) *Scandal Key*	true

Special Keys:
Opposition Implausibility Bonus Key 4A

balance of negative keys: 2

campaign differential: + 2-3 seats for Conservatives

forecast: Conservative majority of 80

tally: Conservatives: 365 Labour: c. 200

actual result: Conservative majority of 80

Conservatives 365 seats Labour 202 seats Liberal Democrats 11
SNP 48

The election saw the Tories win a crushing victory against the unpopular Labour party of Jeremy Corbyn. The Tories gained their biggest win since 1987, with the highest share of the vote since 1979. Labour suffered their worst electoral drubbing since 1935. The Liberals also failed to secure a breakthrough with their leader Jo Swinson losing her seat.

With such a thumping victory, Boris Johnson had secured a mandate for Brexit, which would now be all-but guaranteed to happen in some form or the other. As Britain was poised to enter a new decade, it seemed to many that the Tories would be in power longer than their eighteen years between 1979 and 1997. It seemed that Labour would be in the wilderness for many years and perhaps might never return as a party of government. It was claimed that this would be a Conservative decade.

However, once again, the long-term picture was to prove illusory.

2019- 2024: THE OMNICRISIS TERM
'My ideal world is, we're there, we're in the EU, trying to make it better. Boris Johnson 2015 [470]

Following the near-landslide win in December 2019, the government moved fast on Brexit. The European Union (Withdrawal Agreement) Act 2020 was passed in the Commons on its second reading by 358-234. It became law on 23rd January 2020 and Britain officially left the European Union on 31st January 2020. However, the transition period would continue until 31st December 2020, after which the UK left in practice as well as in name. This was sufficient to turn Policy Change key eleven. It would not in itself turn Foreign Policy Success key seven, as the public were still bitterly divided on the issue.

After this, the government appeared to be resting on their laurels. Labour appeared to be knocked into a cocked-hat, the Liberals still irrelevant and a decade in power was seen as highly probable for the Tories. There was much talk of 'levelling up' for the forgotten north, but little apparent substance. Boris Johnson pursued grandiose plans such as a bridge between Northern Ireland and Scotland, as well a the HS2 rail link between London and the North. All of these dreams would eventually turn to dust.

Indeed, no party is ever destined to be in power for longer than a term (and perhaps not even for as long as that) and consequently no opposition is ever destined to be in the wilderness for more than five years either. What could possibly upset the applecart of Conservative hegemony? Well, as Harold Macmillan used to say, 'Events dear boy, events.'

Events were not too long in coming. By the end of January, reports were coming in of an infectious, respiratory, viral disease that was spreading in the Wuhan province of China. Initially, the mood was complacent in the west, but as cases were recorded in increasing numbers of countries, anxiety began to mount. Boris Johnson did not attend many of the early COBRA meetings in late winter 2020, and in fact was on holiday for some of that time. It was towards the end of February, with COVID-19, (Coronavirus disease 2019) being reported in the UK, as well as a major outbreak in Italy, that the SAGE committee began to realise there was an approaching epidemic wave that could no longer be stopped.

However, even into early March the Prime Minister went on TV to play down the idea of nation-wide restrictions, and speculate that we should 'take it on the chin.' [471] However, the single most important influence in changing the Prime Minister's thinking seems to be the model by Neil Furguson in March, which predicted half a million deaths unless drastic action was taken. The top team were divided, with Michael Gove and Dominic Cummings proponents of lockdown, and Rishi Sunak sceptical. The Prime Minister oscillated between the two positions, being swayed this way and that by those around him. Apparently, Cummings used to call him the 'shopping trolley' as he continually veered direction. [472]

Then, on the 23rd March, the Prime Minister announced a full lockdown, the like of which had never been seen in the United Kingdom before. Everyone but 'key workers' were ordered to stay at home. People were banned from entering other people's homes and were only allowed to leave their home twice a day - once for shopping and once for exercise on foot. Pubs, restaurants and non-essential shops were forced to close. Although the government initially attempted to keep schools open, with schools being closed in Scotland and many parents withdrawing their children from school independently, pretty soon all schools and colleges were forced to shut.

The Prime Minister appeared on a national broadcast - the first since Tony Blair's invasion of Iraq in 2003. He said, 'From this evening, I must give the British people a very simple instruction - you must stay home.' [473] In addition to these measures, the government announced a policy of 'Social Distancing' in which individuals had to stay at least two metres away from each other. The measures were enforced by law, with police having the power to issue fines and disperse gatherings. The measures were enacted with the Coronavirus Act 2020. This got the royal ascent on 25th March. However, many of the restrictions were enforced under the much earlier 1984 Public Health Control of Disease Act.

Britain therefore was thrust into her worst crisis since the Second World War. The Chancellor Rishi Sunak announced a 70 billion-pound furlough scheme which paid eighty percent of effectively curfewed workers' wages.

The disruption to healthcare was shattering. Operations were cancelled without warning and thousands of patients were transferred to care homes to free up more beds. This unfortunately spread the disease to the care homes, as well as resulted in the deaths of many of the discharged hospital patients. Even dentists shut down.

Although there was early cynicism about the reality of COVID-19, with absurd conspiracy theories abounding that it was caused by 5G phone masts, the rapid rise in deaths and cases was undeniable. At the first-wave peak in April, there were more than 1500 deaths per day and hospitals pushed to breaking point. In Birmingham, mass graves were dug as so many died in a very short space of time.

The Prime Minister himself fell ill with COVID, and narrowly avoided passing it on to the Queen. He had to work in isolation from his cabinet colleagues, joining meetings via Zoom. This was far from easy. Anthony Seldon recounts the experience in his book, *Johnson at 10*.

'His fumbling constantly disconnected his iPad from Zoom and he was clueless as how he could rejoin the meeting, so a series of iPads connected to the calls were placed outside his room. Once he had broken the first, he could grab the second, then third, then fourth.' [474]

Some speculated that he caught the illness from foolishly shaking the hands of everyone in a hospital a few weeks before; an act which provoked a public headshaking from Chief Scientific Adviser Patrick Valence.[475] However, the timing would suggest he contracted the virus a little later.

Johnson's condition suddenly deteriorated and he was admitted to Guy & St Thomas's Hospital on 5th April. The situation became even more grave when he was put into intensive care. Roughly half of all ICU patients were put onto ventilators and half of those died. So, the Prime Minister now had a twenty-five percent chance of death.

Due to Britain's lack of a proper written constitution, the procedure in these kinds of situations is a little unclear. Dominic Raab, the Foreign Secretary had also been made First Secretary of State, and so took over cabinet meetings. Many apparently found his more orderly approach a breath of fresh air. Fortunately, Johnson began to recover and was soon out of hospital.

He did still need a few weeks at Chequers to fully recuperate.

As the first wave of the epidemic passed its peak and began falling back in May, the government announced some partial restrictions on allowing people to return to work. This was followed by the beginning of a phased re-opening of schools in June, together with the re-opening of 'non-essential' shops. Many of the restrictions were eased off during the summer, with the government even promoting an 'Eat out to help out' scheme which offered people discounted meals in restaurants.

However, as some restrictions were easing, another was coming into force. The government mandated the wearing of masks on public transport in June and in shops a month later. At around this time the policy of local and regional lockdowns was introduced, with a four-tier system. Unfortunately, this had the effect of only suppressing the virus when it had already reached epidemic proportions in a region - therefore too late.

One disastrous aspect of the COVID policy was in schools. With pupils' education being abruptly terminated in March, exams would be impossible to hold. So, the decision was for teachers to award grades based on their predictions for what the pupils would have achieved. This had to be moderated downwards by the exam boards in a bid to avoid grade inflation. The result was bitter disappointment for thousands of school children.

The most powerful figure in the government during this whole COVID period was neither an elected official nor a civil servant. Dominic Cummings, Boris Johnson's chief advisor was described by Anthony Seldon as the most powerful political adviser in Britain since William Cecil during the reign of Elizabeth I. [476]

Cummings was effectively the driving force behind achieving Brexit in 2019 and was a man who held parliament, cabinet and the civil service in contempt, and who wanted to drastically re-order the political world. Cummings was an almost Nietzschian elitist, who wanted education to advance the top one percent, whilst not really caring about the masses. His dismissiveness of the civil service was blatant: 'It cannot manage public services... it concentrates power in a small number of people who are increasingly crap.' [477]

In January 2020, Cummings actually advertised for, 'Weirdos and misfits with odd skills to apply for number 10 jobs' 'Public school bluffers,' were advised that they need not bother to apply. [478]

After winning the election and the battle for Brexit, Cummings' influence continued to increase, with Boris Johnson being easily swayed by the opinions of others, partly because of his own lack of strategic clarity, and therefore unable to rein in his Machiavellian adviser.

The power wielded by Cummings is best exemplified by his conniving to have Chancellor Savid Javid removed in February 2020. Relations between the two men had been poor since Cummings had ordered one of Javid's aides to be escorted out of the building in 2019.

The conflict was brought to the boil early in the new year when Cummings and Johnson demanded that Javid fired six of his advisors. Javid refused, and when Johnson refused to climb down, his Chancellor resigned, telling journalists that, 'I do not believe any self-respecting minister would accept the conditions.'[479]

When a special adviser at DEFRA criticised Cummings for publicly humiliating young aides to both Theresa Villiers the DEFRA Secretary and Andrea Leadsom the Secretary for Business, Energy and Industrial Strategy, it is perhaps no coincidence that both these cabinet ministers and their respective aides were fired in the February reshuffle.

Cummings became increasingly contemptuous and overtly disrespectful of senior cabinet ministers and civil servants, calling them, 'Useless f***pigs, morons, c***s' in emails and WhatsApp messages. [480]

Cummings was even instrumental in driving from office the Chief Secretary to the Cabinet Mark Sedwill in the late summer of 2020.[481] They had earlier clashed over the COVID response, with Sedwill outraged by the overweening power of the adviser and the almost total breakdown of cabinet government. Sedwill told Cummings; 'We are not running a dictatorship here and the PM is not taking nationally significant decisions with a bunch of Number 10 SPADS (Special Advisers) and no ministers, no operational experts and no scientists. If necessary, I will take over the 8:15 slot and chair a daily meeting myself.' [482]

Cummings' position in the government was brought into great peril by his escapades during the lockdown. In May 2020 it transpired that he had driven his wife and son from London to his parents' house in county Durham whilst feeling unwell. He had then driven them to Barnard's castle - ostensibly in order to have his eyesight tested; which he thought had been affected by COVID. This resulted in a torrent of public criticism and cross-party demands that Cummings be sacked. Yet Johnson held onto him in the teeth of condemnation.

However, the scandal surrounding the comings and goings of Mr Cummings refused to die down and the moral authority of the government to impose further restrictions on the public was undermined.

The end for Cummings was brought about by this and by the growing disagreement between him and the Prime Minister over the need for fresh lockdowns, with

Cummings suspected of leaking government plans for an autumn lockdown, in an apparent bid to bounce the Prime Minister into enforcing one. [483]

Cummings was fired on November 14th and was pictured leaving Downing Street with a box of his belongings. Following his departure, there were multiple changes in Downing Street personnel, but alas no real improvement in its effectiveness, with the cabinet divided into feuding cliques until the very end.

Then, as cases began to rise in late summer, more restrictions came into force. These included the 'Rule of six' whereby no more than six people could gather indoors, and the rather odd 10 PM curfew for the hospitality sector. With deaths steadily rising in October, the Prime Minister announced a second Lockdown on October 31st.

There had been considerable cabinet conflict however. Michael Gove had apparently told Boris Johnson, 'Prime Minister, if you don't do this, then ambulances will be arriving at hospitals and getting turned away because they don't have the space. We will be sending in soldiers to guard hospitals to keep people out if we don't lock down now.' [484] Johnson had reportedly exploded, shouting, 'No more f******lockdowns. Let the bodies pile high in their thousands.' [485]

Although the second lockdown was lifted in early December, the rise in cases led to regional lockdowns being implemented in London and the South East over Christmas, precipitating a mass exodus from the capital that doubtlessly spread the disease far and wide. These restrictions extended to a full nation lockdown in early January, which lasted until April.

Amidst the gloom, there was one crucial event that became the light at the end of a very dark and seemingly very long tunnel. On the 9th November the big pharma company Pfizer announced the development of a vaccine with a ninety percent efficacy. The UK vaccine taskforce ordered forty million doses. Then on the 23rd November, Oxford University announced an Anglo-Swedish Astro-Zeneca vaccine. 100 million shots of that were ordered too.

Speaking to the Commons, Health Secretary Matt Hancock described the day of the vaccine's approval as, 'a day to remember, in frankly a year to forget.' [486]At last Boris Johnson could boast one clear-cut advantage of leaving the European Union. If we had stayed in, we could not have independently have ordered so much of the vaccine so quickly. There is agreement on this at least.

The following month saw the discovery of a new strain of Corona virus - Alpha. In January of 2021 the mass dissemination of the vaccine began, with the oldest age groups receiving them first. There was at last a way out of COVID, though it would undoubtedly take time whilst the virus took more lives.

The second wave peaked in January 2021 with a similar mortality rate to the first and fell away by March. In April the lockdowns were lifted and most restrictions were finally lifted on so-called 'Freedom Day'- July 19th.

The first straw in the wind that the government's popularity might be suffering, came in the shocking Amersham by-election of June 2021, when the safe Tory seat was taken with ease by a resurgent Liberal Democrat party. Part of the anger was about the environmental damage caused by preparations for HS2, (ironically later abandoned.) This occurred just three months after the Conservatives took the Labour seat of Hartlepool from Labour. If a week is a long time in politics, then three months can be an aeon.

The government's authority to impose lockdowns was dealt another blow when The Sun newspaper revealed in June 2021 that the Health Secretary Matt Hancock had breached the COVID rules with CCTV footage of him kissing one of his advisers, with whom he was having an affair. Intimate contact with people outside your household was still prohibited at the time. Hancock soon resigned, and was replaced by the former Chancellor Sajid Javid. Although embarrassing, this was not quite sufficient to topple Scandal key thirteen.

However, in November the Conservative MP and former minister Owen Patterson was found guilty of multiple breaches in the advocacy rules by the Parliamentary Commissioner of Standards, who said that; 'No previous case of paid advocacy has seen so many breaches or such a clear pattern of behaviour in failing to separate private and public interests.' [487]

The Commons Select Committee on Standards recommended that Patterson be suspended from the Commons for thirty days -sufficient to trigger a recall petition in his constituency. However, with Patterson still refusing to admit wrongdoing, a backbench amendment, supported and whipped by the government, sought to replace the current Standards Committee with a new, Tory-dominated one. Although the vote was carried by the house, the opposition parties refused to participate in it - effectively scuppering the move. The government backed down in the face of cross-partisan criticism and offered a Commons vote on whether Patterson be suspended; whereupon he simply resigned from the house.

This severely damaged Boris Johnson's credibility as Prime Minister. Worse was to come. At the end of November, the country was shocked by the scandal of 'Partygate,' in which the Prime Minister and many of his team had broken lockdown restrictions by indulging in Downing Street parties, while the rest of the country were prevented by law from mixing with people from different households and indeed from visiting dying residents in hospitals and nursing homes.

Initially the Prime Minister denied that any such illegal gatherings had taken place and insisted that the rules had been followed at all times. However, video footage emerged of the Downing Street Director of Communications Allegra Stratton staging a mock press conference in which she made joking remarks about the parties. She resigned the next day.

More evidence followed, including a number of photographs of the twelve illegal gatherings - three of which had been attended by Boris Johnson himself. Despite this, Boris Johnson continued to publicly deny that he or his team had done anything wrong. He told the House on December 8th 2021 that; 'There was no party and no COVID rules were broken.' [488] He then shifted tack, describing the gatherings as 'a work event.' [489]

The government launched an inquiry into the scandal that was headed by top civil servant Sue Gray. However, the Metropolitan police launched their own investigations which delayed the Gray report. Operation Hillman ended with penalty notices being handed out to eighty-three individuals, including Boris Johnson, his wife Carrie Symonds and Chancellor Rishi Sunak.

Sue Gray's report was published in May 2022, and it found a culture of drinking, rowdiness and disrespect for cleaning and security staff. It concluded that political and civil service leadership, 'must bear responsibility for this culture.'[490]

This episode and the Owen Patterson affair before it clearly cost the Conservative government Scandal key thirteen. It also had the effect of torpedoing Johnson's moral authority to enact any more restrictions. It is due to the early revelations that the dynamic of the cabinet conflict over lockdowns was flipped on its head. Boris Johnson, with Gove, wanted another Christmas lockdown in the face of the more infectious but thankfully milder Omicron variant. However, they faced a libertarian rebellion led by Chancellor Sunak and had to back down. In January 2022 Johnson announced the end of all state-mandated COVID restrictions.

The impact of the lockdowns on the economy was vast, with the steepest drop in GDP ever recorded, at 9.9% in 2020. [491] The cost of government borrowing to pay for the furloughs and other measures is still not known, but thought to be between £310 and £410 billion pounds - the greatest real-terms debt since World War Two. [492] This level of economic damage therefore easily cost the Conservatives the Long-Term Economy Key seven for the next election - whenever it will be.

The short-term economy, at the time of writing, has been effectively flatlining since 2022, and when population growth is factored in, GDP per capita has suffered the longest period of decline since the measure was introduced in 1955.[493] In February 2024, a recession was officially announced, as two consecutive quarters of contraction were recorded. However, there has not been a big wave of business failures, nor a surge in unemployment, as had been the hall marks of previous recessions. Therefore, do we turn key seven against the Tories? Even before the recent bad news, according to a poll in the summer of 2023, sixty-one percent of people believe the economy was already in recession.[494] Therefore, I have decided to call the short-Term Economy key, half-turned against the government, as it is difficult to call.

The scale of the restrictions - unknown in history, even surpassing the wartime restrictions of 1939-45 would also have won the government the Policy Change key, had it not already been won by Brexit.

The long-term damage caused by the lockdowns, especially to children's education and upon mental health are serious. There are still many unanswered questions at the time of writing. Did the virus originate from the Wuhan laboratory in China, or was it merely a natural phenomenon? To what extent did the lockdowns actually control the spread of the disease? Did they do as much harm as good? Why are there still excess deaths in the UK? (and elsewhere) Perhaps the perspective of time will yield more illuminating answers.

During this turbulent and dystopian era of the pandemic, Brexit was temporarily eclipsed in the news agenda. However, a deal on the post-transition relationship between the UK and Europe was finally agreed at the eleventh hour in December 2020. The EU-UK Trade and Cooperation Agreement was signed on December 30th, and proved successful enough to at least partially satisfy the Brexiteers whilst avoiding the direst consequences warned by many Remainers.

Although Northern Ireland technically left the EU Customs Union, in practice a customs border was placed across the Irish Sea. There would be no restrictions on traffic from Northern Ireland to Great Britain, but there were vice versa. Although the British government had tried to effectively annul the Northern Ireland Protocol with the UK Internal Markets Bill, this would effectively have broken internal law, and the border down the Irish Sea had to remain in practice. Northern Ireland Secretary Brandon Lewis admitted that the bill would 'Break international law in a specific and limited way.' [495] However, with opposition from both the EU and House of Lords, the legislation became heavily watered down before reaching the royal ascent.

Other controversial aspects of the final deal included a five-and-half-year transition period before Britain could reclaim greater access to shipping around British waters.

One undeniable achievement that resulted directly from Brexit, was the unilateral purchase and distribution of the COVID vaccines. Had Britain remained in Europe, this process would have been significantly delayed and more lives lost.

The impact of the deal on Northern Irish politics was rather less good. It led directly to the collapse of power-sharing in February 2022.

One event that helped to lift Boris Johnson's flagging premiership, albeit briefly was Ukraine. On 24th February 2022, Russia invaded Eastern Ukraine, with air attacks against the capital Kiev and elsewhere. This was the greatest military conflict in Europe since 1945, and brought the world closer to nuclear war than at any time since the mid-1980s.

Boris Johnson did show genuine leadership and strategic clarity on this issue, being the first foreign leader to publicly talk of arming Ukraine during the build-up to war in January. He also played a major role in galvanising European opposition to Putin and the ejection of Russia from the international SWIFT payment system. He was also one of the very first foreign leaders to visit Ukraine, and presented Ukraine President Zelensky with the Churchill medal in the country's parliament.

Unfortunately, he did also make a stupid gaffe in March 2022 when he tried to compare Ukraine's struggle for national survival with Britain's Brexit drama.

Although it has to be acknowledged that Britain's military contribution to Ukraine is dwarfed by that of the United States, the UK did at least play a significant part in defending the country from Russian aggression. However, this achievement - real though it is, falls somewhat short of toppling Foreign Policy Success key nine. At the time of writing, the military situation appears to be a bloody stalemate. If western military aid runs out, then how much longer can Ukraine hold the line?

One significant development in British domestic politics that was initially overshadowed by all the drama, was the change in the leadership of the Labour party. After the crushing defeat of December 2019, Jeremy Corbyn signalled his intention to step down, which he did after the election of the former Director of Public Prosecutions Sir Keir Starmer in March 2020, at the start of the pandemic. Starmer began to move the Labour party towards the political centre, eschewing the radical leftism of the Corbyn years. One of Starmer's key aims was to confront and defeat anti-Semitism within the Labour party, vowing to 'tear out this poison by its roots.' [496] His reforms still proved controversial however, and the party lost 100,000 members during 2021.[497]

In October 2020 the Equality and Human Rights Commission (EHRC) found Labour guilty of illegal acts of anti-Semitism and discovered evidence that Corbyn and his team tried to interfere in the complaints process. Starmer apologised to British Jews, describing the findings as 'a day of shame' [498] for the Labour party. Corbyn attacked the report and its response by Starmer as an over-statement of the problem for politically motivated reasons. This cost Corbyn the Labour whip.

The changes in the Labour party and the steady move towards the centre, illustrated by Starmer's refusal to reverse the Tory cap on child benefit for larger families, is reminiscent of Neil Kinnock's and then Tony Blair's similar journey a generation earlier. Although Starmer is no charismatic performer, the changes he has implemented mean that Labour will no longer be gifting the Conservatives the Opposition Implausibility bonus key 4A.

Despite success in Ukraine, Boris Johnson's support at home was crumbling in spring 2022. With the UK now in the grip of a cost-of- living crisis, as a knock-on effect of COVID, Brexit and the Russia-Ukraine war, the floundering and disintegrating government was becoming seen as an out-of-touch, self-serving circus, deaf to the real needs of ordinary people. A crisis-point was reached in June 2022 when the sufficient number of MPs' letters triggered a confidence vote in the Prime Minister. Johnson survived, winning by 211 to 148 votes. However, as with Theresa May who actually did slightly better than that, the pyrrhic victory was merely a short stay of execution. Johnson's hubristic celebration of their 'win' was the writing on the wall.

This vote was followed up by a shocking by-election defeat for the government at Tiverton and Honiton. It was the largest ever parliamentary majority to be overturned in a by-election.

The next scandal to hit the already punch-drunk government was the resignation of Deputy Chief Whip Chris Pincher, over allegations of the sexual assault of younger male colleagues. Number 10 tried to claim that the Prime Minister had been unaware of the allegations, before having to admit that he had been aware, but that no formal complaint had been made. This story too was contradicted by the BBC, who confirmed that official complaints had been made and the Prime Minister informed. Ex-mandarin Simon McDonald said publicly that, 'Number 10 keep changing their story, and it's still not telling the truth.' [499]

These disastrous events led to the simultaneous resignations of the Chancellor Rishi Sunak and Health Secretary Sajid Javid on the fifth July 2022. The next day, the Local Government Secretary Michael Gove was sacked for telling the Prime Minister that he had to resign. At Prime Minister's Questions, Labour leader Keir Starmer asked, 'Is this the first recorded case of the sinking ship fleeing the rat.' [500] This was followed by the resignations of the Education Secretary Michelle Donelen, the Welsh Secretary Simon Hart and the Northern Ireland Secretary Brandon Lewis. By the evening of the sixth of July there had been a total of thirty-one ministerial resignations.

The following day Boris Johnson announced that he was stepping down from the steps of Downing Street with the boos of protestors clearly audible in the background. He acknowledged the rebellion of MPs by saying, 'when the herd moves, it moves.' Although he remained technically in office until his successor could be appointed on the sixth of September, he had lost so much political capital, that the country was effectively leaderless during a period of hiatus and paralysis.

This was the downfall of a man who blamed everyone else for his political implosion. He blamed Remainers in the civil service, his cabinet, his backbenchers, the business world, the biased BBC and media, the Labour party.... The simple truth is that Boris Johnson destroyed himself.

Following Johnson's resignation as Tory leader, the party was once again thrown into contest mode. In the parliamentary battle Chancellor Rishi Sunak narrowly beat Foreign Secretary Liz Truss by 137 to 113. However, the former Liberal Democrat Truss found favour amongst the grassroots members and trumped Sunak by fifty-seven to forty-three percent of the vote.

Truss was appointed Prime Minister on sixth of September 2022 by Queen Elizabeth II, two days before the monarch's death at the age of ninety-six. Government was suspended for ten days during the period of official public mourning. However, political life was to return with a vengeance.

The first serious problem that the Truss government had to face was the mounting cost of living crisis, with food, fuel and energy prices surging as the result of COVID, Brexit and the war in Ukraine; in which Russian gas and the Russian economy in general were being sanctioned. UK inflation as measured by the Consumer Price Index was about to peak at 11.1% in October 2022 - the highest for forty years. Standing outside Downing Street on the 6th September, Truss declared that, 'I am confident that together we can ride out the storm.' The policy response was to announce the Energy Price Guarantee, which sought to cap annual household energy costs at £2,500 for the next two years. So far, so good.

However, the Truss administration caused controversy by firing the Permanent Secretary to the Treasury, Tom Scholar within a few days of taking power. Truss attacked the Treasury for believing in 'abacus economics' - focussing too much on balancing the books at the expense of growth. [501] The sacking of the well-respected and experienced civil servant was widely criticised and was described as an 'ideological purge' by Dave Penman, general secretary of the civil servants' union, the FDA.

On September twenty-third, Chancellor Kwasi Kwarteng unveiled his growth plan to the House of

Commons. This was instantly referred to as the 'mini-budget' in the media. This plan was the most audacious package of tax cuts since Anthony Barber's 'Dash for growth' in 1972. The package included the abolition of the forty-five percent top rate of income tax, a cut in the basic rate, the cancellation of the Social Care Levy that had been recently announced by the Johnson administration, and the cancellation of a proposed rise in corporation tax. All of this, in addition to the Energy Price Guarantee was to be paid for by additional borrowing.

This plan was immediately attacked as tone-deaf and unfair. Large swathes of the electorate simply could not stomach the prospect of big corporations and millionaires benefiting from tax cuts whilst millions struggled to put food on their tables or heat their homes. This kind of criticism though, could perhaps be shrugged off.

However, this plan also seriously spooked the markets, which feared that it would be simply unsustainable. This was not least because of a glaring lack of an independent forecast by the Office for Budget Responsibility (OBR). Within a few days, the cost of government borrowing soared, putting pressure on mortgages. The pound dropped to its lowest ever level [502]against the dollar- at a near parity of $1.033. The IMF openly criticised the budget, warning that it would, 'likely increase inequality.' [503] The Bank of England even took the extraordinary step of buying up £65 billion of government bonds to prop up sterling, protect pensions and counter what they described as, 'a material risk.'

The Conservative party conference in October saw harsh criticism of the new Prime Minister's policy from Michael Gove. In a BBC interview with Laura Kuenssberg, Gove said, 'I think there is an inaccurate realisation at the top of government of the scale of change required... Using borrowed money to fund tax cuts: that is not Conservative.' [504]

On October 12th, Sanjay Raya, chief economist at Deutsche Bank told a committee of MPS that on the back of the problems caused by the war in Ukraine, "You throw on the 23 September event, you've got a sidelined fiscal watchdog, lack of a medium-term fiscal plan, one of the largest unfunded tax cuts that we've seen... since the early 1970s and it's sort of the straw that broke the camel's back." [505]

Despite initially trying to defend the package, the government reversed the abolition of the top rate of income tax and then the cut in corporation tax. With plummeting poll ratings and a widely hostile media, Truss fired Chancellor Kwarteng on 14th October and replaced him with Jeremy Hunt, who reversed most of what was left of the mini-budget.

Christopher Hope, the Associate political editor of the Daily Telegraph described Hunt's Commons statement as 'a political disembowelment I've never seen in twenty years of covering politics.' [506] Truss failed to inspire confidence with her wooden and shambolic fielding of a press conference in which she refused to apologise for her mistakes and robotically repeated the same lines about 'delivering stability'. She hesitated awkwardly over the selection of journalists to take questions from and appeared to scurry away from them at the end. It surpassed even the very worst of Theresa May.

Matters deteriorated even further with the resignation of Home Secretary Suella Braverman on the 18th October after a breach of data security. (She had sent ministerial documents to an MP on an insecure server.) The Labour party also exploited the Tory chaos and division by tabling an amendment on a bill about fracking. The issue was divisive for the Tories as it was being supported by Truss despite having been ruled out in the last manifesto. The vote effectively became a confidence vote, with the result that there were allegations of MPS being manhandled and the false announcement that the Chief and Deputy Chief whips had resigned.

After Truss tried to defend her failing position before a meeting with Tory MPs, one of them described the encounter as, 'The first time I heard a corpse deliver its own eulogy.' [507] At this time YouGov registered the worst Prime Ministerial approval ratings ever recorded - at ten percent. [508]

On the 20th October, after being advised by Graham Brady, Chairman of the 1922 committee that she could no longer salvage her premiership, Truss announced her resignation. When she formally resigned as Prime Minister after forty-nine days in the post, she became Britain's officially shortest-served Prime Minister - beating the previous record of 119 days with George Canning in the early nineteenth century. He at least had the excuse of dying in office. The Daily Star had even featured a live stream of a lettuce from the 14th October, to which the likely longevity of Truss's premiership was being compared.

The tragedy for Truss was different from that of May or Johnson. Both of those Prime Ministers foundered in part because of their lack of strategic clarity. Truss, despite her more considerable ministerial experience, imploded because of her extreme ideological rigidity. Dressed in blue during the televised leadership debates, to signal a kind of second coming of the Iron Lady, Truss's eighties tribute act proved out of touch and out of time.

Her strategy of transplanted Thatcherism failed to adequately recognise the historical context of her heroine's premiership and that of her own situation in 2022. In 1979 with a ninety-eight percent top rate of tax, there was a very plausible argument for cutting taxes. Forty-three years later, with the top rate set at forty-five percent, and huge debts incurred by COVID - and that after a lost decade of poor growth following the 2008 crash, the same prescription was never going to work on repeat.

In the wake of the chaos created by Liz Truss's car crash premiership, a new leader had to be elected. The revolving door of Downing Street had become a national joke, and there was a feeling that if Prime Ministers were randomly selected from the general public, the outcome could not be much worse.

In the wake of the problems caused by a divergence between what the Tory MPs wanted and what the membership wanted, the Conservative 1922 committee decided to change its rules for leadership elections, by making it a requirement that candidates needed at least 100 MPs to recommend them. It also shortened the timeframe for membership voting to a week, through digitalising the process. This was to effectively screen out any candidates with limited support in the Commons. Two candidates emerged; the former Chancellor Rishi Sunak and Leader of the Commons Penny Mordaunt. Former Prime Minister Boris Johnson considered running, but decided not to stand, perhaps fearing the results of the House of Commons inquiry into his conduct over Partygate and the Pincher affair.

However, Mordaunt withdrew her nomination just two minutes before the nomination deadline, thereby making Sunak Prime Minister uncontested. Rishi Sunak became the first British-Asian Premier, the first Premier of colour, and at forty-two, the youngest Prime Minister since Lord Liverpool in 1812.

One of the first acts of his administration was the autumn statement by Chancellor Jeremy Hunt. Although this statement was reminiscent of the austerity budgets of George Osborne, with its desire to cut borrowing, the actual policies marked a sharp departure from that of recent Tory Chancellors. He reduced the tax threshold for the top rate from £150,000 to £125,000. Other income tax thresholds were frozen as was that for Inheritance Tax. He also announced windfall taxes for the big utility companies that would raise £14 billion. This was effectively steadying the ship after the Truss trauma.

Although Hunt declared that the UK economy was already sinking into recession, the economy actually managed to avoid it, and has simply flat-lined ever since. Thus, Short-Term Economy key eight is true - just.

The high cost of living resulted in the biggest upsurge in British industrial action since 1990. Numerous strikes erupted in 2022, including in the railways, hospitals and Royal Mail. There have also been protests by environmental group Just Stop Oil, who have blocked roads in and around London in a bid to raise awareness of climate Change. These strikes and protests though, fall well short of the threshold necessary to topple Civil Unrest key twelve.

On the Brexit front, the Sunak government made some progress with the Windsor Framework of March 2023. This eased some of the restrictions on goods being transported from Great Britain to Northern Ireland, allowing the UK more control over VAT rates in Ulster, as well as control over the regulation of medicines in the country. Although Ulster Unionists see the arrangement as an improvement on the original Northern Ireland Protocol, there is still much opposition to it.

Overall, though, Brexit is seen as unsuccessful by the British public as well as by most of the commentariat. In May 2023, only eighteen percent of people thought Brexit was being handled well, as against seventy-two percent who thought it was being handled badly. When asked in hindsight whether leaving the EU had been the right thing to do; only thirty-one percent thought it was still the right thing and fifty-six percent thought it had been a mistake. When asked whether Brexit had been a success or failure overall; only nine percent judged it a success, compared to sixty-two percent who deemed it a failure. [509]

In a poll by Statistica, published in October 2023, only thirty-three percent of the British people thought leaving had been the right decision, as against fifty-seven percent who thought it had been the wrong decision. [510] Therefore, it is fair to say that Brexit has cost the Conservatives Foreign Policy Failure key ten, and has failed to win them key eleven.

There have been growing problems with illegal immigration, with tens of thousands of migrants crossing the channel in small boats. The government proposed the bizarre solution of flying them to Rwanda, though this has led to conflict with the European Court of Human Rights (ECHR). This is combined with net legal immigration of more than 600,000, which many feel to be unacceptably high.

Although the continued pro-Ukrainian stand has improved Britain's standing internationally, it falls well short of securing key nine.

The Conservatives have suffered a simply catastrophic series of by-election defeats starting with

Amersham in 2021. Therefore, key one is irredeemably lost.

The Conservative party is riven by factions, some loyal to Boris Johnson, some loyal to Liz Truss. There is also a growing move towards a Trumpian style of conservatism that is defined by nationalism and a right-wing traditionalist stance on cultural and identitarian issues such as transgenderism and race. The sacking of outspoken Home Secretary Suella Braverman in November 2023 for, among other things accusing the police of bias against right-wing protests is undoubtedly worsening the divide between liberal Conservatives and national conservatives.

There has even been talk in the autumn of 2023 of Nigel Farage joining the party and even becoming leader. Such ideas are more likely to gain the upper hand the worse the Tories fare in the next election. Certainly, the level of division is now sufficient to cost the government unity key number two.

Whilst Sunak has proved so far to be more competent, honest and sensible than his two immediate predecessors and having far better communication skills than either May or Truss; he certainly falls far short of winning the Incumbent leadership key for his party. He is neither charismatic, a national hero or strong and dominant.

The Tories also have something to fear from the rice of Richard Tice's Reform Party, which grew out of Farage's Brexit party. It is (at time of writing) getting around seven or eight percent in the polls. If it grows a little more, it will be enough to topple a second Third Party key five. This is because although the Liberal Democrats have already toppled that key with their impressive string of by-election wins since 2021, they are not gaining significantly in terms of votes, but are gaining locally in rural/small town seats in England.

Reform on the other hand, are gaining in the different sense of a general swing in the polls. They very likely will not be able to take seats off the Tories directly, but they will inordinately drag the Tory vote down, leaving them vulnerable to the other parties. Reform are also on the other side of the political spectrum to the Liberals on both the economic and identitarian-cultural spectrums. The key is hard to turn at the moment, because Reform are bordering on the level of increased support necessary to turn the key) an increase in five percentage points.) Thus, a double key is a distinct possibility.

The Sixth key - Cyclical Incumbency is also a tricky one to call. The keys have accurately predicted the results of elections in years when the incumbent party has been in power for three terms (thirteen years) in 1964, 1992 and 2010. The 1997 election, when the Conservatives had been in power for eighteen years was only forecast correctly with key six turning against the Major administration. Will the coming election be different? If it goes ahead in 2024, then the Tories would have been in power for fourteen years. If it is postponed to the last possible date of January 2025, they will have been in power for fourteen years eight months. Due to the two very short terms in the 2010s it is harder to turn this key. Certainly the 'time for a change' motif is getting louder.

One factor that will make little difference to the Conservatives directly, but will aid Labour, is the implosion of the SNP. There seemed to be three triggers for this state of affairs. The first was the repeated failure of the SNP to get the Westminster government to allow a second independence referendum. The SNP argued that Brexit changed the terms of Scotland's membership of the United Kingdom. The Westminster government argued that the 2014 referendum had always been billed as a once in a lifetime event.

The second was the Gender Recognition Bill of 2023, which sought to ease the process of legally changing one's gender, without the need for gender realignment surgery. Concerns arose that a prominent rapist had identified as a woman in order to be housed in a women's prison. The outcry was so great, with fears that such people could move from Scotland to elsewhere in the United Kingdom, that the British government directly prevented the bill from getting the royal ascent and becoming law. The official reason was that it violated the 2010 Equalities Act.

Very soon after this crisis, Nicola Sturgeon resigned as First Minister of Scotland. In her resignation statement she affirmed the need to, 'reach across the divide in Scottish Politics. And my judgement is that a new leader will be better able to do this. Someone who is not subject to the kind of polarised opinions, fair or unfair, that I now am.' [511]

Two months after Sturgeon's resignation, her husband who was also the party's former Chief Executive was arrested as part of a police investigation into possible misuse of SNP campaign money. Sturgeon herself was arrested later in the year along with the party treasurer: although in all three cases were released without charge.

Sturgeon's successor Humza Yousaf has so far struggled to attain the same level of popularity that Sturgeon and before her Salmon used to enjoy. Multiple opinion polls have shown the SNP and Labour roughly neck-and-neck in Scotland, suggesting considerable gains for Labour.[512]

Sunak has also been fighting to overcome the ethics crisis of the Boris Johnson years, but here he has struggled. Several of his appointments drew criticism, including the decision to re-appoint Suella Braverman after her resignation only days earlier following a security breach. He also appointed Dominic Raab as Deputy Prime Minister and Gavin Williamson as Minister without Portfolio, after both had been accused of bullying. Williamson resigned within a few weeks and Raab resigned the following Spring after being found guilty of bullying by an inquiry. The party Chairman Nadhim Zahawi was sacked the following January after the dishonest handling of his tax affairs was criticised by an ethics adviser.

Like Cameron with Andy Coulson, Sunak was criticised for appointing these people in the first place.

Meanwhile, the reputation of Boris Johnson was on the line in 2023, when the Commons Privileges Committee was investigating whether he had deliberately misled the House over Partygate. When Johnson received early intelligence on 9th June that the verdict would be damning, he resigned his seat. On the 15th, the committee found him guilty of deliberately lying to Parliament, and added that if he had still been an MP they would have recommended a ninety-day suspension from the house - sufficient to trigger a recall petition. They also recommended the denial of his Parliamentary pass. If the Tories harboured any hope that their sleazy image could be expunged, such hopes now seemed forlorn.

<u>*Next general election 2024?*</u> (assessed March 2024)

1) *By-election key*   false

2) *Unity Key* false
3) *Incumbent Leadership Key* false
4) *Opposition Charisma Key* true
5) *Third Party Key* false (x2)
6) *Cyclical Incumbency Key* true
7) *Short-Term Economy Key* Half-turn
8) *Long-Term Economy Key* false
9) *Foreign Policy/Military Success Key* false
10) *Foreign Policy/Military Failure Key* false
11) *Policy Change Key* true
12) *Civil Unrest Key* true
13) *Scandal Key* false

balance of negative keys: 9 ½

campaign differential?

forecast: Labour majority of c. 100

tally: Conservatives: 188 Labour: c. 375 SNP 25-30 Liberal Democrats c 25-30

2010-2024?
the government that lost its way

When contemporary Conservatives like David Starkey attack the Conservatives as simply carrying on with Blairism, they are partially right, but miss out the fact that the Cameron project originally intended to be much more like Blair than it eventually became in reality.

During the first three years of Cameron's leadership of the party, the Conservatives appeared fully committed to continuing with New Labour spending plans. However, they were blown off course by the Global Financial Crisis of October 2008 and almost immediately had to abandon that pledge.

Whether the crisis gave them a way out of honouring a pledge that they never believed in is hard to say. However, the reality of the Cameron - Osborne tenure is fiscally speaking, a very sharp departure indeed from the spending boom of the second and third Blair terms. Yes, they brought in gay marriage, but the harsh reforms of the welfare system and squeeze on the NHS were tougher than anything even by Mrs Thatcher.

The next massive derailment of the Cameron agenda was his decision to call a referendum on EU membership. This huge gamble backfired and catapulted Mr Cameron from power and scuppered the trajectory of Britain's European policy of the past forty years. The Tories cannot really claim this as an achievement however, as it was essentially the result of a rebellion by right-wing backbenchers who despised Cameron as not being a real Conservative and by Nigel Farage and his UKIP party. Cameron misjudged public opinion and his government was blown off-course. The basically New Labourish, pro-European, liberal and big state heirs to Blair, now found themselves presiding over a shrunken state, being pulled out of the European Union, amid bitterness, acrimony and deep cultural division. In the late autumn of 2023, and in the late autumn of Tory rule, Cameron returns to cabinet to play mortician to a dying government.

When Boris Johnson finally managed to 'get Brexit done' by forging an alliance between culturally conservative Tories and equally culturally conservative red wall Labour supporters, there seemed to be a historic opportunity to do something with it. This was of course partly blown off course by COVID but equally by Johnson's inept leadership of the government, lack of vision and narrow focus on his own self-interest.

As things stand in the autumn of 2023, it seems the Conservatives could be splitting between liberal free-market Tories and culturally conservative nationalist Tories. The two are simply incompatible. The Thatcherite free-market Conservatives want open borders and globalism because big business wants it. The nationalists want to restrict the flow of people which is entirely in conflict with the globalist, free-market agenda, as is social conservatism in general. One is essentially collectivist, the other essentially individualist.

With Reform now snapping at their heels, a heavy defeat seems likely. Whatever new form the new Conservative party decides to take, it seems pretty sure that future historians will look back on the last thirteen years as ones of initial purpose under a Cameron-Clegg coalition, achieving a lot, on its own terms at least, but which got blown off course by Brexit. The years since 2016 will be seen as ones of historic failure, under a succession of disastrous Prime Ministers leading a rudderless, incompetent government.

Chapter 8: questions and criticisms

WHY THE KEYS DON'T WORK BEFORE 1945

The keys system was originally designed to work for the United States' political system, which is of course a binary contest. Therefore, it only works in the UK and indeed elsewhere, if that binary two-party dynamic is present.

Between 1931 and 1945 Britain was ruled by coalition governments. In the 1930s there was the National government formed in 1931 in response to the chaos caused by Britain's exit from the Gold Standard and the deepening Great Depression. Led by Labour Prime Minister Ramsey MacDonald, the ministry was mostly comprised of Conservatives and a faction of the Liberal party, which became known as the National Liberals. Conservative leaders Stanley Baldwin and then Neville Chamberlain succeeded the ailing MacDonald, and in May 1940, a new wartime coalition was formed, led by Winston Churchill and governed until 1945.

During this time the binary dynamic ceased to operate and all elections in this era, including the 1945 election could not have been predicted with the keys model.

In the 1920s, Britain briefly had a tripartite system with the fading Liberals, insurgent Labour and strong Conservative party. Therefore, the keys would not work in this decade either.

Between 1916 and 1922 Britain had a wartime coalition led by David Lloyd George: again, not predictable with the keys.

Prior to this, the exclusion of the poor and to some extent the young (young men living with parents or paying rents below a certain threshold could not vote) would inevitably skew the predictability of the system more so than the exclusion of women. The keys system worked in the States before the political emancipation of women, as voting rights for men were not dependent on wealth or property ownership.

Historically, gender has not been a consistently strong factor in predicting voting intentions, though class and age have been much more so. After all, economic downturns hurt the poor the most. Unemployment hits the poor and the young the hardest. Military conscription is usually for young men. Before the 1918 Reform Act that gave voting rights to all males over twenty-one and to women over thirty with property qualifications, (the rest had to wait until 1928) only around sixty percent of men could vote. [513]Before the 1884 Reform Act that extended the franchise to rural voters, only around a third of adult males could vote.[514] Prior to the 1867 Reform Act only about one in six men could vote, and prior to the 1832 Act, only about a tenth of men had the vote. This was because voting rights were dependant on property ownership in a world where most people were poor.[515].

Obviously, with only the propertied classes having the franchise, it is hard to see how the keys system could accurately predict elections, when only those most cushioned from hardship and vicissitudes of crises could participate in elections.

In addition to the extremely restricted size and composition of the electorate, there were other factors that would make these early elections unforecastable with the keys. One was the heavily distorted nature of geographical representation. This was brought about partly by the existence of 'rotten boroughs' in which virtually uninhabited constituencies were awarded an MP whilst heavily populated cities that had expanded during the Industrial Revolution over the previous forty years, had no representation at all. For example, the constituency of Old Sarum, consisting largely of prehistoric ruins and seven constituents had its own MP, whereas the burgeoning towns of Manchester and Birmingham had not one MP between them.[516]

There are other factors that would militate against the successful deployment of the keys system. One was the level of corruption and intimidation that was commonplace. In addition to the aforementioned 'Rotten Boroughs' there were also the 'Pocket Boroughs,' in which a powerful employer, who was boss to most of his constituents, chose the candidates and demanded voters supported them. Since secret ballots would not be introduced until 1872 and bribery of voters not outlawed until 1880, a powerful figure who controlled his voters' economic purse-strings could effectively impose a candidate of his choosing. It is estimated that well over half of such boroughs saw uncontested elections.

There were also huge imbalances in the ability of the major parties to fund election campaigns and field candidates. During the late nineteenth century, there were up to thirty percent of seats that were uncontested. As late as the general election of 1900, the Conservative majority was hugely boosted by the fact that there were 163 seats in which the Conservative candidate was the only one. The situation was even worse in the earlier decades of the century. [517]Clearly, no keys-based system could work in the face of such an uneven electoral playing field.

Finally, prior to the 1911 Parliament Act, parliamentary terms could be up to seven years long.

This would increase the probability that events earlier in the term would be forgotten or overshadowed by its end. A twenty-one-year-old first-time voter would have been only fourteen at the previous election for example.

WHY DON'T THE KEYS WORK IN THE DEVOLVED PARLIAMENTS OR IN REFERENDA?

There are two reasons for this. Firstly, that the devolved parliaments are only semi-autonomous. They have considerable domestic autonomy, but foreign policy is outside their remit; therefore, keys nine and ten do not really apply. Their control over domestic and fiscal policy is also limited - thus problems can always be blamed on Westminster.

Secondly, the elections in the devolved parliaments, especially in Scotland and Northern Ireland are largely about the constitutional question - of whether the country should remain within, or break away from the union. Therefore, many SNP voters will vote for that party come what may, as their desire for independence trumps their desire to reward or punish executive successes and failures at home.

The keys could not predict a referendum result like Brexit for essentially the same reasons. It would be almost impossible to determine how much economic success was down to EU membership and how much was down to UK government policy. Also, with the 2016 referendum being forty-one years since the previous one in 1975, the period of membership would be far too long - with many voters not yet born when we voted to remain in 1975.

COMMON CRITICISMS OF THE KEYS

The keys method in the United States has long been criticised on a number of grounds. The most common criticism is that the method is too subjective. There is certainly a degree of subjectivity, but how could it be otherwise? If the model is based upon government performance in office, then any assessment of it will necessarily contain an element of judgement and therefore of subjectivity.

However, the subjectivity is less than many believe. Take for example the charisma key. Only a churlish observer would deny that Tony Blair was charismatic in 1997, and no one would seriously suggest that John Major, Ed Miliband or Liz Truss were ever charismatic, so the consensus is much stronger than appears at first glance.

Polling is of course a useful tool for determining public perception of national or foreign policy, but even here judgement is needed. Instinct is frequently a good guide, but must be accompanied by very considerable reading and thought. Ultimately a judgement must be made.

It is important to look at a broad range of data and listen to a similarly wide range of opinions. As Allan Lichtman said himself, the hardest part of turning the keys is the need to set aside personal bias. Of course, political historians can be good authorities on this kind of judgement, but in the end, you have to use your own when turning the keys.

The 'Primaries method' of Helmut Northpol, attempts to forecast US Presidential elections by looking at just two factors: cyclical incumbency and candidate performance in the Primaries. Although Northpol has a strong record, it is not as strong as Lichtman's; he wrongly predicted a Trump re-election in 2020, as well as predicting Trump to win the popular vote in 2016 and Gore to win in 2000. The latter is understandable as the result was so close as to be lost in the margin of error. He also would have failed to predict Kennedy's razor-edge win in 1960. Therefore, although objective quantitative data can get one so far, it seems to be ultimately insufficient.

Another criticism of the model has been that it does not allow differential weighting for the keys. If one failure or success is majorly important, then surely there ought to be a double key? Not so, because if one key is weightier, then it will automatically trigger other keys. For example, the Thatcher government's victory in the Falklands War was a big event. Yet it only directly turned one key - Foreign Policy/Military Success in the government's favour. However, this is not the whole story. It indirectly led to a transformation of Thatcher's status which secured the Incumbent Leadership key. It also united the Tory party- thus securing Party Unity key two.

The reverse of the situation can be found a decade later with Black Wednesday; when Britain was forced to withdraw from the European Exchange Rate Mechanism (ERM) after barely two years of membership. This directly cost the Foreign Policy Failure key, but indirectly led to a breakdown of party discipline which robbed the Conservatives of the Party Unity key.

Sometimes the effect of a big disaster can be limited by skilful political handling. The Suez conflict is one such event. Although it was undoubtedly a major crisis of national confidence, the swift defenestration of Anthony Eden and the calm, confident stewardship of his successor Harold Macmillan, prevented the Party Unity key from being lost. The subsequent restoration of

Anglo-American relations succeeded in winning Foreign Policy/Military Success key nine.

WHAT IF SOMETHING HAPPENS THAT IS OUTSIDE THE KEYS?

If a situation develops that is not covered by the keys, then I will mint a new key. This is a significant departure from Allan Lichtman's original method. One example of a new key being pressed for use is the situation following the Iraq war in 2003. The Conservative opposition under two leaders had first enabled, then publicly defended this unpopular policy. Although the opposition were already weak and implausible, thus winning bonus key four A for the government; they had compounded their ineffectualness with complicity in a highly unpopular government misadventure. Therefore, a new bonus key – Opposition Complicity key four B was created.

It is perfectly possible that other such keys could be made in the future. If for example there was some special unique achievement which did not fit into any existing category, then a Special Achievement key could be forged.

what if a government suddenly lost or gained popularity too near to the election for the By-Election key to register the change?

This is a feasible question, but one without modern precedent. If I genuinely felt that a government had lost (or less likely) gained a dramatic degree of support too quickly for it to have affected by-election results, then I might decide to turn Key one anyway. It would be an interesting situation.

I did wonder that if the government had been forced to call an election whilst Liz Truss was still Prime Minister, whether the keys would have coped. We shall never know, but it seems that very extreme, short-term swings in the polls might not fully materialise when people actually walk into the polling booths. A real example here is the long-forgotten Clegg-mania of the 2010 campaign. The surge in Liberal Democrat support did not materialise in the actual result.

Chapter 9: Counterfactuals

In this chapter, I will use the keys to predict what would have happened in various counterfactual political situations since 1945. It is the 'what ifs?' chapter. Obviously, my retrospective and hypothetical forecasts can never be verified, but it is interesting to try and gain a glimpse into the parallel universe of political destiny.

(1) ANTHONY EDEN DIES DURING AN OPERATION IN 1953: HAROLD MACMILLAN IS PRIME MINISTER IN 1955

This first counterfactual scenario involves Eden dying during the botched operations he underwent for a blocked bile duct in April 1953. This far from improbable scenario would very likely have resulted in Harold Macmillan being appointed Prime Minister two years early in April 1955. Indeed, Churchill was not that confidant in Anthony Eden, despite the outward show of two leaders changing guard smoothly. Churchill was reported to have said that, 'I don't believe Anthony can do it.' [518]

If Macmillan had been Prime Minister in 1956, there is still the strong probability that he would have pursued Eden's aggressive foreign policy towards Egypt. He was vocally supportive of intervention from the start, writing in his diary that, 'If Nasser "gets away with it," we are done for. The whole Arab world will despise us ... Nuri (es-Said, British-backed Prime Minister of Iraq) and our friends will fall. It may well be the end of British influence and strength forever. So, in the last resort, we must use force and defy opinion, here and overseas.' [519]

Following a meeting with Churchill he recorded the following in his diary: 'Surely, if we landed, we must seek out the Egyptian forces; destroy them; and bring down Nasser's government. Churchill seemed to agree with all this.'[520]

Then on 6th November when the invasion had taken place and the Americans were threatening to squeeze the economy, Macmillan performed a volte face and issued the dire, but actually exaggerated news to the cabinet that Britain had lost $370 million dollars since the start of the month and that the war would have to be abandoned. [521] Shadow Chancellor Harold Wilson said that Macmillan was 'first in last out' on the war. [522]

If Macmillan had led Britain into a disastrous war in 1956, he would surely have had to pay the political price for it. Not even he could have talked his way out of Suez and almost certainly would have to have resigned like Eden did in reality. Who would have succeeded him? The likely candidate would have been the Lord President of the Council, and de facto Deputy Prime Minister Raab Butler.

Butler, who had served for four years as Chancellor of the Exchequer had been expected by many to succeed Eden in January 1957. In reality, Macmillan succeeded in wrong-footing him during a speech in front of the 1922 committee when he urged that Britain be 'Greeks in the Roman Empire.' Enoch Powell recalled that Macmillan, 'with all the skill of the old actor manager succeeded in false-footing Rab. The sheer devilry of it verged upon the disgusting.' [523]

However, with Supermac destroyed as a political force, it seems more than likely that Rab Butler would have become Britain's next Prime Minister. Butler had always expressed scepticism about the Suez operation, so was not so badly tarnished with its failure. Butler had been distinguished with his earlier role as Education Secretary, bringing in the Butler Act of 1944. He was also one of the leading moderate forces that helped define the post-war consensus - so much so that the term 'Butskellism' was often used - a portmanteau fusing his name with that of Labour's moderate leader Hugh Gaitskell.

However, would Raab have been so successful at repairing the political damage caused by Suez as Macmillan? For a start he did not quite have the presence and confident manner of Harold Macmillan. He had also been badly affected psychologically by the premature death of his wife from cancer in 1954. It is probable that he would have held office at least until the end of the term and that the big economic and geopolitical picture would have remained broadly the same as in reality.

However, the Incumbent Leadership key would have likely been lost, and quite possibly the Foreign Policy/Military Success key not been gained with a more cautious leader. It is difficult to predict how a different leader would have fared over a long period of time, but it seems reasonable to suppose that a Butler-led Conservative party would have been re-elected in 1959, probably with a somewhat smaller majority, and that Butler would have been damaged by the Profumo affair in 1963, before losing power to the energetic Wilson opposition in 1964.

(2) THE SUEZ CONFLICT AVERTED

There are two ways for this eventuality to have taken place. The first is for Anthony Eden to have been somehow dissuaded from his bellicose course of action in 1956, and the other is of Nasser being dissuaded from nationalising the canal in the first place.

If we take the first possibility, of drawing back from military action, then it would be very likely that Eden's premiership would have been a far longer one than the twenty-one months he had in reality and that he would be quite differently remembered today. Would it have been a realistic possibility? Certainly, Eden seemed consistently determined on using force, not merely to seize back the canal, but also to remove Nasser from power. There was widespread cabinet support for his actions, including from Chancellor Harold Macmillan.

However, it is also true that Macmillan completely misread President Eisenhower who had serious reservations about military action, as did the British Ambassador Sir Roger Makins. He also failed to convey to Eden the message of US Secretary of State John Foster Dulles, who warned him that Britain should abstain from any kind of military intervention until after the US presidential elections in early November.

It is also the case that when the two French emissaries first proposed the scheme of collusion to Anthony Eden at Chequers, the Foreign Secretary Selwyn Lloyd was at the UN HQ in New York, and apparently getting quite close to finding a diplomatic solution with his Egyptian counterpart. Even if a permanent solution had not been agreed, there was still the chance that action in Suez could have been delayed until the American elections, providing more time for some kind of settlement.

The second idea is of Colonel Nasser deciding against the nationalisation of the Suez Canal. The main reason for his decision to do this in July 1956, was the Anglo-American withdrawal of an offer to fund the building of the Aswan dam. This action had been precipitated by several aspects of Nasser's foreign policy that the west found deeply objectionable. One was his support for the Algerian nationalists, which naturally offended the French who still controlled the colony. Another was Nasser's opposition to the Baghdad pact, which was a Cold War military alliance between Britain, Iran, Iraq, Turkey and Pakistan.

A third was his acceptance of Soviet arms via the Czechoslovakian deal, and a fourth was his recognition of communist China.

Nasser argued that the nationalisation of the canal would help pay for the dam by depriving Britain and France of the profits. Perhaps had Britain and the US continued to fund the dam, the conflict could have been prevented.

If either of these perhaps unlikely eventualities had transpired, how would the rest of the Eden premiership have panned out and how would the 1959 election have looked? Although not really charismatic, Eden was popular, and indeed enjoyed quite good approval ratings even during the Suez debacle itself. [524]Although he probably would have disappointed some supporters - indeed there were even 'Eden must go' placards being waved months before Colonel Nasser nationalised the Suez Canal, and[525] well before Suez could have been foreseen. However, with a relatively strong economy, the lack of a charismatic opposition figure or strong third party and the absence of a foreign policy disaster or major ideological division within the party, there is no reason why Eden could not have been re-elected with a handsome majority in 1959.

Suez averted: general election 1959 with Eden as Prime Minister

1) *By-election key*: true
3) *Incumbent Leadership Key* false
4) *Opposition Charisma Key* true
5) *Third Party Key* true
6) *Cyclical Incumbency Key* true
7) *Short-Term Economy Key* true
8) *Long-Term Economy Key* half-turn
9) *Foreign Policy/Military Success Key* false
10) *Foreign Policy/Military Failure Key* true
11) *Policy Change Key* false
12) *Civil Unrest Key* true
13) *Scandal Key* true

<u>*Special Keys:*</u>

Third Party key 5a true

<u>*balance of negative keys:*</u> 2½

<u>*result:*</u> Conservative majority of 60

<u>*tally*</u> : Conservatives 345 seats Labour 248

With the Suez war having been averted, the Foreign Policy Failure key has been salvaged. Yet Macmillan's real-life success in repairing Anglo-American relations would not have been needed and therefore would have cost Foreign Policy Success key ten. The acquisition of the H-bomb alone would perhaps not have been quite sufficient to win that key in itself. It is likely that Eden would have lasted until the Profumo scandal derailed his government in 1963.

His episodic fevers were not really life-threatening and he lived until 1977. Illness provided a dignified exit for Eden in 1957, as it would for Macmillan in 1963. Overall, this different timeline does not drastically alter the development of British or global events. Suez was not so important in itself, merely a historical marker, showing that Britain was no longer a world power and that her colonial ambitions had now reached the end of the line. One could probably add that it was a catalyst for African decolonisation too, and perhaps for the moves to join the EEC. However, these new realities would have simply unfolded more gradually without it.

(3) HUGH GAITSKELL LIVES TO FIGHT THE 1964 ELECTION:

In January 1963, the moderate Labour leader, Hugh Gaitskell died from the immunological disease Lupus at the age of fifty-six. This was an event that shocked the nation and propelled the Shadow Chancellor Harold Wilson into the role of Leader of the Opposition. What would have been had Gaitskell lived? Obviously, the long-term pattern of events would be hard to predict, but the election of October 1964 would have been much less so.

Gaitskell was a competent leader but not really charismatic, and would therefore have allowed the Conservative government to keep Opposition Charisma key four. Nothing else would have changed, since the election is overwhelmingly about the state of the government and the nation. Therefore, the electoral outcome in October 1964 would have looked like this.

1964 General Election

1) *By-election key* — true
2) *Party Unity Key* — true
3) *Incumbent Leadership Key* — false
4) *Opposition Charisma Key* — true
5) *Third Party Key* — false
6) *Cyclical Incumbency Key* — true
7) *Short-Term Economy Key* — true
8) *Long-Term Economy Key* — true
9) *Foreign Policy/Military Success Key*: true
10) *Foreign Policy/Military Failure Key* — true
11) *Policy Change Key* — false
12) *Civil Unrest Key* — true
13) *Scandal Key* — false

balance of negative keys: 4

result: Conservative majority of 15

tally: Conservatives 323 seats Labour 297

In this scenario, Gaitskell's lack of charisma leaves the Conservatives in power with a much-reduced majority. It therefore is likely that they would have remained in power for the rest of the decade. The scorecard for a late Sixties election is of course impossible to be sure about, but I will have a go.

One of the uncertainties of this prediction, is how the Conservatives would have handled the balance of payments situation and the weakening pound. Would they have gone for an early controlled devaluation, or would they have delayed the inevitable until they were caught out like Labour in 1967? Let's assume the latter, or a botched version of the former possibility, which in both cases would damage growth and cost the Long-Term Economy key eight.

In foreign policy, it is hard to see the Tories achieving anything dramatic. How would they have handled the Rhodesia question? It seems likely that they would have been caught out in the same predicament that blighted Wilson's tenure as Prime Minister. Regarding Vietnam, Heath had been more vocally supportive of the American war than Harold Wilson, but was equally opposed to sending any British troops. Therefore, a sixties Tory government's policy on Vietnam would have differed very little in practice.

It would seem clear that even with the relatively liberal Rab Butler as Home Secretary, a Conservative government in the 1960s would not have offered anything to rival the liberal reforms of Labour Home Secretary Roy Jenkins. Ergo the Policy Change key would have been wholly lost.

An increasingly unpopular Tory government with a shoe-string majority would have been a good background for the Liberals to continue building their support, therefore key five would likely be lost. Finally, by 1969 the Tories would have been in power for eighteen years, equalling their later tenure under Thatcher-Major. Thus, the cyclical Incumbency key would also have turned against them. If they had proved unpopular, the By-Election key would also have fallen and probably necessitated a national poll around 1968 or '69 - perhaps earlier if the initial majority was tiny. Let us examine the counterfactual scorecard.

One final question is whether Labour would have continued with Hugh Gaitskell if he had led them to a second electoral defeat in a row, after nine years as leader - especially when expectations of a Labour win would have been so high? The answer is probably not. Most likely, Harold Wilson would have challenged Gaitskell again in the wake of the defeat and would have won, becoming leader in late '64 or early '65.

CONSERVATIVES WIN THE 1964 ELECTION: ALEC DOUGLAS HUME AS PM. WILSON AS OPPOSITION LEADER: 1968 GENERAL ELECTION:

1) *By-election key*	false
2) *Party Unity Key*	True
(uncertain)	
3) *Incumbent Leadership Key*	false
4) *Opposition Charisma Key*	false
5) *Third Party Key*	false
6) *Cyclical Incumbency Key*	false
7) *Short-Term Economy Key*	true
8) *Long-Term Economy Key*	?
9) *Foreign Policy/Military Success Key*	false
10) *Foreign Policy/Military Failure Key*	false
11) *Policy Change Key*	false
12) *Civil Unrest Key*	true
13) *Scandal Key*	true
(probably)	

balance of negative keys: 8 (At least)

result: Labour majority of 140.

tally: Conservatives 233 seats. Labour 385

In this outcome, even if the Tory term had been cut short before the currency devaluation had led to the loss of Long-Term Economy key eight, the outcome would have been a Labour landslide, just shy of Atlee's win in 1945. If by some chance the Conservatives had been able to hold on until 1969, the loss of key eight would have given Mr Wilson a majority of 195 the greatest single party landslide in modern times - outstripping even Blair in 1997.

Labour would therefore have dominated British politics for at least five years and have implemented the liberal social policies and educational reforms just three or four years later than in reality. Then, they would have run into the recession sparked by the Yom Kippur war and the industrial unrest and inflation of the 1970s. Probably, the Tories would have returned to power later in that decade, just a year or two earlier than happened in reality.

In this counterfactual, the historical change is not prevented from happening, merely delayed by three or four years, but made more dramatic by having been dammed up that bit longer. In this case, the pattern is eerily similar to the real-life situation thirty years later, with 1964 and 1992 being elections to lose for the Tories.

(4) HAROLD MACMILLAN STAYS ON TO FIGHT THE 1964 ELECTION

In October 1963 Harold Macmillan resigned the premiership from his hospital bed after being taken ill with prostate disease during the party conference. This was used as an excuse for a dignified way out following the terrible battering the Tories had taken from the bad publicity arising from the Profumo affair that had gripped the nation during 1963.

Although illness was given as a reason for his decision to step down, he did not, as has sometimes been claimed, believe himself to have inoperable cancer. His condition was never thought to be terminal or untreatable. His doctor Richard Lamb was of the opinion that Macmillan could easily have carried on. [526]He could have soldiered on - at least for another year until the election. What would have happened had he done so? One possibility is that the party would have been less able to move on from the Profumo scandal without the swift change of leader. Just as with Eden's defenestration in 1957, the replacement of the somewhat tired and tarnished Macmillan by Home did draw a line under the unfortunate episode. If Macmillan had continued, the questions surrounding Profumo would probably have dogged the Tories significantly more.

General election 1964:

1) *By-election key*   true
2) *Party Unity Key*   ?
3) *Incumbent Leadership Key*   false
4) *Opposition Charisma Key*   true
5) *Third Party Key*   false
6) *Cyclical Incumbency Key*   true
7) *Short-Term Economy Key*   true
8) *Long-Term Economy Key*   true
9) *Foreign Policy/Military Success Key* false
10) *Foreign Policy/Military Failure Key* true
11) *Policy Change Key*   false

12) *Civil Unrest Key*   true
13) *Scandal Key*   false

balance of negative keys: 5/6
result:

knife-edge Labour victory or small Labour majority

tally: Labour: 317/327 seats: Conservatives 304/294 seats

In this counterfactual, absolutely nothing changes. Although Harold Macmillan was once seen as a strong and dominant figure, by the end of his premiership this was no longer the case. Already the butt of mockery from TW3, the elderly Edwardian was looking like a figure from another age, and a 'failing representative of a decadent elite.' [527] The Profumo scandal had made his party look sleazy and him look weak and lacking grip. Therefore, he would not have won the Incumbent Leadership key and would not have fared significantly better in the election than Sir Alec Douglas Hume, and possibly even worse.

If Macmillan had been faced by Gaitskell then we would have been either the same or perhaps one-key worse than the result as outlined in the last counterfactual.

In the latter eventuality, the by now septuagenarian Macmillan would probably have retired almost immediately following his defeat and would have been replaced by either Home or Heath. Either of these men would have led the Conservatives to pretty much the same outcome in 1966.

(5) HAROLD WILSON POSTPONES THE 1970 ELECTION BY ONE YEAR:

In June 1970, Labour's five-and-half-year era was unexpectedly terminated, when the party was defeated at the polls by Edward Heath's Conservatives. Yet Wilson had not needed to call an election that early. One of the reasons that he did, was that he feared that the new decimalised currency that was coming into force early in 1971 would prove to be very unpopular. He could have held off until April 1971. Would this have made any difference to the outcome?

The main issue would have been the economy. Although the UK had avoided outright recession during this period, the currency devaluation in November 1967 had severely shaken the government's economic credibility and had led to a period of mild austerity, low growth and pessimism. By 1970 though, things had improved; the unemployment rate had dropped, the balance of payment figures had been getting much better and growth was at least reasonable. Would having another ten months in office have improved the public perception of economic confidence?

The answer as far at least as the keys are concerned is a resounding no. Economic growth did not pick up much during 1970-71, and so Long-Term Economy key eight would still have been lost. Additionally, unemployment was climbing during this period.

Internationally, there would almost certainly have been no great triumph in Rhodesia, and the situation in Northern Ireland hardly improved either. There would certainly not have been time for Wilson to bring Britain into the European Economic Community in the space of just ten more months in power, so the foreign policy keys would not have been any different.

With Heath still as opposition leader and no great change in the strength of third parties, keys four and five would also have looked no different. The government's shocking record of by-election defeats could not have been reversed in the extra time, nor would Harold Wilson suddenly have become charismatic or regained the air of invincibility he had briefly enjoyed in the mid-sixties.

The strikes that bedevilled the nation during the term would not have gone away, and on the other hand, the situation with party unity and the lack of major scandal would have looked pretty much the same.

Overall, an April 1971 general election would have produced virtually identical results to the one fought in June 1970.

(6) EDWARD HEATH HOLDS ONTO POWER UNTIL JUNE 1975:

In February 1974 Ted Heath went to the country more than year early in a bid to resolve the industrial disputes that were paralysing Britain. He asked the electorate, 'Who governs?' and they replied with the answer, 'Not you.' Yet, had he held on for another year, would a 1975 election have given him a fresh mandate to govern? Or would it have compounded the scale of his defeat?

In terms of GDP, had the Heath administration hung on until June 1975, the average growth over the term would have been significantly worse than in the reality of a shorter term. Therefore, doing so would have cost them key eight. Key seven would still have been forfeited, as the economy had not yet recovered from recession:

unemployment would have been over a million, house prices falling, and the national mood one of economic and political pessimism.

It is of course possible that the Heath government could have come to some sort of arrangement with the striking miners as Harold Wilson did in reality, and thus have salvaged the Civil Unrest key. Yet even if this had been the case, they still would have needed another success to have any hope of holding onto office.

The Sunningdale agreement of 1973 unravelled disastrously in the face of Protestant opposition during the spring of 1974. It is hard to see how the situation could have been salvaged by a Heath government, and so key ten would still have been lost.

It is highly improbable that the resurgence in Liberal party support would have faded away during a longer Conservative term, and with the two-party leaders remaining in office, and the economic situation bleak, keys one to six would have likely been the same.

Overall, a delayed election in 1975 would most probably have yielded exactly the same result as it did in 1974, with the possibility though, of a small outright win for Labour if the industrial unrest had continued full-pelt.

general election 1975:

1) *By-election key* — false
2) *Party Unity Key* — true
3) *Incumbent Leadership Key* — false
4) *Opposition Charisma Key* — true
5) *Third Party Key* — false
6) *Cyclical Incumbency Key* — true
7) *Short-Term Economy Key* — false

8) *Long-Term Economy Key*   false
9) *Foreign Policy/Military Success Key*   true
10) *Foreign Policy/Military Failure Key*   false
11) *Policy Change Key*   true
12) *Civil Unrest Key*   ?
13) *Scandal Key*   true

<u>*balance of negative keys:*</u>   6/7

<u>*forecast:*</u> knife-edge Labour victory or small Labour majority

<u>*tally:*</u> Conservatives 265 or 290 seats. Labour 326 or 301 seats

(7) <u>HAROLD WILSON CONTINUES AS PM UNTIL 1979:</u>

When Harold Wilson announced his resignation from out of the blue in March 1976, he did something that no other modern premier has managed to pull off: he stepped down at a time of his own choosing. Many premiers have had their time in office terminated abruptly by the electorate. Attlee in 1951, Hume in 1964, Wilson himself in 1970, before returning four years later, Callaghan in 1979, Major in 1997, Brown in 2010, and of Course Cameron in 2016. The last example was of a different character; getting on the wrong side of public opinion in a referendum.

Others had been forced out by collapsing support within their own parties: Eden in 1957, Macmillan in 1963, Thatcher in 1990, Blair in 2007, May in 2019 and both Johnson and Truss in 2022. In Thatcher's case there was a formal challenge, in Blair's case, mounting opposition and junior ministerial resignations forced his hand – though there was still a compromise with Blair agreeing to go within a year. Johnson was forced out by mass resignations from his government, including at the highest levels, whereas Truss was effectively sacked by the markets.

Winston Churchill reluctantly relinquished control due to the pressures of old age and ill health (he was eighty and had suffered a stroke.)

Wilson however, had decided a few years in advance that he would retire at sixty - and he did. It is a feat that is deceptively hard for leaders addicted to power and all its trappings. Yet what if he had stayed for another three years?

His First Secretary Barbara Castle was of the clear opinion that him staying on would have proved decisive: 'I have no doubt at all that if Harold Wilson had not suddenly and mysteriously resigned in 1976, we would never have lost the '79 election and Margaret Thatcher would never have entered Downing Street.' [528]

However, it seems rather doubtful that the problems surrounding industrial unrest would have been avoided or mitigated very much. With the social contract breaking down and no majority, any government and any Prime Minister would have struggled. Even Callaghan with his strong relationship with the unions was powerless in the end to rein them back. Wilson was certainly not charismatic or a truly commanding figure in his later years and would not have secured key three. Unless he had been able to secure the deals necessary to defuse the Winter of Discontent, then his continuation in office would have made no difference.

(8) CALLAGHAN CALLS AN EARLY ELECTION IN AUTUMN 1978:

In the late summer of 1978, expectation was building that the Labour government was about to go for an early general election. After a turbulent four years, growth was reasonable, unemployment had stopped rising, inflation had fallen back and following the 1976 bailout by the IMF the pound had stabilised and the level of borrowing three years earlier was now known to be an over-estimate. With a government cutback in overall spending, the country seemed at last on the path back to fiscal responsibility. Also, with the Lib-Lab pact now finished, the impetus to appeal to the public for a fresh mandate was that much stronger.

Callaghan kept the public in suspense about his plans for an early election, even making light of it at the TUC conference by singing the Edwardian musical hall song, 'Waiting at the church.' In retrospect, this looks like a hubristic mistake, almost on a par with Neil Kinnock's Sheffield rally during the closing days of the 1992 general election campaign.

Yet would an early election have saved Labour's bacon in October 1978? Might it perhaps have prevented the Thatcher revolution from ever taking place?

Certainly, the economic keys would not be altered by going to the polls seven months early. Foreign policy too would neither have seen a disaster, nor missed out on a triumph by having an early poll. The leaders facing one another would have remained the same and no great policy change or scandal would have been either precipitated or avoided.

However, one thing is certain. The Winter of Discontent would not have happened before the election and so this would have had the effect of salvaging Civil Unrest key twelve. Thus, calling an early election would have finally made a material difference in the balance of keys.

<u>*general election October 1978:*</u>

1) *By-election key* — false
2) *Party Unity Key* — true
3) *Incumbent Leadership Key* — false
4) *Opposition Charisma Key* — true
5) *Third Party Key* — false
6) *Cyclical Incumbency Key* — true
7) *Short-Term Economy Key* — true
8) *Long-Term Economy Key* — false
9) *Foreign Policy/Military Success Key* — false
10) *Foreign Policy/Military Failure Key* — true
11) *Policy Change Key* — false
12) *Civil Unrest Key* — true
13) *Scandal Key* — true

<u>*balance of negative keys:*</u>   6

<u>*result:*</u> knife-edge Conservative victory

<u>*tally:*</u> Labour 290 seats Conservatives 318 seats

In this scenario, Mrs Thatcher would either scrape home with a shoe-string majority, or fall just short of it. In either case there would almost certainly be a Conservative government. In the latter situation, the Tories would probably have been propped up by the Ulster Unionists. What would follow such an election would be interesting.

It is almost certain that the Winter of Discontent strikes would have happened, and the new Thatcher government have cast them as the visible manifestation of the new ideological battlefield. It is highly probable that the Conservatives would have appealed to the electorate for a fresh mandate in spring 1979, around the time of the real-world election. Here is the guestimated scorecard for that.

general election May 1979:

1) *By-election key* — true
2) *Party Unity Key* — true
3) *Incumbent Leadership Key* — false
4) *Opposition Charisma Key* — true
5) *Third Party Key* — true
6) *Cyclical Incumbency Key* — true
7) *Short-Term Economy Key* — true
8) *Long-Term Economy Key* — n/a
9) *Foreign Policy/Military Success Key* false (discounted)
10) *Foreign Policy/Military Failure Key* true
11) *Policy Change Key* — false (discounted)
12) *Civil Unrest Key* — false
13) *Scandal Key* — true

balance of negative keys: 2

Conservatives 340 seats

Conservative majority of 75

So ultimately, calling an early election would have made little difference except to slightly increase the Thatcher majority. Her mandate would have been more or less the same as in reality. The Liberal showing would be reflective of the Labour government recently removed; so as in October 1974 would not count against the very recently elected government. So far, it seems as if fate is sealed for our national political trajectory, that although details and timing can be changed, the main course of history is inevitable - or at least becomes so.

(9) THE FALKLANDS WAR DOES NOT HAPPEN

One of the great pivotal events in modern political history is the Falklands war. The invasion of a small, sparsely populated piece of territory, 8,000 miles away in the South Atlantic that most Britons were only dimly aware of, led to the complete turnaround of the political fortunes of the Thatcher government. It created the tough, larger than life political figure that we remember today. Yet what if it had not happened? What if Galtieri and his junta had called off their plans for the invasion of the Falklands Islands as being too risky?

The Thatcher government was deeply unpopular in the period before the invasion. Unemployment had just topped three million for the first time since the Depression era. The previous summer had seen Britain's inner cities scarred by weeks of rioting. The battle between union militancy and capitalism had not yet been resolved and the UK was still very much the sick man of Europe. Within a few months the perception had changed drastically. Thatcher had gone from being seen as an out-of-touch, callous and ideologically-possessed premier, to a strong war leader, who was reinvigorating national self-confidence after decades of national decline. Yet, is all this the result of the war?

Much of it is. The success in the South Atlantic certainly won Foreign Policy Success key nine for the government. It certainly transformed Mrs Thatcher into a strong, dominant leader securing key three. It also united the Tory party around her, further marginalising the 'wets' who were opposed to her austere monetarist policy.

However, the economy - at least as measured by GDP, was already slowly recovering in early 1982, and the Policy Change key had already been secured by Thatcher's radical policies. Although there were critics in the party, the 1981 reshuffle had sidelined them, significantly strengthening the Prime Minister's hand, with the Heathite old guard seriously on the back foot. The opposition under Michael Foot was neither credible or popular, gifting the Tories Opposition Implausibility key 4a, and the SDP-Alliance was doing the same for Third Party Bonus key 5a.

Let's look at the alternative scorecard.

1983 general election

1) *By-election key* — false
2) *Party Unity Key* — false
3) *Incumbent Leadership Key* — false
4) *Opposition Charisma Key* — true
5) *Third Party Key* — true
6) *Cyclical Incumbency Key* — true
7) *Short-Term Economy Key* — true
8) *Long-Term Economy Key* — false
9) *Foreign Policy/Military Success Key* — false
10) *Foreign Policy/Military Failure Key* — true

11) *Policy Change Key*	true
12) *Civil Unrest Key*	true
13) *Scandal Key*	true

Special Keys:

Opposition Implausibility Bonuskey	true
Third Party Bonus key	true

<u>*balance of negative keys:*</u>   3

Conservatives 348 seats

Conservative majority of 45

If the Falklands War had never happened, we can see that the Thatcher government would still have won the 1983, (or perhaps 1984) election with a workable majority. This would be thanks to the weak and divided Labour movement gifting the Tories two whole keys. Yet, the government would not have gained the huge confidence that victory in the South Atlantic gave them in reality. Would they have had the strength to defeat the miners, pursue their privatisation agenda or Big Bang regulatory bonfire in the city? We will never know for sure. Yet what we do know with reasonable confidence is that they would still have remained in power - probably for the rest of the decade.

(10) <u>BRITAIN LOSES THE FALKLANDS WAR:</u>

Although Britain achieved a clear-cut victory over Argentina in the Falklands war, with around a third of their losses, things could have turned out very differently in May and June 1982. There were several factors that could have turned Britain's fortunes completely on their head. Firstly, the Argentine navy did not significantly engage with Britain after the sinking of the Belgrano. What if they had chosen a bolder course? Could this have significantly impacted the course of the war?

Secondly, because of the Argentine tactic of flying very low in order to avoid British radar, around sixty percent of their bombs did not explode. [529] This is because the bombs were designed to be dropped from a greater height, and therefore requiring a greater impact for their detonation. What would have been the outcome had the Argentine air force used a different class of bomb, or had had flown at a slightly greater height? Certainly, more British shipping, and therefore lives and equipment would have been lost.

Thirdly, there were mistakes in Argentine targeting. The air force primarily targeted British warships, whereas targeting the two aircraft carriers, landing craft and troop ships, such as the requisitioned QE2 would have been far more effective at stopping a British invasion. Speaking in 1991, Admiral Sir John Woodward said that the loss of the aircraft carrier Hermes, 'would I am inclined to say have certainly altered the outcome.' [530] There were additionally technical problems with Argentina's lone submarine San Luis, which despite being able to evade British depth charges and torpedoes, nevertheless proved unable to land a killer blow on British vessels.

Fourthly, the Argentine army relied heavily on inexperienced conscripts to defend the islands. More experienced troops would have fared better.

Fifthly, British forces were simply becoming exhausted and running out of supplies. Had the Argentinians been able to hold on for another week, the final outcome might have been quite different. This view was expressed by Admiral Sir John Woodward, who told the Guardian in 2002 that the eventual British victory was 'a lot closer run than many would care to believe.' He added that, 'We were on our last legs...If they had been able to hold on another week it might have been a different story.' [531]

With more experienced troops, a more aggressive use of the navy and more effective use of the air force, it is far from inconceivable that Argentina could have won the Falklands war in 1982. With the theatre of war 8,000 miles away from home, it would not have been possible for Britain to replenish her losses, and with no other power willing or able to take up the fight, the taskforce - or what little remained of it, would have limped back to Albion with its tail between its legs.

Even with the bad news delivered dryly by government spokesman Ian MacDonald, the political repercussions would have been immense. It would almost certainly have led to the swift resignation of Margaret Thatcher and probably also that of the Foreign Secretary Francis Pym. The successor could well have been the Chancellor Geoffrey Howe, who would have been seen as a safe pair of hands to steady the ship.

However, such a disaster would have cost the Conservatives Foreign Policy/Military Failure key ten as well as Foreign Policy/Military Success key nine. With the moderate 'wet' faction using defeat as an opportunity to repudiate both Thatcher and Thatcherism, Party Unity key two would undoubtedly have been forfeited. No successor to Thatcher would have looked at all charismatic or dominant in such circumstances, so key four would also have been lost.

Such a disaster would additionally have led to many moderate Tory voters fleeing the Conservatives for the then up-and-coming SDP-Liberal-Alliance. Therefore, the Third Party Bonus key would have been lost, since the Alliance would have been taking votes from both main parties as well as representing serious fractures within both main parties. Overall, the position would have looked something like this.

Falklands War defeat: 1983/84 general election

1) *By-election key*	false
2) *Party Unity Key*	false
3) *Incumbent Leadership Key*	false
4) *Opposition Charisma Key*	true
5) *Third Party Key*	true
6) *Cyclical Incumbency Key*	true
7) *Short-Term Economy Key*	true
8) *Long-Term Economy Key*	false
9) *Foreign Policy/Military Success Key*	false
10) *Foreign Policy/Military Failure Key*	false
11) *Policy Change Key*	true
12) *Civil Unrest Key*	true
13) *Scandal Key*	true

Special Keys:

Opposition Implausibility key   true

balance of negative keys: 5

result: hung parliament with the Conservatives eight seats short of a majority.

tally: Conservatives 318 seats Labour 290

In this scenario it is difficult to predict exact seat totals for Labour, due to the significantly higher vote share of the Alliance. However, in this scenario the weakened Conservative government would have been able to hold out until the last possible date for the election - June 1984. This would have entailed fighting an election campaign during the miners' strike.

With such a weakened and discredited government, Arthur Scargill would have been emboldened, with a higher percentage of miners joining his strike and a strong possibility that sympathy strikes would have been considerably more widespread and aggressive than was the case in reality. In that case the Civil Unrest key could easily have been jeopardised, thus costing the Tory government another twenty seats.

In such a scenario, the outcome would likely be some kind of rickety Lib-Lab coalition with Michael Foot in Downing Street.

Even if the Tories had just managed to hold onto office with the help of Ian Paisley, the sympathy strikes that largely failed to materialise in reality, would have been far stronger in this counterfactual summer of 1984; probably bringing down the government and leading to fresh elections in the autumn. These would result in a Foot minority or coalition government.

With the bitter divisions within the Labour movement at the time, it is hard to see Foot securing a clear majority in a follow-up election. Owing to his age and lack of credibility, Foot would most likely have been eased out in a few years and replaced with Neil Kinnock. He might then be able to win a small majority, but it is far from certain.

This fractious left-wing coalition would have squabbled over many things, but would almost certainly have repealed the Thatcherite anti-trade union laws and reversed the tax cuts and monetarism of the previous half-decade.

A strong and united Labour movement would at least have gained the upper hand and used a subsequent election to get a real majority. In this counterfactual world, we would have been treated to a prolonged and open-ended period of chaos and drift; the Thatcher revolution would have been aborted, but a coherent and stable socialist order would be stillborn.

This is so far, the most dramatic of the counterfactuals. In such a world, the eighties that we know and recognise today would never have existed. Previous scenarios have all, more or less yielded up only a relatively small change in historical details; this one derails the entire trajectory of an era as well as uprooting much of the historical infrastructure present in the early twenty-first century.

(11) MARGARET THATCHER IS KILLED IN THE 1984 BRIGHTON BOMBING:

In October 1984, an IRA bomb devastated the Grand Hotel in Brighton, where the cabinet were staying during their party conference. Five people were killed and many others badly injured. Although Mrs Thatcher escaped unscathed, a bathroom that she had been in only minutes before the blast was wrecked. What would the political fallout have been from the first British Prime

Minister to be assassinated since Spencer Percival in 1812?

A leadership contest would have inevitably followed. Who were the likely candidates? The hard-line Thatcherite Norman Tebbit would have probably been ruled out as both he and his wife had been so badly injured. The arch-Thatcherite Sir Keith Joseph did not have the common touch, was rather too peculiar. The Foreign Secretary Geoffrey Howe was a safe pair of hands but too dull. In June 1978, Dennis Healey likened an attack by Howe to being 'savaged by a dead sheep.' Nicknamed 'Mogadon Man,' he was never going to be able to connect with the public and enthuse people. Cecil Parkinson had the communication skills and charm, but he had been damaged by a sex scandal the previous year.

The Chancellor Nigel Lawson was a strong contender, though perhaps lacked the ability to connect with the public as leader. Leon Brittan the Home Secretary likewise was not a sufficiently good communicator. Douglas Hurd the Northern Ireland Secretary lacked sufficient support - when he actually stood in the 1990 leadership contest, he only got fifty-seven votes.

This leaves one charismatic and compelling candidate - Michael Heseltine. Heseltine was also quite experienced, having spent four years as Environment Secretary and then a year-and-a-half as Defence Secretary. At fifty-one, he could neither be said to be too young or too old. He was a Thatcherite, but a reasonably pro-European, moderate one, so had wide appeal.

A leader taking office from an assassinated predecessor naturally receives initial goodwill and can retain it if they do not betray the fallen leader's vision. A Heseltine Britain in the mid-eighties would have probably followed a similar trajectory to the real one under Thatcher. A charismatic and imposing figure, Heseltine would likely have secured the Incumbent Leadership key. Thus, the 1987 electoral scorecard would probably have looked pretty much the same as the real one.

Beyond 1987, Heseltine would probably have brought Britain into the ERM a year or so earlier than happened in reality. (As would Lawson) Would this have brought forward Black Wednesday? It is of course impossible to know, but it is a strong possibility. Had this disaster occurred before the 1992 election, then the loss of the Foreign Policy key, combined with the loss of Incumbent Leadership key and probably Party Unity key would have undoubtedly cost the Tories that election.

However, a Kinnock win in 1992 would have meant that the Blair project would never have happened. A defeat in 1992 would have not been as bad as the actual defeat in 1997, and the Tories' spell in opposition, perhaps correspondingly shorter.

(12) <u>THATCHER NARROWLY SURVIVES THE 1990 LEADERSHIP CONTEST:</u>

In November 1990, Mrs Thatcher came first in the first ballot against Michael Heseltine by 204-152 votes; four-short of the winning threshold. Had two MPs changed their minds she would in theory at least have been home and dry. How would the next election have panned out?

The first major challenge awaiting a re-elected Thatcher would have been the impending war in the Gulf. Britain had already committed forces to the Gulf before Thatcher's defenestration and the looming UN deadline for Saddam Hussein to withdraw from occupied

Kuwait was 15th January 1991. If Thatcher had survived her political assassination, then further action by rebels would have been difficult with the clock ticking down to war. There was great uncertainty as to the real strength of the Iraqi armed forces, with hospital wards in the UK being cleared for potential casualties of chemical warfare.

Victory in the Gulf at the end of February 1991 would have dramatically shored up Thatcher's position, at least temporarily. She in fact would have advised George Bush Snr to continue the war for longer, in order to destroy more of Saddam's forces. Whether the Bush administration would have done so is impossible to say. However, victory of some kind would have been assured and backbench rebels pacified - for now.

There is a real possibility here that Thatcher would have called an early election to capitalise on victory in the Gulf and to gain a fresh mandate. A new majority would considerably strengthen her position against the rebels. A May 1991 election would have looked like this.

Thatcher survives to fight a spring 1991 election:

1) *By-election key* — false
2) *Party Unity Key* — false
3) *Incumbent Leadership Key* — false
4) *Opposition Charisma Key* — true
5) *Third Party Key* — true
6) *Cyclical Incumbency Key* — true
7) *Short-Term Economy Key* — false
8) *Long-Term Economy Key* — true
9) *Foreign Policy/Military Success Key* — true
10) *Foreign Policy/Military Failure Key* — true
11) *Policy Change Key* — false

12) *Civil Unrest Key*   true
13) *Scandal Key*   true

<u>*balance of negative keys:*</u> 5

<u>*result:*</u> hung parliament

Conservatives: 318 seats   Labour: c. 290

This result would see a minority Thatcher government. Such an inconclusive result would very likely have further emboldened the rebels and a new leadership contest would have been on the cards. In this scenario, Mrs Thatcher would very probably have been overthrown and replaced in the immediate aftermath of the election.

Unlike May's similar predicament a quarter of a century later, there were viable successors waiting in the wings. If Major had become leader in May 1991, the remaining years in office would have resembled those after September 1992 in the real world. Black Wednesday would have happened when it did, and this would have been the likely moment for a no confidence vote and fall of his government.

In the second possibility of Thatcher hanging on until 1992, the next real hurdle for Thatcher would have been the Maastricht treaty of December 1991. This is the treaty that led to further European integration and the official foundation of the European Union, as opposed to the looser European Community. Thatcher had been bitterly opposed to it and had lambasted her successor John Major for signing it, accusing him of doing, 'the equivalent of putting your head in the fire,' and of 'living in cloud-cuckoo land.'[532] If Margaret Thatcher had been Prime Minister at the time, it seems likely that she would have refused to take Britain into the Maastricht Treaty. Yet how would her cabinet and MPs have reacted?

Cabinet resignations would have been a distinct possibility. However, two of her earlier euro-rebels had already resigned; Nigel Lawson in 1989 and Geoffrey Howe before the leadership contest in 1990. In this counterfactual, Heseltine would still have been on the backbenches and Ken Clarke not yet the big beast he was to become in the Major years.

By this point there were only six months left till the last possible date for a general election, and many rebels would have thought twice about destabilising the government with so little time left before going to the country. Any potential successor would also have faced the distinct prospect of becoming a five-month Prime Minister. The economy was mired in recession and the outcome of the next election was far from assured.

Would such a refusal to sign the Maastricht treaty have turned the Foreign Policy Failure Key? Probably not, as it was not at all popular: a telephone poll in 1993 registered ninety-three percent of respondents in opposition to it. It would however have cost the Conservatives the Party Unity key two. The Euro-civil war which is still running in the party, began in earnest after Mrs Thatcher's Bruges Speech of 1988. In reality, Major salvaged that key long enough for the election, by securing a British opt-out for the single currency and the Social Chapter. Thatcher's outright hostility to the treaty would have done the reverse.

With it being too late to change leaders, Thatcher would have led the Tories into the 1992 election. However, with all the acrimony and internecine conflict in her party, the two leadership challenges, the continuing unpopularity of the Poll Tax, recession and sheer length of her tenure at number 10, the Incumbent Leadership key would have very probably been lost. Here is a look at the counterfactual scoreboard for the election in spring/early summer 1992.

THATCHER SURVIVES TO FIGHT THE 1992 ELECTION:

1) *By-election key*   false
2) *Party Unity Key*   false
3) *Incumbent Leadership Key*   false
4) *Opposition Charisma Key*   true
5) *Third Party Key*   true
6) *Cyclical Incumbency Key*   true
7) *Short-Term Economy Key*   false
8) *Long-Term Economy Key*   true
9) *Foreign Policy/Military Success Key* true
10) *Foreign Policy/Military Failure Key* true
11) *Policy Change Key*   false
12) *Civil Unrest Key*   true
13) *Scandal Key*   true

balance of negative keys: 5

result: hung parliament

Conservatives: 318 seats   Labour: c. 290

In this scenario, the Conservatives would be just short of a majority. A deal with the Ulster Unionists would almost certainly keep the Tories at number 10, but for how long? One obvious possibility is an internal coup to replace Thatcher in the aftermath of the election. If she somehow survived, another disaster coming over the horizon would have been Black Wednesday. It would have been too late for Thatcher to voluntarily withdraw Britain from the ERM, as such a dramatic reversal of policy less than two years after its implementation would have been a disastrous volte face in itself.

With Britain expelled from the ERM in September 1992, the Foreign Policy Failure key ten would have fallen. Opposition leader Neil Kinnock (whom having wiped out the Tory majority, would have elected to stay on as Labour leader) would have tabled a motion of no confidence, triggering an election in late October/early November 1992. Here is the scorecard for that.

<u>*Thatcher's second general election 1992:*</u>

1) *By-election key* — false
2) *Party Unity Key* — false
3) *Incumbent Leadership Key* — false
4) *Opposition Charisma Key* — true
5) *Third Party Key* — true
6) *Cyclical Incumbency Key* — true
7) *Short-Term Economy Key* — false
8) *Long-Term Economy Key* — true
9) *Foreign Policy/Military Success Key* — true
10) *Foreign Policy/Military Failure Key* — false

11) *Policy Change Key*   false
12) *Civil Unrest Key*   true
13) *Scandal Key*   True

balance of negative keys: 6

result: hung parliament

Conservatives: 298 seats   Labour: c. 310

In this situation of an existing government forced to go the polls in under a year, the whole of the previous term is counted with the months since the last election simply added onto it. In this outcome, Labour are now the largest party in a hung parliament. With the Liberal Democrats a little stronger, with say - twenty-five seats, a Lib-Lab coalition is on the cards. Neil Kinnock would have finally become Prime Minister. This would have necessitated a third election - probably in spring 1993. Here is the likely result.

Neil Kinnock appeals for a majority: 1993 general election:

1) *By-election key*   n/a
2) *Party Unity Key*   true
3) Incumbent Leadership Key   false
4) *Opposition Charisma Key*   true
5) *Third Party Key*   true
6) *Cyclical Incumbency Key*   true

7) *Short-Term Economy Key* false
8) *Long-Term Economy Key* n/a
9) *Foreign Policy/Military Success Key* false (discounted)
10) *Foreign Policy/Military Failure Key* true
11) *Policy Change Key* false (discounted)
12) *Civil Unrest Key* true
13) *Scandal Key* true

<u>*balance of negative keys:*</u>   2

Labour majority of 75

Labour: 364 seats Conservative: c. 240

This counterfactual example highlights how new governments appealing for a mandate after less than a year in office, are given the benefit of the doubt by the electorate. The lack of a foreign policy success or radical policy change are not counted against the new government. They have not been in power long enough to face many by-elections - if any at all. The opposition are in disarray, with the ideological battle over Europe clouding the party's judgement as to which leader to pick. In this situation, a Kinnock administration would have had a good chance of dominating the 1990s, and the Blair Labour party might never have existed.

(13) <u>JOHN SMITH LIVES TO FIGHT THE 1997 ELECTION</u>

On May 8th 1994, John Smith the leader of the Labour party, collapsed and died suddenly of a heart attack, less than two years into the job and three years before the next election. Smith had suffered heart problems before, but had seemingly bounced back, and his sudden death - like that of his predecessor Hugh Gaitskell thirty years before, took everyone by surprise.

His passing paved the way for Tony Blair's swift succession to the Labour throne, but what would have been had Smith lived? As I am sure you are aware by now, this method is principally focused on government performance, so opposition performance is only a relatively minor factor. However, Blair in 1997 was genuinely charismatic, whereas Smith, though a competent communicator was not. Few politicians are. Apart from this, it seems reasonable to suppose that the performance of the Conservative government would have been no better and no worse than it was under Blair. Therefore, the scorecard for 1997 would have looked like this.

John Smith Lives: 1997 general election:

1) *By-election key* — false
2) *Party Unity Key* — false
3) *Incumbent Leadership Key* — false
4) *Opposition Charisma Key* — true
5) *Third Party Key* — false
6) *Cyclical Incumbency Key* — false
7) *Short-Term Economy Key* — true
8) *Long-Term Economy Key* — true
9) *Foreign Policy/Military Success Key* — false
10) *Foreign Policy/Military Failure Key* — false
11) *Policy Change Key* — false
12) *Civil Unrest Key* — true
13) *Scandal Key* — false

balance of negative keys: 9

result: Labour majority of c. 100

Conservatives: 208 seats   Labour: c. 375 seats

It is clear from the keys that John Smith would have won a handsome majority in 1997. His government would have been significantly different from Tony Blair's and significantly to the left on economic policy. Smith would not have abolished Clause four and would most likely have raised income tax for the rich and possibly even reversed some of the privatisations - perhaps the railways.

Given Smith's heart problems, he would probably not have lasted as leader for very long. Mr Blair would have been his most probable successor. Yet, he would have been taking over the leadership in a very different context to the one he faced in reality in 1994. In this situation he would be taking over in government with a strong majority. The argument that Labour had to change in order to survive would not have worked. It is very likely that the government he would have led, would have looked quite different to the one that he led in reality.

(14) THE FUEL PROTESTERS REFUSE TO BACK DOWN IN SEPTEMBER 2000

In September 2000, the relative tranquillity of the early Blair years was briefly upended by a series of protests by truckers and farmers, who blockaded oil refineries in a protest against high fuel duties. The protests were effectively imported from France and took the nation by surprise. Nothing quite like it had been seen before or since. Although the protesters humiliated the Labour government, they backed down, largely in fear of the consequences of paralysing the country, and so Labour were able to head off a repetition of the crisis, with some moderate cuts in fuel duty in the autumn statement. Yet what would have been the result had the strike continued for several more days?

The government could have used the police and even the army to tow away trucks and tractors, but that might well not have been enough. The tanker drivers themselves had joined the dispute - ostensibly over concerns about their own safety, with talk of the possibility of concrete slabs being thrown off bridges. If they had refused to come out to work - and there is good reason to suppose that a heavy-handed government crackdown might have strengthened their solidarity, then it would have proved to be no solution at all.

Likewise, the solution of seizing individuals' bank accounts like in Justin Trudeau's crackdown on anti-Vaxxers in 2022 would not have been possible then in Britain. It would also not have been possible for military personnel to drive the tankers, as there simply were not enough of them trained to do it.

The only option left on the table would have been a government climb-down over fuel duty. Although the Chancellor Gordon Brown would have been adamantly against such an idea, Blair's advisers and top civil servants in his COBRA meetings would have told him that there was no other course of action available. He might well have had to sack his chancellor in order to find someone more biddable to replace him. Alistair Darling would have been the most likely contender.

A Blair climb-down, combined with the dismissal of the second most powerful man in government, would have been a disastrous misadventure for New Labour. Even though the protesters would have had to accept a far smaller cut than what they had demanded, it would still have been a huge victory for them and a grave humiliation for a government that had seemed like it had the world at its feet.

The result would have been the swift and probably irreparable loss of the Incumbent Leadership key, and probably the Party Unity key as well. The Blair-Brown feud, already becoming a problem by this time, would have really ignited and come into the open following Brown's dismissal. The Scandal Key would likely have been wholly lost, as the damage to Blair's standing would mean that the government's Teflon coating would have been entirely erased. The government would probably have made rapid contingency plans for any repetition of the protests, so the Civil Unrest key would most likely have been salvaged long before the election.

That election would almost certainly have been delayed until May or June 2002. Blair's response to 911 and the Afghan war would have helped him shore up some support, but would likely not have restored key three. Here is the likely result.

fuel protesters Refuse to back down: 2002 general election:

1) *By-election key*   true
2) *Party Unity Key*   false
3) *Incumbent Leadership Key*   false
4) *Opposition Charisma Key*   true

5) *Third Party Key* true
6) *Cyclical Incumbency Key* true
7) *Short-Term Economy Key* true
8) *Long-Term Economy Key* true
9) *Foreign Policy/Military Success Key* true
10) *Foreign Policy/Military Failure Key* true
11) *Policy Change Key* true
12) *Civil Unrest Key* true
13) *Scandal Key* false

<u>*Special Keys*</u>

Opposition Implausibility Bonus Key 4A   true

<u>*balance of negative keys:*</u>   2

<u>*Result:*</u> Labour majority of c. 75

Labour: c. 380 seats. Conservatives: 210 seats

Such an outcome would still have been historically very impressive for Labour, but would nevertheless have seemed like a bit of a coming down to earth, following the euphoria of 1997. Most likely, Blair would have continued as Prime Minister for about as long and Brown would simply have scowled and skulked from the backbenchers. Brown's paralysing over-caution and indecisiveness preventing him from launching any effective challenge against Blair.

(15) <u>KEN CLARKE WINS THE 2001 CONSERVATIVE LEADERSHIP CHALLENGE</u>

In July 2001, the Conservatives were electing a new leader to get them out of the political wilderness to which they had been relegated for the past four years. The 2001 election had seen them make only a pitiful gain of just one seat - whilst losing a million votes, with the result that William Hague immediately fell on his sword. Two months on and the battle was now between the leadership candidates. The third and final ballot of MPs was between the ebullient, left-leaning and pro-European former Chancellor Ken Clarke, the formerly right-wing but now born-again social liberal, former Defence Secretary Michael Portillo and the Shadow Secretary of State for Social Security and arch Euro-sceptic Ian Duncan Smith.

In reality, the MPs narrowly eliminated Michael Portillo and the members plumped overwhelmingly for Ian Duncan Smith. However, the third ballot saw only one vote separating IDS and Portillo, with the latter being eliminated from the contest with fifty-three votes against Ian Duncan-Smith's fifty-four. Yet what if one Tory MP had changed his mind and switched from IDS to Portillo?

In that hypothetical but highly possible scenario, the mostly elderly, right-wing, Euro-sceptic and socially conservative Tory membership would have been placed in something of a quandary. Either to go for the pro-European, well-known, relatively popular and massively experienced former chancellor, or for the man who many now saw as a political turncoat, after talking about the need of the Conservative party to change and to embrace social liberalism.

In 1999, Portillo had been forced to publicly respond to growing rumours about his sexuality. In an interview with The Times, he stated that, 'I had some homosexual experiences as a young person.' 533 All this severely damaged his right-wing reputation and exposed him to charges of hypocrisy due to his earlier opposition to the expansion of gay rights when in government.

In this hypothetical scenario, would Tory members have gone for homophobia or Europhobia? In the real-life membership vote, Clarke still managed to win 100,000 votes to Duncan-Smith's 155,000. Although Portillo was a Euro-sceptic, he was not as strongly Euro-sceptic as IDS by this point. With Clarke able to secure thirty-nine percent of the vote against an ideologically correct opponent, it seems highly probable that he would have gained an outright majority against a man who was ideologically and personally tainted in the eyes of the right-wing party faithful.

With Clarke elected leader in September 2001, Tony Blair would have been faced by an opposition party whose leadership would be opposed to the war in Iraq eighteen months later. In the Commons vote in March 2003, 149 MPs voted against the authorisation of military force against Iraq, as opposed to 412 who supported it. The Conservatives under Ian Duncan Smith had given their staunch support to Tony Blair, but if only 132 of the 166 Tory MPs had voted against the war, then the motion would have been defeated. Could Ken Clarke have successfully whipped eighty percent of his MPS to oppose the war?

If Clarke had successfully defeated the government over Iraq, it is almost certain that Blair and a number of other cabinet ministers would have resigned. In an interview for The Guardian, the Home Secretary David Blunkett told the paper that cabinet ministers close to Blair would, 'go down with him.' The Foreign Secretary Jack Straw added that, 'I knew there would be a point at which Tony would resign and I would resign as well. I told my wife I might well have to go over this. I think Tony assumed that I would go.' 534

The overwhelmingly likely successor to Tony Blair would of course have been his Chancellor Gordon Brown, who had been sitting at the Treasury waiting, but not very patiently, for the top job since May 1997. Yet he would still have been damaged, since he had publicly supported the war. It would have been a very difficult job - perhaps an impossible job for him to reunite a party torn apart and traumatised by such a disaster. It is this hypothetical Brown government facing re-election in 2005 or 06 that we must now look at.

In terms of the military situation, the Americans would have gone ahead without us. In fact, the US Defence Secretary Donald Rumsfeld even offered Britain a way out, saying that if Britain could not participate in the invasion, 'there are work-arounds and they would not be involved, at least in that phase of it.'535 The British role was to take the southern Iraqi city of Basra. It seems that the Americans would have airlifted a few units to the Saudi border – probably delaying the start of the conflict by a few weeks.

With the dramatic resignation of Blair and division in his party, both the Party Unity key and Incumbent Leadership keys would have been lost. This of course happened anyway. The defeat would be followed by a bitter debate on the intelligence used to convince MPs and the public of the case for war, and very likely the Scandal key would have fallen as a result - as it did in reality.

The economic and Policy Change keys would have performed as they did in reality as well. Clearly, if a Tory opposition had succeeded in bringing down a sitting Labour Prime Minister, then they would no longer be an implausible opposition and that bonus key would disappear, and with it the Opposition Complicity key. Although perhaps not charismatic enough to topple Key4, Ken Clarke would have undoubtedly been a more effective campaigner than Michael Howard and for that matter Gordon Brown.

The scorecard for 2005 or 2006 would have looked like this.

Ken Clarke as Tory leader, government defeated on Iraq: 2005/06 general election:

1) *By-election key* — true
2) *Party Unity Key* — false
3) *Incumbent Leadership Key* — false
4) *Opposition Charisma Key* — true
5) *Third Party Key* — true
6) *Cyclical Incumbency Key* — true
7) *Short-Term Economy Key* — true
8) *Long-Term Economy Key* — true
9) *Foreign Policy/Military Success Key* — true
10) *Foreign Policy/Military Failure Key* — false
11) *Policy Change Key* — half-turn
12) *Civil Unrest Key* — true
13) *Scandal Key* — false

balance of negative keys: 4 ½

result: knife-edge Labour victory

Labour: 325 seats. Conservatives: 205 seats

The aftermath of this election would be interesting. If Labour managed to scrape home with any kind of majority, and bearing in mind Sinn Fein won five seats, reducing the threshold for a de facto majority to 323, then Brown could have continued in office, but with clipped wings and a great sense of deflation. If he fell a little below this, then it would have to have been a minority government propped up by the Ian Paisley's DUP. A slow death would have awaited New Labour

(16) 911 IS FOILED

If the September 11th attacks had been foiled - which is not inconceivable, the history of the 2000s would have been a very different one; in fact, it would have been a smooth continuation of the post- Cold War 1990s, giving some credence to Francis Fukuyama's 'End of History' doctrine. However, it was not to be, and September 11th 2001 now seems like the beginning of a period of ominous decline for western power and enlightenment values. Yet, what if world politics took a different, more benign course?

No 911 would mean no war in Afghanistan or Iraq. It would have deprived Tony Blair of his opportunity to fight against evil on the global arena, yet it would have saved him from the greatest single mistake of his premiership - the invasion of Iraq.

Here is the scorecard for the election of 2005 after the more peaceful and halcyon hypothetical second Labour term.

911 is foiled – no Afghan/Iraq Wars. General election 2005:

1) *By-election key*	true
2) *Party Unity Key*	true
3) *Incumbent Leadership Key*	true
4) *Opposition Charisma Key*	true
5) *Third Party Key*	true
6) *Cyclical Incumbency Key*	true
7) *Short-Term Economy Key*	true
8) *Long-Term Economy Key*	true
9) *Foreign Policy/Military Success Key*	true
10) *Foreign Policy/Military Failure Key*	true
11) *Policy Change Key*	half-turn
12) *Civil Unrest Key*	true
13) *Scandal Key*	true

Special Keys

Opposition Implausibility key 4A

balance of negative keys: ½ key

Result: Labour majority of 150

Labour: 405 seats. Conservatives: 170 seats

As we can see, had 911 been foiled, and with it the train of invasions, extraordinary renditions, Guantanamo and authoritarian security measures, Blair would have achieved a wholly unprecedented landslide hat-trick. Marginally smaller than the 2001 majority, this, nevertheless would have been the third largest majority ever, by anyone.

(17) GORDON BROWN CALLS AN EARLY ELECTION IN 2007

During the heady political summer of 2007, new Prime Minister Gordon Brown allowed expectations to build up of a snap autumn election. The pre-electioneering reached a peak in early October with Lady Thatcher being invited to tea at Downing Street. Brown seemed to be sending a signal to middle England that he was just as right wing as Tony Blair - if not more so.

Yet, in the wake of a small post-conference poll bounce for the Tories, following their proposal to cut inheritance tax, Brown lost his nerve and bottled out of an early poll. His disingenuous explanation, that he wanted more time to set out his vision instantly made him look weak and dishonest. It immediately cost him key three. Yet, what would have happened had he been a little bit bolder? Would an election in November 2007 have given Brown a fresh mandate of his own? Or could it have gone horribly wrong?

At that point in time, the Global Financial Crisis had not yet happened. Yes, there was a pre-cursor of it with the shockingly sudden collapse of Northern Rock in September 2007, but this was not enough to push the UK economy into recession. Growth was a bit anaemic but most experts were not forecasting a recession. Ergo, both economic keys would be positive.

Tony Blair's recent historic success in ending the political conflict in Northern Ireland was enough to secure key nine. However, the increasingly unpopular war in Afghanistan as well as the continuing involvement in Iraq would have cost key eight. The government had not effected much policy change, so key eleven would be forfeited. The cash for coronets scandal had already toppled key thirteen, but the new-found affection for Brown in the party was enough to temporarily heal key two. The worst by-election defeats were still ahead of Labour and so key one was still true.

David Cameron was seen as superficial and as trying too hard to be 'heir to Blair.' However, he was leagues ahead of his three immediate predecessors and with the invasion of Iraq fading into the rear mirror, did not gift Labour any bonus keys either.

The Labour vote would also have been helped by the very poor state of the Liberal Democrat polling under leader Menzies Campbell. The weak state of the third party would have meant that an election at this time would have seen both main parties benefit at the Liberals' expense.

Brown seemed strong and popular. Would key three be with Labour? As was the case a decade later with Theresa May, Brown's early popularity was a mirage resulting from novelty in the post and the projections of false hopes. Had Brown actually fought an election campaign in the autumn of 2007 his lack of communication skills would have been quickly exposed in the same cruel fashion as later proved the case for Mrs May. Let's take a look at the scorecard.

<u>*Gordon Brown calls an early general election:* November 2007</u>

1) *By-election key*   true

2) *Party Unity Key*	true
3) *Incumbent Leadership Key*	false
4) *Opposition Charisma Key*	true
5) *Third Party Key*	true
6) *Cyclical Incumbency Key*	true
7) *Short-Term Economy Key*	true
8) *Long-Term Economy Key*	true
9) *Foreign Policy/Military Success Key*	true
10) *Foreign Policy/Military Failure Key*	false
11) *Policy Change Key*	false
12) *Civil Unrest Key*	true
13) *Scandal Key*	false

balance of negative keys :4 keys

Result: Labour majority of 15

Labour: 333 seats. Conservatives: c. 235 seats

In this scenario, Brown would have won a mandate of sorts, but it would have been a pyrrhic victory. He could theoretically have continued in office until the autumn of 2012, but his government's increasing unpopularity would have meant a steadily dwindling majority and growing impotence.

Cameron's performance here is only slightly better than that of Neil Kinnock's Labour party in 1987. It may still have led to a sigh of relief in Conservative central Office, since polls and pundits at the start of the campaign would have been predicting a stronger Brown majority. Perhaps the game of expectation management would have made it feel like a victory for Cameron and a defeat for Brown. It would have been eerily similar to the real life 2017 election in that regard.

The subsequent election in 2012 would be harder to predict, but here goes. After the recession, the Long-Term Economy Key would be lost. Political division in Labour combined with Brown's failings as leader would also cost the first three keys. It is probable that Britain would be sufficiently extracted from Afghanistan to salvage key ten.

The expenses scandal in 2009 would have robbed Labour of key thirteen and after fifteen-and-a-half years in office, the Cyclical Incumbency key would probably be lost too: especially after several years of near-paralysis and drift. Any Olympics boost would be very short-lived. Here is the scorecard. There is a risk that the Liberals would be making big gains as voters tired of Brown - and the by then, not very new Labour.

Gordon Brown hangs on: general election 2011/12

1) *By-election key* — false
2) *Party Unity Key* — false
3) *Incumbent Leadership Key* — false
4) *Opposition Charisma Key* — true
5) *Third Party Key* — true
6) *Cyclical Incumbency Key* — true
7) *Short-Term Economy Key* — true (probably)
8) *Long-Term Economy Key* — false
9) *Foreign Policy/Military Success Key* — true
10) *Foreign Policy/Military Failure Key* — true (probably)
11) *Policy Change Key* — half-turn

12) *Civil Unrest Key* true
13) *Scandal Key* false

<u>*balance of negative keys:*</u> 5½ keys

<u>*result:*</u> hung parliament with Labour as largest party.

<u>*tally:*</u> Labour 308 seats. Conservatives: 261.

In this scenario, the Cameron- Clegg coalition would simply have been delayed by one or two years. It is another counterfactual which changes details, but not ultimately the major trends of political history.

(18) <u>DAVID CAMERON RESISTS CALLING AN EU REFERENDUM</u>

In January 2013 David Cameron bowed to growing Euro-sceptic pressure from his backbenchers and announced in what came to be called his Bloomberg speech, the intention of renegotiating the terms of Britain's EU membership, before calling an in-out referendum on whether Britain should remain in the EU. What if he had resisted the pressure to do this and publicly ruled out such a vote? It would not have affected the 2015 election, and after gaining a small majority he could have relied on Labour votes to block any backbench bills and amendments aimed at triggering such a vote.

Yet in the last days of the 2015 election campaign, Cameron had publicly ruled out running for a third term. Assuming he honoured the pledge, this would have meant him stepping down, probably in the autumn of 2018. The most likely candidate to replace him would have been Boris Johnson. Johnson of course had calculated that in order to get the votes of the party membership it would be necessary to appear highly Euro-sceptic. Therefore, his 2018 leadership pitch would have involved pledging to offer Britain a referendum on continued EU membership.

Johnson's anti-EU noises would very probably have given him the leadership and the keys to Number 10. If he held an election in 2019, he would have been buoyed up by a relatively strong pre-Brexit economy, a relatively stable international scene and an implausible opposition. Had he gone for a five-year term, he would have found the election delayed because of COVID and the term becoming the longest since the war. The poll could have been delayed till autumn 2021.

Boris Johnson: general election 2019

1) *By-election key*	true
2) *Party Unity Key*	false
3) *Incumbent Leadership Key*	true
4) *Opposition Charisma Key*	true
5) *Third Party Key*	true
6) *Cyclical Incumbency Key*	true
7) *Short-Term Economy Key*	true
8) *Long-Term Economy Key*	true
9) *Foreign Policy/Military Success Key*	false
10) *Foreign Policy/Military Failure Key*	true

   11) *Policy Change Key*   false
   12*) Civil Unrest Key*   true
   13) *Scandal Key*   true
(probably)

<u>*Special Keys*</u>

Opposition Implausibility key   true

<u>*balance of negative keys:*</u>   2 keys

<u>*result:*</u> Conservative majority of 75 seats
<u>*tally:*</u> Conservatives 363 Labour 204 seats

If the election had been delayed by two years because of COVID, then the Long-Term Economy key would have been lost, but the Policy Change key gained, as the Lockdowns were a major form of policy change. Therefore, the result would have been the same. Boris Johnson's government would have called the Brexit referendum at some point in the early 2020s. Yet would this have delivered the same result that was achieved in 2016? The demographic changes, with elderly Brexiteers dying off and being replaced with young Remainers might suggest not. However, with such a close outcome in 2016, we can never be sure. So again, this could be another example of history deferred and not cancelled, but ultimately, we can never be sure of this.

(19) <u>BORIS JOHNSON STAYS IN THE 2016 LEADERSHIP RACE AND WINS</u>

In the 2016 Conservative leadership challenge, Michael Gove effectively sabotaged Boris Johnson's chances of becoming Prime Minister by standing against his former friend. However, I believe that Johnson could still have won if he had continued to stand. Gove did not get that many votes and the final two candidates would have almost certainly have been Johnson and May. Alternatively, Gove could have decided not to stand against his friend.

It is quite possible that Johnson could have defeated May in the membership ballot. If he had, how different would the next few years have been? One possibility is that Johnson, like May would have been sorely tempted to call a snap general election to gain a mandate. With the Remainer rebels in his own party, and the difficulties with the Northern Ireland Backstop potentially costing Unionist support in Ulster, the early election gambit would very likely have been taken. How would it have played out with Boris Johnson as PM?

Boris Johnson calls early general election: spring 2017

1) *By-election key*   true
2) *Party Unity Key*   false
3) *Incumbent Leadership Key*   true
4) *Opposition Charisma Key*   true
5) *Third Party Key*   true
6) *Cyclical Incumbency Key*   true
7) *Short-Term Economy Key*   true
8) *Long-Term Economy Key*   true
9) *Foreign Policy/Military Success Key* false
10) *Foreign Policy/Military Failure Key* false
11) *Policy Change Key*   false
12) *Civil Unrest Key*   true

13) *Scandal Key* true

balance of negative keys: 4 keys

result: Conservative majority of 15

tally: Conservatives: 333. Labour 247

In this scenario, Boris Johnson simply ends up with about the same sized majority as David Cameron secured two years earlier. The difference with the actual vote under May, is that Boris Johnson had a kind of anarchic charisma, whereas May had none at all. That one key would have given him a majority, but a rather disappointing one. Ergo, he would still have struggled to get a majority to vote for his Brexit deal in the Commons. He still would have faced the problem of the Northern Ireland Backstop and thus have lost the support of the DUP. The final outcome of another election in 2019 might well have been the same in this counterfactual time stream. So, another counterfactual leading to the same destination through a slightly different route.

(20) <u>THERESA MAY LOSES A NO CONFIDENCE VOTE IN JANUARY 2019</u>

On January 15th 2019, a motion of no confidence was tabled against Theresa May's ministry. The motion was rejected by 325 to 306. If ten MPS had changed their minds or twenty abstainers voted against the government, then it would have fallen. If no one had been able to gain the confidence of the House within fourteen working days an election would have been called. What would have happened?

The failure of May to get a deal approved in Parliament more than two-and-half-years after the referendum would have cost her administration both the Foreign Policy keys, the Policy Change key and the Party Unity key. The Incumbent Leadership key would, it goes without saying be for the birds - possibly vultures. Brexit uncertainty in the markets would also have cost the Long-Term Economy key eight.

However, the implosion of UKIP and the non-recovery of the Liberals would have preserved key five, and Corbyn's by now diabolical public standing, would not only have saved key four, but gifted the Conservatives Opposition Implausibility key four A. In Mid-March, his net favourability rating according to IPSOS-MORI stood at minus fifty; twenty percent approving and seventy percent disapproving. [536]

May loses No Confidence Vote Early Election: March 2019

1) *By-election key*   true
2) *Party Unity Key*   false
3) *Incumbent Leadership Key*   false
4) *Opposition Charisma Key*   true
5) *Third Party Key*   true
6) *Cyclical Incumbency Key*   true
7) *Short-Term Economy Key*   true
8) *Long-Term Economy Key*   false
9) *Foreign Policy/Military Success Key*..false
10) *Foreign Policy/Military Failure Key* false
11) *Policy Change Key*   false

12) *Civil Unrest Key*   true
13) *Scandal Key*   true

<u>Special Keys</u>

Third Party Implausibility   true

<u>balance of negative keys:</u>   5 keys

<u>result:</u> hung parliament with Conservatives largest party

<u>tally:</u> Conservatives: 318. Labour 262

We can see here, that if Corbyn had successfully brought down the May government with a motion of no confidence, then the ensuing election would have exactly recreated the previous parliamentary arithmetic. Nothing would have changed.

In summary then, most political counterfactuals change only the details of the main trajectory and some barely even that. However, there are a smaller number of events that seem to be genuine game changers. The Falklands war is one. To a lesser extent (for Britain that is) is 911. The hypothetical assassination of Margaret Thatcher at Brighton also would seem to change the course of history, through possibly bringing Black Wednesday forward in time to scupper the 1992 Tory victory. That election was a game changer too, but not in the sense we might have thought at the time. It was important because it led directly to the creation of New Labour, which might very well never have occurred had that election been lost to the Tories.

The various postponed elections of the 1970s and changes of leadership personnel of the sixties and seventies changed almost nothing. The counterfactual surrounding the 2007 'bottled' election only delayed the future course of history by a little more.

The importance of Suez was merely in highlighting Britain's relative decline in the world which had already taken place, rather than actually changing anything much per se.

In the future, it might be interesting to do a counterfactual in which the Chinese authorities had succeeded in suppressing COVID as the start and a world pandemic avoided. It certainly would have seen Donald Trump win a second term, but it is a bit too early to draw up a counterfactual for the UK. Enough.

Chapter 10: The lessons of the Keys

(1) oppositions don't win elections, governments lose them

This is an old adage and is very largely true. The election is essentially a referendum on government performance in office since the last election. If they have handled the economy well, achieved foreign policy success, avoided foreign policy failure, scandal, civil unrest and division, they will be re-elected. If they achieve these things, it is also unlikely a third party will gain much traction, unless it is at the expense of the main opposition. Charismatic opposition leaders tend to emerge when the government is unpopular and failing; so, governing effectively, can ward off threats to keys four and five like a lucky talisman.

If the opposition neither have a charismatic leader, nor are widely regarded as hopeless, then nothing they say or do will make any real difference. It may seem negative from the opposition party's point of view, but it is also liberating. There is no need to undergo radical transformations in order to become electable. The opposition's electability is mostly a reflection of government popularity or the lack of. The keys instead allow opposition parties to relax a little and take a more philosophical view of things.

From the government's point of view, it focuses their minds on what they can control; their own performance, and not on what the opposition are doing and not on what the media are saying about them.

(2) the electorate cannot distinguish between governmental performance and governmental luck

There is a lot of luck in politics; that cannot be denied. Tony Blair was a lucky politician. He became opposition leader when the Conservative government was self-destructing but the economy beginning to improve. He reached office when the economy had entered a boom and the Tories had reached maximum unpopularity. He also inherited a relatively tranquil international scene. He was then gifted a series of hopeless Tory leaders, none of whom the country was really interested in listening to. He left office just before the greatest financial crisis since the 1930s was about to hit.

Gordon Brown was an unlucky politician; at least as Prime Minister. He reached Number 10 just before the Global Financial Crisis and just after the Tories had chosen a young and plausible leader who seemed to represent the future.

The public do not take such factors as luck into account. If your government presides over a recession of your own making, it will turn the economic keys no more or less than if the recession was brought about by global forces beyond your control. If you have inherited a bad economic situation, it is now your problem and no amount of blaming the last government will make any difference. The obvious example here is of Wilson's Labour government, which inherited the balance of payments crisis from the Tories; it resulted in a devaluation that badly damaged Labour.

The corollary is also the case. Blair inherited a booming economy, low interest rates and low inflation from John Major. Yet Mr Blair still reaped the electoral rewards. Trump was taken out by the economic effects of COVID; if the pandemic had struck in 2021, he would still be in the White House.

(3) the electorate do not take the merits of opposition parties sufficiently into account: Almost any opposition can win

This is perhaps the scariest lesson of the keys. The election is overwhelmingly about the performance of government and therefore, if a government is sufficiently unsuccessful, then any kind of opposition could win. Yes, there is the bonus key four A that penalises a terrible opposition, but it is only one key. An extremist opposition could suffer a split and then trigger the bonus key five A too. This happened in the 1983 elections, yet even this double bonus would not be enough to keep out an extremist party if the government of the day was as unpopular as say - that of John Major in 1997.

When this finding is combined with that of the public not being able to distinguish between governmental incompetence and governmental bad luck, there is the distinct possibility that a basically decent and competent administration could be brought down by bad luck and replaced by a terrible opposition.

The corollary to this is that even a brilliant government-in-waiting would be left to moulder on the opposition benches if a weak, visionless and maybe corrupt sitting government were lucky enough with the world economic trends and a period of global peace.

(4) no party is ever destined to be in office, or in the wilderness for longer than a single term

It is often said after a crushing victory that the opposition will be out for a generation. Nobody ever seems to learn! In 1945, a Labour MP boldly predicted that his party would be in government for the next twenty years. In fact, they were out of office in a little over six. In 1970, the Labour campaign attacked the Tories as 'Yesterday's men' trapped in the black and white past: yet they still managed to defeat Labour in the polls. In the 1980s and especially after the 1992 election, it became popular to ask that if Labour could not win with nearly three million on the dole, then when could they win? Many speculated that Britain was becoming a one-party state, doomed to vote Tory for ever. Five short years later, Labour were returned to power with the greatest landslide in modern British political history.

Then the cycle repeated. In the late 90's and 00's it was widely believed that the future would be New Labour rule stretching over the horizon into infinity. Yet, at the time of writing, they have been shut out of power for thirteen-and-a-half years. The ex-Labour deputy leader Roy Hattersley opined in 2006 that the next Tory Prime Minister had not been born yet and they would not return to power in his lifetime. In 2023, Hattersley has lived through thirteen years of Tory rule under a grand total of five Prime Ministers. (And possibly another by the time you are reading this.)

After the 2019 election result, many were predicting a long period in the wilderness for Labour, who would need at least a couple of electoral cycles to get back into power. At the time of writing, only four years later, there are polls predicting 400 seat Labour majorities.

All this goes to show that every election is only about the government's record since the last one. The current state of the opposition party also matters a bit, but events prior to the last election do not directly matter at all in themselves. The slate is effectively wiped clean every four or five years. This of course means that on the one hand the public are ultimately forgiving; they do not vote on the basis of old wrongs. It also means that they are ultimately ungrateful, and it is no use reminding them of the great things your party has done in the past.

This does mean though that everything is to play for, and no opposition party should sink into dejection, believing that is doomed to wander in the wilderness for a decade. It also warns against government complacency; nothing is taken for granted by the electorate.

(5) campaigns are nearly always an irrelevance

The conventional wisdom holds that election campaigns start like a horse race, where although some horses are stronger and faster than others, ultimately anything can happen during the race as individual parties and leaders surge ahead or fall behind. This is a complete myth. Rarely in election campaigns is there much of a narrative at all. Pundits consistently expect the poll leads to either narrow or widen and are continually dumbfounded by their failure to do so. Events during the campaign are awarded enormous importance, with commentators saying that one party or another has 'blown' the election by making this gaffe or that gaffe.

One example was the infamous Sheffield rally of 1992, in which the Labour leader Neil Kinnock chanted 'We're alright!' with the crowd of supporters chanting it back to him. This was subsequently blamed for 'throwing' the election. In reality, the keys would have forecast the result to within a handful of seats, foretelling that Kinnock had not the remotest chance of winning a majority. Unless an event impactful enough to turn one of the keys occurs during the election campaign, then no amount of campaigning or gaffes can cause the movement of more than about ten seats at the extreme end of the range.

One apparent exception though is the election of 2017, when Theresa May's disastrous campaign seemed to cause the loss of Incumbent Leadership key three. However, the poor campaign only exposed the serious weaknesses in May's leadership that were already there - just not yet visible to the electorate. Her inability to connect with people, the wooden, uncomfortable, self-consciousness of her performances and her inflexibility were cruelly exposed for all to see. Yet they were there before the campaign. It was not a matter of bad luck during the campaign, rather it being the accident waiting to happen.

The other problem during that particular election was the extreme inaccuracy of the polls throughout it, with pollsters overcompensating for the errors of two years earlier, creating the opposite problem. Ergo, even had May turned out to be a great campaigner, she would only have succeeded in getting roughly the same sized majority as David Cameron in 2015. It was an election that should never have been held.

Conversely, the stunning Labour triumph of 1997 is often ascribed to the brilliant campaigning skills of Tony Blair. This too is false. Although Blair undoubtedly had charisma and was able to connect with the general public, most of those Labour gains had already been decided in advance by the poor performance of John Major's Conservative government.

One final example of this fallacy is the oft repeated adage that in 1987, Labour won the campaign but lost the election. It happens to be true. Although Peter Mandelson created a very polished, professional and up-to-date campaign for Labour, they only gained around twenty new seats and failed to break out of their Scottish, Welsh, Northern and inner- city strongholds.

With this over-estimation of the importance of campaigns is an exaggeration of the importance of events. Although they were the bane of Macmillan, the majority of events that create a headline splash, are soon forgotten. I remember so many hyperbolic headlines in the 2000s about 'Blair's worst week,' but when it came to the election, the old adage that 'Today's headlines are tomorrow's fish & chip wrappers' still held true. Basically, if it does not turn the keys then it probably does not much matter.

(6) manifestos are not worth the paper they are written on

Elections are often thought of as beauty contests between the different parties and manifestos are consequently designed to strategically appeal to different sections in the electorate. We hear people say things like, 'This will win the pensioner vote' or 'This is aimed at people with children,' and suchlike. Although the policies may well be targeted at differing groups in this way, the whole exercise is one of futility.

The reason for this is that people vote retrospectively, not prospectively. They do not vote on the basis of a shopping list of promises that they either like or do not like. They vote on the basis of government performance. What has the government achieved over the course of the term? What has happened since the last election? In particular, what are things like at the moment? The state of the opposition parties only matters at all, if they are on the extreme ends of the performance spectrum; if the leader is charismatic or a national hero on the one end, or if the party appears deeply implausible as a government-in-waiting, on the other.

The examples of this are in the Labour manifestos of 1983 and 2019.[537] In both cases the manifestos themselves were quite popular with the general public. In both cases many people supported nationalising/maintaining nationalisation of public utilities, but in both cases the Labour party suffered historic defeats. This is because in both cases the Tory governments were deemed to be successful and the Labour party extreme, divided, and shambolic, with leaders seen as unfit to be Prime Minister.

(7) the need to triangulate and capture the centre ground is a big myth, it does not work

During the new Labour years and the overlapping Clinton years in the United States, there was much talk of triangulation. It was the idea that if a party on the left steal the more successful policies of its conservative counterpart, then they will also steal its voters. The existing core voters may not like the new centrist policy, but they have nowhere else to go to and so can be safely ignored. This is fallacious, because if it were true, New Labour and indeed the Democrats would never have left office.

The Blair government stuck to the old Tory spending plans for two years, despite the unpopularity of that defeated government and deep public concerns over the quality and future viability of the public services. New Labour refused to give the public what most of them had voted for, out for fear of looking 'loony left' or profligate with the public purse.

The Tories embraced a similar notion under David Cameron, with the party initially pledging to match Labour's spending plans until the Global Financial Crisis hit. They also copied the social liberalism of New Labour and interventionist foreign policy.

However, it is worth pointing out that Cameron failed to win a majority against an unpopular Labour Prime Minister in a recession. The keys would have predicted the exact result in advance, without any new keys being minted for triangulation.

Did Clement Attlee win from the centre ground in 1945? Did Margaret Thatcher win from the centre ground in 1979, '83 and '87? Did Boris Johnson win from the centre ground in 2019? The answer to all three questions is no. In fact, clinging nervously to the centre ground will make it harder for governments to effect radical policy agendas. As the keys show, radical, activist governments do better.

It is fair to say that any party offering dangerous extremism such as fascism or communism will suffer at the polls. However, within the very wide spectrum of sensible and respectable ideas there is much more room than the centrists believe.

(8) electoral coalition building is an illusion: Demographics are not destiny

Politicians often talk in terms of building together a coalition of categories. They want to get the working-class vote, the aspirational vote, the female vote, the black vote, the gay vote, the youth vote, the metropolitan vote, the grey vote. Yet, there is very little evidence that pitching policies at a particular demographic actually wins the votes of that demographic, still less hold if for long. In the late 2000's Gordon Brown intoned incessantly about 'hard working families,' yet it did nothing to save his party's grip on power.

Many times left-wing commentators complain bitterly about how the working class are manipulated by the Tories to 'vote against their own interests.' Yet this very sectional way of looking at politics is very flawed, for people vote on the basis of a broad perception of governmental competence, not specifically on how the government is delivering for themselves.

In the 2000s, Labour was genuinely improving the NHS, yet respondents in polls did not seem to acknowledge it for many years, often saying things like 'I must be lucky' to explain the discrepancy between their own positive experience of the National Health Service with their negative perception.

(9) personality matters a little, character matters a lot

So much is written about charisma and often the lack of it in our politicians. All we have to do is find a leader with charisma and then we will win. It is not that simple. The keys show that having a charismatic leader can turn one key for each party. However, having a leader with strategic clarity, ability to delegate, manage a team and having sound judgement is more important still.

Clement Attlee was often the butt of cruel and unfair jokes about his lack of charisma. One joke goes like this: 'An empty taxi drew up outside 10 Downing Street and Clement Attlee got out of it.' [538] This is wrongly attributed to Churchill who strongly denied using it and disapproved of the sentiment. However, it is a good illustration of how much weight we attach to the more superficial aspects of personality. We are impressed with entertaining people who have big personalities. Yet in the case of Attlee, though a mild-mannered man, what he achieved in those six years was quite extraordinary, whether you agree with it or not. No one since transformed the country so much as Prime Minister - though Thatcher came close.

Though Attlee had no charisma, he did have vision and the practicality and experience to see how his ideas could be implemented. He was a man of unimpeachable ethical integrity, and was a good judge of character, had sound judgement and a stable temperament for the job. These things are the most important things we require in a Prime Minister. Yes, the ability to connect with the public, to wow the party conference and deliver political theatre in the commons are important too, but they are often overrated.

The polar opposite of Clement Attlee is Boris Johnson. Here is a man with a big personality, who can capture the public imagination, make people laugh, talk his way out of most problems and employ clowning and his natural scruffiness to humanise himself and disarm opponents. All very useful attributes.

However, he had no real vision, supporting Brexit as a calculated stepping stone to winning the leadership, which was and is decided by the culturally right-wing membership. He had no real ideas for a post-Brexit Britain, beyond vacuous slogans such as 'levelling up.' Nor did he have any interest in making the most of the opportunities afforded the country by leaving the EU. He was indecisive and lacked sound judgement, being easily swayed by others, especially by the Machiavellian Dominic Cummings. He had no real intellectual curiosity about the history of the office he held or of the workings of government. He did not listen to or trust his civil servants, preferring instead the very unelected advisers who mostly let him down. He broke his own rules and then lied about doing so to the Commons. His partying under Lockdown contrasts sharply with Attlee's spartan lifestyle in Chequers during the darkest days of post-war austerity. Boris Johnson lasted barely three years in office, and apart from breaking the Brexit deadlock, achieved really very little.

Therefore, we require both a deeper and a broader assessment of leaders' qualities than just the charisma or otherwise that meets the eye.

<u>(10) it's not just the economy, but the economy matters a great deal</u>

It was Bill Clinton's strategist James Carville who uttered the phrase, 'It's the economy stupid!' back in 1992. [539] It is partly true but it is not the whole truth. Ergo, it is incomplete as a model for political forecasting. If it were true, then John Major's Tories would have lost the 1992 election, but conversely would have won the 1997 election. The Tories also should have won the 1964 election. The fact that they did not, clearly shows that there are other factors than the economy that matter to voters.

The cynical aphorism that, 'people vote with their wallets,' is simplistic and not really true. As Allan Lichtman has pointed out, people are just not that single-minded. The Brexit referendum and Trump victory in 2016 were also indicators of this truth. It is simply not credible to claim that the people who voted for right wing populism did so because they thought it would boost their bank accounts. They voted on the basis of cultural identity and values that they clearly felt were being undermined by the status quo and ignored by mainstream politicians.

People sometimes wrongly claim that the public do not care about foreign policy. This supposes a navel-gazing lack of intellectual curiosity and imagination on the part of the electorate which is simply not the case. Can anyone claim with a straight face that the Falklands victory made no difference to the outcome of the 1983 election? Was Iraq an irrelevance to the 2005 election? Was Vietnam of no consequence in the 1968, '72 or '76 US Presidential elections? Of course not.

However, it would be equally absurd to pretend that the economy is of no importance. It is rare for governments to be re-elected with an economy mired in recession. Apart from Harold Wilson's minority government that took power during an economic crisis, John Major's surprise win is the only one. Economic performance is simply part of a package, though a very important part.

(11) the press and the media are not electoral kingmakers and they never were, therefore spin is a complete waste of time

In 1992, the Sun newspaper hubristically declared, 'It's the Sun wot won it!' This assumes that newspapers control the public mind. Yet, there is no evidence to suggest this is true, at least in terms of voting behaviour. It is more likely a case of reverse causation. Canny newspaper editors like Kelvine Mackenzie know which way the wind is blowing and back the winner. Governments should stop pandering to them in the false belief that they have all the power; they do not. Politicians hold far more of their destiny in their own hands than is held by editors.

The phrase 'spin doctor' first appeared in the US during the 1980s and became popular in the UK during the following decade. Its epitome was New Labour's Alistair Campbell, who was Blair's Director of Communications at Number 10. The main assumption behind the deployment of spin was that the electorate are easily influenced by the media, and that as Jim Morrison once put it, 'Who controls the media controls the mind.'

This is certainly true to an extent, but only if you go towards the absolute extreme of totalitarianism. In a totalitarian state like the Soviet Union or communist China, the government exerts complete control over the media. No opposition parties are permitted to exist and no criticism of the government is allowed either. Politically inconvenient facts are suppressed and replaced with lies or silence, while gaffes by government ministers are simply not reported. Yes, in such a set up, the public mind can be controlled, yet such a situation is rightly regarded as simply intolerable by most people in Britain and anywhere else in the west.

Unless the government can exert absolute control over the media, or something approaching it, spin cannot work. Bad news will be reported come what may. Gaffes by government ministers will be played and replayed ad nauseum on TV and will live in perpetuity online. Comedians and impressionists will mock and impersonate ministers and the opposition parties and pressure groups will have their say. Anti-government newspapers and online commentators will flourish.

Basically, the philosophy of spin is one that only works in a totalitarian state; it will not work in any kind of functioning democracy.

You can only spin when you're winning, and when you're winning you don't need spin.

One example of the pernicious effects of pandering to the media, was the Blair government's fear of holding cabinet meetings for longer than an hour, lest the media saw it as evidence of splits in the cabinet.[540]

Did the New Labour majority decline in 2005 and then disappear in 2010 because the spin doctors were not doing their jobs properly? Was the only factor in Blair's 1997 landslide that he had Alistair Campbell and Major did not? No one can seriously believe that. Certainly, Blair had charisma in 1997 but it had nothing to do with spin. If it had then why was he less charismatic in 2005? If politician's charisma was just down to spin and marketing, then they all could be charismatic, and of course they are not.

It is a lotus eating delusion that wastes a great deal of time, energy, mental health and ultimately conspires to prevent politicians from taking radical choices and doing what they believe to be right, through fear of short-term unpopularity.

The American cartoonist turned political commentator Scott Adams has published books such as *How to Win Bigly*, arguing that winning in life and in elections is all about persuasion and that base reality does not much matter. Now, persuasive skills are of undoubtedly great value in many situations, and certainly were very valuable for Trump in securing the Republican nomination in 2016, but when it comes to winning general elections, they are only a few tools in a much bigger tool bag.

Adams' view is but a variation of the fashionable catchphrase of the last seven years, that we are in a 'post-truth world' in which 'the facts don't matter anymore.' This is simply refuted by the keys. Trump did not win in 2016 because he was the great persuader (although he was very effective) he won almost entirely due to the failings of the Obama administration and Democratic party.

This kind of trope becomes merely a way for people to dismiss their political opponents as charlatans conning the gullible masses. Another phrase used to dismiss the views of people voting the 'wrong way' is 'low information voters.' This all too easily can mean, voters with different opinions to our own and therefore, 'wrong' opinions; sadly, uncorrected by our brilliant advocacy.

These are ways of ignoring the real reasons why people vote the way they do and to avoid confronting the failings of our own side of the political spectrum. Other popular ideas have been to blame election results on Russian interference or on domestic vote rigging. In a polarised climate, all fault is with the other side and never on our own.

(12) pollsters and pundits can be taken with an industrial-sized drum of salt

This should go without saying really, but let's say it again. Polls are at best a roughly accurate snapshot of where public opinion lies at a given point in time. Polls many months or years in advance of an election are of almost no value. This is not only because the situation on the ground could change, but at least equally because people are poor at predicting how they will respond to future hypothetical events. The pollsters ask how people will vote if an election were to be held tomorrow. However, the respondents know that an election will not be held tomorrow. The election does not become real in people's minds until it has been called. Therefore, they can register a kind of protest vote against the government without real consequence.

This is why governments tend to perform badly in by-elections and local elections during mid-term and then seem to recover by the election. It is not that they are genuinely recovering their popularity, more that people are only taking the choice of parties seriously as the election looms near. Of course, the causality can work the other way; governments call elections when the numbers look good and postpone them when they do not.

The other problem will all polls is that there are two main fields of error. The first is sample error; that is selecting too many young people, too many old people, too many white people, working class people, etc. The other is response error. Sometimes people say they will vote for party x and then vote for party y. This can be a conscious lie, when people are embarrassed to admit to the pollster their real preference, for fear of judgement or ridicule, or even their choice being overheard by others or somehow leaked out to the wider world.

The other possibility is a head-heart split, a battle between the conscious and unconscious minds. Sigmund Freud once said that the Ego, or conscious mind is 'not master in its own house.' [541]That is, if the conscious and the unconscious minds come into conflict, then the unconscious will nearly always win. It can be that if people are asked by a pollster whom they want to vote for, then they will answer with their rational mind. However, when they get into the polling booth and the situation becomes real, the powerful unconscious mind takes over and they simply cannot vote for the party they said they would.

Short of pollsters employing lie detector test, there is little that they can do about it.

There is a similar problem with predicting turnout. Polls nearly always overstate the turnout. Even polls that filter out all respondents who are not absolutely certain to vote, still overstate the turnout. This could be because people want to sound civically engaged and public spirited - fearing sounding lazy, selfish and apathetic.

The dismal performance of most polling companies in the 2015 and 2017 general elections, as well as in the 2016 Brexit referendum, underline how polling is never going to be particularly accurate, except in very obvious elections like 1997, when the outcome casts such a big shadow before it, that only the truly delusional can miss it.

(13) the First Past the Post system works well (for the main parties)

Every so often, people start talking about reform of the electoral system. When New Labour came to power, they asked Roy Jenkins to draw a model of Proportional Representation for them. He did, but it was shelved indefinitely. This is hardly surprising when one considers Labour's huge majority of 179 at the time. Now, there is talk of it again. The main argument against FTFP is that it is unfair, that some parties are over-represented, others are discriminated against and marginalised by it, and that there are millions of 'wasted' votes that do not count.

It is certainly the case that minor parties are effectively shut out of power through this system, but as the keys amply demonstrate, the two main parties are equally affected by comparable events, and that they are assessed by the public equally in terms of their performance.

This is vividly highlighted by the fact that the keys still predict the seat tallies even when the share of the popular vote does not match the changes in performance reflected in the keys. For example, in the 1951 election, five-and-half- keys are turned against the Labour government, compared to just four in the previous election in February 1950. This would suggest that the Attlee government had declined in effectiveness over the short, twenty-month term. However, their share of the popular vote actually increased marginally in the second election. Yet, the decline in fortunes was reflected in the parliamentary arithmetic as the keys would have foretold.

In the 1992 election, the keys showed four negatives against the Major administration, compared to just one against the Tories five years earlier. However, the popular vote held up pretty well - in fact marginally increasing under Major. Yet, the majority was cut from 102 to twenty-one as the keys would have predicted.

These two examples suggest that the British public know how to make the FPTP system work, and that neither of the two main parties are disadvantaged by it.

However, the argument that minor parties are excluded is still a valid one. In 2015, UKIP won over twelve percent of the vote but won not a single MP. Nevertheless, they still made their influence count in spectacular fashion.

The counter-argument in favour of the current system, is that it leads to strong government and not an endless succession of unstable and short-lived coalition governments. There is some truth to this, but the weakness of the current government despite its eighty-seat majority, plus the occurrence of two hung parliaments in the last fifteen years might mitigate against it.

Does this system prove the wisdom of crowds? This theory asserts that a collective choice that is made by many individuals, though deciding as individuals and not as a mob, is more accurate than one made by individual experts, or even a small group of experts. This still holds true even when the most ignorant people are allowed to vote, and even if the specific experts are brilliant.

A critic of this comparison might argue that in elections, although people are voting individually, they are in fact not really choosing individually, but are allowing themselves to be swayed by their family, friends, peers and by the mass media and social media. Therefore, the people do not vote as individuals but vote as a collective herd, with groupthink taking over.

This is hard to entirely refute. However, the record of the keys does show people respond to government performance rationally and proportionately and do not hold grudges against parties after they have punished them at the polls.

In practice though, only a minority of people make the keys truly work. In an election, most people vote tribally or through habit. We must all have heard people say things like, 'I vote Conservative because I've always voted Conservative.' Therefore, people like this are not voting pragmatically at all but out of tribal loyalty or long-ingrained habit. When one also takes into account that in recent years almost a third of the electorate elected not to vote at all, it is only a small minority of 'switchers' who help the seats change hands at each election.

It is therefore only this select few, who effectively operate the changing of the keys. With around forty-six million people on the electoral role, around fifteen million do not vote, around eight-and-a-half million people voted for Michael Foot in the low water-mark for Labour in 1983, and about the same for the Tories at their low-water mark, when led by William Hague in 2001, and with two-and-a-half-million for the Liberals in their disastrous election of 2015. We can see therefore that there are maybe thirty-six million people who either vote tribally or do not vote at all. That leaves only about ten million 'switchers' who vote pragmatically, changing sides. Ergo, just over a fifth of the electorate are the true operators of the keys.

THE VALUE OF THE KEYS

The greatest value of the keys is to steer politics away from spin and dishonesty and back to ideas and competent governance. If politicians realised that there is no quick fix to the nation's problems and only effective governance can get them re-elected, then an enormous amount of time and money would be saved and we would be better governed as a result of it.

A second value of it would be to act as a canary in the coal mine for fraud. If one party used fraud to actually overturn the democratic will of the people, then the key system would simply stop working. This would be a red flag for fraud. The fact that Allan Lichtman correctly predicted the last two presidential elections in the United States proves that if fraud did occur it was not decisive. The Russians did not steal the 2016 election for Trump, nor Democrat vote-riggers for Biden in 2020.

The keys would partially put the pollsters out of business - but not completely. There is still considerable value in polling on leader approval ratings and on specific issues. It is just the horse-race polling which is obsolete and discredited.

Perhaps the greatest value of the keys is to prove that democracy works. People are not gullible enough to be fooled by demagogues and charlatans. They vote pragmatically on the basis of the competence of the sitting government.

I hope that the impact of this book will be to focus the minds of everyone - public, politicians, academics and the media on the important stuff and away from here today gone tomorrow trivia. If the lessons of the keys are widely learned, then it will be mean governments become more motivated to raise their game, and see the futility of trying to control and manipulate the news cycle. It would also reduce the amount of time and money blown on campaigning, since this hardly makes a difference. Instead, there would be greater focus placed on good governance.

What is more, the Keys would puncture the dreary consensualism of the 'centre ground.' It is largely a myth. The keys show that radical governments tend to do better, whether they are of the right or of the left.

The media would also have to take a longer, broader view of the news, instead of attaching great importance to fleeting, ephemeral events such as gaffes. It would help reduce the overblown importance attached to the most superficial aspects of personality and leadership. Above all, it would lead to a re-evaluation of the true importance of substance, competence and integrity. These are the qualities that are most seriously missing today.

Notes

How popular are Labour's radical manifesto policies? – LabourList

[1] Conservatives unlikely to win over Reform UK supporters at next election | YouGov
[2] Allan J Lichtman, Predicting the Next President:The Keys to the Whitehouse 2012: p14-16: Rowman & Littlefield publishers inc: 2012
[3] Anthony Seldon, *Johnson At Ten: The Inside Story*, Atlantic Books, 2023, p 443.
[4] Peter Hitchens, The Abolition of Britain, Bloomsbury Continuum, 2008, p29
[5] Ibid, p30
[6] Charm vs Charisma: Fundamental Differences Of These Terms (thecontentauthority.com)
[7] *British Political Opinion: 2937-2000 The Gallup Polls*, Ed Anthony King & Robert J. Wybrow, The Gallup organisation, 2001, p 185-86
[8] *British Political Opinion: 1937-2000 The Gallup Polls*. Ed Anthony King, Gallup, 2001, p 191-95
[9] Presidential Approval Ratings | Gallup Historical Statistics and Trends
[10] Geoffrey Evans, John Curtice, Pippa Norris, *New Labour, New Tactical Voting? The Causes & consequences of Tactical Voting at the 1997 General Election*: Journal of Elections, Public Opinion & Parties. 1998

chapter 2

[11] Ibid
[12] Clement Attlee, *Clem to Tom*, 2nd April 1918, MS EngC-4792, quoted in *Citizen Clem*, p405.
[13] House of commons official report, 24/10/50
[14] 1945 United Kingdom general election - Wikipedia

[15] Andrew Marr, *A history of Modern Britain*, 2001, Pan Macmillan Ltd, p5-6
[16] *Manchester Guardian*, 4th July 1945
[17] *Chronicle of the Twentieth Century*, editor-in-chief Derrick Mercer, Dorling Kindersley Ltd, 2000. p 629

[18] Ibid
[19] ? *Chronicle of the Twentieth Century*, editor-in-chief Derrick Mercer, Dorling Kindersley Ltd, 2000. p 629

[20] W.K. Hancock & M.M. Gowing, *The British War Economy*: HMSO 1949
[21] Alan Bullock, *Ernest Bevin, Foreign Secretary 1945-51*, Heinemann, 1983 p121
[22] Dr Alfred Cox, British Medical Journal, 6/4/46
[23] Nye Bevan, quoted by Brian Abel-Smith, *The Hospitals, 1800-1948*, Heinemann, 1964, p480.
[24] Peter Hennessy, *Never Again*, Penguin, 1992, p144
[25] Peter Hennessy, Never Again: Britain 1945-51, Penguin books, p 94.
[26] Harold Macmillan, The Blast of War 1939-45, Macmillan, 1967, p326.
[27] Harris, *Attlee*, p371
[28] Attlee, *A PM remember*, Williams, p202
[29] *Manchester Guardian*, 16th April 1947
[30] Meeting of cabinet. 25th October 1946, CAB 130/2. Quoted in Peter Hennessey's *Cabinets and the bomb*. Oxford: Clarendon Press, 2007, p44-59
[31] Lord Jay, Change & Fortune, p135. Conversation with Lord Jay 10/08/90
[32] Michael Jago, *Clement Attlee: The Inevitable Prime Minster*, Biteback Publishing Ltd, 2014,p264

[33] Quoted by Michael Jago, Clement Attlee: The Inevitable PM, 2014, Biteback, p308.
[34] 1983, Attlee Foundation lecture.
[35] Trevor Burridge, *Clement Attlee- A Political Biography*, Cape, 1983, p856

[36] Michael Jago, *Clement Attlee: The Inevitable Prime Minster*, Biteback Publishing Ltd, 2014,p314
[37] 'Duty of ruthless sacking.' *The Times*, 15/06/57
[38] *Chronicle of the Twentieth Century*, editor-in-chief Derrick Mercer, Dorling Kindersley Ltd, 2000. p 699.
[39] Max Hastings, *The Korean War*, Pan, 1988, p261.
[40] Hansard, House of Commons, 07/08/47, Vol 441, col 1766
[41] Aneuran Bevan, Tribune Rally, 29/09/54
[42] Isaiah Berlin, *Enlightening: letters 1946-60*, P38.
[43] 1951 United Kingdom general election - Wikipedia
[44] Douglas Jay, *Change & Fortune: A Political Record*. Hutchinson 1980, p131

chapter 3

[45] Churchill speech at Press Association annual lunch, quoted in Gilbert, *Never Despair*, p733
[46] Lord Chandos, *The Memoirs of Lord Chandos*, p343
[47] Charles Webster, Problems of Healthcare, 1988, HM Stationary Office p208
[48] George Tomlinson, Heinemann, 1954, p202
[49] Harold Macmillan, *Tides of Fortune; 1945-55*, Macmillan, 1969,p491
[50] Martin Gilbert, Winston Churchill Vol VII, Road to Victory 1940-45, Heineman, 1986, p254
[51] Charles De Gaulle, War memoires Vol II: Unity; 1942-44, Weidenfield & Nicolson, 1956, p227.
[52] *Chronicle of the Twentieth Century*, editor-in-chief Derrick Mercer, Dorling Kindersley Ltd, 2000. p 768
[53] Lord Moran, Winston Churchill: the struggle for survival 1940-65, Constable, 1966, p366 – diary entry 22nd February 1952.

[54] Montague Browne, *Long Sunset*, p14
[55] Having it So Good: Britain in the Fifties. Peter Hennessy, Penguin, 2006, p179
[56] Ibid

[57] *The Times*, 6/10/52

[58] *Political diaries of Hugh Dalton* 1918-49, 45-60, ed by Ben Pimlott, p598
[59] Butler, Britain and Empire, p186
[60] Anthony Eden, *Full Circle: The Memoirs of Anthony Eden*, Cassell, 1960, p426
[61] Quoted in Butler, *The Art of the Possible*, Penguin 1973, p188
[62] Channel 4 documentary, *End of Empire*, 1984
[63] NA,PRO,PREM 11/1152.
[64] NA,PRO,PREM,11/1177
[65] Kyle, Suez, P411-413
[66] AnthonyNutting, *No end of a lesson: The Story of Suez*, 1967, p95.
[67] Russell Braddon, *Suez: Splitting of a nation*, Collins, 1973, p11.
[68] Kyle, *Suez*, p456-57
[69] NA,PRO,AIR 8/1940. 'Operation Musketeer General Papers 1956-58.' DH Message 41329, 6th November 1956.
[70] Iverach MacDonald, *A man of the times,* Hamish Hamilton, 1976, p153
[71] Hennessy, *The Prime Minister*, p209.
[72] House of Commons official report, 20.11.56, Col 1493
[73] Edward Heath, *The Course of My Life*, p176-77
[74] Peter Hennessey, *Muddling through: Politics & power & the quality of government in Postwar Britain.* Gollancz, 1996, p201
[75] Anthony Sampson, *Macmillan: A Study in Ambiguity*, Allen Lane, 1967.p124.
[76] Harold Macmillan - Wikipedia
[77] Howard, 1987, p240-41
[78] Goodlad & Pearce, British Prime Ministers from Balfour to Brown, Routledge, 2013, p 170
[79] Windscale fire - Wikipedia
[80] A.J.P. Taylor, *A Personal History*, p227.
[81] Michael Foot, *Aneurin Bevan: A Biography Vol II 194-60*, Davis Poynter, 1973, p574.

[82] Ashton, *Harold Macmillan and the 'Golden Days' of Anglo-American relations revisited*, 2005, p 699.
[83] D.R. Thorpe, Eden: *The Life and Times of Anthony Eden, ist Earl of Avon, 1897-1977*, Chato, 2003, p 368

[84] Charlton, Michael (1983). *The Price of Victory*. London: BBC. p. 274.
[85] NA,PRO,CAB 134/1226 EP (55) 11th Meeting
[86] Horne, *Macmillan, 1957-1986*, p15
[87] Harold Macmillan, Bedford Speech, 1957
[88] Ibid
[89] D.R. Thorpe, Supermac- The life of Harold Macmillan, Pimlico, 2010, p441
[90] *Chronicle of the Twentieth Century*, editor-in-chief Derrick Mercer, Dorling Kindersley Ltd, 2000. p921
[91] Angela Partington, The Oxford Dictionary of Qoutations (4th edition) Oxford University Press 1996.
[92] Harold Macmillan speech, Parliament of South Africa, 03/02/60.
[93] Dr David Butler file of interviews for his book on the 1964 election, Nuffield College, Oxford.
[94] Harold Macmillan to John F Kennedy, 25th October 1962, PREM 11/3690, telegram 24040 loc.cit.
[95] Telephone conversation, 26th October 1962, quoted by D.R. Thorpe, *Supermac- The life of Harold Macmillan*, Pimlico, 2010, p532

[96] Harold Macmillan obituary | Politics | The Guardian
[97] Ben Pimlott & Peter Hennessey, *Wilson*, Collins, 2016, p 295-96
[98] D.R. Thorpe, Supermac- The life of Harold Macmillan, Pimlico, 2010, p547
[99] Philip Norman, *Shout!,* Elm Tree Books/Hamish Hamilton Ltd, London , 1981, p178
[100] Denning report paragraphs 283 & 286.
[101] Goodlad & Pearce, British Prime Ministers from Balfour to Brown, Routledge, 2013, p180
[102] Philip Norman, *Shout!,* Elm Tree Books/Hamish Hamilton Ltd, London , 1981, p179
[103] D.R. Thorpe, Supermac- The life of Harold Macmillan, Pimlico, 2010, p558

[104] Peter Hennessy, The Prime Minister: The Office and its Holders Since 1945, Penguin Books, 2001, p 275-76.
[105] Harold Wilson, Scarborough conference 1963.

[106] Nick Thomas-Symonds, *Harold Wilson the Winner*, Weidenfeld & Nicholson, 2022
[107] Labour Party conference 1963
[108] Harold Wilson: The Unprincipled Prime Mnister?: A reappraisal of Harold Wilson: Andrew S. Crines & Kevin Hickson, Biteback Publishing, 2016, Chapter 3
[109] Anthony Seldon, *The Impossible Office?,* Cambridge University Press, 2021, p 159
[110] *Chronicle of the Twentieth Century*, editor-in-chief Derrick Mercer, Dorling Kindersley Ltd, 2000. p921

[111] Lord Home, *The Way the Wind Blows*: an autobiography, Collins, 1976.
[112] *Pierce, Andrew (14 April 2008). "How Alec Douglas-Home foiled student kidnappers with beer". The Daily Telegraph.*
[113] Opinion polling for the 1964 United Kingdom general election - Wikipedia
[114] Harold Wilson - Whichever party is in office, the Treasury... (brainyquote.com)
[115] Harold Wilson's 1963, conference speech Harold Wilson talking about a new Britain devoid of restrictive practices - YouTube
[116] Hansard, House of Commons, 03/11/64, Vol 701, col 71.
[117] 1964 United Kingdom general election - Wikipedia

chapter 4

[118] *Chronicle of the Twentieth Century*, editor-in-chief Derrick Mercer, Dorling Kindersley Ltd, 2000. p932
[119] John Lennon returns his MBE in protest at British foreign affairs – archive, 1969 | John Lennon | The Guardian
[120] The Beatles, 'Taxman' from the *Revolver* LP, 1966.
[121] Royal Society report, 'Emigration of scientistsfrom the United Kingdom.' 1963
[122] Butler & King, *General Election of 1966*, p111-12
[123] Anthony King & Robert J Wybrow, British Political Opinion 1937-2000, The Gallup Polls, 2001, p 188.
[124] Nick Thomas-Symonds, Harold Wilson The Winner, 2022, p231
[125] BBC documentary, Harold Wilson: British Prime Minister 1964-70 & 1974-76, BBC 2, 1995

[126] Harold Wilson - I'm an optimist, but an optimist who... (brainyquote.com)
[127] *Chronicle of the Twentieth Century*, editor-in-chief Derrick Mercer, Dorling Kindersley Ltd, 2000. p945

[128] Nick Thomas-Symonds, Harold Wilson The Winner, Weidenfeld & Nicolson, 2023, p244
[129] Harold Wilson: The Unprincipled Prime Mnister?: A reappraisal of Harold Wilson: Andrew S. Andrew Crines & Kevin Hickson, Biteback Publishing, 2016, Chapter 7

[130] *Chronicle of the Twentieth Century*, editor-in-chief Derrick Mercer, Dorling Kindersley Ltd, 2000. p979

[131] Ibid
[132] From the archive, 5 May 1969: Harold Wilson shrugs off plotters with a joke | Labour | The Guardian
[133] George Brown, Hansard, 19th December 1966.
[134] C Benn & C Chitty, *30 years on*, Penguin, 1997, p86
[135] Harold Wilson, The New Britain, p 10.
[136] Anthony Crossland, *Crossland,* p148
[137] Henry Pelling & Alistair J. Reid, *A Short History of the Labour Party,* Palgrave Macmillan, 2005
[138] Harold Wilson - Wikipedia
[139] Andrew Crines & Kevin Hickson, Biteback Publishing, 2016, Chapter 9
[140] Harold Wilson, Broadcast speech, 19th November 1967. BBC ON THIS DAY | 19 | 1967: Wilson defends 'pound in your pocket'
[141] *Chronicle of the Twentieth Century*, editor-in-chief Derrick Mercer, Dorling Kindersley Ltd, 2000. p975

[142] Interview with Lord Glenamar, Ben Pimlott, *Harold Wilson*, William Collins, 1992, p 500
[143] Cecil King's Diary, 01.11.67, p153
[144] Roy Jenkins, *A Life at the Centre*, Macmillasn, 1991, p203
[145] *Chronicle of the Twentieth Century*, editor-in-chief Derrick Mercer, Dorling Kindersley Ltd, 2000, p1017

[146] Anthony King & Robert jJ Wybrow, *British Political Opinion 1937-2000 The Gallup Polls,* Politico Publishing, 2001, p207
[147] Nora Beloff, *The Observer*, 07/06/70
[148] Marcia Falkender, *Downing Street in Perspective,* London, George Weidenfeld & Nicholson Ltd, 1983, p12
[149] ? Harold Wilson: The Unprincipled Prime Mnister?: A reappraisal of Harold Wilson: Andrew S. Crines & Kevin Hickson, Biteback Publishing, 2016, Chapter 1

[150] Lynton Crosby's Ten Rules for a Successful Campaign | HuffPost UK Politics (huffingtonpost.co.uk)
[151] (2) 1966 General Election - Part 1 of 2 - YouTube
[152] House of Commons debates, 5th series Vol 805, col 1211, 4th November 1970.
[153] Minutes of the 6th session, 1st February 1970, shadow cabinet weekend, Selsdon Park Hotel, CPA Selsdon Park papers.
[154] Arthur Scargill, *New Left Review*, quoted in *When the lights went out*, Andy Beckett, 2009, Faber & Faber, p73.
[155] D. Hurd, *An end to promises*, London 1979, p103.
[156] J. Jones, *Union Man*, London, 1986, p259.
[157] M. Thatcher, *The Path to Power*, 1995, p224.
[158] *Public Expenditure & Social Policy*, London, 1982, p30. Also *Economic Trends*, London 1990, p95.
[159] HC Debs, 5th series, Vol 837, cd,1096, 22nd May 1973.
[160] Stuart Ball, *The Heath Government 1970-74*, Longman, London & New York, 1996, p343
[161] Stuart Ball, *The Heath Government 1970-74*, Longman, London & New York, 1996, p325
[162] *When the lights went out*, Andy Beckett, 2009, Faber & Faber, p131

[163] *Chronicle of the Twentieth Century*, editor-in-chief Derrick Mercer, Dorling Kindersley Ltd, 2000, p1072.
[164] Ibid
[165] Edward Heath, National TV broadcast, 7th February 1974

[166] *Chronicle of the Twentieth Century*, editor-in-chief Derrick Mercer, Dorling Kindersley Ltd, 2000, p1072
[167] John Campbell, *Edward Heath: A Biography*, 1993, p589
[168] *Peter Hennessey: The Office and its Holders since 1945*, Penguin Books, 2001, p332
[169] February 1974 United Kingdom general election - Wikipedia
[170] 1973 Conservative party conference.
[171] *The Heath Government 1970-74*, Stuart Ball & Anthony Seldon. Longman, London & New York, 1996, p27,

[172] Dominic Sandbrook, State of Emergency: The Way We Were: Britain 1970-74, Allen Lane, 2010, p 611-645
[173] *Tony Benn diaries*, 10.02.74
[174] *Daily Mail*, 28th February 1974
[175] *When the lights went out*, Andy Beckett, 2009, Faber & Faber, p151.

[176] The Strategic/tactical situation in 1973, memo by SirFraser et al. 14/02.73SC/73/17.
[177] *Chronicle of the Twentieth Century*, editor-in-chief Derrick Mercer, Dorling Kindersley Ltd, 2000, p1076

[178] William Waldegrave, letter to Dennis Kavanagh, 9th March 1995.
[179] Ibid
[180] Harold Wilson, quoted by Sir John Hunt in the BBC 2 documentary, Harold Wilson: Prime Minister 1964-70 & 1974-76. Broadcast 1995.
[181] Harold Wilson, broadcast speech, 25th May 1974.
[182] Tony Benn, *Against the Tide,* p343
[183] *The Observer*, 29.09.74
[184] *The Observer*, 6.10.74
[185] 1974 uk general election 1974 October part 1 - YouTube
[186] Antonio Gramsci, Passato e Presente, Quadami dei Carcere, Vol 1, c 1930
[187] *When the lights went out*, Andy Beckett, 2009, Faber & Faber, p175-76

[188] *When the lights went out*, Andy Beckett, 2009, Faber & Faber, p117-121.
[189] Bernard Donoughue, Prime Minister: The Conduct of Policy Under Harold Wilson and James Callaghan. London: Jonathan Cape, 1987, p14.
[190] *Financial Times*, 17.03.76
[191] The Times, 20.03.76
[192] *Daily Telegraph*, 25th January 1974
[193] James Callaghan, Speech at Labour Party Conference, 28/09/76.
[194]
[195] Secret History: Winter of Discontent, 1998, Channel 4. Secret History: Winter of Discontent - YouTube
[196] Tony Benn, Conflicts of Interests: Diaries 1977-80, p448
[197] Graham Stewart, Bang! A History of Britain in the 1980s, Atlantic Books, 2013, p22
[198] Peter Shore quoted by Philip Whitehead, *The Writing on the Wall,* Michael Joseph, 1985, p278
[199] Michael Cockerell's documentary on Callaghan, 2004. Michael Cockerell on James Callaghan - YouTube
[200] Quoted in *The General Election of 1979,* Butler & Kavanagh, 1979
[201] *When the lights went out*, Andy Beckett, 2009, Faber & Faber, p473.
[202] What Margaret Thatcher's Voice Really Sounded Like, Since All 'Crown' Fans Want to Know (yahoo.com)

chapter 5

[203] Butler & Kavanagh, The British Gernal Election of 1979, p265.
[204] Bernard Donoughue, Prime Minister: The Conduct of Policy under Harold Wilson and Jim Callaghan, 1987, p191.
[205] The Times, December 31st 1976.
[206] Margaret Thatcher, The Downing Street Years, HarperCollins, 1993, p9
[207] Margaret Thatcher, Downing Street statement, May 4th 1979.
[208] Margaret Thatcher, The Downing Street Years, HarperCollins, 1993, p29-30
[209] Margaret Thatcher, The Downing Street Years, HarperCollins, 1993, p18

[210] Margaret Thatcher, The Downing Street Years, HarperCollins, 1993, p11
[211] Thornton, Richard C, *The Reagan Revolution: Re-building the Western Alliance*, Trafford, 2004
[212] CBI annual dinner, London Hilton, 19th April 1983
[213] Anthony Seldon & Daniel Collings, *Britain Under Thatcher*., Longman, 2000.
[214] Margaret Thatcher, The Downing Street Years, HarperCollins, 1993, p104
[215] Norman Tebbit. Speech at Conservative Party Conference, September 1981.
[216] Peter Hennessey, The Prime Minister: The Office and its Holders since 1945, Penguin Books, 2001, p422. (A conver4sation between Hennessey and Dr John Ashworth, on 06/05/98
[217] The Thatcher Years; Part 2. The Thatcher Years 2 of 4 (youtube.com)
[218] Archive: Thatcher 'rejoices' at Falkland victory - YouTube
[219] Speech at Cheltenham, 3rd July 1982
[220] Margaret Thatcher, The Downing Street Years, HarperCollins, 1993, p184
[221] David Steel speech at Liberal Assembly 1981
[222] Graham Stewart, Bang! A History of Britain in the 1980s, Atlantic Books, 2013, p173

[223] Gerald Kaufman, quoted in Bang! A History of Britain in the 1980s, by Graham Stewart, Atlantic Books, 2013, p171
[224] British *Political Opinion: 1937-2000 The Gallup Polls*. Ed Anthony King, The Gallup Organisation, 2001, p214
[225] Roy Hattersley, *Fifty Years on*, Little, Brown and Co, 1997
[226] Neil Kinnock Speech, Bridgend, June 1983.
[227] Margaret Thatcher, 1983, *Chronicle of the Twentieth Century*, editor-in-chief Derrick Mercer, Dorling Kindersley Ltd, 2000, p1228

[228] Graham Stewart, Bang! A History of Britain in the 1980s, Atlantic Books, 2013, p173

[229] *Chronicle of the Twentieth Century*, editor-in-chief Derrick Mercer, Dorling Kindersley Ltd, 2000, p1225

[230] Margaret Thatcher, The Downing Street Years, HarperCollins, 1993, p339

[231] Margaret Thatcher, The Downing Street Years, HarperCollins, 1993, p374.

[232] Norman Tebbit, *Upwardly Mobile*, 1989, p302

[233] Margaret Thatcher, The Downing Street Years, HarperCollins, 1993, p377-78

[234] Tony Ben, quoted in Alan Sked & Chris Cook, *Post-war Britain: A Political History*, 1993 p452

[235] Nigel Lawson, *The View from No, 11*, p224

[236] Bob Geldof asserts why he sees Mrs Thatcher as a punk - YouTube

[237] Single European Act, HMSO (cmd 372) 1985.

[238] Graham Stewart, Bang! A History of Britain in the 1980s, Atlantic Books, 2013, p216

[239] Margaret Thatcher, The Downing Street Years, HarperCollins, 1993, p461

[240] Taylor, Peter (2001). Brits: *The War Against the IRA*. Bloomsbury Publishing. p. 265

[241] Anglo-Irish Agreement - Wikipedia

[242] Labour Party conference, 1985

[243] Graham Stewart, Bang! A History of Britain in the 1980s, Atlantic Books, 2013, p325

[244] Interview with *Woman's Own*, September 1987

[245] Margaret Thatcher, The Downing Street Years, HarperCollins, 1993, p626

[246] Everything You Know About The Future is Wrong | Aaron Bastani meets John Gray - YouTube

[247] Whitehead, *The Writing on the wall,* p333

[248] Butler, Adonis & Travers, *Failure in British Government*, p259

[249] Cole, J, *As it seemed to me*, Phoenix, 1996

[250] *Chronicle of the Twentieth Century*, editor-in-chief Derrick Mercer, Dorling Kindersley Ltd, 2000, p1324

[251] Margaret Thatcher's speech to the college of Europe at Bruges, 20/09/88
[252] From the archives: Ridley was right | The Spectator
[253] Margaret Thatcher, The Downing Street Years, HarperCollins, 1993, p721
[254] Margaret Thatcher, The Downing Street Years, HarperCollins, 1993, p834
[255] *Geoffrey Howe, Personal Statement,* Parliamentary Debates (Hansard). *House of Commons. 13 November 1990. col. 461. Retrieved 26 April 2021.*
[256] Ibid
[257] Margaret Thatcher, The Downing Street Years, HarperCollins, 1993, p851
[258] Anthony Seldon & Daniel Collings, *Britain Under Thatcher*, Longman, 2000, p92
[259] Desert Island Discs, BBC Radio 4, January 1992. John Major on Desert Island Discs - 1992 | BBC Radio 4 | wisGEMS - YouTube
[260] John Major, Statement in Downing Street, 28/11/90
[261] Chris Pattern, quoted by Bagehot in 'Selling a new spirit', *The Economist*, December 1990
[262] Anthony Seldon, *Major: A political life*, Weidenfeld & Nicolson, 1997, p174
[263] Norman Lamont, *In Office*, Little, Brown & Company, 1999, p140-41
[264] HC Debs, 6th series, Vol 108, cols 164-66
[265] John Major, Bonn speech as reported in *The Guardian*, 12th March 1991.
[266] *consequences of Tactical Voting at the 1997 General Election*: Journal of Elections, Public Opinion & Parties. 1998
[267] *The Observer,* 15th March 1992.
[268] *Daily Telegraph*, 20th March 1992.
[269] UK General Election 1992 - Neil "We're Alright" Kinnock at the 1992 Sheffield Rally - YouTube
[270] *Daily Telegraph*, 11th September 1992.
[271] The Major Years Part 1 The Major Years | The Complete Series | BBC Documentary 1999 (youtube.com)
[272] Anthony Seldon, *Major: A political life*, Weidenfeld & Nicolson, 1997, p322.

[273] Norman Lamont, 'Out of the Ashes', *The Chancellor's Tales: Managing the British Economy*, ed Howard Davies, London, Polity, 2006, p147
[274] Peter Hennessey, *The Prime Minister: The Office and its Holders since 1945*, Penguin Books, 2001, p466.
[275] *The Times*, 23rd September 1992.
[276] Gyles Brandreth, *Breaking the Code, Westminster Diaries, 1992-97*, Weidenfield & Nicholson, 1999.
[277] Anthony Seldon, *Major: A political life*, Weidenfeld & Nicolson, 1997, p382.
[278] *Daily Telegraph*, 10th October 1994.
[279] Paul Johnson, *The Spectator*, 8th January 1994.
[280] Norman Lamont, *In Office*, p269
[281] Norman Lamont, Press conference, May 1993
[282] Norman Lamont, resignation speech, House of Commons, 9th June 1993. (1) Norman Lamont Resignation Speech - YouTube

[283] Tony Blair, Hansard, 24th April 1995
[284] *The Times*, 26th July 1993
[285] *The Major Years,* part 3. 1 The Major Years | The Complete Series | BBC Documentary 1999 (youtube.com)

[286] *The Independent*, 21st September 1993.
[287] Geoffrey Evans, John Curtice, Pippa Norris, *New Labour, New Tactical Voting? The Causes & consequences of Tactical Voting at the 1997 General Election*: Journal of Elections, Public Opinion & Parties. 1998
[288] John Curtice, Michael Stead, *The results analysed.* In David Butler, Dennis Kavanagh (eds) *The British General Election of 1997*, 1997, Macmillan.
[289] Ian McAlister & Donley T Studler, Conservative Euroscepticism and the Referendum Party in the 1997 British General Election. Party Politics 6 (3) 359-71
[290] *The Times*, 22nd June 1995.
[291] HC Debs, 6th series, Vol 262, col 1078.
[292] *The Guardian*, 17th April 1997.
[293] *Sunday Times*, 20th April 1997.
[294] Tony Blair, Speech at Stevenage, April 22 1997.

[295] *The Major Years,* part 1. 1 The Major Years | The Complete Series | BBC Documentary 1999 (youtube.com)

[296] John Major. Final Downing street statement, May 2, 1997.

chapter 6

[297] Speech at European Socialists' Congress in Mälmo, Sweden, June 1997
[298] *The Guardian*, December 1995
[299] Speech outside Downing Street, 2nd May 1997.
[300] Ed Balls, speech at King's College London, 20/11/2020
[301] Andrew Rawnsley, Servants of the People, Penguin Books, 2001, p38
[302] Peter Riddell, 'cracks in the cabinet cement', *The Times*, 10th November 1997.
[303] Seminar organised by Peter Hennessy. Quoted by Andrew Rawnsley, Servants of the people, Penguin Books, 2001, p27
[304] Rawnsley, Servants of the People, Penguin Books, 2001, p353
[305] UK Public Opinion toward Immigration: Overall Attitudes and Level of Concern - Migration Observatory - The Migration Observatory (ox.ac.uk)
[306] Andrew Rawnsley, Servants of the People, Penguin Books, 2001, p312
[307] Tony Blair, The Third Way: New politics for the new century, Fabian Pamphlet, 1998
[308] Roy Hattersley, St Catherine's lecture, Cumberland Lodge, 24th January 1998.
[309] David Marquand, The Progressive Dilemma
[310] Blair speech at Sedgefield, August 31st 1997.
[311] Andrew Rawnsley, Servants of the People, Penguin Books, 2001, p71
[312] Tony Blair's remarks at Hillsborough castle, 7th April 1998
[313] Tony Blair's remarks at castle Buildings, 10th April 1998
[314] Andrew Rawnsley, Servants of the People, Penguin Books, 2001, p99

[315] Tony Blair, interviewed on the BBC's *On the Record*, 16th November 1997
[316] Margaret Cook, *A Slight & Delicate Creature*.
[317] NOP poll for *Powerhouse*, Channel 4, January 2001.
[318] Andrew Rawnsley, *The End of The Party*, Penguin Books, 2010, p6
[319] Andrew Rawnsley, Servants of the People, Penguin Books, 2001, p199
[320] Andrew Rawnsley, *The Observer*, 10th June 2001.
[321] Tony Blair, Downing street statement, 11th September 2001
[322] Tony Blair, speech at the Labour Brighton Conference, October 2001.
[323] Statements of the Director General of the IAEA, 6th March 2003
[324] Jack Straw, quoted in Andrew Rawnsley, *The End of The Party*, Penguin Books, 2010, p180
[325] Jack Straw, quoted in Andrew Rawnsley, *The End of The Party*, Penguin Books, 2010, p247
[326] *Daily Mail* headline, 19th July 2003.
[327] Yougov poll for ITV, 1st February 2004
[328] Yougov poll for *The Telegraph*, March 2005.
[329] Yougov polling. Memories of Iraq: did we ever support the war? | YouGov
[330] Andrew Rawnsley, *The End of The Party*, Penguin Books, 2010, p195
[331] Tony Blair, Hansard, 20th April 2004.
[332] Economic Optimism Index (EOI): State of the Economy 1997 - present | Ipsos
[333] Gordon Brown, Hansard, 16th March 2005.
[334] Widdecombe goes for the jugular | The Independent | The Independent
[335] Robert Peston, *Brown's Britain*, 2006, p347.
[336] Andrew Turnbull, interviewed byAndrew Rawnsley, End of the Party, Penguin, 2010, p277.

[337] Tony Blair on *Ask the leader*, ITV, 2nd May 2005
[338] BBCs John Simpson Iraq War Worst Foreign Policy decision since the 2nd World War - YouTube
[339] Andrew Rawnsley, End of the Party, Penguin, 2010, p275

[340] David Cameron, Hansard, December 2005
[341] On your bike: Cameron the green is forced to backtrack | Travel and transport | The Guardian
[342] Gordon Brown, Downing Street speech, 27th June 2007.
[343] Political Monitor: Satisfaction Ratings 1997-Present | Ipsos
[344] Vince Cable, Hansard, 28th November 2007.
[345] Tessa Jowell, 'Blair Government', Queen Mary University, March 2011.
[346] Quoted in Andrew Rawnsley, End of the Party, Penguin, 2010, p521.
[347] Andrew Rawnsley, End of the Party, Penguin, 2010, p520
[348] Andrew Rawnsley, End of the Party, Penguin, 2010, p552
[349] Polly Toynbee, 'This buffeted Prime Minister must stop scrambling at every puff of wind.',*The Guardian,* 11th Appril 2008.
[350] 'Britain was hours away from breakdown of law and order during GFC: Ex-Chancellor' Alistair Darling interviewed by Will Martin for ***BusinessInsider.com.au***
[351] Paul Krugman, 'Gordon does Good', *The New York Times*, 12th October 2008
[352] Tom Dewton Dunn, 'PM couldn't even get our name right.' *The Sun,* 9th November 2009.
[353] The 2008 recession 10 years on - Office for National Statistics (ons.gov.uk)
[354] Andrew Sparrow, 'Sullied' members suspended two peers. *The Guardian,* 21st May 2009.
[355] BBC NEWS | Politics | No 10 official quits over e-mails
[356] Civil servant quoted by Andrew Rawnsley, End of the Party, Penguin, 2010, p471.
[357] Populus Poll for *The Times*, May 2009.
[358] (1) Gordon Brown 'Smile' MP's Expenses video with comments allowed! - YouTube
[359] Hazel Blears, 'Youtube if you want to', Observer, 3rd May 2019
[360] Opinion polling for the 2010 United Kingdom general election - Wikipedia
[361] Gordon Brown calls Labour supporter a "bigoted woman" - YouTube

[362] Polly Vizard & Polina Obolenskaya, *Labour's Record on Health, 1997-2010, Social Policy in a Cold Climate,* Working Paper 2, London, CASE, London School of Economics, 2013.
[363] David Cameron, Conservative Party Conference, 2006
[364] ?Cameron at 10: The Verdict, Anthony Seldon & Peter Snowdon,William Collins, London, 2015, p365
[365] Spending Review (CM7942) Table I
[366] Public Sector Employment, Quarter 2. September 2014.
[367] David Cameron, The Sun, 01/02/12.
[368] ? Polly Vizard & Polina Obolenskaya, *The coalition's record on Health*, London,CASE, London School of Economics, 2015,
[369] David Nicholson, 'The year: NHS chief executive's annual report 2008-09, London, NHS 2, p47.
[370] Conservative Party Conference, 02/10/2013
[371] Daily Mail, 23/03/2013
[372] (1) Nick Clegg - Say goodbye to broken promises - 2010 Election Broadcast - YouTube
[373] Daily Telegraph,06/10/12
[374] Interview with Alan Duncan, in Cameron at 10: The Verdict, Anthony Seldon & Peter Snowdon,William Collins, London, 2015, p277
[375] Edward Leigh, *New York Times*, 06/02/13
[376] Cameron at 10: The Verdict, Anthony Seldon & Peter Snowdon,William Collins, London, 2015
[377] Mathew D'ancona, *In it Together: The Inside Story of the Coalition Government*, 2013, p186
[378] Anthony Seldon & Peter Snowdon, *Cameron at 10: The Verdict*, William Collins, London, 2015, p258.
[379] David Cameron, Bloomberg Speech, 23/01/2013
[380] Interview in Cameron at 10: The Vedict, Anthony Seldon and Peter Snowdon, William Collins, London, 2015, p382
[381] *Sunday Telegraph*, 08/06/14
[382] Cameron speech, Scottish widows, 10/09/14sn
[383] I want to push this all the way, declares Clegg | The Independent | The Independent
[384] Richard Keen, Membership of UK political parties, Parliamentary standard no, SN/SG/5125, 2014, p6
[385] Nick Clegg statement, BBC News, 06/08/12

[386] Cabinet Secretary's review of papers relating to the release of Abdelbaset Al-Megrahi, Cabinet Office, 07/02/11
[387] Reuters/Ipsos International poll on Libya | Ipsos
[388] Yougov poll, 28/08/13
[389] *The Spectator,* 29/08/13
[390] *The Times*, 17/-4/13
[391] Press release, The Trussel trust, 16/10/13
1.[392] "Cut to top rate of tax helped raise an extra £8bn, Osborne claims". Archived from the original on 2 March 2016.

[393] Hansard, 19/03/14, column 785.
[394] Cameron at 10: The Vedict, Anthony Seldon and Peter Snowdon, William Collins, London, 2015, p xxxiv

[395] Guardian website, 21/01/11
[396] David Milliband, 'What responsible capitalism is all about', *The Guardian*, 22/05/12
[397] https://www.youtube.com/watch?v=Se_qAXc4VgM
[398] 'Coherent and together, but not yet looking the part.' The Guardian, 23/09/14
[399] *The Guardian*, 07/10/12
[400] *Daily Telegraph*, 16/05/15
[401] Did David Cameron Get His Football Team Wrong? - YouTube
[402] David Cameron 'pumped up' by small business revolution - BBC News - YouTube
[403] "Hell yes, I'm tough enough." Ed Miliband to Jeremy Paxman | Battle For Number 10 - YouTube
[404] Cameron at 10: The Vedict, Anthony Seldon and Peter Snowdon, William Collins, London, 2015, p 518
[405] TOP 25 QUOTES BY NIGEL FARAGE (of 71) | A-Z Quotes (azquotes.com)
[406] Barack Obama, Press Conference, 20/06/16
[407] Sky News, 03/06/16 Michael Gove vs The Experts™ - YouTube
[408] A correspondence with Will Walden, 29th November 2022, quoted in Anthony Seldon & Raymond Newell, *Johnson At 10: The Inside Story*, Atlantic books ltd, London 2023

[409] Cameron at 10: The Vedict, Anthony Seldon and Peter Snowdon, William Collins, London, 2015, p 554

[410] The Standard, 25/06/16
[411] David Cameron tells Jeremy Corbyn to GO #PMQs - YouTube
[412] Being a mother gives me edge on May — Leadsom (thetimes.co.uk)
[413] *The Spectator's* Politician of the year award, , 2nd November 2016
[414] May at 10: The Verdict. Anthony Seldon, Biteback publishing ltd, 2020, p77. Interview with George Osborne.
[415] *Daily Mirror*, 11/07/16
[416] ? May at 10: The Verdict. Anthony Seldon, Biteback publishing ltd, 2020, p80 Interview with Gavin Williamson.
[417] Ibid
[418] 'Britain's Brexit Crisis', BBC *Panorama*, 18/07/19
[419] ?Michael Gove 09/04/16, quoted in May at 10: The Verdict. Anthony Seldon, Biteback publishing ltd, 2020, p119
[420] Ibid
[421] in May at 10: The Verdict. Anthony Seldon, Biteback publishing ltd, 2020, p121

[422] Conservative Party Conference, 04/10/16
[423] *Daily Mail*, 03/11/16
[424] Tim Shipman, *Fallout*, p149
[425] Andrew Marr interview BBC , 30/06/16 Theresa May rules out snap general election in interview #Election2017 #UTurn - YouTube
[426] Dennis Kavanagh and Philip COwley, *The British General Election of 2017*, p170
[427] Theresa May said 'nothing has changed' after her dementia tax U-turn. Oh yes it has | The Independent | The Independent
[428] What is the naughtiest thing Theresa May has ever done? - Daily Mail - YouTube
[429] Fiona Hill, interviewed in *May at 10: The Verdict*. Anthony Seldon, Biteback publishing ltd, 2020
[430] Lynton Crosby, interviewed in *May at 10: The Verdict*. Anthony Seldon, Biteback publishing ltd, 2020

[431] Turning Points - Unscripted Reflections by Steve Richards - 6 - 2017 Election - YouTube
[432] Political Monitor: Satisfaction Ratings 1997-Present | Ipsos
[433] *May at 10: The Verdict*. Anthony Seldon, Biteback publishing ltd, 2020, p665.
[434] Theresa May - The Government cannot just be consumed by... (brainyquote.com)
[435] *The Andrew Marr Show*, BBC1, 11/06/16
[436] *The Financial Times*, 20/06/17
[437] Prankster interrupts Theresa May's conference speech to hand her fake P45 - YouTube
[438] *May at 10: The Verdict*. Anthony Seldon, Biteback publishing ltd, 2020, p435.
[439] Politico, 03/07/18
[440] *The Sun*, 16/07/18
[441] *Sky News*, 17/08/18
[442] *Mail on Sunday*, 09/09/18
[443] All the times EU has said 'no' to Theresa May's Chequers Brexit trade plan | The Independent | The Independent
[444] *The Times*, 23/10/18
[445] Windrush: only one in four applicants have received compensation | Windrush scandal | The Guardian
[446] *The Guardian*, 23/03/18
[447] *Evening Standard*, 15/11/18
[448] *The Spectator*, 14/12/18
[449] Yougov/Best 4 Brexit, 10-11/01/19
[450] *The Guardian*, 16/01/19
[451] BBCNews, 14/03/19
[452] Interview with Ian Duncan Smith, *May at 10: The Verdict*. Anthony Seldon, Biteback publishing ltd, 2020, p589
[453] *May at 10: The Verdict*. Anthony Seldon, Biteback publishing ltd, 2020, p619
[454] *May at 10: The Verdict*. Anthony Seldon, Biteback publishing ltd, 2020, p629
[455] *May at 10: The Verdict*. Anthony Seldon, Biteback publishing ltd, 2020, p633

[456] *May at 10: The Verdict.* Anthony Seldon, Biteback publishing ltd, 2020, p628
[457] *May at 10: The Verdict.* Anthony Seldon, Biteback publishing ltd, 2020, p671
[458] ,Interviewed for *Johnson At 10: The Inside Story*, Atlantic books ltd, London 2023, p25.

[459] Ibid
[460] Johnson *At 10: The Inside Story*, Atlantic books ltd, London 2023, p27.
[461] Johnson *At 10: The Inside Story*, Atlantic books ltd, London 2023, p73-73.
[462] Johnson *At 10: The Inside Story*, Atlantic books ltd, London 2023, p 84
[463] Young, A. (13 September 2019). "Prorogation, Politics and the Principle of Legality". *U.K. Constitutional Law Blog.*
[464] Political Monitor: Satisfaction Ratings 1997-Present | Ipsos
[465] Geoffrey Cox: "this Parliament is a disgrace" AG launches searing attack - YouTube
[466] Johnson *At 10: The Inside Story*, Atlantic books ltd, London 2023, p 29
[467] Johnson *At 10: The Inside Story*, Atlantic books ltd, London 2023, p 572
[468] Jeremy Corbyn: I was present at wreath-laying but don't think I was involved | Labour | The Guardian
[469] Political Monitor: Satisfaction Ratings 1997-Present | Ipsos
[470] TOP 25 QUOTES BY BORIS JOHNSON (of 98) | A-Z Quotes (azquotes.com)
[471] Boris Johnson: UK will "Take it on the chin". - YouTube
[472] COVID inquiry reveals a uniquely toxic, destructive set of individuals trying to work through crisis (msn.com)
[473] Coronavirus: PM Boris Johnson's lockdown statement @BBCNews - BBC - YouTube
[474] Anthony Seldon & Raymond Newell, Johnson At 10: The Inside Story, 2023, Atlantic Books, London, p 207-08
[475] 'I shook hands with everybody,' says Boris Johnson weeks before coronavirus diagnosis - YouTube

[476] [476]Anthony Seldon & Raymond Newell, Johnson At 10: The Inside Story, 2023, Atlantic Books, London, p 238.

[477] www.theguardian.com/politics/2019/Jul/26dominiccummingscareerpsychopathindowningstreet

[478] [478]Anthony Seldon & Raymond Newell, Johnson At 10: The Inside Story, 2023, Atlantic Books, London, p 288.

[479] Sterling jumps after UK finance minister resigns (rte.ie)

[480] 10 minutes of Dominic Cummings rinsing the Tories at the Covid Inquiry - YouTube

[481] Anthony Seldon & Raymond Newell, Johnson At 10: The Inside Story, 2023, Atlantic Books, London, p 295.

[482] The Independent, 08/11/23

[483] Anthony Seldon & Raymond Newell, Johnson At 10: The Inside Story, 2023, Atlantic Books, London, p 231-32.

[484]Anthony Seldon & Raymond Newell, Johnson At 10: The Inside Story, 2023, Atlantic Books, London, p 231.

[485]Ibid

[486] Covid vaccine rollout a 'day to remember in a year to forget', says Hancock - YouTube

[487] Committee on Standards publish report on the conduct of Rt Hon Owen Paterson MP - Committees - UK Parliament

[488] Boris Johnson lies to parliament about partygate - YouTube

[489] Boris Johnson apologises over Downing Street party: 'I believed it was a work event' - YouTube

[490] Partygate - Wikipedia

[491] UK economy suffered record annual slump in 2020 - BBC News

[492] Public spending during the Covid-19 pandemic - House of Commons Library (parliament.uk)

[493] Overall GDP hasn't had 'seven consecutive quarters of no growth' - Full Fact

[494] Three in five people think the UK is already in recession – poll | The Independent

[495] Northern Ireland Secretary admits new bill will 'break international law' - BBC News

[496] New Labour leader Keir Starmer vows to lead party into 'new era' - BBC News

[497] Labour loses nearly 100,000 members and makes £5 million loss in 2021 | The Independent
[498] Keir Starmer: EHRC antisemitism report is day of shame for Labour | Antisemitism | The Guardian
[499] Twitter.com/simonMcDonalduk/status/1544206976820854784
[500] 'Sinking ships are fleeing the rat': Jeering Keir Starmer slams Boris Johnson in brutal PMQs - YouTube
[501] Tom Scholar: Former top civil servants hit out at Treasury boss sacking - BBC News
[502] Liz Truss savaged by journalists after horror show press conference - YouTube
[503] IMF warns UK against mini-budget that will 'likely increase inequality' | Business News | Sky News
[504] Liz Truss's WORST Moments In Kuenssberg Interview - YouTube
[505] How much market chaos did the mini-budget cause? - BBC News
[506] Why did Liz Truss's time as UK prime minister end? - BBC News - YouTube
[507] The untold story of Liz Truss's chaotic 49 days in No 10 - YouTube
[508] Yougov poll, 18/10/22
[509] Yougov Poll, 31/05/23
[510] Brexit poll 2023 | Statista
[511] Nicola Sturgeon resigns as first minister of Scotland - YouTube

[512] Polling in Scotland for next United Kingdom general election - Wikipedia

[513] Reform Act 1867 - Wikipedia
[514] Anthony Seldon, *The Impossible Office?* Cambridge University Press, 2021, p111
[515] Ibid
[516] Britain's road to democracy: slow and not always steady | HistoryExtra
[517] Ibid
[518] Colville, The Fringes of Power, entry for 4th April 1955.

519 Bertjan Verbeek, Decision-making in Great Britain during the Suez crisis (2003) p. 95

520 Toye, Richard Churchill's Empire: The World That Made Him and the World He ade (2010) p. 304

521 Howard, 1987, p237
522 Harold Macmillan obituary | Politics | The Guardian
523 Harold Macmillan - Wikipedia
524 British Political Opinion 1937-2000: The Gallop Polls, Ed. Anthony King, 2001, The Gallop Organisation, p185-86/

525 James Margach, The Abuse of Power, W.H. Allen, 1978, p106

526 Lamb, Richard (1995). The Macmillan Years 1957–63: The Emerging Truth. London: Murray.

527 Goodlad & Pearce, 2013 p.180

528 HAROLD WILSON: British Prime Minister; 1964 - 70 and 1974 - 76. - YouTube

529 Falklands War – Argentine Perspective – An Inevitable Defeat? – Military History Visualized – Offical Homepage for the YouTube Channel

530 What If? The Falklands Conflict - YouTube

531 Falklands victory 'a close run thing' | UK news | The Guardian
532 *The Independent*, 07/05/93
533 Portillo speaks of gay experiences 'in past' | The Independent | The Independent
534 When Blair stood on the brink | Politics | The Guardian
535 US defence secretary Donald Rumsfeld's comments about UK involvement in war | UK news | The Guardian

536 Political Monitor: Satisfaction Ratings 1997-Present | Ipsos
537 How popular are Labour's radical manifesto policies? - LabourList | Latest UK Labour Party news, analysis and comment
538 An Empty Taxi Arrived and Clement Attlee Stepped Out of It – Quote Investigator®
539 It's the economy, stupid - Wikipedia
540 Peter Hennessey, The Prime Minister: The Office and its Holders since 1945, Penguin Books, 2001, P524. (Private information of Hennessey.)

[541] Sigmund Freud, A Difficulty in the Path of Psycho-Analysis, 1917